Unto Every
NATION

Unto Every NATION

GOSPEL LIGHT REACHES EVERY LAND

DONALD Q. CANNON
RICHARD O. COWAN

CONTRIBUTING AUTHORS
R. LANIER BRITSCH
DAVID F. BOONE
FRED E. WOODS

DESERET
BOOK

SALT LAKE CITY, UTAH

All photographs are used by permission of the photographer, the owner of the photograph, or The Church of Jesus Christ of Latter-day Saints. Images from the Church are courtesy LDS Church Archives or Intellectual Reserve, Inc.

Library of Congress Cataloging-in-Publication Data

Cannon, Donald Q., 1936-
  Unto every nation : gospel light reaches every land / Donald Q. Cannon, Richard O. Cowan ; contributing authors, R. Lanier Britsch, David F. Boone, Fred E. Woods.
     p.   cm.
  Includes bibliographical references and index.
  ISBN 1-57008-948-5 (alk. paper)
  1. Church of Jesus Christ of Latter-day Saints—History.   2. Mormon Church—History.   I. Cowan, Richard O., 1934-   II. Britsch, R. Lanier   III. Boone, David F.   IV. Woods, Fred E.   V. Title.
  BX8611.C29   2003
  289.3'32'09—dc21   2003012510

Printed in the United States of America   70582-7062
Phoenix Color Corporation, Hagerstown, MD

10   9   8   7   6   5   4   3   2   1

Contents

PREFACE

In 1980 the Department of Church History and Doctrine at Brigham Young University launched a new course. The course was originally called "International Church History," but the name was later simplified to "The International Church." In the department's regular Church history courses, students had learned about and studied the Church's beginnings in Palmyra, New York, its struggles in Kirtland and Missouri, its exodus from Nauvoo, and its grounding and growth in the Salt Lake Valley. Little attention was given to events in other parts of the world. The department felt that because the Church had become global, important and unique events and moments in the Church's history throughout the world were worthy of study. That would become the subject matter of this new course.

This course was taught by a team of professors headed by James R. Moss, who had worked with the Church Educational System in Britain. Others participating included James R. Christianson, Richard O. Cowan, and R. Lanier Britsch. By 1982 these brethren had prepared a text that was issued in paperback by BYU Publications.

Many inspired and far-reaching developments have occurred in the Lord's worldwide kingdom since 1980. The present editors, therefore, undertook to bring the story up to date. While there are excellent books that treat Latter-day Saint history in general or developments in one particular area, there is no volume that looks at the fascinating and inspiring events in all of the areas around the world. We hope this book will fill that important niche.

We appreciate the encouragement received from Sheri Dew and Cory Maxwell at Deseret Book, as well as the privilege of working with Janna DeVore, our chief editor. We also value the pioneering work of Brother Moss and the others; their volume provided the inspiration as well as the foundation for this present work. We are also grateful to Lanier Britsch (recently retired from BYU's History Department), David F. Boone (associate professor of Church history), and Fred E. Woods, each of whom have contributed chapters to this book. Patty Smith, director of Religious Education's Faculty Support Center, provided valuable assistance with this project. Marisa Price and Carly Andelin worked with us in researching and refining the material in this volume. Finally, we especially express our thanks to Kirstin Price, who has provided excellent editorial help and who prepared the final manuscript.

We have one more hope for this book. Our faith is that The Church of Jesus Christ of Latter-day Saints is God's kingdom foreseen by the Prophet Daniel, and that it is fulfilling the Savior's injunction to carry his gospel "unto every nation" (D&C 133:37). We hope that in these pages you will find material that will strengthen your testimony and inspire you to play your part in accomplishing God's purposes in these latter days.

—Donald Q. Cannon and
Richard O. Cowan

GLOBALIZATION OF THE CHURCH

DONALD Q. CANNON

In 1842, John Wentworth, editor of a Chicago newspaper, asked Joseph Smith to provide a brief history of the Church and a summary of its major beliefs. To epitomize the Church's teachings, the Prophet provided thirteen brief statements we now know as the Articles of Faith. In what came to be known as the Wentworth Letter, the Prophet concluded his review of the Church's history with this bold assertion: "The Standard of Truth has been erected; no unhallowed hand can stop the work from progressing; persecutions may rage, mobs may combine, armies may assemble, calumny may defame, but the truth of God will go forth boldly, nobly, and independent, till it has penetrated every continent, visited every clime, swept every country, and sounded in every ear, till the purposes of God shall be accomplished, and the Great Jehovah shall say the work is done."[1]

The globalization of the Church as described in this volume represents the fulfilling of the Prophet's declaration.

Globalization is an oft-mentioned, all-important matter in today's world. News media, special-interest groups, and governmental bodies regularly apply it to economics, law, ethics, political science, and sociology.

For The Church of Jesus Christ of Latter-day Saints, globalization is more than just an interesting topic; it is an urgent priority. The mission of the Church is to bring all people everywhere to Jesus Christ so that they might enjoy the eternal fruits of his gospel. A worldwide Church is certainly in a better position to accomplish this mission than one that is only local or even regional.

Additionally, Church members view the process of globalization as the fulfillment of prophecy, both ancient and modern. Daniel's prophecy in the Old Testament anticipated the time in latter days when God's kingdom would roll forth as a stone. Daniel prophesied that "the God of heaven" would "set up a kingdom, which shall never be destroyed" (Daniel 2:44), but would roll forth and fill the whole world (see Daniel 2:26–44). In the modern era the Lord likewise affirmed, "The keys of the kingdom of God are committed unto man on the earth, and from thence shall the gospel roll forth unto the ends of the earth, as the stone which is cut out of the mountain without hands shall roll forth, until it has filled the whole earth" (D&C 65:2).

Not only does globalization fulfill prophecy; it is something the Lord has commanded of his followers. To his ancient disciples he directed, "Go ye therefore, and teach all nations, baptizing them in the name of the Father, and of the Son, and of the Holy Ghost" (Matthew 28:19; see also Mark 16:15). In the latter days, the Lord has again given the same directive: "Send forth the elders of my church unto the nations which are afar off; unto the islands of the sea; send forth unto foreign lands; call upon all nations, first upon the Gentiles, and then upon the Jews" (D&C 133:8). Globalization, therefore, takes on a truly miraculous character. It is the fulfillment of the will of God.

For Latter-day Saints, globalization concerns both the internationalization of the Church and its ability to adjust to different cultural conditions. Both processes can be seen in the history of The Church of Jesus Christ of Latter-day Saints.

EARLY GLOBALIZATION

The first significant period of growth in the Church outside the United States occurred in eastern Canada. Conveniently located next door to the birthplace of the Restoration in upstate New York, Canada became a natural target for early latter-day missionaries. One of the earliest of these missionaries was Brigham Young, who journeyed to Kingston, Ontario, Canada, to declare the newfound gospel to his brother Joseph. In the fall of 1833 the Prophet Joseph Smith baptized additional converts in Ontario. In 1834 and again in 1836, additional missionaries were sent into Canada. Eventually, Latter-day Saint missionaries also found their way into the Maritime Provinces of New Brunswick, Nova Scotia, and Prince Edward Island.[2]

Conversions in Canada led to conversions in England. Indeed, some of the earliest Canadian members served as missionaries to England. For example, Joseph Fielding, a new Canadian convert, traveled to England in 1837, where he preached to his brother James and his congregation in Preston. Several of Reverend James Fielding's flock were baptized. By the time these early missionaries from Canada and members of the Council of the Twelve returned to America in April 1838, they had baptized more than fifteen hundred people.[3]

A second apostolic mission took place from 1840 to 1841.

Once again, contact with relatives proved fruitful. John Taylor visited his in-laws, the George Cannon family (my own ancestors) in Liverpool, and brought them into the Church. In terms of numbers, Wilford Woodruff must have credit for his remarkable success as a missionary. Working among members of a religious group called the United Brethren in Herefordshire, he succeeded in bringing six hundred new members into the fold. Before sailing for America, the nine Apostles who had labored in England tallied Church membership at 5,864. Many thousands more would follow during the ensuing decades.[4]

Latter-day Saint missionaries also preached in Scotland, Ireland, and Wales. The first preaching in Scotland was done in 1839, when two Scottish-Canadian converts, Alexander Wright and Samuel Mulliner, arrived in Glasgow. These two elders also carried the gospel to Ireland and Wales in 1840. Thus the gospel was introduced to every country in the British Isles.[5]

The Church's first foreign language missions were organized in the South Pacific. Four missionaries arrived at Tubai, an island three hundred miles from Tahiti, in early 1844. One of these missionaries, Addison Pratt, baptized sixty people, a third of the island's population, during the first year of his mission. Meanwhile, others worked on additional islands in French Polynesia, including Tahiti. Thus, the Pacific became an early part of the Church's globalization.[6]

DEVELOPMENTS IN THE LATER NINETEENTH AND EARLY TWENTIETH CENTURIES

In the 1850s, the Church's globalization efforts were centered in continental Europe. The first Latter-day Saint missionaries in Scandinavia arrived in Denmark in the summer of 1850. By the end of the year there were 135 members there. Missionaries also took their message to Sweden, Norway, and Iceland. About this same time, Elder John Taylor of the Council of the Twelve, who had introduced the gospel to Ireland, officially opened France for missionary work. Among the tasks he supervised was the translation of the Book of Mormon into French. Taylor simultaneously supervised the translation of the Book of Mormon into German. And although Taylor himself didn't stay long in Germany, other missionaries took up the work, and at the end of two years, 128 Germans had been baptized.[7] The work in Germany was greatly benefited from one convert in particular: Karl G. Maeser. His education and expertise was such that many fellow Germans were drawn into the fold.[8]

During the latter part of the nineteenth century the Mormons also found new converts in other parts of Europe, including Italy, Switzerland, Austria, the Netherlands, Bohemia (Czechoslovakia), and Hungary. Outside of Europe, contacts were made in Malta, Turkey, South Africa, India, Ceylon, Burma, Siam, Hong Kong, Australia, New Zealand, Samoa, Tonga, Hawaii, and Chile.[9]

The Church looked to Mexico both as a place for colonization and as a mission field. The first missionaries entered Mexico in 1875. Although hunger, drought, and disease accompanied their early efforts, they were able to establish a successful settlement in Colonia Juarez, a village with tree-lined streets, canals, farms, stores, and factories. By the beginning of the twentieth century there were four thousand Latter-day Saints in the area. Most of them abandoned the colonies during the Mexican Revolution in 1912, but more than one-fourth of those colonists later returned and contributed to further growth in the area.[10]

RECENT GROWTH

The globalization of the Church in the twentieth century was interrupted by two world wars, both of which were responsible for a curtailment of missionary activities as well as restricted international travel. World War II, however, brought Church members in contact with people and places that were either untouched by the gospel or had had only brief exposure to it previously.[11]

In the years since World War II the Church has grown rapidly and expanded into new territory. Some of the countries opened or revisited as a direct result of contact with Latter-day Saint military personnel include Japan, the Philippines, Korea, Vietnam, Spain, and Turkey. In addition, many other countries in diverse areas have been opened for missionary work, including Guatemala, Honduras, El Salvador, Costa Rica, Panama, Venezuela, Colombia, Ecuador, Peru, Bolivia, Chile, Argentina, Uruguay, Paraguay, Brazil, Ghana, Nigeria, and Zimbabwe.[12]

Asia and Latin American are home to several "hot spots" (high-growth areas) in the Church, including the Philippines and Brazil. Latter-day Saint servicemen and women preached the gospel in the Philippines during World War II and later during postwar occupation, when they were assigned to naval and air installations on the islands. In 1961 Elder Gordon B. Hinckley rededicated the Philippines for the preaching of the gospel; the first full-time missionaries arrived that same year, and the Church grew at an amazing rate in this unique mission field. One writer has suggested that the complex, multicultural nature of the Philippines—which is rich with American,

Spanish, and Malayo-Indonesian customs and tradition—has enabled the gospel to flourish there.[13] For example, American elders have had great success by taking advantage of several strong American connections to cultural features in Filipino Society. Spanish elders see similarities between their own culture and that in the Philippines and are able to show sensitivity in their approach.

The rapid growth in Filipino membership is reflected in the creation of new missions at an astonishing rate. At first the Philippines were part of the Southern Far East Mission, but in 1967 a separate mission was created just for the islands of the Philippines. By the end of the century, there were thirteen missions and nearly a half million Latter-day Saints in the country.[14] The Manila Philippines Temple is another indication of the Church's influence in the country; temples are built only where there is a substantial Church population and steady growth.[15]

Commenting on the phenomenal growth of Church membership in the Philippines, President Gordon B. Hinckley said: "I do not know of any place in the world where the harvest has been so great in such a short period. The Lord has touched this land in a miraculous and wonderful way."[16]

Another "hot spot," Brazil, had its first contact with Latter-day Saints in 1928, when several German converts immigrated to the southern regions of that vast country. Therefore, when the Church first sent missionaries to Brazil, they spoke German rather than Portuguese. The Church grew very slowly until after World War II. By this time, missionaries were speaking Portuguese and working with the Brazilian majority, using a Book of Mormon translated into their language.[17] Rapid growth began in the mid-1950s, when several specific events helped stimulate expansion in the Church. The first was the visit of President David O. McKay in 1955. He authorized construction of new meetinghouses where the Saints could worship. The first Portuguese translations of the Book of Mormon occurred in 1940. By the 1960s other LDS scriptures, Church magazines and manuals, and a number of other materials were also available in Portuguese. By 1966 the first Brazilian stake was created. In 1978 the first temple was erected in Brazil and located in São Paulo.[18]

In 1987, when the whole world was divided into seventeen huge administrative "areas," Brazil became an area of its own, reflecting its substantial growth. By the early part of the twenty-first century, there were more than three-quarters of a million members, more than two dozen missions, and five temples either functioning or under construction in Brazil.[19] Five native Brazilians have also been called as General Authorities: Helio da Rocha Camargo, Helvecio Martins (the first General Authority of African descent), Claudio R. M. Costa, Athos M. Amorim, and Adhemar Damiani.[20]

MEMBER MISSIONARIES

Many individuals have assisted in the globalization of the Church—too many to mention here. The following two individuals, however, are representative of the faithful and dedicated servants around the world.

KREŠIMIR ĆOSIĆ

Basketball star Krešimir Ćosić was instrumental in spreading the gospel message throughout Yugoslavia. Recruited by Brigham Young University in 1969, Ćosić moved to Provo, where he later joined the Church and became the first foreign player ever to be named an All-American. Rather than staying in America and turning pro in the NBA, Ćosić returned home in 1973. He played on the Yugoslav National Team, helping them win the silver medal in the 1976 Olympics in Montreal. He also spent much of his time at home publicizing his new religion and lobbying for its official recognition by the Yugoslav government. A national hero to the Yugoslavs, Ćosić became prominent even in government circles. He assisted missionaries from America and succeeded in translating the Book of Mormon into Serbo-Croatian. In 1985, when Communist Europe was beginning to crumble, Elder Thomas S. Monson dedicated the land of Yugoslavia for missionary work, evidence of Ćosić's thirteen-year dedication to the work of bringing the gospel to his homeland. When the basketball star died of cancer in 1995, over ten thousand of his countrymen paid their respects on the day of his funeral.[21]

EMMANUEL ABU KISSI

A humble African medical doctor named Emmanuel Abu Kissi helped introduce The Church of Jesus Christ of Latter-day Saints into Ghana. His first acquaintance with the Church occurred during another first—his first trip outside of Ghana. Kissi and his family were living in England, where they had moved so Kissi could pursue additional medical studies. It was there that two missionaries came to the Kissis' home and taught them the gospel. The family returned to Ghana in 1979—only a year after President Spencer W. Kimball revealed that all worthy males could hold the priesthood—where Brother Kissi established a small medical clinic, shared the gospel, and provided leadership as the Church began to grow in his homeland. During a year-and-a-half period in which the Church was banned from Ghana, Brother Kissi served as acting mission president of the area and participated in negotiations with the Ghanaian government. Five months after the ban was lifted, two stakes of the Church were organized in Ghana, and Brother Kissi was called to serve as a Regional Representative.[22]

ACCELERATION OF THE GLOBALIZATION PROCESS

Certainly, the last half century has seen a dramatic increase of globalization. A study completed by Victor L. Ludlow, a Brigham Young University professor of ancient scripture, demonstrates this increase. Dr. Ludlow used the following eight indicators to measure growth rates:

- copies of the Book of Mormon sold (number of copies sold in all other languages compared to number of copies sold in English)
- enrollment of students in seminary and institute classes (enrollment in other nations, compared to USA-Canada enrollment)
- number of General Authorities from foreign countries (according to their place of birth)
- Church membership outside North America (baptized members outside USA-Canada compared to inside)
- missions of the Church (all other nations compared to those inside USA-Canada)
- full-time missionaries (according to their country of origin)

- stakes of the Church (all other nations compared to stakes inside USA-Canada)
- temples of the Church (all other nations compared to those inside USA-Canada)[23]

Among the results of this worthwhile study are two sets of data: one for the above indicators in 1955 and another for the same indicators in 1999. These two sets of data provide a good basis of comparison, which we will use to summarize the Church's growth in the last half of the twentieth century.

FOREIGN LANGUAGE BOOK OF MORMON SALES

In 1955, 20 percent of all Book of Mormon sales were foreign language copies. In 1999, the percentage had grown to 53 percent. One-half of the copies sold in a foreign language were in Spanish, and Dr. Ludlow's study found that "92 percent of the total world population now has the Book of Mormon or 'Book of Mormon Selections' available in their native language."[24]

INTERNATIONAL CES ENROLLMENT

In 1955 there were no students enrolled in Church Educational System (CES) programs outside the United States and Canada. By 1977, however, total enrollment in CES programs was 301,439. Of this number, 83,174 students were enrolled outside the United States and Canada, making international enrollment 28 percent of the total.

In 1999, total CES enrollment was 659,137. Outside the United States and Canada, the number had grown to 298,093, meaning that 45 percent of students enrolled in CES programs were enrolled internationally.[25]

GENERAL AUTHORITIES

Between 1830 and 1955, 167 General Authorities were called to serve. Fifteen of these were born outside the United States and Canada. Thus, only 9 percent of General Authorities were international.

Between 1955 and 1999, 194 General Authorities were called to serve. Twenty-six of these were born outside the United States and Canada. Thus, 13 percent of General Authorities were international.

Factoring in the number of Area Authorities serving at the end of 1999, however, shows a dramatic increase in international Church leadership. Sixty percent of the 150 Area Authorities serving at the end of 1999 were born outside the United States and Canada.[26]

MEMBERSHIP OUTSIDE THE UNITED STATES AND CANADA

Total Church membership at the end of 1955 reached 1,357,274, with total international membership at 150,000. By 1999, total Church membership had climbed to 10,752,986. International membership soared as well, reaching 5,483,002. More than half of all Church members lived outside the United States and Canada, jumping from 11 percent to 51 percent in fewer than fifty years.[27]

INTERNATIONAL MISSIONS

The number of missions throughout the Church totaled 44 in 1955; 24 of those were international missions outside the U.S. and Canada, which made up 55 percent of the total. In 1999, the Church operated 333 missions, 226 of them outside the United States and Canada. Here, again, we see a jump.

Sixty-eight percent of the Church's missions are outside the United States and Canada.[28]

FULL-TIME MISSIONARIES

A large increase in the number of international missionaries is also evidenced in Dr. Ludlow's study. The numbers in 1955 show that the Church had 4,607 full-time missionaries in the field. Of these, only 14 were from outside the United States and Canada—a rate of 0.33 percent. By 1999, 58,593 missionaries were serving; 13,817 were from areas outside Canada and the United States. The rate of international missionaries had jumped to 24 percent.[29]

STAKES

As 1955 came to a close, the Church reported the existence of 224 stakes throughout the world; only one of these was outside the United States and Canada. By 1999, the total number of stakes had increased almost twelve-fold: 2,542 stakes total. In 1955, 0.4 percent of stakes were located outside the United States and Canada. Now that number had climbed to 40 percent, totaling 1,020 stakes.[30]

TEMPLES

As the twentieth century came to a close, the Church saw an amazing number of temples being built and announced. In 1955, the first year analyzed in Dr. Ludlow's study, only one international temple existed: the Bern Switzerland Temple. Temple building was at a virtual standstill between 1955 and 1977. Then, between 1977 and 1999, twenty-four international temples were dedicated. By the end of 1999, twenty-eight additional international temples had been announced.[31] At the end of 1999, sixty-eight temples were in operation throughout the world. Twenty-seven of these were outside the United States and Canada—40 percent of the total. Between 2000 and 2001, forty-seven temples were built.[32] As of early 2003, 114 temples were in operation and fourteen more had been announced.

ANALYSIS

The foregoing data from the Ludlow study demonstrates that the globalization or internationalization of the Church increased significantly during the last fifty years of the twentieth century. Furthermore, growth outside the United States and Canada is likely to increase even more rapidly in future years.

THE INFLUENCE OF GLOBALIZATION

As The Church of Jesus Christ of Latter-day Saints expanded into countries around the world, it adjusted and adapted to new cultural environments. Sometimes these adjustments came in teaching material; at other times adjustments occurred in building construction or missionary attire. As globalization occurred there was always mutual interaction between LDS doctrine and practices and native customs.

A symposium called "The Expanding Church," held at Brigham Young University from 30 March to 9 April 1976, was among the first evidence that the LDS Church recognized the need for cultural adaptation and adjustment in non-doctrinal policies. On that occasion, Latter-day Saint scholars and Church leaders from around the globe came together to discuss the challenges of globalization. Elder Gordon B. Hinckley, who would later become the president of the Church, delivered the keynote address. His topic: "The

Expanding Church among the Nations and Cultures of Man." Elder Neal A. Maxwell, who was then an assistant to the Quorum of the Twelve, spoke of the challenges facing Latter-day Saints as they interacted with different countries. Elder Maxwell said he believed that the Latter-day Saints would succeed because "the Lord is helping us in transculturization in the Church."[33] In the twenty-five years after the symposium was held, numerous changes occurred as the Church expanded into and adjusted to foreign cultures around the world. Church magazines, for example, now include pictures of Latter-day Saints from all over the world rather than just Anglo-Saxons from Utah.[34]

In the Philippines, several key adjustments in Church operations and procedures have been made. For example, even though standard plans and building materials were generally sent out from Salt Lake City in the past, the Church buildings in the Philippines were constructed from native materials. One LDS scholar and author writes of another interesting adjustment in the Philippines regarding the beautiful Makati Chapel:

> The chapel's beauty and functional utility notwithstanding, it has taught local leaders and administrators in Salt Lake City many lessons. One was that even though Church leaders wanted to show the Filipino Saints they were equals with members elsewhere in the world and demonstrated this fact by building a large air-conditioned chapel, the local Saints could not afford to pay the electricity bill to run the air-conditioning system (approximately U.S. $500 to $1,000 per month). Moreover, they were not accustomed to air conditioning and found it too cold. In the 1980s the Church Building Committee approved the construction of much less expensive chapels that have louvered windows to allow the breezes to blow through.[35]

Harold B. Lee (middle), chairman of the Church's Servicemen's Committee, meets with military officials in Pusan, Korea, in 1954. Almost three decades later, Koreans received their own temple, and membership flourished in that Asian nation. (LDS Church Archives)

Another Philippine example of accommodation is the heavy emphasis on educational programs. The members needed educational assistance to develop the skills necessary for productive employment, so the Church responded by providing both religious and secular education and materials.[36]

Yet another example of the Church's ability to adapt were the changes made to the required missionary "uniform" in various countries throughout the world. Instead of the traditional dark suit that missionaries wore in Germany in the 1950s, for example, missionaries in Tahiti were instructed to wear slacks and a short-sleeved white shirt and sandals. The climate and the culture demanded a different type of clothing.[37]

An inspired change of much greater significance occurred in

1978. Prior to this time, the Church did not ordain members of black African descent to the priesthood. On 8 June 1978, the Church announced a new revelation about the priesthood, calling for no restrictions as to race, color, or nationality. Henceforth, all worthy male members could be ordained to the priesthood. The revelation provided an inspired solution to one of the Church's biggest growth issues at the time: rapid expansion in Brazil. In that country, it was almost impossible to determine whether someone had a trace of African lineage. Inspired revelation led to the means for cultural adaptation.

CONCLUSION

The growth and globalization of the Church between 1830 and 2000 is truly astonishing. Today, Latter-day Saints are found on every continent. Growth in Asia and Latin America in the twentieth century superseded earlier growth in Europe. Globalization has brought Latter-day Saints into contact with the world and the world in contact with Latter-day Saints. Unique and smart adjustments and adaptations have been made—and will continue to be made—as this church that began with just six members in United States of America encounters new cultures around the world. Certainly, the process of globalization will continue as the twenty-first century plays out.

PART I

THE CHURCH
IN EUROPE

From the beginning of the Church's history, Latter-day Saints have been eager to share the restored gospel. In 1836, Moses restored "the keys of the gathering of Israel from the four parts of the earth" (D&C 110:11); the very next year, the Church opened its first overseas mission. It should be no surprise that this initial international venture was directed to Europe, the ancestral homeland of the early North American Saints.

During the middle decades of the nineteenth century, thousands of European converts gathered to "Zion" in America, strengthening the Church there. By the beginning of the twentieth century, however, Church leaders began urging European Saints to remain in their homelands and build up the Church on the European continent. The Saints heeded this counsel, particularly during the second half of the twentieth century, when temples, stakes, and other gospel blessings were made available in Europe. Conversion of European citizens did not occur as rapidly as it had a century earlier; nonetheless, this was the time when the Church in Europe grew more than ever before. As the Church celebrated its sesquicentennial in Europe, new missionary fields were still being opened in response to the duty of carrying the gospel unto every nation.

BRITISH ISLES

Atlantic
Ocean

•Inverness

SCOTLAND

North Sea

•Edinburgh
Glasgow•

NORTHERN
IRELAND •Belfast

•Newry

Isle of
Man

•Milnthorpe
•Downham
•Preston
•Manchester

Liverpool•

Dublin ★

IRELAND

•Potteries

WALES

•Birmingham
•Bedford
•Herefordshire

★London

ENGLAND

English Channel

FRANCE

CHAPTER 1

OPENING THE BRITISH MISSION: 1837 TO 1841

RICHARD O. COWAN

1836	John Taylor and others converted in Toronto (spring)
1837	First missionaries arrive in Liverpool (20 July)
1837	First converts baptized in Preston (30 July)
1837	Preston Branch organized (6 August)
1838	Elders Heber C. Kimball and Orson Hyde sail for America (20 April)
1839	Members of the Twelve assemble at Far West, Missouri, prior to their overseas mission (26 April)
1840	Elders Heber C. Kimball and Wilford Woodruff arrive in Liverpool (11 January)
	Elder Orson Pratt assigned to preside in Scotland (May)
	Elder John Taylor carries gospel to Ireland (July)
	Elders Heber C. Kimball, Wilford Woodruff, and George A. Smith begin preaching in London (August)
1841	Most of the Twelve leave for home (spring)

Although Great Britain was home to the Church's first overseas mission field, opening in 1837, important developments in Canada preceded this landmark development, as did several inspired prophecies. At a meeting in the Kirtland Temple on 6 February 1836, William Smith saw in vision the Twelve gathered in England and "prophesied that a great work would be done by them in the old countries, and God was already beginning to work in the hearts of the people."[1] Two months later Heber C. Kimball, one of the Twelve, unexpectedly visited Parley P. Pratt at his home, and "being filled with the spirit of prophecy," declared to him: "Thou shalt go to Upper Canada, even to the city of Toronto, the capital, and there thou shalt find a people prepared for the fulness of the gospel, and they shall receive thee, and thou shalt organize the Church among them, and it shall spread thence into the regions round about, and many shall be brought to the knowledge of the truth and shall be filled with joy; and from the things growing out of this mission, shall the fulness of the gospel spread into England, and cause a great work to be done in that land."[2]

Within a few days, Parley left Kirtland for Canada. In Toronto, he met John Taylor, an emigrant from England who was a member of a group convinced that no existing churches corresponded to New Testament Christianity; the group had been meeting for two years seeking the truth. At first, Parley was received only coolly. Discouraged, he planned to leave Toronto after being there only one day, but a friend of the Taylors was impressed to invite Elder Pratt to stay and offered her home as a place where he could preach to the group. As the group listened to Elder Pratt, many were convinced that he represented what they had been seeking. Converts included John Taylor and his wife, Leonora Cannon, Joseph Fielding, and his sisters Mary and Mercy.

The year 1837 brought great difficulties to the Church. During the early months of the year the spirit of apostasy was rampant in the Ohio city; this was complicated by the failure of the Kirtland bank that summer, which was part of a nationwide economic panic. In this setting, the Lord revealed to the Prophet

Joseph Smith that "something new must be done for the salvation of His Church."[3] Soon afterwards, on Sunday, 4 June 1837, Joseph Smith met Heber C. Kimball in the Kirtland Temple and without warning announced to Heber: "Brother Heber, the Spirit of the Lord has whispered to me: Let my servant Heber go to England and proclaim my Gospel, and open the door of salvation to that nation."[4] Heber was overwhelmed by this call: "How can I go to preach in that land, which is so famed throughout Christendom for learning, knowledge and piety; the nursery of religion; and to a people whose intelligence is proverbial!" Elder Kimball was also concerned about leaving his destitute family. Nevertheless, he concluded, "The moment I understood the will of my Heavenly Father, I felt a determination to go at all hazards, believing that He would support me by His almighty power, and endow me with every qualification that I needed."[5]

Soon, the First Presidency set Elder Kimball apart to head "the first foreign mission of the Church of Christ in the last days."[6] Orson Hyde, a fellow Apostle, who had been somewhat influenced by the spirit of apostasy and speculation, overheard Elder Kimball's blessing and asked for the privilege of going with him to England.

Five months earlier, Elder Kimball had received a premonition that he would be going on a mission to Europe. When he shared this with Willard Richards, who had just been converted to the gospel, Willard asked if he might go along. Elder Kimball had responded, "Yea, in the name of the Lord, thou shalt go with me when I go."[7] These three missionaries were joined by four others: Joseph Fielding, Isaac Russell, John Goodson, and John Snyder—all Englishmen who had immigrated to Canada where they had been converted to the gospel. By 22 June, only two and a half weeks after Elder Kimball had received his call, he and his associates were in New York City, where they booked passage on the sailing ship *Garrick*.

England would be particularly well prepared to receive the missionaries' message. The elders from America spoke the same language and shared the same cultural heritage as the people they would teach. Many people in the working classes had been left without employment during the Industrial Revolution, so were thus struggling as they sought to discover their new identity. At the same time, clergymen from the established Church of England tended to neglect the working classes, so these people increasingly felt that they had been abandoned. Many groups were looking for something new in terms of faith and, fortunately, enjoyed guarantees of religious freedom. Furthermore, at this time Britain had a stable government and economy.[8] Hence, as the scripture states, "the field" was truly "white already to harvest" (D&C 4:4).

GOSPEL DOORS OPENED IN PRESTON

The missionaries from America arrived at Liverpool, England's main seaport at the time, and went ashore on Thursday, 20 July 1837.[9] The elders undoubtedly were filled with anxiety as they wondered how best to gain a foothold in this new land. They did not stay in Liverpool long, but were impressed to travel a short distance inland to the city of Preston, where Elder Fielding's brother was a Nonconformist Protestant minister. Upon their arrival, the missionaries happened to glimpse an election banner just then being unfurled. In large gold letters it proclaimed, "Truth Will Prevail." Taking this as a good omen, they exclaimed, "Amen! So let it be."[10]

Joseph Fielding took the two Apostles and Elder Goodson to meet his brother, James. The Reverend James Fielding was eager to meet the missionaries, having heard of the Restoration by means of letters written by his brother and sisters in Canada. The four visited far into the night, and the minister invited the elders to attend Sunday services the following morning at his Vauxhall Chapel.[11]

On Sunday morning as the Reverend James Fielding was preaching, the missionaries were secretly "praying to the Lord to open the way for [them] to preach." At the conclusion of the service, therefore, they were surprised yet overjoyed to hear Reverend Fielding announce that the missionaries from America would preach during the afternoon service. Responding to this invitation, Elders Kimball and Hyde bore testimony of the first principles of the restored gospel. Elders Goodson and Fielding preached at yet another service in the evening.[12]

Reflecting on the events of this day, Elder Heber C. Kimball noted how the parishioners "cried 'glory to God,' and rejoiced that the Lord had sent His servants unto them. Thus was the key turned and the Gospel dispensation opened on the first Sabbath after landing in England."[13] Significantly, these events fulfilled a revelation given that very day across the Atlantic in Kirtland, Ohio. Through Joseph Smith, the Lord promised Thomas B. Marsh, then president of the Twelve, that "in whatsoever place ye shall proclaim my name an effectual door shall be opened unto you, that they may receive my word" (D&C 112:19).

The missionaries preached at another service in Vauxhall Chapel the following Wednesday evening. A growing number of the congregation wanted to be baptized into the new church. When the Reverend Fielding realized that he was losing his congregation, he forbade the missionaries to preach any longer in his church, and soon became a bitter opponent. Still,

*Heber C. Kimball baptized
the first nine converts to the
Church in Great Britain. (Photo
courtesy Richard O. Cowan)*

he had provided the elders with the foothold they needed to launch their work in Great Britain.

Heber C. Kimball scheduled the first baptisms for Sunday, 30 July. Earlier that morning, the missionaries had an experience that made them aware of Satan's opposition to the work they were then opening in Britain. Elder Kimball was awakened by Isaac Russell, one of his missionary companions, who urgently asked him to cast out evil spirits that had been tormenting him. Elders Kimball and Hyde arose and gave the requested priesthood blessing. Heber C. Kimball recorded what happened next as the evil spirits overcame him:

> I was struck with great force by some invisible power, and fell
> senseless on the floor. The first thing I recollected was being
> supported by Elders Hyde and Richards, who were praying for
> me. . . . Elder Hyde and Richards then assisted me to get on
> the bed, but my agony was so great I could not endure it, and
> I arose, bowed my knees and prayed. I then arose and sat up
> on the bed, when a vision was opened to our minds, and we
> could distinctly see the evil spirits, who foamed and gnashed

their teeth at us. We gazed upon them about an hour and a half (by Willard's watch). We were not looking towards the window, but towards the wall. Space appeared before us, and we saw the devils coming in legions, with their leaders, who came within a few feet of us. They came towards us like armies rushing to battle. They appeared to be men of full stature, possessing every form and feature of men in the flesh, who were angry and desperate; and I shall never forget the vindictive malignity depicted on their countenances as they looked me in the eye; and any attempt to paint the scene which then presented itself, or portray their malice and enmity, would be vain.[14]

In a letter to Heber C. Kimball, Orson Hyde later gave his account of this terrifying ordeal: "After you were overcome by them and had fallen, their awful rush upon me with knives, threats, imprecations and hellish grins, amply convinced me that they were no friends of mine. While you were apparently senseless and lifeless on the floor and upon the bed (after we had laid you there), I stood between you and the devils and fought them and contended with them face to face, until they began to diminish in number and to retreat from the room."[15]

Much later, after returning to America, Heber spoke with the Prophet Joseph about the experience with the devils. To Heber's surprise, the Prophet remarked, "When I heard of it, it gave me great joy, for I then knew that the work of God had taken root in that land." The Prophet clarified his statement by explaining: "The nearer a person approaches the Lord, a greater power will be manifested by the adversary to prevent the accomplishment of His purposes."[16]

Despite this experience, the elders followed through with their plans. At about nine o'clock in the morning they went to a parklike setting where the River Ribble flows through Preston; a crowd of about eight thousand spectators looked on as Elder

Kimball baptized nine converts. Two of the brethren were so eager to be the first convert baptized in Great Britain in this dispensation that they ran a race to the river's edge to determine which would be first. George D. Watt, the younger of the two, won this privilege.

A week later, on Sunday, 6 August 1837, Elder Kimball officially organized the Preston Branch. At first, the converts held services in the elders' lodgings, but soon their numbers overcrowded these cramped facilities. In September, therefore, the Saints began meeting in Preston's more commodious Temperance Hall. This facility was popularly known as "the Cockpit" because cockfights had been staged there in earlier years. By the following month, the congregation had grown so large that it was divided into five separate branches. Before long, there were 140 members in Preston.[17]

THE WORK EXPANDS

While the Church was coming into being in Preston, the missionaries began carrying the gospel message to other communities. Elders Isaac Russell and John Snyder traveled 150 miles north to Alston, a small town near the Scottish border. Here, they hoped once again to gain an advantage in establishing the gospel by first sharing it with relatives and friends. Several were baptized, and a small branch was organized. At the same time, Willard Richards and John Goodson traveled to Bedford in the south of England, where Joseph Fielding's brother-in-law, Timothy Matthews, was also a minister. The missionaries arrived on 2 August, contacted the Reverend Matthews, and were invited to preach in his church that very evening and the three following nights. As had been the case with the Reverend Fielding in Preston, Matthews supported the elders at first but turned against them when they began baptizing members of his congregation.

Closer to Preston, Elder Heber C. Kimball contacted a family in Eccleston called the Moons. At first the family seemed to be resisting his message, but they subsequently accepted the gospel. Eventually, thirty members of the extended Moon family were baptized. Three years later, John Moon, one of the sons in the family, led the first group of emigrants from Great Britain to America.[18]

Jennetta Richards, who happened to be visiting two of the recent converts in Preston, also accepted the gospel and was baptized on 4 August. The daughter of the Reverend John Richards in Walkerfold, Jennetta wondered how to tell her father about her conversion. Heber Kimball encouraged her to not be afraid and promised her that "the Lord will soften the heart of thy father, that I will yet have the privilege of preaching in his chapel, and it shall result in a great opening to preach the Gospel in that region."[19] In literal fulfillment of Heber's prophetic promise, the Reverend Richards invited Heber to preach during the morning, afternoon, and evening services on Sunday, 13 August. Other opportunities followed during the week, and six were baptized. Even though the Reverend Richards was losing some of his flock, he still remained a friend to the missionaries.[20]

After baptizing Jennetta, Heber C. Kimball wrote to Elder Willard Richards, who was still in Bedford: "Willard, I baptized your wife today." When Willard returned from Bedford, Elder Kimball encouraged him to get better acquainted with Jennetta. Obediently, Willard arranged to attend some meetings in the area where she lived. One Sunday afternoon, while walking through the countryside with her, Willard mentioned that Richards was a good name and remarked that he never wanted to change it. "Do you?" he inquired of Jennetta. "No, I do not," she replied. They were married several months later.[21]

Early in 1838, Elders Heber C. Kimball and Joseph Fielding traveled twenty miles from Preston up the Ribble Valley to the small towns of Chatburn and Downham. The elders had been cautioned that the people there would not be receptive, as ministers from other churches had preached there without any success: "This did not discourage me in the least," Elder Kimball reflected. "I went in the name of Jesus Christ. My testimony was accompanied by the Spirit of the Lord and was received with joy, and these people who were represented as being so hard and obdurate, were melted down into tenderness and love."[22] So great was the interest in the missionaries' message that the elders sometimes had to preach out of doors. On one occasion, Heber C. Kimball stood atop a stone wall while addressing an eager audience.[23] Furthermore, Elder Kimball recorded what happened one day when the elders were seen approaching Chatburn on their way to Downham:

> The news ran from house to house, and immediately the noise of their looms was hushed, and the people flocked to their doors to welcome us and see us pass. More than forty young people of the place ran to meet us; . . . singing the songs of Zion, while their parents gazed upon the scene with delight, and poured their blessings upon our heads, and praised the God of heaven for sending us to unfold the principles of truth and the plan of salvation to them. The children continued with us to Downham, a mile distant. Such a scene, and such gratitude, I never witnessed before.[24]

During the next few days, the elders baptized more than a hundred people in these two towns. Several months later, Elder Kimball would return to these villages for one last visit:

> On the morning when I left Chatburn many were in tears, thinking they should see my face no more. When I left them, my feelings were such as I cannot describe. As I walked down the street I was followed by numbers; the doors were crowded by the inmates of the houses to bid me farewell. . . . While contemplating this scene I was constrained to take off my hat, for I felt as if the place was holy ground. The Spirit of the Lord rested down upon me and I was constrained to bless that whole region of country.[25]

Heber C. Kimball later recalled how he walked through these villages "feeling as I never before felt in my life. My hair would rise on my head as I walked through the streets, and I did not then know what was the matter with me. I pulled off my hat, and felt that I wanted to pull off my shoes, and I did not know what to think of it."[26] He remarked to Joseph Smith that he didn't understand why he felt that way. The Prophet responded: "Did you not understand it? That is a place where some of the old Prophets travelled and dedicated that land, and their blessing fell upon you."[27]

Not surprisingly, the missionaries' success sparked sharp opposition. Clergymen held series of meetings to warn their flocks against "the Mormon menace." Newspapers published articles attacking the Church and portraying Joseph Smith as a fraud. Despite these attacks and record cold winter weather, the elders continued to gain converts:

> Some days we went from house to house, conversing with the people on the things of the kingdom, and would sometimes be instrumental in convincing many of the truth: and I have known as many as twenty persons baptized in one day, who have been convinced on such occasions. I have had to go into the water to administer the ordinance of baptism six or seven times a day, and frequently after having come

out of the water and changed my clothes, I have had to turn back to the water before I reached my lodgings; this, too, when the weather was extremely cold, the ice being from twelve to fourteen inches thick. The weather continued so about twelve weeks, during which time I think there were but ten days in which we were not in the water baptizing.[28]

A mission conference convened in the Temperance Hall at Preston on Christmas Day. Even though the elders had been in the country for only five months, some three hundred Saints crowded the hall to receive counsel and inspiration from their leaders. Nearly thirty branches reported a combined membership of several hundred. "The Spirit of the Lord was with us," Elder Kimball recorded, "and truly the hearts of the Elders were rejoiced beyond measure when we contemplated the glorious work which had been done, and we had to exclaim, 'Blessed be the name of the Lord, who has crowned our labors with such success!'"[29] The missionaries spent the next three months strengthening the new Saints, organizing additional branches, and helping local members assume a greater leadership role.

Another conference met at Preston in April 1838, with seven hundred in attendance. By this time there were fifteen hundred to two thousand members. Before Apostles Heber C. Kimball and Orson Hyde sailed for home on 20 April, they installed Joseph Fielding as mission president with Willard Richards as first counselor and William Clayton, a recent convert who later would compose "Come, Come, Ye Saints," as second counselor.

The next two years were a sifting time for the Church in Britain. As opposition intensified, weaker members were weeded out; those with stronger faith had their testimonies strengthened as they overcame persecution. A leaner but stronger membership would greet the Apostles upon their return.

CALL OF THE TWELVE TO BRITAIN

As early as April 1838, the Lord had revealed that the Twelve would embark on a mission the following spring "to testify of my name and bear glad tidings unto all the world" (D&C 114:1). In another revelation given in July, He specified that the Twelve would "go over the great waters" and should leave on their mission from the building site of the Far West Temple on 26 April (see D&C 118:4–5). This same revelation called brethren to fill vacancies in the Twelve caused by the recent wave of apostasy. These included three who would play a key role during the upcoming mission: John Taylor (the leader of the group converted in Toronto), Willard Richards (who was still in England), and Wilford Woodruff (see verse 6).

Following Governor Lilburn Boggs's extermination order, the Saints were forced to flee from Missouri during the winter of 1838–1839. Some of their enemies vowed that the departure of the Twelve from Far West on 26 April would be "one of Joe Smith's prophecies" that would not be fulfilled. Under the courageous leadership of Brigham Young, however, the Apostles gathered at the temple site in Far West on the appointed date, transacted needed business, and formally departed for their overseas mission.

The Twelve accepted their mission call in the most trying of circumstances. Not only were they impoverished from leaving their Missouri homes behind, but most also were afflicted with the malaria that had swept through the Mormon settlements along the Mississippi River during the summer of 1839. "Early upon the morning of the 8th of August," Elder Wilford Woodruff recorded, " I arose from my bed of sickness, laid my hands upon the head of my sick wife, Phoebe, and blessed her. I then departed from the embrace of my companion, and left her almost without food or the necessaries of life. She suffered my departure with the fortitude that becomes a saint, realizing the responsibilities of her companion."[30]

On 14 September 1839, Brigham Young left Montrose for his mission. His wife was ill in bed, their baby was only three weeks old, and no one in the family was well enough to care for one another. He crossed the river to the home of Heber C. Kimball to prepare for their departure. Three days later, Mary Ann Young was well enough to also cross over to Nauvoo, where she "might nurse and comfort Brother Brigham to the hour of starting."[31] The following day, the two brethren left on their mission. Elder Kimball recalled:

> I went to my bed and shook hands with my wife who was then shaking with a chill, having two children lying sick by her side; I embraced her and my children, and bade them farewell. . . . It was with difficulty we got into the wagon, and started down the hill about ten rods; it appeared to me as though my very inmost parts would melt within me at leaving my family in such a condition, as it were almost in the arms of death. I felt as though I could not endure it. I asked the teamster to stop, and said to Brother Brigham, "This is pretty tough, isn't it; let's rise up and give them a cheer." We arose, and swinging our hats three times over our heads, shouted: "Hurrah, hurrah for Israel." Vilate, hearing the noise, arose from her bed and came to the door. She had a smile on her face. Vilate and Mary Ann Young cried out to us: "Goodbye, God bless you." We returned the compliment, and then told the driver to go ahead. After this I felt a spirit of joy and gratitude, having had the satisfaction of seeing my wife standing upon her feet, instead of leaving her in bed, knowing well that I should not see them again for two or three years.[32]

The Twelve did not travel together as a body, but in groups

of two or three that took various routes to the East Coast. Typically they went without purse or scrip, depending on the generosity of people they met along the way. "We consider that there is no instance on record," Brigham Young wrote from New York, "where men have been called to so great an undertaking, under the same circumstances of poverty, sickness and distress; both ourselves, families, and brethren; but yet through the mercy of God, we think the mission will be accomplished."[33]

The first of the Apostles to arrive in England were Elders John Taylor and Wilford Woodruff.[34] They landed at Liverpool on 11 January 1840 and then traveled to Preston where they met with the mission presidency. This meeting was a reunion between Elder John Taylor and mission president Joseph Fielding, who had been a close associate in Toronto a few years earlier.

Elder Taylor later returned to Liverpool, going directly to the home of George Cannon, his brother-in-law. George was not home, but Elder Taylor spoke to his wife, Ann Quayle, who remarked to her son as the missionary left, "George, that is a man of God."[35] The missionary later returned and taught the family the gospel. After reading the Book of Mormon, George Cannon concluded that "no wicked man could write such a book as this; and no good man would write it, unless it were true and he were commanded of God to do so."[36] Soon, he, his wife, and three of their children, including thirteen-year-old George, joined the Church. Years later, this boy would himself become a member of the Twelve and would serve as a counselor to John Taylor in the First Presidency. Others were also converted in Liverpool, and soon a branch was functioning there.

Meanwhile, Elder Wilford Woodruff was assigned to "the Potteries," a group of small towns south of Preston in

The John Benbow farmhouse in Herefordshire, where Wilford Woodruff preached in 1840. John and Jane Benbow and several members of their church (the United Brethren) were baptized. (Photo courtesy Richard O. Cowan)

Staffordshire, where the clay is ideal for producing fine china. Upon his arrival, he found a small group of people who had already received the gospel, and during the next forty days, forty more converts were added. Preaching every night, Elder Woodruff looked forward to continuing success in that area.

However, on Sunday, 1 March 1840, Elder Woodruff's thirty-third birthday, the Spirit told him, "This is the last meeting that you will hold with this people for many days."[37] When he shared this with the congregation during the evening meeting, they were just as astonished as was he. Praying for further guidance, he learned that he "should go to the south; for the Lord had a great work for [him] to perform there, as many souls were waiting for His word."[38] William Benbow, a recent convert, offered to escort Elder Woodruff to the home of his brother John, who lived further south in Herefordshire.

John Benbow and his wife, Jane, belonged to a group of about six hundred former Methodists who were seeking added religious truth. These "United Brethren" had their own chapel, as well as several homes licensed for preaching, and included several lay preachers. Elder Woodruff arrived 4 March, and two days later John and Jane Benbow were baptized. Other conversions followed, including Thomas Kington, leader of the United Brethren. Elder Woodruff later recalled, "I laid before him the Gospel. He said, 'If it is true, I wish to embrace it; if not, I shall oppose it.' I said, 'That is right.' But I made a covenant with him. I said to him, 'If you will go before the Lord and ask him if this work is true, I promise you in the name of the Lord Jesus Christ that you shall receive a testimony for yourself.'" A short time later, "I asked him if he had enquired of the Lord. He said he had. 'What did the Lord tell you.' 'He told me it was true;' and he then said he was ready to obey the Gospel, and I baptized him."[39]

As members of other faiths also joined the Church, their ministers became alarmed, fearing that they would lose their congregations to the Mormons. Elder Woodruff described how one minister sent a constable, who arrived to arrest Brother Woodruff just as a meeting was about to begin at the Benbow home. "I asked him, 'For what crime?' He said, 'For preaching to the people.' I told him that I, as well as the rector, had a license for preaching the gospel to the people, and that if he would take a chair I would wait upon him after meeting. He took my chair and sat beside me. For an hour and a quarter I preached the first principles of the everlasting gospel. The power of God rested upon me, the spirit filled the house, and the people were convinced." At the end of the meeting, seven—including four preachers and even the constable— accepted Elder Woodruff's invitation to be baptized. He personally baptized them. "The constable went to the rector and told him that if he wanted Mr. Woodruff taken for preaching the gospel, he must go himself and serve the writ; for he had heard him preach the only true gospel sermon he had ever listened to in his life." The rector then sent two clerks to "spy" on the missionaries; they too were converted. "The rector became alarmed," Elder Woodruff concluded, "and did not venture to send anybody else."[40]

Eventually, all but one of the United Brethren were baptized. Hundreds of others followed. Concerning this extraordinary experience, Wilford Woodruff reflected: "The whole history of this Herefordshire mission shows the importance of listening to the still small voice of the spirit of God, and the revelations of the Holy ghost. The people were praying for light and truth, and the Lord sent me to them. I declared the gospel of life and salvation, some eighteen hundred souls received it. . . . In all these things we should ever acknowledge the hand of God, and give Him the honor, praise, and glory."[41]

Upset at such Latter-day Saint success, local ministers joined in petitioning the Archbishop of Canterbury to urge that Parliament pass a law banning the Mormons from preaching. Respecting the British tradition of religious freedom, he refused. Instead, he admonished the ministers to solve their own problem by becoming more faithful pastors.[42]

A MAJORITY OF THE TWELVE IN BRITAIN

On 6 April 1840, exactly one decade after the restored Church's organization in America, five more members of the

Twelve landed at Liverpool: Brigham Young, Heber C. Kimball, Parley P. Pratt, his brother Orson Pratt, and George A. Smith. A week later they met in council at Preston with Elders John Taylor and Wilford Woodruff, who had arrived in England three months earlier. In accordance with the Lord's revelation (D&C 118:6), Willard Richards was ordained to the Apostleship. They promptly convened a general conference of the English Saints. The existing mission presidency was released, Brigham Young and the Twelve assuming leadership. Each of the Apostles received specific assignments and so went their separate ways.

Back in Liverpool, John Taylor rented the largest available building, the Music Hall. Here he gave a series of lectures that attracted large audiences, contributing to the branch's continued growth.

Elder Taylor enjoyed particular success among the city's numerous Irish immigrants. Soon he determined that he should carry the gospel to Ireland itself. On 31 July 1840 at Newry, Elder Taylor baptized Thomas Tait, the first convert in that land.

After returning briefly to Liverpool, Elder Taylor sailed in September to the Isle of Man, the ancestral home of his Cannon in-laws. During his month there, he again gave a series of well-attended lectures. These attracted attacks from the local clergy, with whom he debated successfully.

Brigham Young accompanied Wilford Woodruff back to Herefordshire to continue the work in this fruitful field. In the small town of Dimmock, William Pitt (the parish choir director) and his sister Mary were converted. Mary, an invalid, desired a priesthood blessing. Wilford Woodruff later described what happened: "I told President Young what Sister Pitt wished, and that she believed she had faith enough to be healed. We prayed for her and laid hands upon her. Brother

Young was mouth, and commanded her to be made whole. She laid down her crutch and never used it after, and the next day she walked three miles. This created a great deal of anger and madness in the feelings of the rector of that town."[43] Later, after emigrating from England to Nauvoo, William Pitt would organize the brass band that uplifted the spirits of the pioneers as they crossed the American plains to the Rocky Mountains.

Not surprisingly, opposition continued. After Wilford Woodruff preached an especially effective sermon at Haycross, another small village, several wanted to be baptized in spite of threatened physical violence. Elder Woodruff recalled, "I found a vast assembly of people, the house, yard, and street was thronged, and among the number a mob was collected, determined to break up the meeting; however, I arose and preached the gospel unto the people, many of whom could hear notwithstanding their [sic] was much confusion created by the mob, and when I closed a number wished to be baptized, and I told these who made the request, that notwithstanding the desperation of the mob if they had faith enough to be baptized, I had faith enough to administer the ordinance unto them; and we repaired to the pool, which was surrounded by the mob armed with stones, I walked into water with my mind stayed on God and baptized five persons while they were pelting my body with stones, one of which hit me on the head and came very near knocking me down, however I received no lasting injury."[44]

On 20 May 1840, Elders Brigham Young, Wilford Woodruff, and Willard Richards ascended the Herefordshire Beacon, a prominent hill in the area, to hold a council meeting. Here they made some important decisions. Brigham Young would go to Manchester and publish the first British edition of the Book of Mormon and a hymnal. These significant publications were to be financed with more than three hundred pounds (over $20,000 in today's money) contributed by the United Brethren converts, particularly John Benbow and Thomas Kington.[45]

At Manchester, Elder Parley P. Pratt gave direction to these publication projects. In addition to the Book of Mormon and the hymnal, he published a variety of missionary tracts and launched the *Millennial Star*. Under Pratt's capable editorship, the *Star* appeared monthly, and for a time every two weeks. This British Mission periodical became the only newspaper where the Saints could read anything positive about the Church.

Orson Pratt was assigned by Brigham Young to head the work in Scotland, arriving there 4 May 1840. Two missionaries, Samuel Mollener and Alexander Wright, had already baptized a few converts in that land before Elder Pratt's arrival in May. The first Scottish branch was organized at Paisley just four days after Orson Pratt came to Scotland. On one occasion, Orson climbed Arthur's Seat, a rocky hill overlooking the capital city of Edinburgh, where he pled with the Lord that the missionaries might see at least two hundred converts come into the fold. For the next eleven months Orson Pratt served as president of the Scottish Conference (or district). During that period, he saw more than two hundred baptized.

Elders Heber C. Kimball and George A. Smith traveled together to many parts of Britain, preaching the gospel, strengthening the Saints, and organizing branches. In areas where Elder Kimball had worked during his earlier mission, his converts—especially in the Ribble Valley—were excited to see him again. Some had fallen away in the face of persecution, but the return of their beloved Apostle missionary served to rekindle their faith. Elder George A. Smith, large in stature and the youngest of the Apostles, soon became well beloved by the Saints.

*Heber C. Kimball,
Wilford Woodruff, and
George A. Smith stayed
in this building—The
King's Arms Pub—upon
their arrival in London
in 1840. (Photo courtesy
Richard O. Cowan)*

Brigham Young implemented the principle of the gathering in June 1840 when he appointed John Moon of Eccleston to head the first company of emigrating Saints. These were but the first of thousands of Saints who would sail to America and strengthen the Church there during coming decades.

A new chapter in British mission history opened on 18 August 1840 when three Apostles—Elders Kimball, Woodruff, and Smith—carried the gospel message to London. They found their first lodgings at the King's Arms Pub (or inn), almost in the shadows of the famed London Bridge. The elders did not enjoy success in this neighborhood but were directed to Tabernacle Square a short distance away. There, they found a crowd of about four hundred listening to a Protestant minister who was standing on a chair preaching. When he finished, Elder Kimball called out, "There is a man present from

America who would like to preach." Elder George A. Smith was given this opportunity, and spoke for about twenty minutes on the first principles of the gospel. Upon his conclusion, Elder Kimball then asked if a time might be set when the American preacher could be heard again. Someone in the crowd objected: "I have just learned that the gentleman who has addressed you is a Latter-day Saint"; and he urged the gathering not to listen to him. "We have got the Gospel, and can save the people, without infidelity, socialism, or Latter-day Saints." Another person countered, and said to the missionaries, "You have as much right to preach here as he has." Elder Woodruff, therefore, was given the opportunity to preach that afternoon. Not only was the square full of eager listeners but people in the surrounding buildings also crowded open windows as high as the fourth story to hear what the Mormon elder had to say.[46]

Their first convert was baptized on 31 August; but generally, the work progressed only slowly. Heber C. Kimball lamented, "In our travels, either in America or Europe, we have never before found a people, from whose minds we have had to remove a greater multiplicity of objections, or combination of obstacles, in order to excite an interest in the subject and prepare the heart for the reception of the word of God, than in the city of London."[47] Still, by 14 February 1841 there were enough converts to organize the London Conference headed by Lorenzo Snow, a recently arrived missionary (and future apostle and president of the Church). During the next three years he would see several hundred additional converts join the Church and would even have the opportunity of presenting a copy of the Book of Mormon to Queen Victoria.

During early 1841, Elder Orson Hyde spent three months in England en route to his mission in Palestine. This brought the total number of Apostles in Britain to nine. On no other occasion has there been such a large number of these Brethren serving together in an overseas mission.

In the early spring of 1841, the Prophet Joseph Smith directed the Twelve to return home. In preparation for their departure, they visited the various areas where they had labored, strengthening branches and preparing the Saints to carry on the work even in the face of persecution. At the April conference in Manchester, members of the Twelve instructed the Saints in basic gospel doctrines and on how the Church should be organized.

Several hundred attended a gala farewell dinner at the Music Hall in Liverpool to honor the Apostles before they sailed for home. Elder Parley P. Pratt, who had brought his family from America the previous fall, remained behind to preside over the mission. For nearly a century, the British Mission would almost always be headed personally by a member of the Twelve.

Brigham Young looked back on what had been accomplished:

> It was with a heart full of thanksgiving and gratitude to God, my heavenly Father, that I reflected upon his dealings with me and my brethren of the Twelve during the past year of my life, which was spent in England. It truly seemed a miracle to look upon the contrast between our landing and departing from Liverpool. We landed in the spring of 1840, as strangers in a strange land and penniless, but through the mercy of God we have gained many friends, established Churches in almost every noted town and city in the kingdom of Great Britain, baptized between seven and eight thousand, printed 5,000 Books of Mormon, 3,000 Hymn Books, 2,500 volumes of the *Millennial Star,* and 60,000 tracts, and emigrated to Zion 1,000 souls, established a permanent ship-

ping agency, which will be a great blessing to the Saints, and have left sown in the hearts of many thousands the seeds of eternal truth, which will bring forth fruit to the honor and glory of God, and yet we have lacked nothing to eat, drink or wear; in all these things I acknowledge the hand of God.[48]

Not only had the Twelve fortified the Church in Britain, but this mission experience had also strengthened them as a quorum. Working together for a year in Britain bonded the members of the Twelve and solidified them as a body. When the Twelve were called in 1835, Oliver Cowdery had emphasized the need for them to be united. Historians of the 1837 to 1841 experience have concluded, "Until the mission to England, however, the Quorum had seldom fulfilled this charge. . . . It had often been contentious and divided and sometimes more concerned about prerogatives than about service. By 1841 that situation had changed dramatically, and the apostles returned from the British Isles stronger, more unified, and better prepared for new responsibilities."[49] Significantly, only the nine Apostles who responded to the call and served together in Britain would remain with the main body of the Church as it moved to the West. Among the Saints in Nauvoo who sustained the Twelve as the new leaders in 1844 following the martyrdom of Joseph Smith were hundreds of British converts who had been taught the gospel by these men.

Much remained to fully perfect the Church in Great Britain. Still, a beachhead had been established. As the British Empire extended its influence around the world, faithful Saints from Britain would have the opportunity to plant gospel seeds in many far-flung regions. A beginning had been made in Europe. About a decade after the elders had opened the mission in Britain, others would carry the gospel to the Continent.

CHAPTER 2

THE GOSPEL CARRIED TO THE CONTINENT

DONALD Q. CANNON

1849   Members of the Twelve called to open missions in Continental Europe.

1850   Church established in Denmark, Italy, and France

1851   Church established in Switzerland and Germany

          Book of Mormon published in Danish—first in a language other than English

1852   Missionaries enter Malta

1853   Missionaries reach Gibraltar

1855   Karl G. Maeser baptized

From its very beginnings The Church of Jesus Christ of Latter-day Saints has taught that the gospel should be carried to all the world. While initial international missionary efforts took place in Canada and the British Isles, Joseph Smith also showed a strong interest in taking the gospel to Continental Europe. He was aware of the Norwegian colony called the Fox River Settlement, not far from Nauvoo, where the first Scandinavian converts were baptized. He had been fascinated with Elder Orson Hyde's reports on conditions in Europe while traveling to and from the Holy Land in 1841 and 1842. As a result of this, the Prophet called Orson Hyde and James Adams to preach the gospel in Russia.

Lorenzo Snow, as shown in this Frederick Piercy steel engraving in January 1853, was the first missionary called to preach the gospel in Italy. He found only minor success there. More than a century would pass before missionary efforts resumed. (LDS Church Archives)

This commitment to teaching the gospel in all the world also became a priority for Joseph's successor, Brigham Young. In the general conference held in Salt Lake City in October 1849, the First Presidency called several Apostles on missions to various parts of the world, including John Taylor to France, Lorenzo Snow to Italy, and Erastus Snow to Denmark.[1] Germany and Switzerland were soon added to the list.

SCANDINAVIA

Most of the early European converts came from Scandinavia, which consists of the countries Denmark, Finland, Norway, and Sweden; Iceland is also included on occasion.

Scandinavians who joined the Church in America helped carry the gospel to their ancestral homelands. Thus, Peter Hanson—who had come to America to be baptized after his brother Hans, a sailor, joined the Church and wrote to Peter about it—was called to accompany Elder Erastus Snow to

Denmark, as were several other Saints of Scandinavian heritage.[2]

Elder Snow and the others arrived in Denmark on 14 June 1850. Inasmuch as he was with John Forsgren, who would work in Sweden, and George Dykes, who would work in Norway, Elder Erastus Snow dedicated all of Scandinavia for the preaching of the gospel, praying that each country would be receptive to their message. Eventually, Denmark, Norway, and Sweden all came under the jurisdiction of the Scandinavian Mission.

The establishment of religious freedom was an issue in all European countries at this time. Although Denmark had enacted a freedom of religion law in 1849, the power of the Lutheran Church and the pressure of persecution from every quarter made missionary work very difficult.[3]

In order to fortify the Saints, Elder Erastus Snow promoted publication and dissemination of all kinds of printed material concerning the Church. Elder Peter Hanson was the chief translator. The mission published a hymn book and several tracts, and in 1851 they also published the Book of Mormon in Danish—the first foreign language publication of that book of scripture.[4]

In addition to working in Copenhagen, missionaries preached in the northern part of Denmark, particularly in Aalborg. In this area they encountered opposition and persecution, but also enjoyed considerable success. Among those new converts from Aalborg was the Lund family, including one young boy named Anthon, who was bullied and harassed by his schoolmates because of his interest in being baptized. Anthon later had a notable career in the Church, serving several missions and eventually becoming an Apostle and member of the First Presidency. Elder Lund was the first Scandinavian to be called to serve as an Apostle.[5]

Missionaries called to Scandinavia taught the gospel not only in Denmark but also in Sweden, Norway, and Iceland. John E. Forsgren had been assigned to Sweden and entered that country in June 1850. Although members of his family readily accepted the gospel, Elder Forsgren experienced only a little success among other Swedes. Before the Swedish government ordered his deportation to America for preaching Mormonism, he managed to baptize seventeen people. Following his deportation he was able to work in Denmark.[6]

Among the early converts in Copenhagen were two Icelanders, Thorafin Thorason and Gudmundur Gudmundsson. They had been living in Denmark to obtain vocational training and planned to return to Iceland. When Gudmundsson saw one of the elders preaching on a street corner, a voice whispered to him, "What that man is saying is true; listen to him." He heeded the prompting and was baptized.[7] Before he and his friend left Denmark, Elder Erastus Snow ordained them to the office of priest in the Aaronic Priesthood so they could preach and baptize. They succeeded in baptizing two members before the Icelandic authorities prohibited any further preaching. Unfortunately, Brother Thorason accidentally drowned in December 1851. A Danish Elder, Johan Lorentzen, went to Iceland in 1853 and ordained Brother Gudmundsson to the office of elder. In the mid-1850s, nearly all Church members in Iceland would immigrate to Utah.[8]

In Copenhagen, Erastus Snow had converted and baptized Svend Larsen, a Norwegian ship captain. Svend traveled to Norway in company with Elder Hans F. Petersen, a new Danish elder. Unfortunately, persecution quickly arose, and

Elder Petersen was arrested and placed under order not to preach the gospel in Norway. Nevertheless, he tried to convert Norwegians in private conversation. Eventually Elder Petersen had to leave Norway because of the violent persecution against Mormons. Captain Svend Larsen, however, continued to preach the gospel wherever his ship docked.[9]

By the end of Elder Erastus Snow's term of service as mission president in 1852, seven hundred Scandinavians had embraced the restored gospel. Elder Snow left mission affairs under the direction of John Forsgren.

All through the 1850s, persecution against the Latter-day Saints continued in Scandinavia. Missionaries were imprisoned and/or banished on several occasions. Despite such persecution, the number of converts steadily increased. When the missionaries were called home in 1857 with the approach of a hostile U.S. army during the so-called "Utah War," there were 3,353 Saints in Scandinavia. Eventually, fourteen thousand Scandinavian Saints gathered to Utah.[10]

What caused such success in Scandinavia? Why did so many join the Church when it brought persecution and problems? In his classic work *Homeward to Zion,* William Mulder gave a plausible answer. Professor Mulder believes the answer is in the power of Mormon doctrine, especially the doctrine of gathering. Mormonism gave Scandinavian believers an opportunity to channel their faith into meaningful action. The Saints believed the gathering was a part of the doctrine of perfection and progression.[11]

In addition to these doctrinal points, Mulder's work describes the effect of religious discontent that was rampant in Scandinavia and caused the people to seek for something more.[12]

ITALY

The general conference of October 1849 designated Elder Lorenzo Snow of the Twelve and Joseph Toronto, a convert from Italy, to open missionary work in that land. While in England on their journey to Italy they enlisted the aid of two additional missionaries: Elder T. B. H. Stenhouse and Elder Jabez Woodward. Also while in England, Elder Snow felt impressed to engage in a study of a religious group known as the Waldensians, a Protestant sect founded by French merchant Peter Waldo. Lorenzo Snow believed that a heritage of persecution and spirit of independence made the Waldensians good prospects for accepting the gospel.[13]

Peter Waldo's conversion, religious activity, and subsequent founding of the Waldensians began in 1170. In a sense, the Waldensians were the earliest Protestant Reformers, and when others became involved in the Reformation, the Waldensians joined with them in their efforts. Many Waldensians took up residence in the northwestern mountain valleys of Italy. As Protestants, they suffered attacks from the government of Savoy, under strong encouragement from the Catholic Church. In the Revolution of 1848, the Waldensians received a measure of religious freedom. The Mormon missionaries began their work in these circumstances.[14]

Elder Snow and his companions arrived at Genoa, Italy, in June 1850. On 29 October 1850, the missionaries ascended Mt. Castelluzzo near the village of Torre Pellice. There on top of the mountain peak, which they called Mount Brigham, Lorenzo Snow dedicated Italy for the preaching of the gospel.[15]

As the missionaries commenced their labors among the Waldensians, they blessed the sick child of their innkeeper. The critically ill child soon recovered, and news of this event

Mt. Brigham (or Mt. Castelluzzo) near Torre Pellice, Italy, where Lorenzo Snow dedicated Italy to the preaching of the gospel on 29 October 1850. (Photo courtesy Donald Q. Cannon)

opened many doors for them. Most of the Waldensians spoke French and so they had Church materials translated into that language. [16] Elder Lorenzo Snow also saw the need for Italian materials and so the Book of Mormon was translated into Italian in 1852.

While some of the Waldensians embraced the Church, most did not. Many believed that joining a new religion would be an act of disloyalty toward their ancestors and religious heritage. Thus, the high hopes that Elder Snow had entertained for success among this Protestant group were never realized. Most of those who did join the Church were organized and prepared for gathering to Zion. Elder Woodward led the first group of Waldensians to Salt Lake City in 1854. Although their numbers were never large, the Waldensian converts have a rather remarkable posterity. Waldensian names common among the Saints of today in Utah include Beus, Cardon, Malan, Bertoch, Pons, and Chatelain.[17]

Armed with an Italian Book of Mormon, some of the early missionaries made an effort in Genoa and other cities populated by Italian Catholics. Despite their best efforts no one entered the waters of baptism.

In 1854 the Swiss and Italian missions were consolidated. Some sporadic work continued in Italy, but most missionary efforts and success would not take place until the twentieth century.[18]

SWITZERLAND

Famed for its Alpine scenic attractions, policy of neutrality, and spirit of independence, Switzerland was opened to missionary work in December 1850 as an outgrowth of earlier activity in Italy. Because he knew some French, Elder T. B. H. Stenhouse was assigned to Geneva in the French-speaking portion of Switzerland. His wife and daughter joined him there and assisted in preaching the gospel.[19]

Elder Lorenzo Snow joined Elder Stenhouse in February 1851 and dedicated Switzerland for the preaching of the gospel. Early missionary efforts were undertaken in the face of considerable opposition from the Calvinist Protestants of Geneva. Reflecting their resistance to Mormonism, Elder Stenhouse described Geneva as "The Protestant Rome." Despite widespread resistance, a few brave souls joined the Church. By the end of 1851 two small branches had been established, one in Geneva and one in Lausanne.[20]

Among the early converts in Lausanne was the Ballif family. Serge Ballif, former minister and publisher and a man of some considerable wealth, became a powerful missionary himself after his own conversion. He preached in his native Lausanne and assisted in opening missionary work in the German-speaking area of Switzerland. In this effort the missionaries were assisted by the German translation of the Book of Mormon.[21]

Although the Church grew, opposition and persecution also occurred. Elder William Budge, for example, was arrested thirteen times in less than a year while laboring in the Zurich region. A British citizen, he finally appealed his case to the British ambassador in Bern, who told him the actions against him were appropriate, as the LDS Church was "opposed to civilization and religion."[22]

In common with other early converts, the Saints in Switzerland learned about the gathering and responded to the call. In February 1854, T. B. H. Stenhouse led the first group of fifty-eight Swiss members to Zion by way of Liverpool. An example of an early Swiss emigrant is Jacob Spori. Born in Oberwyl, Switzerland, in 1847, he showed a marked interest in learning at an early age. The recipient of several academic degrees, Spori could speak nine languages. He taught school and served as principal of a high school as well as city clerk. Having become dissatisfied with the Reformed Church, he was eager to accept the message of the Restoration presented by the missionaries. He was baptized in 1877 and immigrated to Utah two years later. Jacob later helped establish the Bannock Stake Academy, which later became Ricks College, now BYU—Idaho. He was one of many Swiss converts who helped build Zion in the American West.[23]

GERMANY

At the time Germany received missionaries from the Church it was not a single unified country, but a federation of thirty-one independent German states. During the 1840s the Church had made some effort to bring the gospel to Germany. James Howard, an English convert, did some missionary work in Hamburg in 1840, but no conversions resulted from his efforts. Elder Orson Hyde spent several months in Germany in 1841–42 en route to Jerusalem and on his return trip. His efforts resulted in the publication of a pamphlet entitled *Ein Ruf Aus der Wueste (A Cry from the Wilderness),* which told the story of Mormonism and its beliefs.[24]

A missionary assigned to Denmark, Elder George P. Dykes, preached in the adjoining Schleswig-Holstein area of northern Germany and baptized a few converts. Banished from that area in 1851, he later linked up with Elder John Taylor in London. Together, they began a German translation of the Book of Mormon. Traveling together, Elders Taylor and Dykes landed in Hamburg in October 1851. They began publication of a monthly periodical, *Zions Panier (Zion's Banner),* and by 1852 had published a German language translation of the Book of Mormon.[25]

During that year, Church Authorities appointed Daniel Carn as the first official German mission president. He arrived in Hamburg in mid-1852 and by August had baptized twelve people and organized a branch. Early in 1853 seven more elders joined President Carn.[26] As success came, so did persecution and opposition. Whether in Hamburg, Prussia, Saxony, or Wuerttemberg, Mormon missionaries, and even President Carn, were arrested and then banished from German territory. Despite such harassment, the Church continued to grow. By

1854, 128 persons were baptized. Many of these members immigrated to America.[27]

In the midst of these difficulties, an outstanding convert, Karl G. Maeser, came into the fold. Unlike most early German converts, Maeser belonged to the German aristocracy. He would make a significant contribution to the Church, both in Germany and in America.[28]

FRANCE

Unlike Italy and Germany in the mid-nineteenth century, France was a unified nation. It was also one of the most powerful countries in the world. However, there were two forces that thwarted proselytizing efforts: an atmosphere of skepticism and the powerful Catholic Church.

Missionary work in France began in 1849, when William Howells of Aberdare, Wales, traveled to LeHavre on the northern coast of France. His first companion was his daughter Ann, who was only nine years old. Because his French was fairly limited, he worked among English families in LeHavre. His first convert was Augustus Saint d'Anna, a young man with skill in multiple languages. Howells was able to organize a small branch of the Church in Boulogne in April 1850. In June 1850, Elder John Taylor of the Twelve arrived in Boulogne, and in company with William Howells and other members dedicated France for the preaching of the gospel. The dedicatory prayer was offered on the seashore near Boulogne. Brother Howells then accompanied John Taylor and the others to Paris, where he continued to preach.[29]

Missionary work in France made some progress, but the opposition was formidable. Elder John Taylor expressed his frustration about the severe restrictions under which missionaries

It was in this building in Paris, France, that the Book of Mormon was translated into French in 1852. (Photo courtesy Donald Q. Cannon)

labored: "'Liberty,' 'Equality,' 'Fraternity,' were written upon almost every door. You had liberty to speak, but might be put in prison for doing so. You had liberty to print, but they might burn what you had printed, and put you in confinement for it."[30]

In addition to preaching the gospel and defending the Church from attack, Elder John Taylor launched a vigorous publishing effort. This was assisted by one highly interesting and intelligent Frenchman: Louis Bertrand, who was baptized by Elder Taylor in December 1850.[31] A brilliant writer involved in the Revolution of 1848, Bertrand had published a Communist newspaper, *Le Populaire*. Using these publication and editorial skills, he helped establish the monthly Latter-day Saint periodical, *Étoile du Deseret* (*Star of Deseret*), in 1851. Bertrand also assisted with the translation of the Book of Mormon, which was published in 1852.[32] Later, he translated the Doctrine and Covenants into French. As a missionary, Bertrand taught the gospel to several French revolutionaries—including the famed Victor Hugo—in the Jersey Isles; none of them joined the Church, however.[33]

Following a few years in Utah, Bertrand was called as a mission president in France. He served from 1859 to 1864, during which time he unsuccessfully petitioned the Emperor Louis Napoleon II for permission to preach the gospel without restriction.[34] Due to such lack of success, the French mission was temporarily closed in 1864. Truly one of the most notable and interesting Frenchmen to join the Church, Louis Bertrand died in Salt Lake City in 1875.[35]

MALTA AND GIBRALTAR

Eager to share the gospel in additional lands, Elder Lorenzo Snow expanded missionary efforts in Italy into nearby Malta—a British controlled island in the central Mediterranean Sea—in 1852. Within a few months, about twenty-six people joined the Church. When Elder Snow left Malta to return to Utah, he appointed Thomas Obray, an English elder, to supervise mission activities. The mission in Malta spawned three branches: a "floating branch" consisting of British naval personnel in the Mediterranean, a branch consisting of people from Nova Scotia, and an Expeditionary Force Branch in Turkey. Unfortunately, this rapid growth did not continue, and Church leaders closed the mission in 1856. Work in Malta would not resume until 1979.[36]

Meanwhile, missionaries had similarly carried the gospel to Gibraltar, a British-controlled island at the western end of the Mediterranean. Elder Edward Stevenson, a native of Gibraltar, returned to his island fortress homeland along with Nathan

Porter in 1853. Eventually, despite opposition, a branch of the Church with ten members came into being. When the Crimean War broke out, some of these members went to fight in that conflict. Discouraged by the lack of results and by military obligations, Elder Stevenson departed for Utah in 1855, pausing to dust his feet as a testimony against Gibraltar's political administration, which had placed heavy restrictions on the missionaries. Thus ended the first and only mission to Gibraltar. Recent success in Spain, however, has led to the re-establishment of a Church presence there; a score of members of the Cadiz Spain Stake now live in Gibraltar. Edward Stevenson, who had pioneered the work, received a call to the First Council of the Seventy in 1894.[37]

CONCLUSION

During the 1850s, Latter-day Saint missionaries introduced the gospel into many countries of Continental Europe. These faithful missionaries reaped their greatest harvest in Scandinavia, especially Denmark. Major success would not come in other European countries until much later (see chapters 6 and 7). The lack of religious freedom played a major role in this occurrence. Many Saints did not remain in Europe, but immigrated to America.

CHAPTER 3

GATHERING TO ZION

FRED E. WOODS

The glorious news of the restoration of the gospel of Jesus Christ included the doctrine of the gathering—the coming together of God's covenant people. Adherence to this doctrine would result in dramatic life changes and, for many, would require an arduous journey to a new homeland. Latter-day Saints regard themselves as literal (or adopted) descendants of the ancient house of Israel and believe in "the literal gathering of Israel."[1] Biblical accounts record God's attempts to gather his people from earliest times. But why?

The Prophet Joseph Smith once asked rhetorically, "What was the object of gathering the Jews, or the people of God in any age of the world?" His answer, "The main object was to

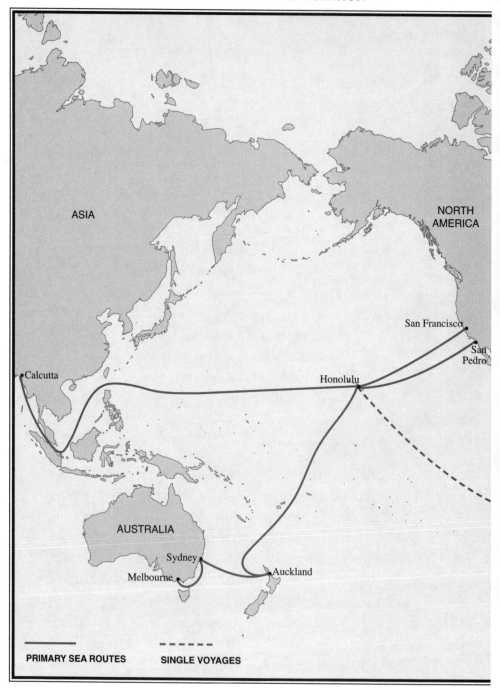

ASIA

NORTH AMERICA

San Francisco

San Pedro

Calcutta

Honolulu

AUSTRALIA

Sydney

Melbourne

Auckland

PRIMARY SEA ROUTES   SINGLE VOYAGES

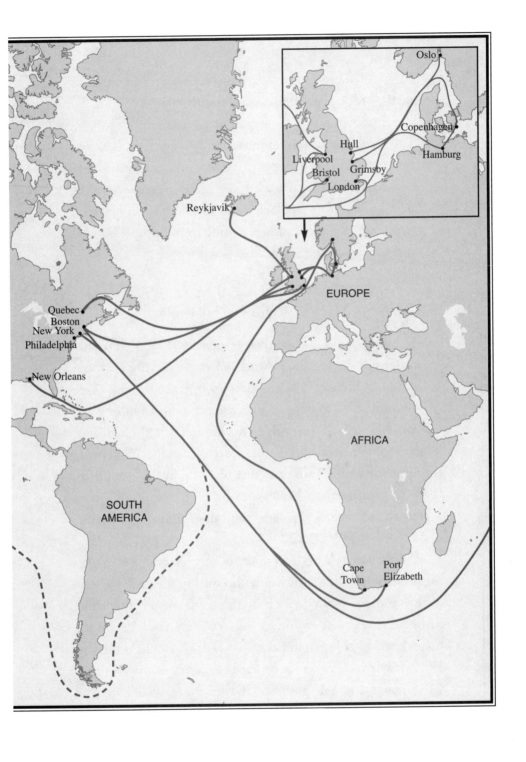

build unto the Lord a house whereby He could reveal unto His people the ordinances of His house and the glories of his kingdom, and teach the people the way of salvation."[2]

The many migrant miles traversed by tens of thousands of Latter-day Saint converts beg yet a second question: Where does the Mormon Trail really begin?[3] We must go beyond the plains in search of the trailhead. For much of the nineteenth century, the people who gathered came from Europe; but this was not the case at the beginning.

GATHERING IN THE EARLY YEARS OF THE RESTORED CHURCH

The universal call to gather was received by the Prophet Joseph Smith during the second conference of the Restored Church, less than six months after its organization in 1830: "And ye are called to bring to pass the gathering of mine elect; for mine elect hear my voice and harden not their hearts. Wherefore the decree hath gone forth from the Father that they shall be gathered in unto one place upon the face of this land, to prepare their hearts and be prepared in all things against the day when tribulation and desolation are sent forth upon the wicked" (D&C 29:7–8).

Yet missionary work and the associated gathering were taking place only within North America during the first few years of the Church's existence. Throughout this period the Saints gathered first in the region of western New York, where the Church was established in Fayette on 6 April 1830. As the year 1831 dawned, they were instructed to gather to the Kirtland, Ohio, region and were given specific reasons for so doing: "And that ye might escape the power of the enemy, and be gathered unto me a righteous people, without spot and blameless—

Wherefore, for this cause I gave unto you the commandment that ye should go to the Ohio; and there I will give my law; and there you shall be endowed with power from on high" (D&C 38:31–32).

From Kirtland, missionary work was launched during the 1830s to various places in the United States as well as Canada. Converts from various pockets of North America were encouraged to gather to Kirtland where the temple was being constructed during the years 1833–36. Once the temple was completed, Church members were enriched by the power they experienced in this sacred edifice. However, social prejudice soon followed, which forced the Saints to leave the Kirtland region. It was not intended that Kirtland be a permanent gathering place for the Latter-day Saints at this juncture in time. In the fall of 1831, God spoke through his servant Joseph, declaring, "I, the Lord, will to retain a strong hold in the land of Kirtland, for the space of five years" (D&C 64:21).

During the decade of the 1830s, some Church members gathered to western Missouri in hopes of establishing Zion in that state as well. In the summer of 1831, the Lord identified Jackson County, Missouri, as the heart of Zion and noted that "the place which is now called Independence is the center place; and a spot for the temple is lying westward" (D&C 57:3). Yet, the Missouri temple was not built in Independence because the Saints were driven out by Jackson County mobocrats at the close of 1833. Five years later, the Missouri Saints—who had generally migrated north to Caldwell and Davies Counties—as well as hundreds of Kirtland Saints who had fled to this region, were exiled from the state of Missouri as a result of the extermination order issued by Governor Lilburn W. Boggs on 27 October 1838.

A new gathering place for these displaced Ohio and Missouri Saints was chosen the following year in western Illinois. Here, Saints from Canada and the eastern United States, as well as foreign converts from abroad, combined their faith and works to build the beautiful city of Nauvoo out of a mosquito-infested swampland on the eastern banks of the Mississippi River.

The gathering of foreign Saints from abroad did not commence until the necessary priesthood keys were restored to the earth. This restoration occurred 3 April 1836, just one week after the dedication of the Kirtland Temple. In this sacred edifice, the ancient prophet Moses appeared and bestowed on Joseph Smith Jr. and Oliver Cowdery "the keys of the gathering of Israel from the four parts of the earth" (D&C 110:11).[4]

The following year, Joseph Smith charged his trusted associate, Apostle Heber C. Kimball, with the assignment of opening up missionary work in Great Britain. Elder Kimball was joined by a fellow Apostle, Orson Hyde, and with five other missionaries.[5] These elders were instructed to teach the message of the Restoration and were also warned by the Prophet Joseph before their departure to "remain silent considering the gathering . . . until such time as the work [is] fully established, and it should be clearly made manifest by the Spirit to do otherwise."[6]

During the space of just nine months (July 1837 to April 1838), these missionaries baptized more than fifteen hundred converts.[7] Their success was augmented less than two years later when other members of the Twelve embarked on another

The Liverpool waterfront was the point of departure for thousands of LDS converts en route to America. (Photo courtesy Donald Q. Cannon)

mission to Great Britain (January 1840 to April 1841). They came not only to expand the work, but also to revive a lethargic spirit that had crept in among some of the British converts.[8] The Twelve reaped great success in the British Isles, and by the spring of 1840, the Church was firmly established in the land. It was in this season that the Twelve decided it was time to commence the gathering of the British converts to America.[9]

THE STRAINS AND GAINS FOR CONVERTS GATHERING FROM ABROAD

The British Saints began their immigration to Nauvoo with the voyage of the *Britannia* on 6 June 1840, with English convert John Moon leading a group of forty Saints from the port of Liverpool.[10] At the time of embarkation, Hugh Moon recalled that members of the Twelve were present to lend their support. Moon wrote, "We found Elders Brigham Young and Heber C. Kimball aboard. They had stretched a curtain across our cabin and commenced blessing the company. They bid us walk in."[11]

Notwithstanding, many experienced the difficulty of leaving their family, friends, and homeland. Reflecting upon her journey to Zion, Priscilla Staines wrote: "I left the home of my birth to gather to Nauvoo. I was alone. It was a dreary winter day on which I went to Liverpool. The company with which I was to sail were all strangers to me. When I arrived at Liverpool and saw the ocean that would soon roll between me and all I loved, my heart almost failed me. But I had laid my idols all upon the altar. There was no turning back."[12]

Yet for Staines and many other converts, such as William Clayton, the sacrifice brought joy: "It is impossible for pen to describe to you the difficulties you will have to endure. You must come or suffer the vengeance of heaven and for my part I will say that if I was in England now and had experienced all the journey it would not in the least deter me from coming for I have often found that in the greatest seasons of suffering we have the greatest cause of rejoicing."[13]

LETTERS AND EPISTLES ENCOURAGE GATHERING FROM ABROAD

After safely arriving in Illinois, Francis Moon wrote back to his British homeland to describe the temporal and spiritual advantages of immigrating to Nauvoo: "What I might say upon this subject [I hope] might have the tendency of encouraging my fellow Englishmen in the point of gathering. . . . And [I] would say if you can get to this land, you will be better off than in England, for in this place there is a prospect of receiving every good thing both of this world and that which is to come."[14]

Letters home bearing glad tidings from British proselytes paved the way for nearly five thousand British converts who would follow and settle in Nauvoo.[15] Such positive feedback was published in the periodical, *The Latter-day Saints' Millennial Star*. For example, in 1841, the *Millennial Star* printed an article titled "Emigration" and commented, "The news from the emigrants who sailed from this country last season is so very encouraging that it will give a new impulse to the spirit of the gathering."[16] In addition, Church leaders also provided written instructions that encouraged immigration to Nauvoo in order for the Saints to build the temple and partake of its blessings.[17]

British converts were also influenced by the excellent organization and dependability of their Church leaders, both at Liverpool and in Nauvoo. Not only did the *Millennial Star* provide useful instructions to departing Latter-day Saint emigrants, but it also published the dates when various trans-Atlantic voyages would depart. In addition, an emigration agent was selected by Church leaders to carry out arrangements at Liverpool. As early as April 1841, an "Epistle of the Twelve" was published in the *Millennial Star* and addressed the appointment and advantages of having a Church agent:

> We have found that there are so many "pick pockets," and so many that will take every possible advantage of strangers, in Liverpool, that we have appointed Elder Amos Fielding, as the agent of the church, to superintend the fitting out of Saints from Liverpool to America. Whatever information the Saints may want about the preparations for a voyage, they are advised to call on Elder Fielding, at

Liverpool, as their first movement, when they arrive there as emigrants. There are some brethren who have felt themselves competent to do their own business in these matters, and rather despising the counsel of their friends, have been robbed and cheated out of nearly all they had. A word of caution to the wise is sufficient.

Furthermore, the letter continued: "It is also a great saving to go in companies, instead of going individually. First, a company can charter a vessel, so as to make the passage much cheaper than otherwise. Secondly, provisions can be purchased at wholesale for a company much cheaper than otherwise. Thirdly, this will avoid bad company on the passage. Fourthly, when a company arrives in New Orleans they can charter a steam-boat so as to reduce the passage near one-half. The measure will save some hundreds of pounds on each ship load. Fifthly, a man of experience can go as leader of each company, who will know how to avoid rogues and knaves."[18]

Later, the Church assigned agents at the ports of New Orleans as well as New York to meet the incoming Saints. As they travelled up the Mississippi during the Nauvoo years (1840–1846), immigrating Saints were also met by other supportive Saints and Church leaders, including the Prophet Joseph Smith.[19]

Despite the best efforts of leaders and Saints, those who gathered were warned by the First Presidency concerning false expectations: "We would wish the Saints to understand that, when they come here, they must not expect perfection, or that all will be harmony, peace, and love; if they indulge these ideas, they will undoubtedly be deceived, for here there are persons, not only from different states, but from different nations, who, although they feel a great attachment to the cause of truth, have their prejudices."[20]

Although there were certainly problems to be dealt with at Nauvoo, the Saints in general met most of the obstacles and labored together to build a splendid temple that adorned the city. However, by the winter of 1846, the Saints were forced to leave Nauvoo, and the following year they made a new Zion in the West.

PROBLEMS AND SOLUTIONS IN GATHERING TO THE WEST

Emphasis on the gathering was continued in Utah with the same amount of energy it had been given in Nauvoo. For example, in 1852, when Latter-day Saint Scandinavians began to immigrate to Utah, the First Presidency declared to the Saints abroad, "It is time for them to gather, without delay, to Zion."[21] Some Scandinavians who endured the long Atlantic voyage aboard sailing vessels found obstacles crossing the American plains that delayed them and that they found more difficult than their ocean travels. One author noted, "Some of the Scandinavians, disliking the American way of driving oxen in yokes, hitched up the beasts of burden in regular Danish fashion. But they had forgotten one little thing—that the oxen were American. . . . It was decided that it would be easier for the emigrants to learn American ways than it would be for the oxen to learn the Danish harness."[22]

Many Scandinavian and British Saints faced serious delays, which kept them from reaching Zion in a timely fashion. Economics was the primary challenge and difficulty for many converts seeking to gather resources for themselves and their families. This problem was partially resolved by the windfall of resources brought to the Salt Lake Valley by those heading West in the gold rush, bringing a certain degree of wealth to the Valley.[23] Such a windfall provided means for missionary work to be opened in more areas of Europe. It also allowed resources for the launching of the Perpetual Emigrating Fund, which helped provide a way for the poor to be financially assisted in their journey to Zion. This revolving fund, generally called the PEF, was launched in 1849 and continued until 1887. It provided assistance for thousands of Saints who gathered to Utah Territory during the nineteenth century. This fund was called "perpetual" because it was established with the idea of allowing immigrants to have a temporary loan that was to be paid back to the PEF as soon as possible once the migrants reached Utah.[24]

ROUTES OF TRAVEL

Notwithstanding such assistance, there were various factors which influenced the number of European immigrants that came to Utah during the nineteenth century as well as the route they took and their mode of transportation. During the years of Brigham Young's administration as Church president (1847–1877), he made the final decisions regarding migration routes, but only after gathering all the information he could. For example, due to health risks, in 1854 he rerouted the Saints through select eastern ports instead of New Orleans, which had been the Saints' principal port from 1841 to 1854. In a letter of that year, Brigham directed Elder Franklin D. Richards, stationed in Liverpool, as follows: "You are aware of the sickness liable to assail our unacclimated brethren on the Mississippi river, hence I wish you to ship no more to New

Orleans, but ship to Philadelphia, Boston, and New York, giving preference in the order named."[25]

President Young also listened attentively to his emigration agents at various ports and posts; they often had valuable suggestions. For example, in 1859 the Mormon immigrants' railway transport route through the States changed as a direct result of a letter New York emigration agent George Q. Cannon sent to Brigham Young. In this letter, Cannon proposed that the Saints be rerouted through Quincy, Illinois, (instead of Iowa City) before getting on board the Hannibal and St. Joseph Railroad, which the Saints used from 1859 to 1866.[26] In 1866, New York emigration agent Thomas Taylor chose a more economic route from New York to Chicago, which the Church supported.[27]

MODES OF TRANSPORTATION

The changing circumstances of the immigrants also affected their means of travel. For example, the destitute British Saints resorted to handcarts to reduce the cost of their journey. In a letter dated 30 September 1855, Brigham Young wrote: "I have been thinking about how we should operate another year. We cannot afford to purchase wagons and teams as in times past. I am consequently thrown back upon my own plan to make hand-carts, and let the emigration foot it, and draw upon them (the carts) the necessary supplies, having a cow or two for every ten. They can come just as quick, if not quicker and much cheaper."[28]

Although nearly two hundred died as the Willie and Martin handcart companies suffered in the winter of 1856, overall this handcart experiment proved successful as nearly three thousand Saints crossed the plains in ten companies using 662 carts during the years 1856 to 1860.[29]

A significant change in the mode of travel resulted from a suggestion contained in a letter George Q. Cannon wrote to Brigham Young dated 18 January 1860. He suggested, "I have thought that a good many of the poor Saints might be taken through who otherwise have to remain, if they [the emigrants] could go through with part rations and be met with teams with provisions from the Valley."[30] Beginning the next year, therefore, immigrants were met at the Missouri River by Utah teamsters who brought wagons and provisions. During the next several years, nearly twenty thousand migrants crossed the plains with these "Church Trains."[31]

GATHERING DURING THE CIVIL WAR YEARS

Although it seemed unlikely, during the Civil War (1861–1865) Mormon immigration heightened, rather than declining.[32] A *Millennial Star* headline printed just one month after the war commenced read, "Civil War in America—Its Importance As a Warning to the Saints." After recounting the war's commencement, the article pointed to the event as the fulfillment of Joseph Smith's prophecy given nearly three decades earlier, which declared that a war beginning in South Carolina would be "poured out upon all nations" (D&C 87:2). The article then stressed that those gathered out West in Zion "shall be the only people that will not be at war," and those who journeyed Zionward would be nestled "in the bosom of a vast continent, far removed from the scene of strife, and encompassed by lofty mountains and interminable deserts and plains, the country they inhabit will be but little affected by the battles and dissensions of the outer world."[33] Such information appears to

Steamships such as this one—the S. S. Wyoming, *which carried 10,473 LDS emigrants in 38 voyages between 1871 and 1890 from Liverpool to New York—cut travel time across the Atlantic by more than three weeks. (Photo courtesy Peabody Museum of Salem)*

have motivated more than eleven thousand European Saints to cross the Atlantic on thirty-two voyages and then to travel across America during the Civil War. This was a very adventurous period for the immigrants, who were threatened both on land and sea by Confederate warships and American soldiers. In fact, while crossing the Plains these European converts actually feared the soldiers more than the Indians.[34]

IMPROVEMENTS IN TECHNOLOGY

Progress in the area of transportation technology also had a tremendous impact on the gathering. For example, during the years the Saints crossed the Atlantic on sailing vessels (1840–1867), the average time for a voyage from Liverpool to New York was about five weeks. The earlier route to New Orleans lasted more than two weeks longer. With the advent of steamships, the Saints could make the journey from Liverpool to New York in about eleven days.[35]

Steam power had the same impact on land. With the completion of the Transcontinental Railroad (10 May 1869), travelers could cross the United States from coast to coast in less than ten days. This was in stark contrast to traveling ten to twelve weeks just from the Missouri River to the Great Basin during the wagon train years. For the complete story of the migration, one must include the sail and rail, as well as the trail.

CONCLUSION

At the close of the nineteenth century, immigration to Zion began to decline. During the years 1840 to 1890, more than eighty-five thousand Mormon converts crossed the Atlantic, with most coming from Great Britain, the second largest group from Scandinavia, and smaller numbers from Germany and Switzerland. In addition, there was a sprinkling of others who crossed the Pacific from various countries.[36] In the twentieth century, Church leaders began to emphasize that the Saints were not to move to Zion (America), but rather to build Zion where they were.[37] In 1911, for example, the First Presidency counseled that "under present conditions" gathering to America was "not urged" because it was preferable "that our people shall remain in their native lands and form congregations of a permanent character to aid in the work of proselyting."[38] However, for some Saints the urge to gather was too strong, especially because there were no temples overseas for many years. This drain of faithful converts posed one of the greatest challenges the Church in Europe faced during the later nineteenth century.

CHAPTER 4

THE EUROPEAN CHURCH BECALMED

DONALD Q. CANNON

1840	The *Millennial Star* published in England
1851	Pearl of Great Price published in England
	Étoile du Deseret published in France
1861	First missionaries enter Belgium
1864	Netherlands mission opened
1865	Mission organized in Austria
1875	First missionaries enter Finland

The somewhat unusual title for this chapter is derived from the tremendous differences that existed between the early and late nineteenth-century history of the Church. For example, in the 1830s and 1840s the Church grew very rapidly in the British Isles, especially in England. The phenomenal success of Wilford Woodruff's mission, with his conversions running into the hundreds, is matched by other successful missionary efforts.[1]

In stark contrast, the work in the British Isles suffered a severe decline in the last half of the nineteenth century. Thus, the Church in Europe, like a vessel at sea without any wind in its sails, was becalmed. Several factors contributed to this predicament.

THE CHURCH IN EUROPE

FACTORS INHIBITING CHURCH GROWTH

Between the years 1851 and 1859, membership in Great Britain dropped from 33,900 to 13,000, a decrease of 60 percent. Obviously, the immigration of thousands of Latter-day Saint converts to America contributed to this decline. While many converts added to the Church's growth in Europe by coming through the front door of baptism, a comparable number took away from it by leaving through the back door of emigration. Settlements in western America were being strengthened, but the Church in Europe was losing not only most of its members, but particularly its capable leaders. And still, other factors presented further obstacles for the Church to overcome. The public announcement of plural marriage in 1852 and ensuing press coverage and judicial proceedings fostered a negative image of the Church. This undoubtedly contributed to the decline in baptisms. Between 1851 and 1859, baptisms fell by 88 percent in Europe.[2]

Apathy among the British Saints was another significant factor. Visiting his native England in the 1870s, George Reynolds, one of Brigham Young's secretaries, said: "Many of the folks have degenerated into old sing along sectarians. . . . They are so fast asleep that you can't wake them up."[3]

In society, challenges to religion posed by science—particularly Darwinism—caused a loss of faith and the rise of doubt. Darwin's *Origin of the Species* appeared in 1859. Church leaders, sensing the potential dangers in his theories, responded in print. Additionally, George Q. Cannon (who continually sought to refute Darwinism in the 1860s while in England, and throughout the remainder of the century) delivered a conference address in the 1880s in which he said:

Books have been written and years of time spent by learned men to establish what is called Darwinian theory, while others have endeavored to combat that theory. It has disturbed the whole religious world. Many preachers of the Gospel have adopted this theory. The result is, infidelity has spread. Doubt has been thrown upon the Mosaic account of creation, the whole religious world has been agitated, and in many instances faith in the scriptures has been destroyed by this theory of the eminent philosopher, Charles Darwin. I suppose the majority of the theologians who have been trained in the universities during the last quarter of a century, are inclined to look upon the Mosaic account of the creation as mythical in character. Men will try to show—and apparently succeed—that this earth and its inhabitants have existed for a far longer period than the Bible warrants us in believing.[4]

Emigration, polygamy, apathy, and Darwinism combined to take their toll, and the growth of the Church in Great Britain declined sharply.

While the Church continued to grow for a time in Scandinavia, eventually some of the same factors that had earlier slowed progress in Great Britain had a similar effect in Scandinavia and Continental Europe. In these areas, though, additional factors presented challenges to the Church. For example, the Franco-Prussian War (1870–71) disrupted the work in many countries of Europe, but the impact was not uniform. Growth in Denmark, which had been continuing solidly throughout the 1860s, declined; nevertheless, growth accelerated in Sweden.

Even though the Church's progress in Europe during the later nineteenth century was generally slow, there were, nevertheless, some bright spots representing significant accomplishments.

The Karl G. Maeser home in Meissen, Germany. Maeser was one of the most influential converts from Europe. (Photo courtesy Donald Q. Cannon)

These included expansion into new areas, as well as the impact of key individuals and important Church publications.

KARL G. MAESER

Missionary work in Switzerland and Germany received a boost from Karl G. Maeser. During his term as president of the Swiss-German Mission from 1867 to 1870, the number of new members increased sharply, in contrast to the decline elsewhere. Part of this growth came from the publication of a mission periodical called *Der Stern* (*The Star*). Enthusiasm for gathering to America also stimulated Church growth. The story of Karl G. Maeser is unique in the history of the Church. He came from the upper strata, something very unusual in the early days of the Church. While teaching at the prestigious Budich Institute in Dresden, Germany, he read a tract written by an anti-Mormon. The illogical nature of the pamphlet caused him to desire to know the truth about Mormonism. Eventually his inquiries led to a visit by a Mormon missionary, William Budge. After being taught the gospel and meeting with Franklin D. Richards, the European Mission President, Maeser was baptized in 1855. Following his immersion in the Elbe River near Dresden, he received a miraculous confirmation of his decision to be baptized. Elder Budge had been acting as interpreter between Karl G. Maeser and President Richards, but following his baptism, Karl G. Maeser and President Richards were able to understand each other without the translation efforts of Elder Budge. Maeser was thus convinced of the correctness of his decision to be baptized.

Brother Maeser continued to help in the building of the Church in Germany before gathering to Utah. After a few years in America, Karl G. Maeser returned to Germany, where he served effectively as mission president. Later, he helped found Brigham Young Academy in Utah, which eventually became Brigham Young University.[5]

NEW FIELDS OF LABOR

THE NETHERLANDS

Commonly called Holland, the Netherlands has twelve provinces, and Dutch is the official language. A small country of only 13,000 square miles, it gained its independence in 1648.

Although Elder Orson Hyde visited the Netherlands in 1841 while on his way to the Holy Land, the first full-time missionaries, Paul Schettler and W. Van der Woude, did not arrive until October 1861. The first branch was organized the following year in Amsterdam, and the first mission president, Joseph Weiler, began serving in Holland in 1864.

Missionary work in the Netherlands was difficult because the Dutch tend to cling tightly to their traditions. The crusade against polygamy in America also had its negative effect in the Netherlands. Prejudice against the Church became so widespread that many years passed without any baptisms. After the Manifesto in 1890 announced the end of plural marriages, the number of converts increased dramatically. That same year, the Book of Mormon was published in Dutch, a factor that also increased missionary success. By 1900 there were nearly seventeen hundred members in Holland.[6]

AUSTRIA

In the nineteenth century, Austria was part of the Austro-Hungarian Empire, which had a dozen ethnic groups and at least that number of languages. The official language of Austria was German, and most Austrians were Roman Catholics.

Orson Hyde visited Austria en route to the Middle East in 1841. In 1865, Elders Orson Pratt and Willam Ritter began missionary work in Austria. Working in Vienna, they encountered religious intolerance and a people not especially interested in a new American religion. They left after a short time with no converts to the Church.

The first missionary effort to bear fruit was that conducted by Paul Hammer and Thomas Biesinger, who were sent from the Swiss-German Mission in 1883. Later that year they baptized Paul Haslinger. While they enjoyed some limited success, they were also harassed, placed in prison, and eventually banished; Austria was not a land of religious freedom at that time.

Finally, in 1902 a branch was organized in Haag am Hausruck, when Johann Huber—a prominent citizen—was baptized. Huber taught the gospel to all who would listen, and succeeded in bringing family, friends, and others into the Church. Almost alone, he built a solid foundation for Church growth in Austria.[7]

FINLAND

In the country of Finland, located in northern Europe between Sweden and Russia, 90 percent of the population was Lutheran in the nineteenth century. In that era, Finland was under Russian control. Finnish, the official language of the country, is very difficult for foreigners to master.

The first Mormon missionaries in Finland were Carl and John Sundstrom, who were sent from Sweden in 1875. Because religious freedom was not established in Finland, progress for the Church was very slow. The first convert was Johann Berg, and eventually a few other members were added and various branches established. The first permanent branch was established in Larsmo in 1880. In 1903, Elder Francis M. Lyman of the Quorum of the Twelve dedicated Finland for the preaching of the gospel. Significant progress in the Church in Finland would not come until much later, however.[8]

BELGIUM

Belgium was created as a buffer state between France and the Netherlands in 1830. The northern section of Belgium is Dutch speaking. Wallonia, the southern part, is French speaking. Louis Bertrand, president of the French Mission, sent Gustav Chaprix to Belgium to preach the gospel in 1861. He apparently had no success. The Swiss Mission later sent Octave

Ursenbach to Belgium in 1868. As will be seen, Mischa Markow, a Serbian convert from Constantinople, introduced the gospel to Antwerp and baptized a few people there in 1888. Administration of missionary work in Belgium alternated between the Swiss-German, Netherlands, and French missions. By 1912 there were 179 members in Belgium.[9]

Missionary work in these new countries during the second half of the nineteenth century might be compared with a military invasion in wartime. The most difficult operation is usually establishing a beachhead. In missionary work the beginning stages are also generally the hardest.

IMPORTANT PUBLICATIONS

During the nineteenth century, mission periodicals were published as soon as practical in most European countries. The *Millennial Star,* published in Manchester, England, beginning in May 1840 became a major source of information both for the Saints in Britain and for members in America. It contained sermons by Church leaders in both countries as well as policy statements and general news of the Church. It was published continuously until 1970, when the Church replaced existing magazines with the *Ensign,* the *New Era,* and the *Friend.* The *Millennial Star* constitutes a major source for the study of the Church in the nineteenth century.[10]

Foreign language periodicals followed. In France, Louis Bertrand, a convert with editorial experience, began the *Étoile du Deseret* (*Star of Deseret*) in 1851. Germany's *Der Stern* was first published in 1869 under the skillful editorship of Karl G. Maeser, who wrote most of the material for the early editions himself. Eventually other European countries began publishing

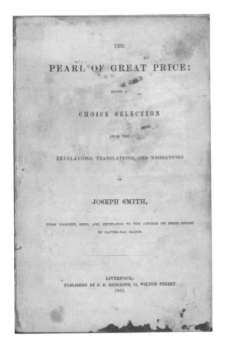

In 1851, Elder Franklin D. Richards compiled a number of materials into a pamphlet for the British Saints. He titled the pamphlet The Pearl of Great Price. *The small volume became the foundation for the book of the same name, which became a standard work of the Church in 1880. (LDS Church Archives)*

mission periodicals. These Church magazines gave a sense of national identity to members in each country.[11]

What eventually became known as the Pearl of Great Price was originally published in England in 1851 by Elder Franklin D. Richards, president of the British Mission. Because of the dearth of printed material available to Church members, President Richards put together a pamphlet, which later became a book of scripture. The first editions published in the United States occurred in 1878 under the editorship of Elder Orson Pratt. In October 1880 Church members voted to accept the Pearl of Great Price as part of the standard works of the Church. Eventually, the Pearl of Great of Price included selections from the Book of Moses, the Book of Abraham, Joseph Smith–Matthew, Joseph Smith–History, and the Articles of Faith.[12]

Dr. James E. Talmage's eloquent addresses on Mormonism did much to soften ill feelings about the Church in London in the 1890s. (© by Intellectual Reserve Inc.)

Another important publication that came to light in England was the *Journal of Discourses*. It contained stenographic reports of talks given by Church leaders in America during the period 1851 to 1896. Originally it was published in individual numbers twice a month. Later it was bound in a set of twenty-six volumes. The *Journal of Discourses* does not contain official policy or doctrine, but it constitutes an important source of history and doctrine for the nineteenth century.[13]

NOTED VISITORS

Several members of the Quorum of the Twelve presided over the European Mission in the late nineteenth and early twentieth centuries. In that role they countered anti-Mormon articles found in the European newspapers and magazines. As opportunities afforded, they attempted to set the record straight by presenting lectures and publishing articles. Dr. James E. Talmage was at the forefront of this work. Talmage, a native of England, was a skilled and prodigious writer. In 1891 he was invited to speak about the Great Salt Lake at the meetings of the Royal Microscopical Society in London. He regarded this invitation as a significant breakthrough for the Church. While in England, he visited his boyhood home, but was generally shunned by his relatives. Nevertheless, when he spoke on "Utah and the Mormons" at the town hall, he addressed a full house; his remarks were so well received that even his relatives insisted he stay with them if he ever came back to the area. Seven years later, Talmage returned to Britain and gave a series of eight lectures on Mormonism in leading cities. Some newspapers that had attacked the Mormons now praised Dr. Talmage's eloquence; audiences appreciated his accounts of Brigham Young's leadership as the Saints overcame obstacles in colonizing the Rocky Mountains.[14]

Latter-day Saints in the British Isles and on the European Continent often had the privilege of being visited by leaders from Church headquarters. In 1906, President Joseph F. Smith traveled to Europe, becoming the first prophet to visit the Saints on this continent while serving as president of the Church. On that occasion, he called upon the members to stay in their own countries and not to gather to Zion as they had done in the past. This constituted a turning point in the international history of the Church. During the two-month period of his visit, he met with missionaries and Church members in the Netherlands, Germany, Switzerland, France, and England. President Smith made an important prophecy while visiting Bern, Switzerland. He declared that the time would come when the world would be dotted with temples. That prophecy has found literal fulfillment in the temple-building work accomplished nearly a century later by President Gordon B. Hinckley. Significantly, the first European temple would be built in the suburbs of the very city where President Smith made his prophecy.[15]

"A REMARKABLE CONVERT-MISSIONARY"

One of the most fascinating people ever caught in the gospel net was Mischa Markow. While the Church was barely holding its own in western Europe, he was carrying the gospel to new areas in the eastern part of the continent. Fortunately, he wrote a life history and some reminiscences that have been preserved and are now available in print.[16]

Mischa Markow was born 21 October 1854 in Serb Zornia, Hungary, of mixed parentage (his father was Serbian and his mother Romanian). Raised in the Eastern Orthodox Church, Mischa attended a Serbian school and worked on the family farm. Along the way he learned the barber trade. His religious inclinations motivated him to undertake a pilgrimage to Jerusalem in 1886. From Jerusalem he went to Alexandria, Egypt, where he opened his own barber shop. In Alexandria, Mischa began a systematic search for the true church. His study centered in the Bible, and he prayed earnestly for guidance. As a result of study and meditation he concluded that he should travel to Constantinople, where he thought he would find a variety of religious denominations.[17]

In this same period, Jacob Spori, president of the Latter-day Saint Turkish Mission, was in Palestine doing missionary work among Germans living there.[18] While in the Holy Land, Jacob was directed by the Spirit to travel to Egypt. In a vision, President Spori saw Mischa Markow in Alexandria, and accordingly traveled there to find him. When he failed to do so, he disappointedly embarked on a steamer bound for

Constantinople. Mischa relates their meeting in this fashion (original spelling and punctuation preserved):

> I sold my Barber Shop and bought a Ticket on the Arabik Steamer to sail for Konstantinople and by that time Brother Spory arived to Alexandria and he look for me Three Days, but Alexandria is a Big City and he could not find me. than he bought a Ticket for Konstantinople on the Arabik Steamer and that was in January 1887. and when I come on the Steamer, Brother Spory was allready on the Steamer and when he saw me he look at me and ask me where was I from. I told him I am from Hungary and he ask me what is my Religion. I told him I belong to the Ortodox church and I am a Serbien by birth. and he Speak to me in German Language. than he said to me, "I did not find you, but you found me." then he said to me that the Lord did revealeth to him in a Vission and he was told to go to Egipt to Alexandria and look for me, and he said to me, "I look for you Three Days in Alexandria and I could not find you and now you found me."[19]

Upon their arrival in Constantinople, President Spori introduced Mischa Markow to two other Mormon missionaries, Ferdinand Hintze and Joseph M. Tanner. Together they taught Mischa the gospel and then baptized him in the nearby Black Sea.

Mischa was later ordained to the office of elder, and was thus authorized to preach the gospel to others. From the beginning, he was endowed with a special missionary zeal. As he wrote in his life history: "My duty was to preach everywhere."[20]

Elder Markow traveled first to Odessa, Russia, where he earned money to finance his missionary labors. Proceeding to London, he went to the Hungarian Consulate to obtain

Mischa Markow, a Serbian born in Hungary, joined the Church through miraculous events in 1887. He went on to serve missions in Belgium, Serbia, Hungary, Romania, Bulgaria, Germany, Russia, and Turkey. (LDS Church Archives)

permission to preach in countries under their jurisdiction. On his way east, he stopped in Belgium.

Once in Antwerp, Belgium, Elder Markow prayed that the Lord would direct him to those seeking the truth. Soon thereafter he met Karl Beckhaus, who invited him to meet his "wife," Henrietta Esselman. In the meantime, she had a dream in which she saw Mischa. At this time Henrietta was living with Karl Beckhaus without benefit of marriage. Nevertheless, recognizing her deep religious nature, Mischa taught her the gospel and counseled her to marry Karl. As Elder Markow taught the family the gospel, the following situation developed (original spelling and punctuation preserved):

> I start to Preach the Gospel to them. they all believe and they want to be Baptised. but inesmuch the Devil he knows that the Lord God will use me as a instrument in his

Hands to make a first opening in Belgien, so the Satan start to work on Karol Beckhaus to persecute me that I may leave Belgien and not Start. then he said to me, "Mr. Markow, I believe the church you advocate is the true Church, but at the present time I don't want to be Baptised, but my Wife she is free. she can be Baptised if she want to." now Mr. Beckhaus try it in every way to persecute me and Stop me.[21]

Eventually Elder Markow baptized Sister Esselmann, her son, and finally, Karl Beckhaus, who had seen the error of his ways and repented. Mischa promised the family that he would meet them in Zion, and in 1892, he did see them in a meeting for German Saints in Salt Lake City.

Between 1892 and 1899, Mischa Markow resided in Salt Lake City. Earning his living as a barber, he met and married Jonetha Hansen, a convert from Norway. They were sealed in the Salt Lake Temple and had three children.

By 1899 Mischa was on the road again, returning to Europe as a missionary. This time he had an official "seventy's license," or formal mission call, signed by Elders Seymour B. Young and Joseph W. McMurrin, two members of the First Council of the Seventy. He traveled to Romania, working in the capital city of Bucharest, and baptized nine persons. Unfortunately, he was banished from Romania, a common experience for nineteenth-century missionaries. Preaching for a time in Bulgaria, he was again banished.

Following this banishment, Elder Markow traveled to Hungary, his native land. He worked in the city of Temesvar and requested that the president of the German Mission, Arnold Schulthess, send him a missionary companion. His new companion, Elder Hyrum Lau, joined him in Hungary.

Although faced with official government opposition, they succeeded in baptizing thirty-one people.[22]

Two years later he began another mission, this time in Russia and Turkey. He received an assignment from European Mission President Francis M. Lyman to open missionary work in Russia. President Lyman warned him to be cautious and to leave Russia if he encountered serious opposition. Mischa Markow began his mission in Warsaw, which was then part of Russia. Leaving Warsaw after a short stay, he traveled to Riga, where he began to preach to the extensive German population in that city. Relating some of his experiences with the Germans in Riga, he wrote (original spelling and punctuation preserved):

> and I start right away to work among the Germans, and they were Baptists. and I had German Tracts with me. and the Lord was with me and I was blessed and I distributed about 150. Tracts among the German people. and I have had many conversation with Russians so that 3. Germans Family ask for Baptism. and I Preach to the Russian People and I told them that their Priests did not have Authority from God because the Gospel was taken from the earth, and now in our Days the Gospel is Restored Again. then One German Lady said to me, "Sir, you dont need to tell that Russian Priests dont have Authority. if you tell them that, they will surely take you from the Streets and send you to Siberia.[23]

Elder Markow did not end up in Siberia, but he did encounter fierce opposition from Russian government officials. He tried to hire a lawyer to defend him, but the lawyer refused, telling him that it would be too dangerous to defend a Mormon. Mischa left Russia and went to Austria.

His next assignment took him to Turkey, where he worked in Aintab and Alexandretta, now known by the Turkish names of Gaziantep and Iskenderon. Most of the people in these cities were Armenian, and Mischa was able to teach and baptize some converts during his sojourn.

Upon leaving Turkey, he spent a little time in Athens, Greece. He was then released from his mission and returned to Salt Lake City in December 1905. He resided in Salt Lake City and attended the Fifteenth Ward. Once again, he earned a living for him and his family as a barber. He died in 1934.

This is but a brief summary of the life and missionary labors of this most remarkable man. In the words of the translator and editor of his life history, Mischa Markow "was a visionary man, a courageous man, a man of great faith and missionary zeal."[24]

CHAPTER 5

THE CHURCH AND THE WORLD WARS

DONALD Q. CANNON

1914	World War I begins (August)
1918	Armistice ends World War I (11 November)
1920s	Germany called the most successful mission field
1930	Hitler comes to power in Germany
1939	Latter-day Saint missionaries evacuated from Europe at outbreak of World War II
1940	Pearl Harbor attacked; U.S. enters World War II (7 December)
1945	World War II ends (May–August)
1946	Ezra Taft Benson's mission of mercy to Europe
1948	Berlin airlift

WORLD WAR I

When Archduke Franz Ferdinand of Austria was assassinated in Sarajevo, Bosnia, in July 1914, a war began that pitted Austria and its ally, Germany, against Serbia, Russia (Serbia's protector), and France (Russia's ally). In a matter of days, the British joined the war on the side of Serbia, Russia, and France. The conflict lasted four years, eventually drawing in the United States of America in 1917. It became known as World War I— the Great War.

Among the Latter-day Saints killed in World War I was Stanford Hinckley, President Gordon B. Hinckley's brother. His grave, shown here, is among 1,541 American dead buried in Suresnes, France. (Photo courtesy Donald Q. Cannon)

For the first time, Church members faced each other in battle. Missionary work slowed—American missionaries, of course, had been evacuated from the war zone—leaving members in Europe with more responsibility. Members of the Church in England and Germany were heavily and directly involved in the war.[1] One example of the patriotism of the English Saints appeared in the British press: "The Pudsey Branch has a record of patriotism which will be hard to beat, as every man of military age, with the exception of those engaged in government and munitions work has enlisted. Whatever we may say about the so-called 'Mormons,' we must admit they are certainly very patriotic at Pudsey."[2]

On the other side of the war, German Saints fought for their own country, and many members supported their soldiers by sending packages to the front lines. By the end of World War I in 1918, seventy-five German Latter-day Saints had lost their lives. Sixty-five British Latter-day Saints were killed.[3]

Even though the war disrupted the Church's correspondence and American presence abroad, the members in both Germany and England continued to carry out their responsibilities, including missionary work. New members did come into the fold. The conversion story of Gustav Weller illustrates this process of growth in the midst of conflict. Serving as a pilot in the German Air Force, he suffered an accident that freed him from military service. Returning home to Chemnitz, Germany, he accompanied his sister to meetings of the Church. Within a short time, Gustav was baptized and then moved to Schneidemuehl, Germany, where he had taken a job as a buyer for a pilot training school. Filled with a special zeal to share the gospel, Gustav Weller brought several families into the Church during the war. Some of his converts included Otto Sasse, Walter Stover, Otto Sonnenberg, Emil Wirkus, Max Hohman, and Karl Otto Wegner. Brother Weller and his family later moved to Utah, where he founded Zion's Bookstore, now known as Sam Weller Bookstore.[4]

HITLER AND THE NAZIS

Desperate economic conditions at the close of World War I challenged the Saints in Germany, as well as all citizens of the country. Severe inflation and high unemployment made the German mark virtually worthless. These troubled times, however, paralleled a phenomenal period of growth for the Church. There was a marked increase in baptisms, and Germany had the highest number of Church members in any mission; there were 11,102 members in the German-speaking countries of Germany, Austria, and Switzerland.[5]

During this time, Adolf Hitler—with the National Socialist Party (or the Nazis)—began his rise to power, a climb that can be linked to the desperate economic conditions in Germany resulting from the war. Hitler, after all, had fought along with the Germans in the trenches, and he used his experiences to develop a connection with the people of Germany. Hitler was appointed Chancellor of Germany in 1933. His Third Reich aimed at destroying Communism and the Jews, as well as other "undesirables."

In the beginning, Latter-day Saint activities did not interfere with Hitler's operations. American missionaries were even invited to teach German youth how to play basketball. The Nazis hoped such coaching would enhance Germany's chances in the Olympics of 1936. Another area where Mormon and Nazi programs converged was in genealogical research. Both groups avidly pursued such studies, but for vastly different reasons: Latter-day Saints hoped for salvation for their ancestors, while Nazis wanted to determine who had Jewish blood.

A number of myths about Mormons and Nazis have been created and circulated over the years. Some myths claim that many members of the Church were high-ranking members of the Nazi Party. Others stress that the National Socialists consciously modeled their youth programs after those of the Church. Still others maintain that the Nazi practice of having only one meal on designated days had its roots in the Mormon fast day. None of these can be substantiated in fact. They are simply the product of fertile imaginations.[6]

Eventually, Nazism and Mormonism collided. While some German members became Nazi Party members, most did not, and little by little freedom was curtailed. Boy Scouts and Primary were discontinued under government pressure so they would not compete with Nazi youth organizations. Church songs with references to "Zion" or "Israel" could no longer be sung. Hymn books, and even *The Articles of Faith* by James E. Talmage, were confiscated by the police because they contained such references.[7] Despite such pressures, the Church continued to operate because of its emphasis on the separation of church and state.

During this period of anxiety, the Saints were reassured by a visit from President Heber J. Grant. In 1937, he and other Church leaders visited the Saints in Belgium, Switzerland, Czechoslovakia, Germany, Holland, Sweden, Denmark, Norway, and England. For many Church members, this visit from the prophet was a fulfillment of their dreams. President Grant encouraged the Saints to remain in their home countries and build up Zion. The President also urged that responsibility for leadership in branches and districts be taken from the missionaries and turned over to local members. Also, in most areas, the Church was blessed with genuinely favorable publicity in the media.[8]

A specific reason for President Grant's European visit was to participate in celebrations of the British Mission's centennial. J. Reuben Clark, President Grant's first counselor, joined him for this occasion. Never before had two members of the First Presidency been in Europe at the same time.

MISSIONARIES WITHDRAWN

Adolf Hitler's ambitions extended beyond the borders of Germany. He felt that all German-speaking peoples should belong to one great *Reich,* or state. In 1937, Germany used political and economic pressure to accomplish the *Anschluss,* or union, with Austria. The following year, Hitler sent troops into western Czechoslovakia, supposedly to protect German people in that region but in actuality to be in a position to annex Czechoslovakia into Germany. It appeared that war might break out once again in Europe. Church leaders became concerned about the safety of missionaries serving in Germany and

Four German missionaries pose in front of an anti-Jewish display before the out-break of World War II. The sign reads: "The race question is the key to world history! Jewish women and girls are your undoing!" (LDS Church Archives)

Czechoslovakia, and thus evacuated them. When the Western Allies caved in to Hitler's demands of annexation at Munich, however, hostilities were averted, at least for a time. The evacuated missionaries were allowed to return to their fields of labor after an absence of only two or three weeks and felt an increased sense of urgency to share the gospel effectively. Experience gained in this brief evacuation would be very valuable the following year. As German aggression continued and tensions increased, President J. Reuben Clark, a former high official in the United States State Department, monitored conditions in Europe and kept Church leaders posted on an almost hour-by-hour basis. In late August 1939, orders were given to pull the American missionaries out of Germany and Czechoslovakia once again. Elder Joseph Fielding Smith of the Council of the Twelve was already in Europe visiting the missions there. He therefore was in a position to take personal charge of the evacuation.

The evacuation of Latter-day Saint missionaries from Germany proved to be quite an adventure. As President M. Douglas Wood of the West German Mission directed the evacuation of his missionaries, he was able to confirm that most had made it out safely, but could not account for the location or condition of thirty-one elders. President Wood instructed Elder Norman Seibold to find these missionaries and help them get out of the country. As time was short and he wasn't sure of the exact location of these missionaries, Elder Seibold used an imaginative approach. When he arrived at a railroad station, he would climb up on a baggage cart and begin whistling "Do What Is Right," a favorite hymn among the missionaries. Elders who had come to the station hoping to find help responded and joined him. Eventually, all thirty-one remaining missionaries arrived safely in Holland or Denmark.[9]

Meanwhile, in Czechoslovakia, mission president Wallace Toronto sent his wife with most of the missionaries to Denmark. He and four elders remained behind to wind up some essential business. For nearly a week, Sister Toronto was not able to contact her husband. Seeing preparations for war accelerating on every side, she expressed her concerns for her husband's safety to Elder Joseph Fielding Smith. The Apostle assured her, "Sister Toronto, this war will not start until Brother Toronto and his missionaries arrive in this land of Denmark." Completing their business in Prague, President Toronto and the elders left Czechoslovakia late Thursday evening, 31 August, on the last available train. They caught a ferry across an arm of the Baltic Sea and arrived in Denmark

Friday afternoon.[10] On that very day, 1 September 1939, Hitler invaded Poland. This is generally regarded as the beginning of World War II in Europe. Thus, Elder Smith's prophecy was very precisely fulfilled. Soon, Latter-day Saint missionaries would be evacuated from all the missions of Europe.

WORLD WAR II

In 1940, Hitler invaded Norway, Denmark, the Netherlands, Belgium, and France. Nazi forces also began air strikes in the British Isles. Switzerland and Sweden somehow managed to maintain their neutrality. Still, the war had an enormous impact upon the Saints in Great Britain and throughout the Continent.

For example, though all American missionaries had been evacuated from the British Mission, it remained intact. It was presided over by Andre K. Anastasiou, an immigrant to England from Russia. Some British Saints were not eligible for military service because of physical disabilities, and so served as missionaries. Wartime also meant deprivations of goods and services. Destruction in England caused by German air raids contributed to the hardships faced by the British Saints during the war. Church schedules and routines were affected. Most Church meetings were attended primarily by women and children.

Some German members resisted Hitler and Nazism. Such was the case with a group of teenage members in Hamburg. The leader of the group was Helmut Huebener, and he was assisted by two others, Rudolf Wobbe and Karl-Heinz Schnibbe. Helmut and his friends clandestinely listened to radio broadcasts of the BBC (British Broadcasting Corporation). They took notes and then typed leaflets that were distributed in the area where they lived. These leaflets or pamphlets contained information that was counter to the official Nazi view. In February 1942 the Gestapo arrested Helmut and his friends. Schnibbe and Wobbe were sentenced to hard labor, while Helmut Huebener was incarcerated in Ploetzensee prison and eventually executed.[11]

In the Third Reich, all able-bodied men were required to serve in the armed forces of Germany. This duty, of course, could not always be performed without some conflict of conscience. Such was the case with Walter Krause. Walter had been a member of the Church since 1926 and had served in many Church callings, including work as a missionary. On 26 January 1940, Walter went on active duty with Feldpolizei (Military Police). He was married, had three children, and would not have chosen to serve. Despite this, Walter made every possible effort to live his religion. For example, in his first meeting with his military police unit, he announced that he did not use tobacco and did not drink alcoholic beverages. Apparently they respected him for his standards and accepted him as a comrade in arms.

However, conflict arose as Krause refused to carry out orders to execute prisoners of war and military criminals. His commanding officer accommodatingly assigned him to noncombat duty. Walter was able to report gratefully, "I never shed any blood." He was assigned to serve as a cook for his unit. When he received this assignment, he immediately wrote to his wife and requested that she send him cookbooks and recipes. He set a high standard by dressing in a clean apron and cap and by not allowing any non-kitchen personnel in the kitchen area. He prepared tasty and nourishing meals and received commendation for his ability to prepare them rapidly and efficiently.

Given his Church experience and basic character, Walter Krause tried sincerely to be honest and forthright in dealing with others. He had the courage to tell a general who inspected the camp that the food supplies were both inadequate and dirty. He was commended for his honesty and integrity.

Because Krause was fortunate enough to have commanding officers who allowed him to serve in a noncombat role, he was able to serve in the Germany Army without compromising his integrity. It is certain that others did not have it so good.[12]

During the war the Saints had to fend for themselves. Accustomed to having missionaries from America take charge, the European Saints now conducted their own meetings and carried on the work of the Church. In some areas they were even able to continue missionary work.

The devastation brought on by the war was without historical precedent. Some 45 million people lost their lives. Physical destruction of homes, churches, and public buildings was almost too horrific to describe. The Saints in Great Britain and Europe were not spared the suffering and devastation caused by the conflict. Allied air campaigns brought heavy destruction to Germany, in particular. Hamburg, for example, was bombed 104 times during a two-week period in 1943. In some areas of Germany, 95 percent of the homes were destroyed. About five hundred German Saints died, which was approximately 5 percent of the Church membership there.[13]

THE AFTERMATH OF WAR

At the end of the war in 1945, General Authorities in Salt Lake City sought to reestablish contact with Church leaders and members in war-torn Europe. The Church drew on its

Elder Ezra Taft Benson (center) stands amidst the rubble and destruction of war in Karlsruhe, Germany. He toured the area with chaplain Howard Badger (left) and mission president Max Zimmer (right) in 1946. Karlsruhe, which lies along the Rhine River in southwest Germany, was hit particularly hard by the Allies. (LDS Church Archives)

welfare supplies and began shipping packages and then railroad carloads of goods to relieve those in need in Europe.

In January 1946, the Church announced that Elder Ezra Taft Benson would preside over the European Mission. Although he was one of the newest members of the Council of the Twelve, his experience in agricultural affairs and his extensive travel prepared him well for this new assignment. Accompanying Elder Benson was Frederick W. Babbel, a military chaplain, who had been a missionary in Germany and Switzerland just before the outbreak of World War II.[14]

Their mission of mercy to war-torn Europe was marked by many miraculous events. As he reported his experiences in General Conference, Elder Benson recalled:

Barriers have melted away. Problems that seemed impossible to solve have been solved, and the work in large measure has been accomplished through the blessings of the Lord. I remember well our first inquiry as to the time we could set sail, either by plane or boat. We were told it would take three months, that all bookings were filled for that period. Yet within twenty-one days from the time our appointment was announced, we landed at Hurn Airport sixty miles south of London. And in spite of a most acute housing shortage in London, two days thereafter suitable headquarters had been established.[15]

Often, as Elder Benson and Brother Babbel met with the Saints, they found them assembled amid bombed-out ruins and rubble. Lack of public meeting facilities, housing, and especially food and clothing made the situation desperate. While Elder Benson made the necessary transportation arrangements, the Church began assembling the commodities needed for war-torn Europe. In addition to supplies on hand in the welfare storage units, the Saints in the Rocky Mountain West contributed clothing and other items. Government officials in Europe were amazed at the speed with which the relief goods arrived.[16]

As Elder Benson visited the various countries of Europe, he felt that he often had divine assistance in making necessary travel connections. For example, on one occasion he needed to travel from France to The Hague in the Netherlands. Officials at the railway station in Paris told him that the direct line was not in service because the bridge at the Dutch border had been bombed. Therefore, they advised him to go by a much longer route that would bypass the problem. Elder Benson, however, felt impressed to catch a train heading directly toward Holland. The railway officials objected, insisting that this would require

Elder Ezra Taft Benson, pictured here with a group of Finnish Saints, dedicated Finland for the preaching of the gospel on 16 July 1946. (LDS Church Archives)

him to backtrack, and would actually delay him significantly. When he reached the border, he found that the bridge was, in fact, out. When he saw a United States army truck approaching, he asked the driver where he was headed. The soldier replied that he was going over into Holland by means of a temporary pontoon bridge erected about a half mile away. Upon crossing into Holland, Elder Benson immediately found a local train about to depart for The Hague. Thus he was able to reach his destination on time.[17]

Elder Benson also felt an urgency to visit German Saints in what had become part of Poland. With some difficulty, he obtained the needed visas. As he and Brother Babbel approached the town of Zelbak in a United Nations jeep, townspeople thought a group of Russian soldiers was approaching and thus ran and hid out of fear. That morning, branch members had met in fast meeting and prayed earnestly that they might once again receive a visit from Church leaders. Frederick Babbel described what happened: "Upon alighting from our vehicle we asked the only woman in sight if this was the Mormon chapel and where we might find the branch president. We had spotted the woman hiding behind a large tree. Her expression was one of fear as we stopped, but upon learning who we were she greeted us with tears of gratitude and joy. . . . Within minutes the cry went from house to house, 'The brethren are here! The brethren are here!' Soon we found ourselves surrounded by about fifty of the happiest people we had ever seen."[18]

Assistance also came from within Europe. One dramatic example involved Dutch Saints helping German Saints–even though they had recently been wartime enemies. Massive shipments of Dutch potatoes were delivered to grateful German families.[19]

Besides reestablishing contact with Church leaders and having relief shipments brought in, Elder Ezra Taft Benson extended missionary work into Finland. In 1946 he dedicated that country for the preaching of the gospel.[20]

In the postwar period, one Latter-day Saint pilot made a rather distinctive contribution. In 1948 the Communist Government of East Germany shut down the borders between East and West Germany. This action essentially isolated West Berlin and cut it off from its supply lines. To counter this move, the Western powers began flying critical goods to Berlin. This operation became known as the Berlin Airlift. An American pilot and Church member, Colonel Gail Halvorsen, volunteered and eventually became one of the most famous airmen to be associated with the lift. He described the difficulty of flying into Tempelhof Airport in West Berlin. This airport was located right in the city, rather than on the outskirts. Consequently, planes had to fly directly over the bombed-out buildings and then quickly land on the runway. He described how grateful the Germans were who received the life-sustaining loads of essential food and fuel. He was especially impressed with the children of West Berlin. They were very hungry, but they would not stoop to become beggars. He told them he would drop some candy and chewing gum for them when he flew over. In order for them to distinguish which plane was his, he said he would wiggle the wings back and forth. He had learned to perform this somewhat bizarre maneuver in his early flying lessons in Utah.

Needless to say, the children were delighted with the presents. Because of his generosity and kindness they called him the Candy Bomber, Uncle Wiggly Wings, and the *Schokoladen Flieger* (chocolate pilot).

Colonel Halvorsen was proud of his contribution to the freedom and independence of West Berlin. But he cautioned that it was not the American pilots who were the heroes, it was the good people of the city.[21]

World War I and World War II had a lasting impact upon history; the world would never be the same. These wars also strongly affected the Church. While there was a temporary slowdown in the work, the eventual impact was highly positive. Most of the growth of the Restored Church took place after World War II.

CHAPTER 6

THE CHURCH COMES OF AGE IN EUROPE

DONALD Q. CANNON

1950s	Church building program begins in Europe
1955	Swiss Temple dedicated
	Tabernacle Choir tours Europe
1958	London England Temple dedicated
1960	First European stake organized—the Manchester England Stake
1965	Missionary work renewed in Italy
1968	Church recognized by government of Spain
1972	Greece dedicated for the preaching of the gospel
1974	Portugal Lisbon Mission organized
1975	Elder Charles Didier called as first European General Authority in twentieth century
1985	Freiberg Germany Temple dedicated
	Stockholm Sweden Temple dedicated
1987	Frankfurt Germany Temple dedicated
1998	Preston England Temple dedicated
1999	Madrid Spain Temple dedicated
	Copenhagen Denmark Temple announced
2000	Helsinki Finland Temple dedicated
2002	The Hague Netherlands Temple dedicated

Europe at mid-twentieth century was far different than it had been fifty or even ten years earlier. World War II had changed the political and economic structure in a dramatic fashion. Europe was now divided between Communist and non-Communist countries, an "Iron Curtain" separating the two spheres. In the heart of Europe, the victorious Western powers had divided Germany in an attempt to prevent future problems such as those Hitler had created. Most of Europe lay in devastation and ruin from the horrible destruction of war.

The Church had also changed. During World War II, membership had been depleted and physical facilities destroyed. Out of this devastation, however, would emerge a much stronger Church. In the next few decades, European Saints would develop their own leadership, and the drain of immigration to America would nearly stop. Many new buildings, including temples, would be constructed to strengthen the kingdom in Europe.

TEMPLES IN EUROPE

The construction of temples in Europe symbolizes the international expansion of the Church and the effects of its positive growth. The first of these temples were built under the direction of President David O. McKay. He was uniquely qualified to direct this task. As one historian explained: "His personal background suited him well to give leadership during an era of expansion. His mission to Scotland, his 1921 world tour, his service as president of the European Mission, and his responsibility for missionary work as a counselor in the First Presidency all made him personally aware of the Church's worldwide responsibilities and opportunities."[1]

The inscription above the doors at the Swiss Temple was the first of its kind: A declaration in a language other than English that this is a house of the Lord. (© by Intellectual Reserve, Inc.)

There was a definite need for a temple somewhere in Europe. The Saints had found it necessary to travel to the United States in order to receive blessings in the house of the Lord. In the Salt Lake Temple on 17 April 1952, the First Presidency and Quorum of the Twelve voted to build a temple in Europe.

In June of that year, President McKay traveled to Europe to select building sites. He selected Switzerland for the first temple because of its peaceful conditions, central location, and multilingual culture. President McKay decided to locate the temple in Bern, the capital of Switzerland. After negotiations for purchasing the site began, long delays ensued. Concerned over the delay, Samuel Bringhurst, president of the Swiss Mission, asked his missionaries to fast and determine the Lord's will in the matter. The next day he learned that the property was no longer for sale. They

The Swiss Temple—the first erected in Europe—set the pattern for making temple blessings available worldwide. (© by Intellectual Reserve, Inc.)

went to work and found a new site in the greater Bern area. When President Bringhurst first inspected the new property he said, "We felt certain we were on the site the Lord wished for the first European temple." The mission president soon "learned why the Lord did not allow us to purchase the first site." A new highway was built through the property that had been under consideration, making it unsatisfactory as a temple site.[2]

The site selected for the temple was in Zollikofen, a suburb of Bern. Behind the property a dense grove of fir trees provided a picturesque setting for this new temple. Groundbreaking occurred in 1953, and, following two days of public tours, President David O. McKay dedicated the temple on 11 September 1955. Dedicatory services in various languages continued for five successive days. Those present said they had never felt the veil so thin.[3]

President McKay was intimately involved in the planning process. He knew that the smaller Swiss Temple could not be like the much larger Salt Lake Temple; it had to meet the needs of Saints with various languages and cultures. Thus, the idea of using motion pictures to be shown in a single ordinance room was conceived. The committee that was to oversee the production of this film consisted of two members of the Quorum of the Twelve—Joseph Fielding Smith and Richard L. Evans—and Gordon B. Hinckley, a Church staff member. The committee decided to produce the films in the large assembly room of the Salt Lake Temple.[4]

This first foreign temple marked the beginning of a new period of spiritual development for the Church in Europe. The temple in Switzerland has not only symbolized but also accelerated this new era of progress for the Church.

When President McKay announced the construction of the temple in Switzerland, he said that it would be just the first of several temples to be built in Europe. In 1953 the Church announced another temple, this one to be built near London. President McKay spoke enthusiastically about the natural beauty of the site and said the Church would preserve the 350-year-old Elizabethan manor house located on the property.

A crowd of one thousand attended the groundbreaking ceremony on 17 August 1955, just one month before the dedication of the Swiss Temple. Three years later, the London Temple was dedicated in six services held between 7 and 9 September 1958. As in the case of the Swiss Temple, ordinance work commenced almost immediately following the dedication. One of the first families to be sealed was that of Derek and Muriel Cuthbert, who had been baptized just a few years before. Brother Cuthbert would be the first resident Briton called as a General Authority (in 1978), though others from Britain had been called after immigrating to the United States.[5]

The London Temple played an important role in missionary work. A young British photographer, John Cox, spent a great deal of time taking pictures of the temple. Selvoy Boyer, the temple president, ordered several copies of his pictures on many different occasions. Each time John came to the temple to deliver his pictures, President Boyer took time to explain a gospel principle. In 1960, Cox joined the Church and later became president of the London Stake.[6]

Six more temples would be completed in Europe during the late twentieth and early twenty-first centuries:

Temple	Year Dedicated
Freiberg Germany	1985
Stockholm Sweden	1985
Frankfurt Germany	1987
Preston England	1998
Madrid Spain	1999
The Hague Netherlands	2002

The Church also announced temples to be built in Copenhagen, Denmark, and Helsinki, Finland.[7]

The Copenhagen Temple is being constructed within the shell of the existing Church meetinghouse, which was erected in the 1930s. This stately building will house the temple, using the Vernal Utah Temple as a model and prototype. The temple in Vernal was built inside the old tabernacle and is furnished in furniture and decorations from the era when the tabernacle was first built in the early twentieth century.

The Copenhagen Denmark Temple is being constructed inside the shell of this pre-existing Danish chapel. (Photo courtesy Donald Q. Cannon)

TABERNACLE CHOIR TOUR

In 1955, the Salt Lake Tabernacle Choir participated in the dedication of the Swiss Temple. In addition to its engagement in Bern, the choir also sang at the groundbreaking ceremony for the London Temple and conducted an extensive concert tour throughout Europe. The choir performed concerts in Brussels, Belgium; Amsterdam, Holland; Copenhagen, Denmark; West Berlin, Germany; Frankfurt, Germany; Zurich, Switzerland; Paris, France; Glasgow, Scotland; Manchester, England; Cardiff, Wales; and London, England. Their concert tour proved to be a powerful and influential public relations tool. The choir and the Church both received very favorable press coverage.

Among their concerts, the one in Berlin stands out, for it happened only by divine intervention. In an uncharacteristic

This building served as the mission home in Berlin-Dahlem (in the American sector of Berlin) during the 1950s and '60s. (Photo courtesy Donald Q. Cannon)

move, the Russian ambassador to Washington issued special travel visas that enabled the choir to travel through East Germany. As they arrived in West Berlin they were serenaded by a local Latter-day Saint choir. As one observer noted: "Each sang in his own language and burst forth in mighty song and the saints of the two great nations were suddenly welded into one people by the spirit of God and brotherhood of man."[8]

President McKay accompanied the choir on some of the tour and attended several concerts. This afforded an opportunity for him to meet with government officials in formal receptions. He contrasted this welcome with his earlier experiences in Scotland as a missionary, when he and his companions met resistance and contempt instead of a gracious reception.[9]

THE BUILDING PROGRAM

During the devastation of World War II, many buildings were destroyed. Others that survived were simply inadequate for Church purposes. Consequently, Church leaders chose to launch an extensive construction program in the British Isles and Continental Europe beginning in the 1950s.

In Great Britain the Church authorized the construction of twenty new meetinghouses or chapels. To create these meetinghouses, the Church often purchased a large home and renovated it for meetings. While members met in these homes, construction of a separate building on the same property would begin. By 1967 the Church owned seventy-three completed chapels in Britain. Other than the temple, one of the most prominent and important buildings constructed during this period was the Hyde Park Chapel in London. President McKay dedicated this building in February 1961. This meetinghouse would serve as a symbol of the permanence and progress of the Church in Europe. As President McKay said: "This building is a monument to progress, progress of the Church numerically, progress of better understanding in all men's minds of the value of the Church of Jesus Christ to the final establishment of peace on earth and goodwill toward men."[10]

Church buildings were also erected on the Continent. For example, Europe's first postwar chapel was built in a beautiful wooded area in Berlin-Dahlem in the early 1950s. Much of the expense for this beautiful edifice was met by the personal funds of Walter Stover, who served as mission president immediately after the war and on into the 1950s.[11]

During the early 1950s, most Church meetings in Germany convened in public schools. Later, a building program was developed that included buying property, as well as designing and constructing new meetinghouses. By 1959 most cities had buildings under construction, or in some cases, completed buildings that had already been dedicated.[12]

Today, the Church has several chapels and stake centers in Germany. Some of these Church buildings are in prime locations. One stake center in West Berlin, for example, is located in the world-renowned Tiergarten Park, midway between the business center of West Berlin and The Reichstag near the former East German border.

CREATION OF STAKES

When a given geographic area of the Church reaches a certain level of development, mission districts may be organized into stakes. This requires not only a certain number of members in the area, but also substantial priesthood leadership, the ability to carry out the programs of the Church, and perhaps even the presence of adequate physical facilities. The designation "stake" is taken from the writings of Isaiah where he likened the growth of the Lord's people to the creation of a large tent. "Enlarge the place of thy tent, and let them stretch forth the curtains of thine habitations: spare not, lengthen thy cords, and strengthen thy stakes" (Isaiah 54:2). The stake was identified as a source of strength and stability. A mission district is a unit that needs to *receive* strength *from* the Church, while a stake is a unit that can *give* strength *to* the Church. Therefore, the formation of new stakes is an indication of meaningful Church growth.

The first stakes in Europe were organized in the 1960s. The first, in Manchester, England, was organized by Elder Harold B. Lee on 27 March 1960. In 1961 several stakes were organized in Continental Europe—in The Hague, Netherlands (the first non–English-speaking stake of the Church); Berlin, Germany; Stuttgart, Germany; Hamburg, Germany; and Zurich, Switzerland. By 2002 many more stakes had been organized, the total in western and southern Europe reaching 102. There were forty-five in the British Isles, nine in Scandinavia, and forty-eight elsewhere on the European continent.[13]

The organization of stakes in Europe brought far-reaching changes for the Church. Principally, it meant that leadership changed from outsiders to local members. In mission districts American missionaries had filled many leadership positions. In stakes, native leaders assumed the responsibility.

EUROPEAN LEADERSHIP

In addition to those serving at the stake and ward levels, Regional Representatives and eventually General Authorities were called from among the local membership in Europe. A review of some of these leaders' biographies sheds light on the growth of the Church as well as the kind of people who received calls to serve.

Charles Didier joined the Church in 1957 and was sustained to the First Quorum of the Seventy 3 October 1975 at age thirty-nine, the first member from a foreign country. He became a member of the Presidency of the Seventy in 1992, serving from 1992 to 1995, and was called again to serve in the Presidency in 2001. Previously, he served as president of the France-Switzerland Mission. Elder Didier is fluent in five languages: Flemish, French, German, Spanish, and English. He holds a bachelor's degree in economics from the University of Liege in Belgium. He served as an officer in the Belgian Air Force Reserve. He was born 5 October 1935 in Ixelles,

Belgium. He and his wife, Lucie Lodomez Didier, are the parents of two children.[14]

Jacob de Jager was sustained to the First Quorum of the Seventy 3 April 1976 at age fifty-three. He and his wife, Bea Lim, joined the Church in 1960 while he was working in Toronto, Canada. They were fellowshipped by Frances Monson, wife of President Thomas S. Monson, who was serving as president of the East Canadian Mission. Elder de Jager served in several positions in the Church while living in Holland and then in Indonesia after leaving Canada. He speaks five languages. He was named an emeritus General Authority 2 October 1993. Elder de Jager was born 16 January 1923 at The Hague, Netherlands. He is the father of two children.[15]

F. Enzio Busche was sustained to the First Quorum of Seventy 1 October 1977 at the age of forty-seven. He served in the German army during World War II and received vocational training in Bonn and Freiberg. He then went to work in his father's printing business. Diagnosed with a liver disease, he recovered in a miraculous manner and then began to search for the true church. He and his wife, Jutta Baum Busche, were baptized 19 January 1958. Busche Printing became one of the largest offset printing businesses in Germany. Elder Busche was born 5 April 1930 in Dortmund, Germany. He became an emeritus General Authority 7 October 2000.[16]

Derek A. Cuthbert was sustained to the First Quorum of the Seventy 1 April 1978. He and his wife, Muriel Olive Mason Cuthbert, were baptized 27 January 1951. During World War II he served with the Royal Air Force. After the war he studied at the University of Nottingham and then started work with the British Celanese Limited. He eventually became the manager of a large factory. The Cuthberts and their five children were the first family to be sealed in the London Temple after its dedication. He served as business manager for the *Millennial Star*. Later he became a Regional Representative and served in many other Church positions. Elder Cuthbert died in Salt Lake City on 7 April 1991 at the age of sixty-four.[17]

Hans Benjamin Ringger was sustained to the First Quorum of the Seventy 6 April 1985 at the age of fifty-nine. He was the first native of Switzerland to become a General Authority. He joined the Church after serving as a colonel with the Swiss Army. He was a noted architect and industrial designer. Before becoming a General Authority he had served as a bishop and stake president. As an area president he was instrumental in opening several Eastern European countries for the preaching of the gospel. He and his wife, Helene, are the parents of four children. He was named an emeritus General Authority on 30 September 1995.[18]

Kenneth Johnson was sustained to the First Quorum of the Seventy 31 March 1990 at age forty-nine. He was baptized in 1959. He served as a Regional Representative and as a stake president. He was educated at Norwich City College and the Guilds of London. He taught college courses and was a partner in a British insurance firm. He was born in Norwich, England, 5 July 1940. He and his wife, Pamela Wilson Johnson, are the parents of one son.[19]

Dieter F. Uchtdorf was sustained to the Second Quorum of the Seventy 2 April 1994 at age fifty-three. He was later sustained to the First Quorum of the Seventy 6 April 1996 and as a president of the Seventy on 5 October 2002. Elder Uchtdorf joined the Church at age eight in Zwickau, East Germany. He and his family later fled to West Germany. He was a fighter pilot for the German Air Force. Later, he was a pilot for Lufthansa, the official German state airline. Eventually, he became the vice president for flight operations and also chief pilot for Lufthansa. He is fond of flying and says this about the perspective it gives him: "I see how beautiful the deserts and the jungles and the seas are. . . . I marvel at the world's different cultures. Everyone is different, and yet we are the same."[20] He served as stake president before his call as a General Authority. Elder Uchtdorf was born 6 November 1940 in Ostrava, Czechoslovakia. He and his wife, Harriett Reich Uchtdorf, are the parents of two children.[21]

GENERAL AUTHORITIES FROM EUROPE CALLED SINCE 1900

1. Charles W. Penrose: Apostle—1904; second counselor in First Presidency—1911; first counselor in First Presidency—1921; died 1925.
2. Charles W. Nibley: Presiding bishop—1907; second counselor in First Presidency—1925; died 1931.
3. James E. Talmage: Apostle—1911; died 1933.
4. John Wells: Second counselor in Presiding Bishopric—1918; died 1941.
5. John A. Widtsoe: Apostle—1921; died 1952.
6. Charles A. Callis: Apostle—1933; died 1947.
7. Charles A. Didier: First Quorum of Seventy—1975; presidency of Seventy—1992.
8. Jacob de Jager: First Quorum of Seventy—1976; emeritus status—1993.
9. F. Enzio Busche: First Quorum of Seventy—1977; emeritus status—2000.
10. Derek A. Cuthbert: First Quorum of Seventy—1978; died 1991.
11. John Sonnenberg: First Quorum of Seventy—1984; Second Quorum of Seventy—1989; released—1989.

12. Hans B. Ringger: First Quorum of Seventy—1985; emeritus status—1995.

13. Kenneth Johnson: First Quorum of Seventy—1993.

14. Dieter F. Uchtdorf: Second Quorum of Seventy—1994; First Quorum of Seventy—1996; presidency of Seventy—2002.

GROWTH IN SOUTHERN EUROPE

In the last half of the twentieth century the Church became established in three Catholic countries near the northern Mediterranean: Italy, Spain, and Portugal. Although each of these countries has a Catholic heritage and a similar climate, they are nonetheless quite distinct.

ITALY

Italy had been one of the earliest non–English-speaking countries to be opened to missionary work. Initial preaching, which began in 1850, resulted in both converts and emigrants, but the Church waned in Italy and was not reestablished until the 1960s. The first twentieth century contacts came from Latter-day Saint sailors who were stationed at Naples and from northern Italian workers who had gone to West Germany as "guest workers" and heard the gospel while they were there. In 1965 a few elders from the Swiss Mission were assigned to the northern part of Italy. In November 1966, Elder Ezra Taft Benson dedicated Italy for the preaching of the gospel, choosing a site in Torre Pellice near the place where Elder Lorenzo Snow had offered his dedicatory prayer in 1850. By 1967, the Italian Church periodical *La Stella* (*The Star*) began to be published and distributed to the Saints throughout Italy. Sustained by steady growth, the Italian Mission was divided in 1971. By 1977 the Church had four missions in Italy: Rome, Catania,

Milan, and Padova. President Spencer W. Kimball visited Italy in 1977, the very first Church president to do so. In 1993 the Italian government granted legal status to the Church. By the end of the century, Italy had three stakes: Milan, Venice, and Puglia.[22]

Joining the Church in Italy requires a great measure of faith. There are formidable barriers to surmount, including the well-established Catholic tradition, the widespread use of tobacco and alcohol, and difficult economic conditions. Despite such obstacles, many Italians have joined the Church. Roberto Asioli, who later served as a counselor in the Padova Mission presidency, met two missionaries when his wife was in the hospital recovering from the loss of a child at birth and he was at home alone, feeling quite low and discouraged. Of the very first meeting with the missionaries, Roberto said, "It was not difficult for me to receive their testimony—it was the right time for me to hear the gospel message."[23] At first, his wife reused to join. Promised by the missionaries that she would join if he was baptized, he went ahead and was baptized without her. She observed her husband carefully and saw how fulfilled and devoted he had become. Two months after Roberto's baptism, he baptized his wife.[24]

Such conversion stories are not uncommon in Italy. Gradually and steadily the Church is growing in that beautiful country, and nearly twenty thousand Italian Saints are a testimony to that growth.[25]

SPAIN

American servicemen stationed in Spain during World War II and after the war constituted the first Latter-day Saint presence in that country. By 1966 two branches of the Church had

Church members and missionaries in Barcelona gathered together on 29 May 1976 for the dedication of the Spain Barcelona Mission. (LDS Church Archives.)

been organized under the direction of the French Mission. In 1967 Spain enacted the Religious Liberty Law, allowing other churches besides the Catholic Church to function in that country. Elders Gordon B. Hinckley and Howard W. Hunter worked together to gain official recognition for the Church, which was granted in 1968. The Spain Madrid Mission was created two years later. Soon, four other missions were formed. The first stake in Spain was organized in Madrid in 1982. By the early years of the twenty-first century, there were seven stakes in Spain. And at the end of the twentieth century, President Gordon B. Hinckley dedicated the Madrid Spain Temple (March 1999).[26]

Spaniards who join the Church in Spain have to surmount significant cultural barriers. Families, friends, and the Catholic

Church combine forces to discourage people from becoming Latter-day Saints. Nevertheless, many valiant members have converted and remain faithful. One such member is Jose Madorran. Raised as a Catholic, Madorran was in training to become a priest when he decided to take a leave and earn some money to assist his struggling parents. He took a job at a hotel in northern Spain which was later destroyed by a terrorist bomb. Jose was severely injured. After several months of physical therapy he was still paralyzed from the waist down.

When two Latter-day Saint missionaries knocked on his door, he was not interested in their message because he wasn't feeling very well. They scheduled an appointment and when they returned, he told them he had a serious liver infection and would probably live for only a few more months.

The missionaries asked Jose if he would allow them to give him a blessing. He consented and later explained that he earnestly desired to have the same spirit these missionaries had brought into his life. Within two hours of the blessing he began to feel his strength returning. Thirty minutes later he could stand on his own without any assistance. Before very long he began to walk again. Jose Madorron was baptized soon after this miraculous healing. He has been a faithful member and has brought many into the Church. Jose is very thankful that the missionaries were worthy to use the priesthood to save his life.[27]

PORTUGAL

The first Latter-day Saints in Portugal were members of the United States armed forces. They came in the early 1970s. In May 1974 the government granted religious freedom to Portugal and soon thereafter David M. Kennedy, the Church's

The first official public meeting of The Church of Jesus Christ of Latter-day Saints in Portugal was held 24 November 1974 in Estoril at the home of Ray Caldwell (back row, first at left). Here, the Caldwell family and other early Portuguese members of the Church pose with Mission President William Grant Bangerter (back row, third from left). (LDS Church Archives)

"ambassador-at-large," received permission for the Church to officially enter the country of Portugal. In November 1974, the Church organized the Portugal Lisbon Mission and called William Grant Bangerter as the first mission president. By July 1978, Portugal had one thousand members, and the first stake was organized in Lisbon three years later. This meant that Portugal had accomplished in a few years what most other European countries had required more than a century to achieve. Growth and expansion came rapidly, and by the year 2000 Portugal had the second largest Church membership of any European country.[28]

Joining the Church in Portugal is difficult because of a

combination of the old Catholic tradition and a new wave of agnosticism and skepticism. Nevertheless, people have joined the Church in large numbers. Hernaldo and Eugenia Grillo were born and raised in the Portuguese colony of Angola (in Africa). They were forced to leave there when this former Portuguese colony became independent through a violent uprising. In October 1975 they fled to Portugal, taking only what they could carry with them. Life was very hard for refugees such as the Grillos; they were very poor and realized that they had to start over. Eventually they earned enough to have a small apartment of their own. In their desperate condition they prayed to God, asking him what he would have them do.

Within two days missionaries were at their door. These missionaries brought answers to many questions that Hernaldo and Eugenia had. They learned about the purpose of life and the possibilities for the eternities. They readily accepted the message taught by the missionaries. They were baptized in November 1977.[29]

GREECE

Missionary work also began in this period in a country that is difficult to categorize. Greece is sometimes considered a part of the Balkans, often as a part of the Middle East, and occasionally as a part of Europe. In this instance it will be placed alongside the three countries just considered.

Before the organization of a separate mission in Greece, Church membership consisted primarily of military and government personnel and their families. In 1972, Elder Gordon B. Hinckley dedicated Greece for the preaching of the gospel. Missionary work followed that event and was placed under the direction of the Vienna East Mission. Greece was organized as a separate mission in 1990. In the year 2001 there were 553 members living in five branches in Greece.[30]

CONCLUSION

The general progress of the Church in Europe in the last half of the twentieth century is miraculous. The consistent growth in the face of obstacles is nothing less than astonishing and remarkable. What had been an obscure religious group became visible and influential all across Europe.

CHAPTER 7

THE CHURCH BEHIND THE IRON CURTAIN

DONALD Q. CANNON

1903   Russia dedicated for the preaching of the gospel

1929   Mission opened in Czechoslovakia

1977   Poland dedicated

1985   Yugoslavia dedicated

        Freiberg Germany Temple dedicated (East Germany)

1987   Hungary dedicated for the preaching of the gospel

1988   First baptisms in Lithuania

1989   Berlin Wall comes down

        First baptisms in Estonia

1990   Czechoslovakia dedicated for the preaching of the gospel

        Russia rededicated

        First missionaries arrive in Bulgaria

1990–91 Revolutions in Eastern Europe in which Communist governments are replaced

1991   Ukraine dedicated for the preaching of the gospel

1992   Missionary work begins in Latvia

1993   Albania dedicated for the preaching of the gospel

        Romania-Bucharest Mission created

During most of the twentieth century, the Church had only limited contact with Eastern Europe. Then, in the 1980s,

several events took place that brought the Church and the people of Eastern Europe into a much closer relationship. In 1974, President Spencer W. Kimball asserted: "I believe the Lord can do anything he sets his mind to. But I can see no good reason why the Lord would open doors that we are not prepared to enter. Why should he break down the Iron Curtain or the Bamboo Curtain or any other curtain if we are still unprepared to enter?"[1]

In 1987, Mikhail Gorbachev, president of the Soviet Union, introduced *glasnost* (openness) and *perestroika* (economic, political, and social restructuring) in the Soviet Union and its satellite nations. These forward-looking policies helped set the stage for monumental changes across all of Eastern Europe. In November 1989 the Berlin Wall fell. During the next two years democratic governments replaced totalitarian regimes in Poland, Czechoslovakia, Hungary, Bulgaria, and East Germany. Other eastern bloc nations also began to change to a more democratic and open system of government. These sweeping changes allowed the Church to enter places where it had previously been forbidden, fulfilling President Kimball's prophecy that the Lord can make anything happen—if his people are ready for it.

EAST GERMANY

Before the fall of Communism, East Germany was home to nearly 3,500 members of the Church. This large body of Saints resulted mostly from missionary work done prior to World War II. After the war these faithful Saints lived under harsh Communist restrictions for more than forty years. In the 1960s, however, a few favorable changes began to take place. In a meeting with Church members in Görlitz in 1969, Elder

The Freiberg Germany Temple, built behind the Iron Curtain through miraculous circumstances, was dedicated in 1985. (Photo courtesy Donald Q. Cannon)

Thomas S. Monson stood before 235 German Saints and made an inspired promise: "If you will remain true and faithful," he said, "every blessing any member of the Church enjoys in any other country will be yours."[2] In 1975 Elder Monson renewed these promises when he dedicated the German Democratic Republic for the preaching of the gospel. These blessings soon found fulfillment: in 1982, the Freiberg Stake was organized, followed by the Leipzig Stake in 1984. And, under miraculous circumstances, in 1985 the Freiberg Germany Temple was dedicated. In April 1989 the first foreign missionaries in more than fifty years entered the German Democratic Republic. And, in November 1989, the Berlin Wall fell. The next year, the two Germanys were reunified and became one nation.[3]

The Freiberg Germany Temple was the result of a genuine miracle. During the days of Communist control in former East

Among those present at the dedication of the Freiberg Germany Temple were President Gordon B. Hinckley (at microphone) and Elder Thomas S. Monson (two individuals left of President Hinckley). Elder Monson was instrumental in much of the work that occurred behind the Iron Curtain in East Germany. (Photo courtesy Richard O. Cowan)

Germany, members were not allowed to travel outside their country to visit the temple. Nonetheless, Church leaders and members frequently petitioned government officials for permission. The government consistently refused. In a remarkable turn of events, the government of the German Democratic Republic eventually proposed that the Church build a temple in East Germany.

This, one government official said, meant Church leaders could "put a stop to the annoying practice by members of resubmitting visa applications to visit the temple in Switzerland."[4] Many miracles followed.

In order to construct the temple, the East German government had to approve building plans, grant permits, allow

Missionaries (back row) pose with a Czech family at baptismal services in Czechoslovakia in 1940. (LDS Church Archives)

building materials to be secured, and authorize the use of natural gas for heat. Church leaders were continually amazed by the cooperation they received from usually rigid authorities.[5]

Ironically, across the border in West Germany, Church leaders were having a terrible time getting permits and other necessary authorizations for construction of the Frankfurt Germany Temple. In fact, that temple, which was announced a year and a half earlier than the Freiberg temple, would not be completed until two years after the temple in East Germany.

Historians David F. Boone and Richard O. Cowan documented the Freiberg temple's impact as follows:

> Some 89,789 visitors toured the temple during its twelve-day open house—about twice the population of Freiberg, double the number visiting the Stockholm Sweden

Temple during the same time, and nearly twenty times the Latter-day Saint membership in the GDR.

Interest increased as the open house period continued. People who had grown to detest standing in line to get almost everything they needed, willingly waited up to four hours, often in the rain, in a line a kilometer long, to visit the new temple. "You know, around here you're forced to stand in so many lines, and we're sick of it," one visitor exclaimed. "But this is the line I chose to stand in, and I'm not budging until I see in there!" Sometimes fathers waited in line while their wives took care of the children in a more comfortable place; then the mothers would switch places with their husbands in order to save the family's place in line. Open house hours were normally from eight A.M. to eight P.M., but at closing time there sometimes were still large numbers waiting to get in. "We simply can't turn them away," [Dresden Mission] President Henry Burkhardt concluded. "Tonight we are going to stay open until every person that wants to see this temple has seen it." On that occasion the tours continued until two A.M.[6]

CZECHOSLOVAKIA

The Czechoslovakia mission was originally opened in 1929, interrupted during World War II, and then closed by 1950, following the Communist takeover. The Church was officially banned from the country. Yet, even though the police occasionally interrogated them, Church members continued to "inconspicuously visit each other in their homes," partake of the sacrament, and pay tithing. These couple of hundred Czech Saints were visited from time to time by Church leaders from adjoining European countries and even occasionally by General Authorities—all entering as tourists.[7] In the mid-1980s Latter-day Saint church leaders began to meet with government leaders

119

in Prague, seeking recognition for the Church in that country. Elder Russell M. Nelson of the Twelve and Elder Hans B. Ringger of the Seventy were told that only a native Czech member of the Church could apply for official recognition. Despite considerable personal risk—including government interrogation and possible imprisonment—Jiří Šnederfler, the district president in Prague, agreed to submit the application. As a direct result of Brother Šnederfler's courageous act, with additional support stemming from the revolution of 1989, recognition was granted by a new democratic government. Elder Nelson offered a special prayer of thanksgiving at the same site where Elder John A. Widtsoe had dedicated Czechoslovakia in 1929.[8]

A new mission opened in that country in July 1990, with Richard K. Winder, who had served as a missionary there forty years earlier, as president. The new mission enjoyed real success as many well-educated people came into the Church. Eventually Czechoslovakia was divided into two missions.[9] In the early years of the twenty-first century, there were more than seventeen hundred members of the Church in the Czech Republic.[10]

HUNGARY

During the 1980s several significant events occurred that enabled the Church's establishment in Hungary. In 1982, the Mormon Tabernacle Choir visited the country. Their concerts aroused interest among those in charge of the Hungarian National Television station, which sent a crew to Utah to film a TV series about the Church in 1984. As this series aired on Hungarian television, nearly every adult in the country saw at least one segment of the production. Following the broadcast

(Left to right) Matthew H. Ciembronówicz, President Spencer W. Kimball, Camilla Kimball, Marian Ciembronówicz, and Fryderyk Czerwiński in front of the Tomb of the Unknown Soldier in Saxon Garden, Warsaw, on 24 August 1977. (LDS Church Archives)

several Hungarians sent queries to the Church's missionary department. One of them, a Hungarian surgeon named Dr. Gedeon Kereszti, wrote to Dr. Kim Davis of the University of Utah Medical School, asking for information concerning the Church. Dr. Kereszti remembered reading an article written by Dr. Davis in a medical journal. The Kereszti family received the discussions from the mission president in Hungary and eventually traveled to Vienna to be baptized.[11]

As a follow-up to these events, Elder Russell M. Nelson of the Council of the Twelve dedicated Hungary for missionary work in a park in Budapest in April 1987. Two days later, Elder Nelson and area president Hans Ringger met with the chairman of the Council of Religious Affairs in Hungary. The council required that a few native Hungarians become Church members before official recognition be granted. To accomplish this, the government allowed a few missionaries to enter Hungary. Converts were baptized, including two more Hungarian medical doctors, and official recognition of the Church came in June 1988.[12]

Church growth continued, and in 1989, the Church purchased a villa in Budapest to accommodate meetings. President Thomas S. Monson dedicated the villa as a meetinghouse in October 1989. By January 1991, there were three hundred members in Hungary. Meanwhile, the Hungary Budapest Mission had been created.[13] By the beginning of the twenty-first century there were more than thirty-five hundred members in Hungary.[14]

POLAND

Prior to World War II, a sizeable number of German Saints lived in the area that later became part of Poland. Some of these remained in the area following the war and provided a foundation for later Church growth in the country. On 24 August 1977, President Spencer W. Kimball visited Warsaw. In a secluded grove of trees in the middle of a beautiful downtown park, he "dedicated the land of Poland and blessed its people that the work of the Lord might go forth."[15] Then, in 1986, President Thomas S. Monson, Elder Russell M. Nelson, and Elder Hans B. Ringger met with Polish government officials in charge of religion. They asked for two things: permission for young missionaries to enter Poland and authorization to buy or build a chapel. The government granted both requests.[16]

Prior to this development, the Church had sent senior couples into Poland to make friends and lay the foundation for regular missionary work. Among those were Juliusz and

Dorothy Fussek. Elder Fussek had been born in Poland and thus knew the language. The Fusseks were real "pioneers" in Poland. They made friends and paved the way for establishing the Church. Their commitment was so great that even though they were originally called for only two years, they stayed for five.[17]

In 1989, the year of freedom in Europe, Lech Walesa, head of the Solidarity Labor movement, and others created a parliamentary government in Poland. As president of Poland, Lech Walesa enacted a religious liberty law. This law was a real boon for the Church.[18]

In 1991, a beautiful chapel in Warsaw was dedicated by Elder Nelson. Following this milestone, Church growth continued at a steady pace. New members came into the Church, and Poland sent its first missionaries abroad.[19]

Although two factors still tended to curtail growth in Poland—the Catholic tradition and a failing economy—by the early years of the twenty-first century, there were just over twelve hundred Church members in Poland.[20]

ROMANIA

The story of the Church in Romania differs markedly from experiences in other Iron Curtain countries. It is a different story because Romania was the only Eastern European country to experience a violent revolution during the fall of Communism. Nicolae Ceausescu, the brutal Communist dictator of Romania, was toppled from power and executed in December 1989. In the weeks that followed, the words of a revolutionary song echoed throughout the land: "Come, Lord, Come." The Christian people of Romania had waited more than forty years to openly express their beliefs.[21] Within six weeks of the overthrow, a party of Latter-day Saint General and Area Authorities entered Romania to meet with government officials and to dedicate the land for the preaching of the gospel. Elder Russell M. Nelson dedicated Romania in Cismigiu Park in Bucharest.[22]

These same Church leaders offered humanitarian aid—medical, dental, and social help—that the country's new government leaders gratefully accepted. Latter-day Saint doctors, such as Dr. Glenn K. Lund, came to provide badly needed medical skill. Other couples set up programs similar to Alcoholics Anonymous and arranged for adoptions by LDS American couples for a large number of Romanian orphans.[23]

These humanitarian efforts led to several conversions; and eventually missionaries from Italy arrived and began to teach the people. Progress came step by step.

One of Romania's earliest converts, Eva Balazs, has an especially interesting converstion story. One day she asked her husband, "Why were we ever born?" Attempting to find an answer to this question, she began a thorough study of religion. She studied about the history of Christianity and about the teachings of several religious denominations. She then concluded that if she had enough faith, God would lead her to the true church.

Not long after reaching this conclusion, she met two LDS sister missionaries. As she interacted with them and studied the gospel, she realized that their beliefs corresponded to her own beliefs. After a period of study and searching, she asked God if the Church was true. When no immediate response came, she concluded that this was another false religion. A few moments later, however, a state of joy came over her and an inner peace entered into her heart. She had received her answer. She was baptized and has been a faithful and contributing member ever since that day.[24]

At first, missionary work in Romania was directed by the Vienna East Mission, then by the Hungary Budapest Mission, but by 1993 the country had a mission of its own—the Romania Bucharest Mission.[25] By the early years of the twenty-first century there were more than two thousand members in Romania.[26]

BULGARIA

As in many other Communist satellite countries, the gospel came into Bulgaria following the revolution of 1989–90. Fortunately, American members with Bulgarian ancestry had already translated the Book of Mormon into Bulgarian years before. This translation facilitated missionary work in a substantial way.[27]

Elders Russell M. Nelson and Hans B. Ringger visited with Bulgarian government leaders soon after the revolution. Bulgarian officials asked the Church if they could provide English teachers. Accordingly, two married couples and two sister missionaries were sent to teach English at the Bulgarian National School of Languages in Sofia. Soon, missionaries transferred from German-speaking missions began teaching German to Bulgarian students. Gradually, these teachers of English and German introduced gospel concepts into their language teaching. The first baptisms were conducted in November 1990.[28]

In July 1991, the Bulgarian government officially recognized the Church. Ten days later, the Church organized the Bulgaria Sofia Mission. As in the case of Romania, the Church first sent in humanitarian missionaries. Among them were ophthalmologists and audiologists who helped meet medical needs.[29]

Although many Bulgarian converts had a difficult time accepting and living the requirements of the Word of Wisdom (drinking and smoking were socially accepted and widespread), members met the challenge, and the Church grew.[30] By the early years of the twenty-first century, there were more than nineteen hundred Church members in Bulgaria.[31]

ALBANIA

Conditions in Albania were somewhat more difficult for the Church than those in other East European nations. First, there existed massive poverty. Second, 70 percent of Albanians were Muslim. Nevertheless, the Church began missionary work in this country following its revolution in 1991.[32] Albania had a tremendous need for humanitarian services, and the Church was willing to help, providing both medical and agricultural assistance.[33]

Elder Dallin H. Oaks of the Twelve dedicated Albania for the preaching of the gospel in 1993. Later, missionaries were sent into the country. At first, the Albanian language had to be learned directly in the mission field, as no training was available in any of the missionary training centers (MTC). In 1994, however, Albanian was introduced at the Provo MTC. Following this, the Book of Mormon was translated into Albanian. As a result of these developments, the number of converts increased.[34] By the early years of the twenty-first century, there were more than eleven hundred Church members in Albania.[35]

YUGOSLAVIA

The nation of Yugoslavia, composed of Serbia, Croatia, and other smaller states, came into being at the end of World

Krešimir Ćosić (back row, second from left) poses with other Church members in Zagreb, Yugoslavia, in October 1982. (LDS Church Archives)

War I. The early history of the Church in Yugoslavia centers around the work of one man: Krešimir Ćosić. As a participant in the 1968 Olympics in Mexico City he came to the attention of coaches at Brigham Young University, who successfully recruited him. While playing basketball at BYU, he joined the Church. His extraordinary athletic skills earned him the status of a world-renowned basketball player and he was a hero to many Yugoslavians. In 1972, Brother Ćosić and Elder Gordon B. Hinckley met and discussed how the Church might be introduced into Yugoslavia. Thus, Krešimir returned to Zadar, Croatia, his hometown, and missionaries from Italy were sent into the part of Yugoslavia where Italian was spoken. Ćosić actively assisted the elders with their work. Soon, Vladimir Peric, a friend of Brother Ćosić, was baptized. Other converts followed. Eventually, Serbo-Croatian began to be taught at the training center in Provo. A much larger missionary force then entered Yugoslavia. In order to succeed in this Communist society, the missionaries had to be innovative. They wore jeans and T-shirts instead of dark suits. One of the early missionaries, Kurt Bestor, gave piano lessons and played the piano in a lounge. Meanwhile, Krešimir Ćosić personally paid for the translation of the Book of Mormon into Serbo-Croatian. President Monson dedicated Yugoslavia for the preaching of the gospel in 1985. Meetinghouses were either built or leased, and the number of members grew.

Upon the disintegration of Yugoslavia, Krešimir Ćosić received an appointment as Deputy Ambassador to the United States for Croatia. Although Ćosić died of cancer in May 1995, his support in these missionary efforts is remembered, and his legacy continues.[36]

Civil wars and political unrest following the fall of Communism led to the breakup of Yugoslavia into separate countries. These conditions have made progress for the Church difficult. Nevertheless, there are members in some countries that were formerly part of Yugoslavia. By the year 2000, Croatia had well over three hundred Church members, and a few members were also found in Bosnia and Kosovo.[37]

THE SOVIET UNION

Latter-day Saint interest in the Soviet Union began early. Mischa Markow preached in the area at the dawning of the twentieth century. Elder Frances M. Lyman, a member of the Twelve, then dedicated Russia in 1903, but no further missionary work took place. Russian translation of the Book of Mormon was completed in the 1920s. But the first meaningful contacts came much later—in 1989—about the same time as in other Soviet satellite countries.[38]

As in so many other cases, Elders Russell M. Nelson and Hans B. Ringger visited the Soviet Union in 1989, explaining to government officials what the Church would like to do in their country. As a result of this contact, the first missionaries to enter Soviet territory went to Tallinn in Estonia and Vyborg and Leningrad, Russian cities close to the Finnish border. These missionaries came from the Finnish Mission. In July 1990, the Finland Helsinki East Mission was created to take charge of all programs in Russia. Gary Browning, a professor of Russian at BYU, was called to be the president. By that time, the Leningrad Branch had one hundred members, Tallinn fifty, and Vyborg twenty-five. After only one visit to these Soviet branches, President Browning was immediately impressed with the deep spirituality of these new members:

> I was deeply moved as I attended church meetings in Vyborg on the first Sunday of my mission. Since 1963, I had visited Russia fairly frequently. In my heart I had felt that the restored gospel would be shared with this deserving people whom I had come to love dearly, but in my mind I could not imagine how our Church could ever be established with that country's government and ruling party so opposed to religion. On that day early in July 1990, I walked into a small music school and was greeted by two legendary missionaries and by nearly two dozen recently baptized members of the Church. Before my sacrament meeting talk, six little girls, ranging from about three to nine years of age, sang, in Russian, "I Am a Child of God." The singing was angelic, as were their radiant, broadly smiling faces. As I watched and listened in my awe, my heart filled with "hosannas" for the blessing of this long-awaited day.[39]

Elder Russell M. Nelson visited Leningrad in April 1990 for the purpose of contacting government officials and rededicating

Russia for the preaching of the gospel. He gave the dedicatory prayer at the same place along the Neva River where Elder Francis M. Lyman had given his prayer in 1903. Later in 1990, a few missionaries from the Vienna Austria East Mission were assigned to Moscow and Kiev. In 1991, a revolution divided the Soviet Union into fifteen separate countries.[40] In that same year, the Church was recognized by the Russian Federation, the largest nation from the former Soviet Union.

THE RUSSIAN FEDERATION

By February 1992, there were 750 Church members in Russia, including three hundred in St. Petersburg (Leningrad). As Sunday was the only day of the week when Russians did not have to work, most Russians did shopping, household tasks, and recreation on that day. Keeping the Sabbath day holy proved to be a serious challenge. Most new members, however, were obedient in this and other commandments. The Church created two missions in Russia in 1992—one headquartered at St. Petersburg and one in Moscow. Both mission presidents, Thomas S. Rogers and Gary L. Browning, had been involved in the pioneering efforts from outside the Soviet Union. Both missions grew rapidly. Success, however, attracted the attention of the powerful Russian Orthodox Church, and soon the Russian Parliament advocated a law forbidding new Christian missionaries from entering the country. For a time, the Latter-day Saints moved cautiously. Nevertheless, the Church continued make new friends and gain respect. In 1993, another mission was added: the Russia Samara Mission.[41] By the year 2002, there were almost seventeen thousand Church members in Russia.[42]

UKRAINE

Ukraine became a separate nation in 1991. Later that year President Boyd K. Packer of the Twelve dedicated this country for the preaching of the gospel. In 1992 the Ukraine Mission opened, with Howard L. Biddulph as president. In 1993, the Ukraine-Donetsk Mission opened. By 1995, most of the basic Church materials had been translated into Ukrainian.[43] By the end of 2002 there were more than eighty-six hundred Church members in the Ukraine.[44]

BELARUS

Formerly known as White Russia, this country gained its independence in 1991 with the breakup of the Soviet Union. Missionaries from the Ukraine Kiev Mission began teaching in Belarus in 1993. It later was administered by the Lithuania Vilnius Mission.[45] By 2002, there were more than four hundred Church members in Belarus.[46]

THE BALTIC STATES

This region—composed of Estonia, Latvia, and Lithuania—was opened for missionary work about the same time as the other states in the former Soviet Union. Progress occurred first in Estonia because Finnish missionaries had been sent there at the same time others went into Moscow and Leningrad.

The Church grew steadily if not rapidly in the Baltic States. Eventually, a separate mission was created to serve all the Baltic States. Originally, mission headquarters was established in Riga, Latvia, but in 1996 was moved to Vilnius, Lithuania.[47] This mission was home to more than two thousand Church members in 2002.[48]

Elder M. Russell Ballard traveled to Lithuania in 1993 to dedicate the land for the preaching of the gospel. Here, he stands with missionaries after the dedicatory services on 20 May 1993. (LDS Church Archives)

CONCLUSION

By the year 2000 President Kimball's prophecies concerning the Iron Curtain countries had been fulfilled to the letter. The political upheavals and reform of the 1980s and 1990s had facilitated the introduction of the Church into many nations in this part of the world. Today, Zion is still growing behind the former Iron Curtain.

CHURCH STATUS IN EUROPE*

GEOGRAPHICAL AREAS	MEMBERS	STAKES	MISSIONS	TEMPLES**
Great Britain				
England	135,819	36	5	2
Ireland	2,610	1	1	—

GEOGRAPHICAL AREAS	MEMBERS	STAKES	MISSIONS	TEMPLES
Northern Ireland	5,332	1	—	—
Scotland	25,622	5	1	—
Wales	7,615	2	—	—
Scandinavia				
Denmark	4,457	2	1	1
Finland	4,497	2	1	1
Greenland	13	—	—	—
Iceland	273	—	—	—
Norway	4,102	1	1	—
Sweden	8,678	4	1	1
Continental Europe				
Andorra	78	—	—	—
Austria	3,996	2	—	—
Belgium	5,979	2	1	—
Corsica	55	—	—	—
France	31,971	8	2	—
Germany	36,704	14	5	2
Gibraltar	19	—	—	—
Greece	591	—	1	—
Italy	20,493	3	3	—
Luxembourg	175	—	—	—
Malta	118	—	—	—
Netherlands	7,899	3	—	1
Portugal	36,546	6	2	—
Spain	34,831	7	5	1
Switzerland	7,418	3	2	1
Eastern Europe				
Albania	1,160	—	1	—
Belarus	403	—	—	—
Bulgaria	1,927	—	1	—

Geographical Areas	Members	Stakes	Missions	Temples
Croatia	379	—	—	—
Czech Republic	1,821	—	1	—
Estonia	677	—	—	—
Hungary	3,784	—	1	—
Latvia	651	—	—	—
Lithuania	735	—	1	—
Moldova	200	—	—	—
Poland	1,296	—	1	—
Romania	2,146	—	1	—
Russia	16,638	—	8	—
Serbia	213	—	—	—
Slovakia	110	—	—	—
Slovenia	286	—	1	—
Ukraine	8,627	—	2	1
Europe Totals:	**426,944**	**102**	**50**	**11**

* Numbers are for year's end 2002

** These numbers represent operating temples and those that had been announced or were under construction at press time.

PART II

THE CHURCH IN
THE PACIFIC

While the Saints were still in Nauvoo, the Prophet Joseph Smith sent missionaries to the Pacific to teach the gospel message to thousands of warm and friendly islanders. Of all the lands in the world, in fact, only the residents of North America and Great Britain received the message of the restored gospel sooner. Today, Latter-day Saint Polynesians—descendants of the first converts in the Pacific—are able to trace their heritage to Book of Mormon times, believing that their ancestors, like Hagoth's colony (Alma 63:5–8), had sailed into the Pacific from ancient America.

The Church and its members face a unique set of circumstances in the friendly isles of the Pacific. Maps of the Pacific reveal that myriad small islands are separated by long stretches of water, posing substantial challenges in transportation and communication. Contemporary visitors to Hawaii, Tahiti, or Fiji hardly comprehend the difficulties of earlier years. Even today a large amount of travel in French Polynesia and Tonga is done by small boat. Mission presidents and missionaries in French Polynesia spend considerable time in small motorized canoes and schooners. Communications between islands are generally conducted by short-wave transmission. Telephone communications are still the exception. Isolation is common.

The geographical restraints and limitations extant in the Pacific world are far different from the romantic notions that film writers, poets, and novelists often portray. Although some islands are indeed lush and verdant and provide a relatively easy life, most islands allow their inhabitants only meager fare. Today, the high volcanic islands of Hawaii, Samoa, and Tahiti are large enough and geologically varied enough to provide a pleasant way of life. But in the mid- to late-1800s, even in these isles, the variety of foods was limited and monotonous. Life must have been boring on the atolls—low coral islands—of the Tuamotu Archipelago in French Polynesia. Even after modern sailors began selling canned goods to the local people to supplement their normal diet of fish and coconut, life on the atolls was far from ideal. Only in New Zealand, where the islands are continental and the climate is temperate, did the Polynesians have a wider range of foods to choose from.

But food is only the beginning. By their nature, the islands limited the kinds of clothes, houses, tools, cooking implements, and so on that people could wear and use. And a limited number of natural resources—for example, the almost complete absence of minerals—has made economic development very difficult. Many island economies are based almost entirely on copra (dried coconut) and fishing. Hawaii, New Zealand, Fiji, and a few other areas are large enough to accommodate sugarcane plantations and large farms, but most island groups are not so fortunate.

In most of the island groups, New Zealand and continental Australia excepted, the weather is warm throughout the year. The heat is frequently debilitating, and work must be done in the early hours of the day or in the evening. Americans sometimes accuse island people of being lazy when, in fact, the local people are using the climate to their best advantage.

Tropical storms and hurricanes frequently bring destruction to the islands. Latter-day Saint missionaries and local Saints have suffered through numerous lengthy storms that have ruined plantations, *homes, boats, and almost everything else above ground. Many missionaries and mission presidents, including David O. McKay, have been caught in storms at sea and have seen their ships driven before the wind for hours or days on end.*

In summary, life in the islands is not as easy as is often assumed by visitors who have not seen its full cycle.

Still, the Prophet Joseph felt it necessary to send missionaries to these sometimes-stormy isles. When the first missionaries reached the isles, they built on foundations that had been laid by Protestant and Roman Catholic missionaries who had come into the Pacific earlier and converted virtually all of the Polynesian people and a high percentage of the peoples of Melanesia and Micronesia to Christianity. The Protestants had also translated the Bible into all of the local Polynesian languages. They had started schools and helped the people become literate. Protestant missionaries had become involved in local governmental affairs, sometimes to the detriment of the local people; but they did introduce many ideas that helped to assure the religious rights of Latter-day Saint missionaries when they came on the scene. Still, ministers of these other faiths regarded the Mormons as rivals. The Catholics and Protestants particularly resented Latter-day Saints taking away converts that they themselves had earlier brought into the Christian fold. Even though the LDS missionaries justifiably considered other ministers of the gospel their competitors and at times even their adversaries, the pioneer missionary efforts of these other churches contributed significantly to the Latter-day Saints' success.

THE PACIFIC

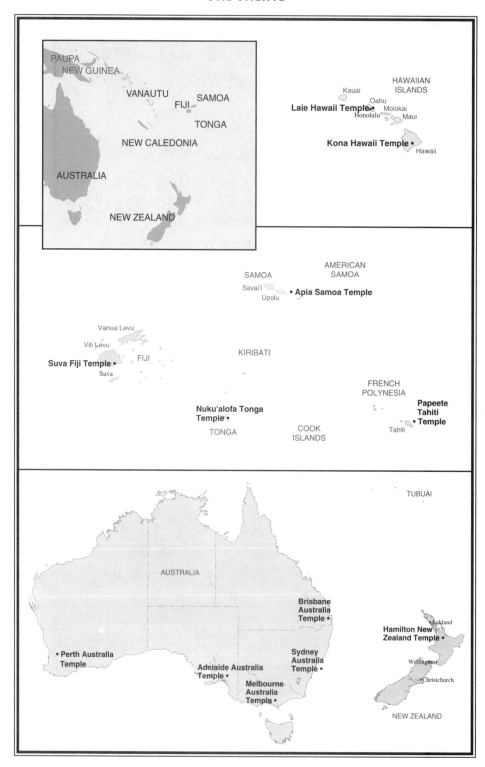

PAPUA
NEW GUINEA

VANAUTU   SAMOA
           FIJI
                 TONGA

NEW CALEDONIA

AUSTRALIA

NEW ZEALAND

HAWAIIAN
ISLANDS
Kauai
        Oahu
Laie Hawaii Temple •   Molokai
         Honolulu   Maui

Kona Hawaii Temple •
              Hawaii

AMERICAN
SAMOA
SAMOA
Savai'i
   Upolu   • Apia Samoa Temple

Vanua Levu

Viti Levu
         FIJI   KIRIBATI
Suva Fiji Temple •
   Suva

                                FRENCH
                                POLYNESIA
                                        Papeete
                                        Tahiti
Nuku'alofa Tonga   • Temple
Temple •   Tahiti
   TONGA   COOK
                ISLANDS

                                TUBUAI

AUSTRALIA

                Brisbane
                Australia
                Temple •
                                        •Aukland
                                Hamilton New
                                Zealand Temple •
• Perth Australia
Temple   Sydney
                 Australia
                 Temple •
   Adelaide Australia   Wellington•
   Temple •
        Melbourne   •Christchurch
        Australia
        Temple •
                                 NEW ZEALAND

CHAPTER 8

BEGINNINGS IN
FRENCH POLYNESIA AND HAWAII

R. LANIER BRITSCH

1843   Four missionaries called to serve in the Pacific

1844   Work opens in French Polynesia

1850   First missionaries arrive in Hawaii

1852–54 George Q. Cannon translates Book of Mormon into Hawaiian

1857   Missionaries withdrawn at outbreak of Utah War

1861   Walter Murray Gibson arrives in Hawaii

1865   Laie purchased as new gathering place in Hawaii following Gibson's excommunication

1873   RLDS missionaries arrive in Tahiti

1892   French Polynesian Mission reopens

THE ESTABLISHMENT OF THE CHURCH IN FRENCH POLYNESIA, 1844 TO 1895[1]

In the spring of 1843, Addison Pratt received a mission call from Joseph Smith. His destination was to be Vermont, an area where a number of his family members lived. It is not clear why or how the old salt's mission call was changed to the Pacific islands, but on 11 May 1843, Addison Pratt was told he should serve there instead. Perhaps his call was the result of his past experience as a sailor. When Addison was a young man, he had sailed across the Pacific and spent time in the Sandwich Islands (Hawaii). Three other men—Benjamin F. Grouard, who had also sailed the Pacific and had lived in Hawaii; Noah Rogers; and Knowlton F. Hanks—were also assigned to take the restored gospel to the peoples of Oceania.

Addison Pratt was set apart by Brigham Young, ordained a seventy, and given power over the elements. In the years that followed, he would need this blessing, as well as Brigham's counsel to avoid haste and passion and to see goodness in all.[2] The little company of missionaries left Nauvoo, Illinois, on 23 May, with no idea, of course, that one of their number, Elder Hanks, would soon die of consumption at sea, or that another of their group, Elder Grouard, would not leave his mission field in the South Pacific until May 1852—nine years later. Elder Rogers alone would briefly see Nauvoo again, only to leave with the Saints and die at Mt. Pisgah. In New Bedford, Massachusetts, the small missionary group looked for a ship bound for the Sandwich Islands (Hawaii); instead, they found a whaling ship, the *Timoleon,* that was bound for the Society Islands (French Polynesia-Tahiti area). Their voyage, which began on 10 October 1843, took them around the Cape of Good Hope, through the Indian Ocean, and finally into the South Pacific.

After six months of sailing, the missionaries sighted the oval-shaped island of Tubuai, 350 miles south of Tahiti. That day, 30 April 1844, marked the beginning of Latter-day Saint missionary work in the Pacific Islands. The bronze-skinned Polynesians of Tubuai were excited to welcome the missionaries into their company. On learning that the Latter-day Saints were missionaries, they pleaded with Elder Pratt to remain among them. The islanders were already nominal Christians, but they wanted a permanent minister.

Elder Pratt was at first torn between their pleas and his

original intention of teaching the gospel in Hawaii and the well-known Tahiti. He did not know if his efforts in such a small island, with such a small population as Tubuai, would be worthwhile. As missionaries are inclined to do, Elder Pratt sought the Lord's opinion. The Spirit told him that, indeed, his efforts would be worthwhile—his duty was to stay. Finding it impossible to turn down their request, Addison removed his belongings from the *Timoleon* and bade his two companions good-bye. They sailed north to Tahiti, which now became their destination.

Pratt, whom the Polynesians lovingly called "Paraita," went to work with a will. Since he could speak but a few words of Hawaiian, he first limited his teaching to a small group of Caucasian sailors who had settled on the island, taken wives, and become shipbuilders. It was one of their number—Ambrose Alexander—who was the first person in the Pacific area to receive baptism from a Latter-day Saint elder. Five weeks later, the first Polynesians were baptized. In late July, Elder Pratt organized the Tubuai Branch of the Church with eleven members.

Although Elder Pratt enjoyed his associations with the Caucasian members of the branch, he believed he had an obligation to teach the local people. Therefore, he moved to a village where no English was spoken. And with the help of an English-Tahitian grammar book and many hours of practice, Pratt was preaching in Tahitian by September 1844.

During Pratt's first year on Tubuai he converted and baptized sixty people—a third of the island's population—including all but one of the Caucasians on the island. Caring for the members of his little flock was a demanding responsibility. Not only did he find himself deeply involved in all religious and spiritual matters but he was also sought out for advice on matters of law and government.

Meanwhile, Elders Rogers and Grouard were engaged in missionary work on Tahiti and other islands to the northwest. They arrived at Papeete, Tahiti, on 14 May 1844 and soon discovered that social and political conditions were tense and unsettled. Tahiti was technically under local Polynesian control, but the French government was daily tightening its authority over the area. Because of these problems, the elders found the local people unwilling to listen to their message. Of course, the elders also had a serious language deficiency.

It was not until 11 August—nearly three months after their arrival—that Rogers and Grouard had their first baptisms. On that day, Mr. and Mrs. Seth George Lincoln, friends from the *Timoleon,* joined the Church. They proved to be loyal members who provided room and board for the elders as well as facilities for church meetings.

When two American sailors joined the Church on 18 August, some members of the foreign community became upset. Representatives of the London Missionary Society (LMS) circulated derisive stories about Joseph Smith and harassed Church members in other ways; but a few other sailors still chose to join with the Saints.

By early spring, the elders were convinced that other areas would be more productive. Their two paths, Rogers's to the Leeward Islands of the Society Islands group and Grouard's east to the Tuamotu Islands, brought contrasting results. "By the middle of June," writes scholar S. George Ellsworth, "Rogers was back in Tahiti, alone, without success, without word from the church or his family, disheartened. American newspapers carried by passing ships confirmed vague news of trouble in Illinois and the death of Joseph Smith. He feared for his family of nine children at Nauvoo. He himself had suffered violence at the hands of Missourians in 1840. He knew what could happen. The opportunity presenting itself he took *The Three Brothers* to the States. He arrived at Nauvoo 29 December 1845 and was united with his family only to die in the spring exodus from Nauvoo."[3]

Benjamin F. Grouard's experience on the low-lying atolls of the Tuamotus was quite the opposite of Elder Rogers's. When he arrived on Anaa on 1 May 1845, Elder Grouard initiated the most productive era of the mission. Anaa, with its population of two or three thousand, offered a bleak existence. The island provided little more than coconuts, and the sea provided fish. The people's ways were still essentially primitive. Although there were one hundred or so nominal Christians on the island, Grouard could not easily distinguish between them and their fellow islanders.

Perhaps because of their circumstances, rather than in spite of them, the people and chiefs of Anaa were eager to have Elder Grouard live among them. No other Caucasian missionary had lived on Anaa. When Grouard arrived he was already fluent in Tahitian and had only to modify his language a bit to speak. His hearers listened well to his sermons. Only six weeks after he commenced his work, Elder Grouard took his first twenty-four converts into the ocean to baptize them. By the end of August there were 355 baptized members of the Church. On 21 September 1945, Grouard organized branches in all five villages. He had baptized 620 Polynesians in four months.

By October, his administrative burdens became too heavy and he decided to call for Elder Pratt's assistance. He sailed for Tahiti on a large double canoe with a crew of eighteen. Unfortunately, the boat was irreparably damaged on a reef off the small island of Mehitia. While waiting for a new ship to be built, Elder Grouard preached the gospel to the natives of the island, baptizing two. Elder Grouard eventually reached Tahiti and sent word to Elder Pratt to come there. By 3 February 1846, the two men were on Anaa. They worked together until

June, when Grouard began a preaching tour that took him to nine other islands. When he returned in September, Grouard reported 116 more baptisms.

When Elders Pratt and Grouard held the first conference of the Church in the Pacific on Anaa on 24 September 1946, they gathered Saints from ten branches. There were 866 members of the Church in the Pacific. Over three years had passed since the elders had left Nauvoo, and there had been only two or three letters from home. Evidently no replacements were on the way. It was therefore decided that Pratt should return to the body of the Saints, wherever that was, and bring other missionaries to help with the work. Grouard, who had married a Polynesian girl in April 1846, would remain in the islands.[4]

When an inter-island ship came to Anaa in November 1846, Elder Pratt took passage on it. "I shall never forget the parting with Brother Grouard," Pratt wrote. "He and I have been yoked together in this mission for three and a half years. We have withstood the frowns of poverty, the opposition of men and devils, . . . the frowns of hunger, traveling over the sharp coral rocks and slippery mountains with our toes out of our shoes and our knees and elbows out of our clothes, living a part of our time on coconuts and raw fish and sleeping on the ground for the sake of obeying the Savior's commandments and preaching the gospel to the natives of these South Sea Islands."[5]

Once in Tahiti, Elder Pratt started looking for a ship that would take him to California. Between November 1846 and 23 March 1847, when he finally sailed, Pratt developed a branch of twenty-seven members at Huau near Papeete. When Pratt arrived in San Francisco on 11 June, he immediately started looking for anyone who could tell him the location of the Saints and where his wife and four daughters might be. He found some Church members who had come to California with Samuel Brannan, and

Addison Pratt, one the the first missionaries to serve in French Polynesia, established a branch in Tubuai in 1844. (© by Intellectual Reserve, Inc.)

they told him that the Saints had been driven from Nauvoo; they were waiting for Brannan to return with better information on the whereabouts of the main body of the Church. It was not until the next spring that Addison was able to travel with a remnant of the Mormon Battalion toward the Great Salt Lake Valley. When he arrived there on 28 September, he was overjoyed to be reunited with his wife, Louisa, and their daughters, who had reached that city only eight days before from the east.

Only a week or two later, Elder Pratt reported on his mission in general conference. The conference voted to send Addison and a contingent of new missionaries back to Polynesia as soon as possible. Louisa hoped that would not be too soon.

During the winter of 1848 to 1849, Addison taught the Tahitian language to prospective missionaries and other interested people. In late summer, Pratt and a young veteran of the Mormon Battalion, James S. Brown, left for California and the Pacific. Twenty-one other missionaries and family members left later, among them Louisa and her daughters. Louisa's sister, Caroline Crosby, and her family also came along.

When Pratt and Brown's ship reached Papeete in May of 1850, they were detained there by the French governor, who demanded written statements about what the Mormons taught. They were finally given permits to travel in the islands, but the government made missionary work difficult. Pratt did not arrive in Tubuai until 28 January 1851, three months later · than his wife's party arrived.

The second period of the mission was neither easy nor successful. By 1850 the Roman Catholic French government was firmly in control, and the edicts of religious toleration of four years before were no longer respected. The government was uneasy about foreigners and gave preferential status to Catholics. These realities combined to create a near-impossible situation for the Mormons. Two missionary families, finding the work too hard, sailed home for America in the spring of 1851. In frustration at the foolishness of these missionaries, Elder Pratt concluded that the mission needed "young men who are neither sugar nor salt, as they are sometimes exposed to the wet."[6] Sisters Pratt and Crosby, who must have been made of something more than sugar or salt, stayed on Tubuai and opened a school for their own and the island children. They also taught homemaking skills to the Polynesian women.

In March 1852 the government placed all matters of religion under state control and created a new office of district minister to direct and correlate religious affairs throughout the protectorate. All missionaries were ordered to keep to one district and to preach only when they had written invitations from their congregations. But neither Mormons nor Protestants followed these laws when they could avoid them. Unfortunately, however, the Latter-day Saints did not have enough missionaries or sufficient financial backing to counteract the French government. Before long, Elder Grouard was summoned to

Papeete on trumped-up charges and acquitted; James S. Brown was deported; and some local Saints lost their lives on Anaa because they insisted on worshiping as Mormons.

Pratt and most of the other missionaries left for home in 1852. For the next four decades, the island Saints, without official leadership, drifted into factions. Still, an important development came in 1867 when the government granted religious tolerance to the people in French Polynesia.

The Polynesian Saints created two gathering places or "Zions." The older was at Mahu, Tubuai. The second Zion, or *Tiona,* was at Faaa, three and one-half miles west of Papeete. There the island Saints built homes, a school, and a meetinghouse. It was into this little community that two missionaries of the Reorganized Church came in December 1873. They were headed for Australia, but during their short visit in Papeete they convinced at least part of the community that they represented the true inheritors of Joseph Smith's authority and church. Before they left they baptized fifty-one people into the RLDS Church. Other RLDS missionaries followed during the next few years and won over half of the remaining Saints in French Polynesia to their church.

Latter-day Saint missionary work in French Polynesia was resumed on 27 January 1892, when Elders William A. Seegmiller and Joseph W. Damron Jr. arrived in Papeete from Apia, Samoa; they had been sent by President William O. Lee of the Samoan Mission. After establishing themselves in an inexpensive cottage, the elders began asking for information concerning any remaining Mormons from the early mission. They were told to go to Faaa, Tiona. When they arrived there on 9 February, they learned that everyone in the village was RLDS, but they were told that there were Mormons in the Tuamotu

Islands and on Tubuai. Not knowing French or Tahitian, Seegmiller and Damron were severely hampered in their work.

Realizing that they needed a connection with the past, the elders wrote to the First Presidency in Salt Lake City to ask whether any missionaries from the first mission could be sent. The First Presidency responded by calling James S. Brown, now sixty-five years old and having lost one leg, to return to French Polynesia as mission president. He, along with his son Elando and another elder, Thomas S. Jones, arrived in Papeete on 1 June 1892. The government had considered him *persona non grata* when he left the islands in 1852, and for a time it appeared that he would bring the new mission more trouble than help. But with the assistance of the American consul in Papeete, Elder Brown convinced the French government that he would cause no problems.

In August, Brown received a letter asking him to visit the Saints in Tubuai. It proved to be the opening the elders had been hoping for. Tehahe, who wrote the letter of invitation, said his people "had been left in the dark many years without one ray of light." At the same time, the elders learned of other groups of Mormons who were still active in the Tuamotus. With Elder Seegmiller, Brown traveled to Tubuai, where they soon baptized sixty-five people into the Church.

Elder Brown returned to Papeete on 1 December and almost immediately learned that the remnant of the Saints in the Tuamotus were going to hold a conference on Faaite on 6 January 1893. Elders Damron and Jones had established contact with these people and strongly encouraged Brown and his son to come to that area as soon as possible.

Not long after James S. Brown stepped ashore, he was confronted by an elderly blind man named Maihea. Maihea was the leader of the Polynesian Saints. He claimed to have received his authority from Elders Pratt and Grouard. Maihea asked Brown several questions to confirm that he was the same missionary that had brought them the gospel forty years before. Satisfied with the answers, he said, "We receive you as our father and leader, but had you not come back personally we would have refused to receive any foreign missionaries, as so many false teachers have been in our midst and decoyed many from the Gospel of Jesus Christ." Maihea then told Brown and his young companions how he and his people had prayed constantly for more missionaries, and now, after forty years, their prayers had been answered.

As the conference proceeded, the elders learned that there were ten organized Latter-day Saint branches, with 425 members. Seventeen members were yet alive who had been baptized before 1852.

In July 1893, James S. Brown and his son sailed for home. Three months before they left, a new contingent of eight missionaries arrived from Utah. Elder Damron was appointed president of the now-stable mission. The work surged forward, and by 1895 the Tahitian Mission of the Church had 1,040 members and children. The Church in French Polynesia was ready to move into its second phase of development.

THE ESTABLISHMENT OF THE CHURCH
IN HAWAII, 1850 TO 1865

When the first ten Latter-day Saint missionaries arrived in Honolulu from the gold fields of northern California on 12 December 1850, they found a mission field that was both similar to and different from Tahiti and its surrounding islands. The Hawaiian people were closely related to other Polynesians, and both island groups had captured the romantic imaginations of sailors around the world. The Tahitians had tried to resist the

French encroachment but had ultimately failed and hence lost the ability to determine their own destiny. The Hawaiians, on the other hand, were able to resist foreign domination until the 1890s and thus enjoyed a vastly different history. In Hawaii the government guaranteed religious toleration during the 1840s and continued this position after the United States government took over near the turn of the century. Obviously, Latter-day Saint missionary work was directly influenced by these contrasting religious policies. The closer proximity of Hawaii to the U.S. mainland also encouraged stronger ties between those islands and the Church than between French Polynesia and the Church.

Compared with the three elders who had arrived in Tubuai and Tahiti six years earlier, the ten missionaries arriving in Hawaii in 1850 enjoyed much greater mutual support. On the morning of 13 December 1850, Hiram Clark, fifty-five years old, veteran of two missions to Great Britain and president of the new mission in Hawaii, led his nine companions up Nuuanu valley and onto a hill (now called Pacific Heights) where they built an altar of stone and offered a prayer of dedication on the islands and on their work. Within a few days the elders were paired off and sent to the outer islands. President Clark and two missionaries stayed in Honolulu, which became the headquarters of the mission.

The elders had little success in the Honolulu area and on the island of Kauai, but the missionaries in Maui, among them George Q. Cannon, had quite a different experience. Within two days of their arrival there they had preached to the few *haole* (Caucasian) people but concluded that their mission would be a failure if they did not turn to the Hawaiian people; hence, they immediately began studying the Hawaiian language. Within three weeks Elder Cannon could understand what he heard, but it took him another two or three weeks before he could speak very well.[7]

At the end of three weeks in the fishing village of Lahaina, the trio were almost destitute of funds and had to leave their rented quarters. It was at that point that Nalimanui, a kind Hawaiian lady, offered a room to them. While staying there Elder Cannon had some powerful spiritual experiences. He received direct instructions from the Lord relevant to the future of the Hawaiian people and the Church. In later years, Elder Cannon, who had become a member of the First Presidency, recalled that he heard the Lord's voice "more than once as one man speaks with another, encouraging me and showing me the work which should be done among this people if I would follow the dictates of His Spirit." It was through such experiences that Elder Cannon concluded that the Hawaiians were of the seed of Abraham. He said he knew it because "the Lord told him so at Lahaina."[8] The firm connection between the Hawaiian Islanders and the Lamanites of the Book of Mormon has been subsequently established by statements of Latter-day Saint authorities. In his dedicatory prayer for the New Zealand Temple, President David O. McKay referred to the Polynesians as "descendants of Father Lehi."[9] By 1852 the missionaries were regularly referring to their Hawaiian converts and proselytes as descendants of Israel, God's chosen people.

When President Clark asked Elder Cannon to return to Honolulu, Cannon was shocked to learn that several members of the group were planning to leave for the mainland. In fact, by the end of April, five of the missionaries, including President Clark, left the mission field. George Q. Cannon and four other elders, however, chose to remain in Hawaii and establish the gospel among those people.

On 4 March 1851, Elder Cannon, who was back in Maui, set out for Wailuku and arrived there three days later. He soon met Judge Jonatana H. Napela, an influential man in Wailuku.

Elder George Q. Cannon was one of the first ten missionaries to arrive in hawaii in 1850. Cannon could understand and speak the language after six weeks in the islands and later translated the Book of Mormon into Hawaiian. (Photo courtesy Cannon family)

Napela, who joined the Church a short time later, listened intently to Cannon's message and introduced a number of his friends to him. The people of Wailuku showed such interest in Mormonism that the local minister became quite upset. Because he did not want to cause problems, Cannon took Napela's advice and moved on to the Kula district at the foot of Mt. Haleakala. Here he organized the first branch in Hawaii on 6 August 1851. More than two hundred members were baptized on the north side of the island, and soon four more branches were organized among them.

On 10 August 1851, another small group of missionaries arrived in Maui. One of the group, Phillip B. Lewis, explained that he had been appointed president of the mission by Parley P. Pratt, who was in charge of the Pacific area. His arrival freed Elder Cannon and his companions to attend to other problems in Maui. For example, the local minister of religion and the *konohiki,* lord of the land or local government official, had stopped all Latter-day Saint religious services and threatened to take away the land of all practicing Mormons. Because

he could not get to the bottom of the problem with any officials on Maui, in October Cannon went to Honolulu. There
he took up the Church's position with the Reverend Mr.
Richard Armstrong, minister of public instruction. Armstrong
assured Cannon and his colleagues that no government official
had the authority to interfere with anyone's right to worship as
he pleased. Elder Cannon also met with Hawaiian Princes Lot
and Alexander and received their assurance that the Mormons
would not be molested. These positive pledges notwithstanding, and even though Cannon solved the immediate problem,
over the next several decades the Church was never accorded
full equality with other faiths. The polygamy issue was at the
center of most of the Latter-day Saint problems.

Despite these difficulties, the Church made remarkable
headway during the first four years in Hawaii.

In 1853, Jonatana Napela organized the first missionary
language-training school in the Pacific when he invited a new
group of missionaries to come live in his home. He began by
having the elders read aloud from the Hawaiian Bible. "I have
bin a hard working man all the days of my life," one of the elders wrote in his diary, "but this is the hardest work I ever dun
to set and study all day. Our teacher is very atentive. Sum of
the Brethring have got so thay can read quite well but cant tell
the mening of what thay read."[10]

By the end of 1854 there were more than four thousand
members in fifty-three branches. Many Hawaiian men had
been ordained to the Melchizedek Priesthood and either given
local leadership responsibilities or called on short-term missions to their own people. By August 1853 there were small
LDS schools under way, and by the end of 1854 there were
schools on Oahu, Kauai, Maui, Molokai, and Lanai. The local

Joseph F. Smith was just fifteen when he sailed for the Sandwich Islands in 1854 to serve a missin. (© by Intellectual Reserve, Inc.)

Saints built chapels—either grass structures or frame buildings with thatched roofs—wherever branches were organized.

One of the new missionaries arriving in 1854 was fifteen-year-old Joseph F. Smith. He was determined to learn the language: "I felt resolved to stay there, master the language and warn the people of those islands, if I had to do it alone; for I felt that I could not do otherwise and be free from condemnation; the spirit of it was upon me." Unlike other elders who thought their mission was only to the whites, young Joseph F. exercised "faith before the Lord to obtain the gift of talking and understanding the language." After being in the islands only one hundred days, he was able to conduct meetings, perform ordinances, and speak "with greater ease then he could when he spoke English." At age sixteen, he was called to preside over the Saints on Maui. Later, on the island Molokai, Joseph became desperately ill with a raging fever that lasted for nearly three months. He was nursed back to health by a woman named Ma Mahuhii, who became like a mother to him. This young boy, son of the martyred Hyrum and nephew of the Prophet Joseph, would later fill the shoes of those who came before him; he was set apart as president of the Church on 17 October 1901 at age sixty-two.[11]

In January 1852, Elder Cannon had begun work on a translation of the Book of Mormon into Hawaiian. Because much care was needed in workings and interpretation, the project took two years to complete. Because Cannon was a printer by trade, he suggested that the Church in Hawaii buy a press and publish the book less expensively then paying someone else to do the job. Unfortunately, Elder Cannon was released before the press arrived from New York and no one else in the Church knew how to operate it. Brigham Young had the elders in Hawaii send the press to San Francisco, where President Young sent Elder Cannon to print his translation. Cannon did his part, but the Hawaiian Book of Mormon was not in print until 1857, and when it arrived in Hawaii the copies were still unbound. The timing was unfortunate because President Young had just called missionaries home because of the threat of war in Utah. Most of the copies of the Book of Mormon were left boxed up and did few people any good.

An interesting but ultimately unsuccessful undertaking was the creation of the Lanai colony.[12] Even before October conference in 1853, President Brigham Young asked the mission leaders in Hawaii to consider establishing a local gathering place. A committee visited a number of sites on different islands during the next eight or ten months and then suggested the Palawai Basin on Lanai as the best place for a settlement. On 28 August 1854, the first group of missionaries and Hawaiian "pioneers" arrived on the island. During the next decade the Church developed a settlement that was not unlike the communities of Utah. The streets were laid out running north, south, east, and west. Crops were planted, cisterns were dug and lined, homes were constructed, and a chapel and meetinghouse was built. At its height, this "City of Joseph" had a population of around three hundred people. They were generally the most active and faithful members of the Church in the islands. The strongest members left many of the branches on other islands to live in the Church settlement. This left weaker people to lead those branches.

The Lanai colony was founded at the very time when interest in the Church was beginning to wane. Between the end of 1854 and late 1857, Church membership dropped from more than 4,000 to 3,122. This general decline was complicated by the increased emphasis on gathering to the Lanai colony, which took strength away from Church branches in other locations. The novelty of the Mormon message also lost appeal during these years.

Unfortunately, like the Saints on other islands, the Saints on Lanai also became discouraged, largely because of crop failures, communal debts, and lack of an adequate water supply. In October 1847, the mission leaders decided to look for a better gathering place, but a month later Brigham Young sent word for the elders to come home and nothing was done about the decision.

Missionaries and members were saddened when they received word from President Young that he thought "it best for all of the Elders (with one or two exceptions) to come home . . . as soon as possible." His request was prompted by the discouraged sounding letters he had been receiving from Hawaii for some time and because (as mentioned before) there was a serious threat of war in Utah. As a result, by 1 May 1858 the Hawaiian Saints were alone.

Three years passed before another authorized missionary from Salt Lake City arrived in Hawaii. Unfortunately the new elder was Walter Murray Gibson.[13] After a life of adventure and world travel, Gibson had joined the Church in Salt Lake City in January 1860. He filled a brief mission for the Church in the eastern states and then convinced President Young that he, Gibson, should fill a mission to Japan and Malaysia. While on his way to Asia, Gibson stopped off in Hawaii and took control of the Church there. Through letters he convinced President Young that what he was doing was in the best interests of the Church and within the limits of appropriate Church procedure.

From September 1861 until April 1864, Walter Murray Gibson ran the Church more like his personal political kingdom than the kingdom of God. He sold offices in the Church, called a first presidency, apostles, and an archbishop, sold Church and private members' lands, managed the people on Lanai more like subjects than fellow Church members, and caused a state of general apostasy. He is most bitterly remembered for his personal acquisition of a large part of Lanai through the use of Church funds.

Early in 1864, some Hawaiian Saints who had become disaffected from Gibson wrote to Church headquarters and explained what was going on. Brigham Young dispatched two Apostles, Ezra T. Benson and Lorenzo Snow, along with three former missionaries—Joseph F. Smith, Alma L. Smith, and W. W. Cluff—to Hawaii to investigate. On personally observing the situation in Lanai and elsewhere, the delegation excommunicated Gibson from the Church on 8 April 1864. Not much time passed before the Saints on Lanai returned to their former homes on other islands and Gibson was left almost alone on Lanai.

Elders Benson and Snow left twenty-four-year-old Joseph

This nineteenth-century chapel on the island of Maui was among the earliest chapels in Hawaii. (Photo courtesy Donald Q. Cannon)

F. Smith in charge of the mission, with Alma L. Smith and William W. Cluff as counselors. They had much to do to effect a reformation among the Hawaiian members and to bring order back into the Church.

Joseph F. Smith had been present at the meeting in 1857 when the missionaries and Hawaiian leaders had decided to look for another gathering place. He did not have to be convinced that Lanai was not suitable. As he thought about the problems the Hawaiian Saints faced, Elder Smith concluded that it would be well if the Church found a new gathering place. He suggested this to Brigham Young, who agreed but suggested that the new island Zion should be bought by the Church and not by the local Saints. In October 1864, President Young called Francis A. Hammond, who had helped choose Lanai, and George Nebeker, Hammond's brother-in-law, who had never been to Hawaii, as co-presidents of the mission. He charged them with finding a new gathering place.

Hammond and Nebeker arrived in Hawaii on 23 December 1864 and immediately started their search for land. They soon learned that the sugar market was in a slump and land prices were low. After looking at properties on Oahu and Kauai, the elders concluded that a six-thousand-acre ranch and plantation on the north side of Oahu was the most suitable for the Church's needs. It was called Laie. On 26 January 1865, the Church purchased the Laie plantation from Thomas T. Dougherty for $14,000.

President Brigham Young told Presidents Hammond and Nebeker that they were to teach the Hawaiian Saints how to labor and how to live the principles of the gospel. The clearest statement of purpose for the new settlement was made in a letter from Brigham Young to King Kamehameha V. "According to the precepts of our religion," wrote President Young, "the spiritual and temporal are so intimately blended that we view no salvation or system of salvation as being complete, which does not provide means for the welfare and preservation of the body as well as the salvation of the Spirit. . . . Mr. Hammond, and my other friends will teach your Majesty's subjects . . . practical salvation."[14]

Laie became a new kind of gathering place, a village where the Hawaiian Saints could live together and learn concerning both their spiritual and temporal salvation. In the future, Laie would prove a blessing to not only the Hawaiian Saints but to people from throughout the world.

CHAPTER 9

BEGINNINGS IN AUSTRALIA,
NEW ZEALAND, SAMOA, AND TONGA

R. LANIER BRITSCH

1851	Missionaries open work in Australia
1853	First company of LDS emigrants leave Australia for Utah
1854	Missionaries carry gospel from Australia to New Zealand; these countries form Australasian Mission
1858	Missionaries called home upon outbreak of Utah War
1863	Samuela Manoa from Hawaii preaches in Samoa
1867	Gospel again taught in New Zealand
1879–98	Three branches operating in Australia
1880s	Great success among the Maoris in New Zealand
1888	Samoan Mission officially organized
1900	Samoa divided between U.S. and German spheres of influence

THE ESTABLISHMENT OF THE CHURCH
IN AUSTRALIA, 1851 TO 1897

The story of the Church in Australia is quite unlike those of the other areas of the Pacific. Each of the island cultures presented the missionaries with ways of life that were different from those of America or Europe. Australia, on the other hand, was simply another "Western" nation, one that offered exotic animals and strange-sounding place names but little else that

160

was very different from the homelands of the missionaries in the 1850s. In fact, the relative newness of the colonies—Sydney, the first colony, was founded in 1788—made Australia seem like home to many of the early Latter-day Saint missionaries who went there from Utah. Since Australia had been founded by immigrants primarily from Great Britain, English was the common tongue, and Christianity was the accepted religion.

When John Murdock and Charles W. Wandell arrived in Sydney on 30 October 1851, spring was coming to the land "down under." Sydney, now sixty-three years old, was a modern and growing city. It did not take the two elders long to learn that stories of Joseph Smith and polygamy had preceded them; yet, not everyone held the Church in disrespect. As they made their way about the city, the elders found many people who were interested in their teachings.

Believing that the printed word would be helpful in conveying the message of the restored gospel, Elders Murdock and Wandell engaged a printer to produce two hundred copies of Parley P. Pratt's pamphlet *A Proclamation to the People of the Coasts and Islands of the Pacific* only two days after their arrival. It sold well. Before long they published three other tracts and pamphlets and a selection of hymns. By 1855 these elders and those who followed published at least twenty-four thousand tracts and sold several hundred pounds sterling worth of books. Anti-Mormon literature was circulated from the first, and some Latter-day Saint publications were produced to counteract such misinformation.

The elders initially preached in public places but soon rented a hall for meetings and the like. By early December 1851, Emily and Joseph Popplewells and Bridget Gallimore asked for baptism, and by the end of that month nine other converts had been brought into the Church. The elders organized the Sydney Branch on 4 January 1852, and by the end of March there were thirty-six members.

Elders Murdock and Wandell met the challenges of a demanding schedule. They directed three meetings each Sunday and preached at publicly advertised meetings five nights a week.

In June 1852, John Murdock, who had presided over the Australia Mission, sailed for home; Elder Wandell took over as president. He was assisted in the work by five local elders and two priests. Together they opened Maitland (eighty miles northeast of Sydney) and Melbourne, Victoria, to missionary work. By March 1853, there were more than one hundred members of the Church in Australia, and Elder Wandell felt it was time for him to return home. Not knowing that ten additional missionaries were on their way from Utah and that they would arrive seven days after his departure, Wandell set apart John Jones as president of the mission and sailed for home. The new elders arrived on 30 March 1853. One of them, Augustus Farnham, had been appointed by Brigham Young to direct the work in the mission.

The new missionaries opened the work in still more cities and districts: Hunter's River district; Moreton Bay (Brisbane) in Queensland; and Adelaide, South Australia. Mormon elders eventually traveled through a large part of southeastern Australia and had considerable success in numbers of baptisms. But two forces worked against the establishment of the Church in Australia: polygamy and emigration. Once the doctrine of plural marriage was established as a tenet of the faith, the missionaries had trouble with anti-Mormon agitation. The polygamy issue remained a problem into the twentieth century.

Emigration was a different kind of problem. From 1852 on, Elders Murdock and Wandell and those who followed them taught their new converts that it was an obligation—a principle of the gospel—to gather to Zion in Utah. Elder Wandell led the first group, thirty Saints, when he departed for America. Between 1853 and 1859, missionaries took at least ten more emigrant companies from Australia to Zion. More than five hundred Saints gathered to Utah during those years, plus another two or three hundred between 1859 and 1900.

Emigration weakened the Church in Australia. Whole branches sometimes migrated together, not leaving a trace of the Church behind. It could be argued, in fact, that the policy of gathering was the main reason for the Church's slow growth in Australia. But there is strong evidence that the members who remained in Australia frequently saw their children marry outside the Church, sometimes to people who were hostile to its purposes. Also, the Australian Saints did much to help build up the Church in Utah. In any event, the Church did not prosper in Australia during the nineteenth century.

In April 1858, the missionaries were told to come home because of the impending Utah War. Local members directed the work as long as there were enough Saints in the country to carry on, but by 1863 there were only two hundred members there, and they were scattered over a vast area. From then until 1898, Australia received only scant attention from Church leaders in Salt Lake City. Missionaries did not serve in the country continuously, and, in fact, until the last two decades of the twentieth century little progress was made. Three or four branches operated between 1879 and 1898.

In summary, it can be said that during the period from 1851 to 1858 the Church supplied a steady number of missionaries to Australia, and those elders baptized between seven hundred and eight hundred people. But after the pullout resulting from the Utah War, matters elsewhere occupied the leaders of the Church, and Australia was given a lower priority until 1898. Only after that time did any significant and lasting growth take place in the land down under.

THE ESTABLISHMENT OF THE CHURCH IN NEW ZEALAND, 1854 TO 1885

The history of the founding of the Church in New Zealand is a story in two parts: first, taking the restored gospel to the *pakeha*—the white people—of New Zealand; and second, taking the message to the Maoris, the native Polynesian people of the area.

In 1854, Augustus Farnham, president of the Australia Mission, reported to President Brigham Young that the Maoris of New Zealand were dissatisfied with Christianity as it had been preached to them. Farnham suggested that the time might be right to introduce the restored gospel to the Maori people. Evidently, Farnham was encouraged to open the work in New Zealand; in the October conference in Australia he proposed that missionaries go to New Zealand to investigate the possibility of establishing the Church there. The motion carried, and on 27 October, Farnham, along with Elder William Cooke (an Australian convert) and Thomas Holden (a priest who was originally from New Zealand) arrived in Auckland. They found the city bustling with activity. New immigrants were everywhere. Failing to establish themselves in Auckland, the elders traveled to

Members of the Australasian Mission between 1885 and 1887. (LDS Church Archives)

Wellington, at the south end of New Zealand's North Island. There, in a little town called Karori, the elders had their first success: Thomas Holden's mother and sister became the first converts to the Church in New Zealand. Elder Cooke eventually helped the new members in Karori establish a branch there. Soon thereafter, Brigham Young heard news of the elders' early success and made the decision to include New Zealand and Australia in a mission unit called the Australasian Mission. The two nations would remain one mission until 1 January 1898.

Elder Cooke taught the restored gospel in New Zealand until 1856, at which time he returned to Australia; he baptized ten converts in that time. Church historical records then become silent regarding New Zealand. In 1867, the silence is broken, and we have record of three local converts teaching the gospel in and around Christchurch, on New Zealand's South Island. Records from the same year show that a schoolteacher named Henry Allington heard about the Church through pamphlets in Karori. He was so enthusiastic that he converted twelve other people by 1870. In April 1870, Elder Robert Beauchamp, who was the only set-apart missionary in Australia or New Zealand, came to New Zealand. In his visits to Karori and Kaiapoi, a village in Christchurch, Elder Beauchamp baptized thirty-two people, organized two branches, and formed the New Zealand Conference. All but one of the members in Karori immigrated to Utah in 1871 and 1872.

Between 1875 and 1880 several Utah missionaries were assigned to New Zealand. They had some degree of success in their work, and by the end of 1880 there were seven branches (three with Sunday Schools and two with Relief Societies), with 133 baptized members and 65 children. Because of this success in New Zealand, headquarters of the Australasian Mission were moved from Sydney, Australia, to Auckland, New Zealand.

The big story in New Zealand, however, was the Church's tremendous success with the Maoris during the 1880s. Despite Elder Farnham's interest in the Maori people in the 1850s, little was done among them until the 1880s. This was due to the social, political, and religious climate of the times. The Christianizing process had begun among the Maoris before the end of the eighteenth century, and by the 1850s most Maoris were nominally Christian. Unfortunately, at the same time well-meaning European missionaries were preaching Christianity to the Maoris, other *pakehas* were engaged in taking the Maoris' lands. Additionally, the Maori population was in decline until the late nineteenth century due to an influx of diseases introduced by colonizing Europeans to which the Maoris had little or no resistance. Between 1860 and 1872, a war ensued between the Maoris and the *pakeha.* Relatively few lives were lost, but the Maoris came out of the experience defeated, depleted, and badly in need of spiritual regeneration. By the 1880s, Maori anger toward white Christian missionaries had been calmed enough for them to listen to a new message.

In October 1880, Joseph F. Smith, who had had great missionary success among the Hawaiians, became a counselor in the First Presidency. He instructed William M. Bromley, who had been called to preside over the New Zealand Mission, that the time had come to start a concerted effort to teach the Maori people the gospel. In March 1881, two months after he arrived in New Zealand, President Bromley began working among the Maoris in accordance with President Smith's counsel. Bromley and some of his companions first met with several Maori chiefs and groups, but had only marginal success. The elders had some tracts and other literature prepared in the Maori language. The first Maori convert was baptized in October 1881. But more than a year passed before anything noteworthy happened among the Maori people.

In December 1882, President Bromley traveled to Cambridge to visit with Thomas L. Cox, a *pakeha* elder in the Church, and his wife. The Coxes were well acquainted with the Maori people of their area and were eager to share the gospel message with them. On the twenty-fourth of that month, William McDonnel, another local elder from Auckland, arrived and told the others that he had a number of dreams that had convinced him the Maori people were

This meetinghouse was home to many of New Zealand's early Maori converts. The chapel, in Karongata, was completed in 1904. (LDS Church Archives)

ready to accept the gospel. That day the three elders visited a Maori village in the area and were returning home in the evening when Elder McDonnel noticed a man standing near a Maori house on the brow of a hill. Elder McDonnel climbed to where the man stood, gave him a Maori tract, and turned to walk away. The man, Chief Hare Teimana, grabbed Elder McDonnel by the collar and asked him to stay and give his message. The three elders taught Hare Teimana and his household and even gave Teimana's daughter a blessing.

The next day Teimana told the elders of a dream, or night vision, he had experienced a month earlier. The message of his dream was that emissaries from God were coming and that these men were working under the direction of the ancient Apostle Peter. Because of the elders' message and because

Teimana's daughter had shown signs of recovery as a result of the priesthood blessing, a number of Maoris were converted to the Church. Three people were baptized on Christmas night. After this beginning, other Maoris came into the Church in that area. By the following March there were sixty-one members in the new Waotu Branch.

During the same month, President Bromley sent Elder Alma Greenwood to preside over the Wellington area of New Zealand. Here, he and his companions, particularly Ira N. Hinckley, had remarkable success among the Maori tribes of the Wairarapa district, where they labored for over a year. They raised up two branches, both of which were presided over by Maori elders.

Leaving more than one hundred Saints behind, Elders Greenwood and Hinckley next traveled northeast to the Hawkes Bay district. There they had immediate success. During May and June of 1884, they taught the Maoris of every settlement in that area, made many converts, and organized two branches.

Elders Greenwood and Hinckley were soon joined by Mission President Thomas Stewart, who personally contributed much to the success of preaching the gospel to the Maoris. During President Thomas' service in Northern New Zealand, nearly 540 people joined the Church. Those Maoris who joined were prosperous, cultivated people who would later become fine leaders for the Church. By the end of 1884, there were 1,076 members in New Zealand; 265 were *pakeha* and 811 were Maoris.

By the end of 1885 there were sixteen Maori and four *pakeha* branches in New Zealand. By the turn of the century there were over seventy-nine branches and four thousand members. Most of these people were Maori. In fact, in New Zealand the Church was considered a Maori church.

There are a number of reasons why the Maoris accepted the restored gospel so readily. The Maoris were prepared for the coming of Mormonism by at least five Maori *tohunga,* or priests. Since pre-Christian times the Maoris had looked to spiritual leaders, who were seers to their people. The *tohungas* acted as mediums for the *atua*—or gods. As oracles, the *tohungas* cured diseases and admonished their people. In some instances, family patriarchs, village elders, and chiefs acted as prophets and were highly regarded by their people for their spiritual powers. Such men made prophecies about the coming of the LDS Church to New Zealand.

The prophecy of Arama Toiroa will serve as an example. In 1830 he gathered his large family and told them that the church they had recently joined, the Church of England, was not the true church.

"There will come to you a true form of worship," said Arama. "It will be brought from the east, even beyond the heavens. It will be brought across the great ocean, and you will hear of it coming to Poneke Wellington, and afterwards its representatives will come to Te Mahia. They will then go northward to Waiapu but will return to Te Mahia. When this 'Karakia,' form of worship is introduced amongst you, you will know it, for one shall stand and raise both hands to heaven. When you see this sign, enter into that church. Many of you will join the Church, and afterwards one will go from amongst you the same way that the ministers came even unto the land from afar off."[1]

Elders Greenwood and Hinckley traversed the same route Arama predicted in his vision. However, it was at Korongata, not at Mahia, that Arama's descendants first accepted the restored gospel. Hirini Whaanga, one of Arama's descendants, who later traveled to Salt Lake City in fulfillment of part of the prophecy, described the meeting of his people with the Mormon elders:

> In journeying northward they [Greenwood, Hinckley, and Stewart] reached . . . Korongata, where many of us were assembled on the Sabbath day.
>
> Amongst the people who were there was a grandson of Arama Toiroa whose name was Te Teira Marutu.
>
> The meeting was conducted by Elder Stewart and his friends. The services were opened with singing and prayer, and a Gospel address was delivered, after which they sang again, and Brother Stewart arose to dismiss with prayer. In doing so he raised both hands and invoked God's blessing upon the people.
>
> As soon as the grandson of Arama Toiroa saw this he arose and declared that this was the Church of which his forefather prophesied which would surely be firmly established amongst the Maori people.
>
> He and his wife applied for baptism, and they and their children were thus initiated into the Church by Elder Stewart.[2]

Because of this prophecy, every person in Korongata joined the Church, and many Maoris in Mahia also entered the waters of baptism.[3]

There were a number of other reasons why the Maoris were attracted to the gospel. Their belief in prophesy among their own people made them appreciate that the Latter-day Saints too believed the heavens were still open and revelation was an important part of the gospel. The Maoris took note of the way Mormon missionaries lived among them, learned their language, slept in their homes, ate their food, and in almost every way learned to accept the Maori way of life. The elders of the Mormon Church, unlike other Christian churches the Maoris had associated with, did not reject all parts of Maori culture. In fact, there was a feeling in the Church that the Maoris were being brought back into a fold from which they had not strayed too far. The Maoris shared the intense interest the Latter-day Saints had in family life. They were also touched by the doctrine of temple work for the dead. Other churches had told the Maoris that their dead, though highly revered, were bound to everlasting burning. The Maoris also believed that priesthood administrations and blessings were signs of the true church. Even the highest ideas the Maoris held about their native god *Io* were somewhat similar to the Mormon concept of Jehovah. Finally, the Mormon elders showed little or no racial prejudice toward the Maoris. The missionaries gave both the Aaronic and the Melchizedek Priesthood to the Maoris almost as soon as they entered the Church.

Even before the Latter-day Saints went among them, the Maoris had identified with the people of Judah. They especially saw a similarity between the persecutions of Judah and themselves. When the Mormon elders came, they told the Maoris that they were descendants of Israel through the Book of Mormon prophet Lehi. This concept, too, appealed to many Maoris and helped bring about the growth of the Church.

The connection between the Maoris and the LDS Church has remained secure ever since the 1880s. Nevertheless, many significant changes and developments have taken place since that time. Several of these, most notably schools, translation work, and the New Zealand Temple, will be discussed in the next chapter.

THE ESTABLISHMENT OF THE CHURCH IN SAMOA, 1863 TO 1899

The Samoan Mission of the Church was officially founded on 21 June 1888. But it might not have been established then if Samuela Manoa, a Hawaiian elder, had not encouraged Joseph Harry Dean to come to Samoa from Hawaii. Manoa's reason for being in Samoa dated back to the era of Walter Murray Gibson, who had used his authority over the Church in Hawaii for his own personal gain and financial success—and who was subsequently excommunicated. While Gibson was in charge of the Church in Hawaii he sent two missionaries, Kimo Belio and Samuela Manoa, to Samoa. They arrived there on 24 January 1863. Because Gibson was not authorized by Church leaders in Salt Lake City to make this move, the mission that Belio and Manoa established was neither sanctioned nor official. Nevertheless, both men had been given the priesthood by legitimate authority and magnified their callings for a time.

The two elders baptized around fifty people during the early years of their mission. Elder Manoa fell out of the Church for a time because of personal transgression. But by the late 1880s, however, he was living with his wife and family on the tiny island of Aunuu, off the coast of Tutuila, and had returned to Church activity. He had done little missionary work since his re-entry into the Church, but he had written to the Church in Hawaii a number of times asking for help. That help finally came in the form of Elder Joseph Harry

Dean, who was accompanied by his wife Florence and their infant son.

Thirty-one-year-old Dean was a man of many talents, and of experience beyond most men of his years.

When he was a called as a missionary to Hawaii in 1887, he was told to go not only to Hawaii, but also to Samoa and any other island that the Lord might dictate through the authorities. When Elder Dean arrived in Hawaii, he immediately began gathering information about Samoa. By October 1887 he had learned about Brother Manoa's presence in Samoa and had made plans to go there.

It was not until June 1888 that the Deans were finally ready to sail for Samoa. Florence's pregnancy and the birth of a ten-pound baby boy in February had delayed travel plans a bit. They set sail in June but were delayed again, when after only eight days at sea, the steamer *Alemeda* shut down its engines and drifted to a stop two miles west of Tutuila. The Deans— including their infant boy and young toddler—were lowered over the side of the great ship into a longboat. Strong Samoan oarsmen sped the boat through the rough sea to the island of Tutuila. After three nights there the ocean was calm enough to proceed on to Aunuu.

Brother Manoa was deeply grateful to have the Deans come to Samoa, for he had been away from the Saints in Hawaii for over twenty-five years. He had done his best to prepare a comfortable western-style home for the new missionaries. Nevertheless, they had "no stove, no cows, no bread, nor anything to make it of. No running water, rainwater being all they use. It seems that we will have to live on straight native fare."[4]

During the Deans' first four months there, Elder Dean

baptized thirty-five or forty people, formed a branch with a Sunday School and a Relief Society, made good progress on the Samoan language, helped five other missionaries get settled on Aunuu, and supervised the construction of a meetinghouse. Unlike some other LDS mission areas in the Pacific, where the Church had difficulties finding a foothold, in Samoa the success of the mission was never in doubt.

Dean, who was soon recognized as presiding over the work in Samoa, had not been on Aunuu long before he realized that it was too small and out of the way to make a good place for mission headquarters. With the arrival of new missionaries in August and October, he felt that he could move to Tutuila without disrupting the work on Aunuu. In January 1889, the Deans moved to Vatia, Tutuila. This new headquarters also proved to be out of the mainstream, and by the next August President Dean extended the mission to the island of Upolu, where he built a mission home at Fagalii, a short distance from Apia, Samoa's consensus capital. Fagalii remained the center of the Church in Samoa for over a decade.

When the Deans arrived in Samoa, they did not know much about the people or their background. They knew that the Samoans were Polynesian and that their language was closely related to Hawaiian, but the Deans and the later missionaries did not understand the social system, nor did they understand the current political and religious situations. The LDS missionaries were pleased to learn that the Samoan people had been Christianized since the 1830s. In fact, Dean and his companions had never seen a people who knew the Bible better or a people who worked more diligently at living Christian lives. Every evening the Samoan fathers gathered their families together for prayer and scripture reading. The

Missionary families, including Sister Dean and her infant son, pose in front of the mission home in Fagalii, Upolu, Samoa, in 1887. (LDS Church Archives)

family was the center of life. Every family was led by a chief, or a *matai,* of some rank. The word *family* referred to extended families, or *aiga,* rather than the western-style nuclear family with only father, mother, and children. Samoan families, the missionaries learned, held all things in common—home (*fale*), land, tools, and even personal property. Almost all decisions were made by the *matai* in council, the *fono.*

The Samoans greatly valued the ability to speak well. They also devoted much time and attention to ceremony and had developed a highly developed system of protocol. The elders soon learned that if they failed to participate in the *kava* ceremony when they entered a village, they were committing a serious social and political offense. Kava is a mild narcotic drink offered to visitors as a way of extending welcome. Etiquette did not require the missionaries to actually drink the kava, but they were expected to at least touch the cup and pass it back. The missionaries were given permission to participate in this way and thus not violate custom.

It did not take the elders long to learn that they had arrived in Samoa during a time of tribal war. Factional disputes had divided the local people, and international competition for influence had involved Germany, Great Britain, and the United States. There was not a stable national government. The three foreign powers brought whatever order existed under the circumstances. Even though the missionaries had some of their property, particularly livestock, destroyed in local battles, they were never in danger themselves.

In June 1889, four new missionaries joined the force. A year had passed since President Dean had opened the work, and by this time the missionaries had experienced almost every problem Samoa could offer them. They had endured war, a hurricane, and a famine in its wake. Rumors had been circulated against them, and Protestant ministers had used newspapers and their pulpits to republish all the old lies about Joseph Smith and the Latter-day Saints. Living conditions resembled a perpetual camping trip. Nevertheless, most of the Samoan people themselves were kind, patient, and willing to accept the missionaries even when they did not believe the message the elders carried. The work of the mission was well established, and only time and additional missionaries were needed before the Church was extended to all parts of the islands.

Upolu was opened to LDS missionary work in the fall of 1889, and the large island of Savai'i was opened in June 1890.

When President Dean turned the mission over to William O. Lee and his wife in August 1890, there were twelve elders and Sister Lee serving in Samoa. Including the children, there were 124 members of the Church.

Between then and 1899, the growth of the Church was generally slow but steady. The year 1894 brought the largest growth: 268 baptisms and 84 children blessed. At the end of 1899 there were 1,139 members of the Church in Samoa. By that time at least seven villages had come into the Church in mass movements. Local leaders were in charge of the branches. Samoan priesthood holders and their wives were serving missions. Schools were operating in a number of villages, and three "central" residential schools had been created on the islands of Tutuila, Upolu, and Savai'i. Wherever branches had been organized, the members had built small chapels.

By the turn of the century the Church was well organized in Samoa, but translation work was noticeably lacking. The standard works were not available in Samoan.

The year 1900 brought major political changes. Because the Samoans were unable to resolve their factional problems, the three foreign powers—Germany, Britain, and the United States— took matters into their own hands and divided the islands among themselves. Germany took over Upolu and Savai'i and the islands nearby. The United States took Tutuila—primarily because it had a good harbor and served well as a coaling station—and its contiguous islands. Tutuila came to be called American Samoa. The Germans controlled Western Samoa until the outbreak of World War I, when New Zealand took possession. In this dividing of the islands, Great Britain took concessions in other parts of the

Pacific. The division of Samoa brought significant changes to the LDS mission. Some of these changes, notably the creation of two gathering places, will be discussed in the following chapter.

ESTABLISHMENT OF THE CHURCH IN TONGA, 1907 TO 1916

From 1891 until 1897 the Samoan Mission operated a conference (district) in Tonga. But because the missionaries made almost no converts there, they were removed for a decade. On 19 March 1907, however, President Thomas S. Court of the Samoan Mission sailed to the Vava'u Group in northern Tonga to investigate the possibility of sending missionaries there again. He returned to Apia on April 11 with the report that the prospects in Tonga seemed excellent and soon sent two missionaries to labor there. By the end of July the elders had established a school that was growing very well.

Between 1907 and 1916, the Church grew considerably in Tonga, creating administrative difficulties. The Tongan area demanded a great deal of each mission president's time, and yet it did not receive as much attention as it should have. It became necessary, therefore, to divide the two areas. In February 1916, President Edward J. Wood of the Alberta Stake, who had served as a missionary in Samoa twenty years earlier; President Joseph H. Dean, the first missionary to Samoa; and Ernest C. Wright, newly appointed mission president in Samoa, arrived in Samoa from America. The First Presidency had given President Wood the assignment to choose a mission president for Tonga from among the elders presently serving in the Samoan mission. He selected Willard L. Smith and his wife, Jenny, to lead the new mission in Tonga. They had already served for a year on Tutuila. The Smiths were set apart on April 3 and sailed for Tonga soon afterward. The new mission was created in this way.

CHAPTER 10

GROWTH AND CHALLENGES IN THE PACIFIC THROUGH WORLD WAR II

R. LANIER BRITSCH

INTRODUCTION

The preceding two chapters surveyed the planting of the restored Church in all of the areas of the Pacific where it was successfully established before or shortly after the turn of the twentieth century. Until after World War II, however, no other

LDS missions were founded in the Pacific. Nevertheless, the Church's postwar ability to move into new areas came after years of struggle and development in the old established mission fields.

The first half of the twentieth century was not an easy time for missionary work. This period was one of destructive wars and a debilitating, worldwide economic depression. Furthermore, relations with some island governments created addition challenges for the Saints. Nevertheless, the Church took significant steps to strengthen its members in the Pacific. These developments will be considered in this chapter.

ISLAND ZIONS OR GATHERING PLACES

When the Prophet Joseph Smith commenced the gathering of the Saints to Kirtland, Ohio, and Nauvoo, Illinois, he created an attitude that influenced the Saints until well into the twentieth century. Until President Lorenzo Snow told the Saints in Europe and other parts of the world to remain in their homelands and build up Zion there, members of the Church gathered to Zion, that is, to Utah and the Mountain West. However, Brigham Young encouraged Polynesian members of the Church to remain in their own lands. Most of them stayed, but by no means all. From the 1870s to 1915, when President Joseph F. Smith announced that a temple would be constructed in Laie, Hawaii, a trickle of Hawaiian members left their homeland and migrated to Utah. Because these people had special financial and social needs, President Smith and other returned missionaries from Hawaii created a gathering place for the Hawaiian Saints in Skull Valley, west of Salt Lake City, Utah. This ranching enterprise was called Iosepa, which means Joseph in Hawaiian, after Joseph F. Smith. But beyond the two hundred or so Polynesians who lived there, there were few other island people who migrated to Utah.

In the islands, however, the missionaries desired to set the new Saints apart from the world. The abortive establishment of a colony on the island of Lanai in Hawaii was one such attempt. The existence of two *Tionas,* or Zions, in Tahiti and Tubuai in French Polynesia were another. But there were three other important gathering places in the Pacific—Laie in Hawaii, and Sauniatu and Mapusaga in Samoa.

The history of the Laie plantation is so important that it is almost coequal with the history of the Church in Hawaii. Laie was purchased for the Church by Francis A. Hammond and George Nebeker in January 1865. The plan for Laie called for worthy Hawaiian Latter-day Saints to move to that village to rent land for their homes for a small amount, and to work on the Church-owned sugar plantation. Laie had its troubles, mostly economic, but it was finally placed on a firm financial footing by President Matthew Noall and his successor, Samuel E. Woolley. President Woolley's name came to be synonymous with the Laie plantation. He served as mission president and plantation manager from 1895 to 1919. By the time he left Hawaii, Laie had grown to a village of about one thousand people, irrigated lands had been greatly enlarged beyond those of earlier times, and most important, the Hawaii Temple had been constructed in the heart of the community.

In 1919 the headquarters of the Hawaiian Mission were moved to Honolulu. Nevertheless, Laie remained the spiritual center of the mission. The Church leased its sugarcane lands to other interests in 1931 and thus went out of the sugar business, but Laie continued to grow. The most notable change during the 1920s was the addition of a number of Samoan families who had come to Laie to be near the temple.

Following World War II, the two most notable changes in Laie would be the creation in 1955 of the Church College of Hawaii, now called the Brigham Young University–Hawaii Campus, and the Polynesian Cultural Center in 1963. Laie no longer serves as an important gathering place. Today it is the Church's major missionary attraction in the Pacific.

The two gathering places in Samoa had a vastly different history from that of Laie. Neither place grew like Laie, and neither plantation was successful financially. The Samoan gathering was influenced in large by the German takeover of Upolu and Savai'i in 1900. The imposition of the German language in schools, along with other restrictions, caused some Samoan members, but especially the missionaries, to believe that Governor Wilhelm Solf was persecuting the Church. During 1901, members and missionaries began talking about the advantages of having the Samoan Saints gathered in one place so that they could withstand the abuses and persecutions they were being subjected to and free themselves from ancient traditions.

Between 1901 and 1903, mission authorities encouraged the Saints to prepare for the gathering. They also wrote to the First Presidency and told them of their plans. But the First Presidency was not quick to accept the idea. In fact, they advised the mission leaders to proceed with care and to study thoroughly the implications of such a move.

It could be said that the gathering began on Tutuila Island even before it was authorized by the First Presidency in July 1903. Around the turn of the century most members of the village of Faleniu joined the Church and gave their chapel and minister's home to the mission. This village became a natural gathering place. So the mission leased twenty-two surrounding acres. In 1903, President Martin F. Sanders dedicated this land as a gathering place and renamed it Mapusaga. In July 1903, the First Presidency suggested that two gathering places, one in American Samoa on Tutuila and the other in German Samoa. These colonies were to consist of good, productive, healthful land, and each was to be at least four hundred acres in size.

Unfortunately, some of the land President Sanders acquired at Mapusaga was tied up in legal proceedings, so the gathering did not move forward rapidly on Tutuila. Thus, until his release in November 1904, President Sanders spent most of his time looking at land in German Samoa. At the end of May 1904, he found a good 725-acre site twenty-five miles east of Apia and several miles inland from the sea. Sanders informed the First Presidency about it and about the financial terms that were available. Because the project was of such magnitude, the First Presidency asked President Samuel E. Woolley of the Hawaiian Mission to go to Samoa and evaluate not only the land but also the whole concept of gathering there. After walking over the land, President Woolley concluded that it was good and that the gathering should proceed. This gathering place was named Sauniatu, which means, "prepare for the things of the Lord."

The development of Sauniatu was a difficult matter. The Saints had to clear the land, plant crops, build roads, plant coconut and other trees, build walls, and found a school. Sauniatu did not grow rapidly, but by April 1906, there were twenty-eight fales (houses) and a meetinghouse on the land, and more than 150 people lived there.

The growth of Sauniatu and Mapusaga brought serious problems to the mission. In brief, the same thing happened in Samoa that occurred in Hawaii when the Lanai colony drew off the best leaders and the most faithful members from the branches of the mission. But in Samoa the effects of the gathering were even more negative than in Hawaii. Many Samoan members left the Church because they did not want to leave their ancestral homes and lands. In his report of 31 December 1908, mission secretary John Q. Adams explained: "Unlike the white foreigners, whose home is as a rule decided by his purse, the native domicile descends as a sacred legacy from father to son. Almost invariably, the piece of land occupied by a family at present is the identical spot on which for generations back, have dwelt their ancestors."[1]

The founding of Sauniatu took a great toll among the members, and a number of branches were closed. It was not until 1908 that the Church began to recover the lost ground. Mission leaders worked to heal the wounds and to build new bridges to the disaffected members.

Although Sauniatu and Mapusaga caused problems for the mission, they have both been important to the history of the Church in Samoa. Residential elementary schools were operated at both sites for many years, and Mapusaga also would become the location of an important modern high school in 1950.

The concept of gathering as it has been applied in the Pacific has not been very successful. The Laie plantation and community have been by far the most satisfactory undertaking. The other gathering places have not contributed much to the building of the kingdom; in fact, despite their best efforts, they have caused difficult problems.

A TEMPLE IN HAWAII

Temples are built not only because the Saints of an area are prepared to use them appropriately but also because the Church leaders see the need to bless and strengthen the members of the Church. The first temple dedicated outside the continental United States was built in Hawaii.

As early as 1900, President George Q. Cannon of the First Presidency had seen the need for the Hawaiians to have the blessings of being sealed as families for time and eternity. He told the Hawaiian Saints to prepare for the time when they would be sealed in the house of the Lord. After that time, temple work was discussed frequently in conferences.

President Samuel E. Woolley regularly told the members of the Church to live good moral lives and to search for the names of their kindred dead. In April 1915 he said, "Have we searched out our genealogies? Are we prepared for a temple to be built? . . . Who knows but what the Lord wants us to build a temple in this land? I tell you that there are people here today who if they continue in the work of the Lord, shall enter into the temple or other temples; and the time will come, in my judgement, that a temple will be built here."[2]

Only two months later, while President Joseph F. Smith was visiting Laie, he chose a temple site and dedicated it to the Lord. Elder Reed Smoot, who was with the prophet, later recounted how he had walked with President Smith to the place where the temple now stands:

Nothing was said of what we were going for until we stood at the back of the meetinghouse, and President Smith then said: "Brethren, this is the birthday of President Brigham Young, June 1, 1915. I feel impressed to dedicate this ground for the erection of a Temple to God, for a place

The Hawaii Temple, dedicated in 1919, was the first temple outside North America. (Photo courtesy Donald Q. Cannon)

where the peoples of the Pacific Isles can come and do their temple work. I have not presented this to the Council of the Twelve or to my counselors; but if you think there would be no objection to it, I think now is the time to dedicate the ground." I have heard President Smith pray hundreds of times. . . . But never in all my life did I hear such a prayer. The very ground seemed to be sacred, and he seemed as if he were talking face to face with the Father. I cannot and never will forget it if I live a thousand years.[3]

The next October, President Smith presented the temple proposition to the Church at general conference. He said the temple was needed "so that the people of those islands may reach the blessing of the House of God within their own borders, and that the people from New Zealand, if they do not become strong enough to require a house to be built there also, by and by, can come to Laie, where they can get their blessings and return home and live in peace, having fulfilled all the requirements of the Gospel the same as we have the privilege of doing here."[4]

When the announcement of the forthcoming temple reached the islands of the Pacific, Saints in New Zealand, Samoa, Tonga, and French Polynesia began saving their earnings and looking forward to the time when they could visit the temple in Hawaii.

Architects Hyrum E. Pope and Harold W. Burton had the plans for the temple completed by early 1916, and in February ground was broken for the building. Three years passed before the magnificent concrete and steel structure was ready for dedication. The temple was dedicated on 27 November 1919 by President Heber J. Grant. In his dedicatory prayer, President Grant expressed gratitude to the Lord for George Q. Cannon, Joseph F. Smith, and Jonatana H. Napela. He gave thanks "that thousands and tens of thousands of the descendants of Lehi, in this favored land, have come to a knowledge of the gospel." He prayed that peoples from all the Pacific would be able to come to "this holy house and become saviors unto their ancestors."[5]

Attending one of the five dedicatory sessions was Ma Mahuhii, the faithful Hawaiian woman who had nursed a young Joseph F. Smith back to health over six decades earlier. She received her endowment a week later, needing to be carried and helped through the ceremony. Within a few days, she returned to her home in Honolulu and soon became very sick. She asked mission president E. Wesley Smith, the son of her beloved Joseph F. Smith, to come see her. Clutching his hand, she said in her own tongue, "It is enough, I am satisfied and ready to go now."[6]

President Grant's prayer has been answered thousands of times over the years. Laie has been a place of pilgrimage for Saints from every part of Polynesia as well as for members from Asia. The Hawaii Temple served the needs of all the Pacific Saints until 1958, when President David O. McKay dedicated the Hamilton New Zealand Temple.

ELDER DAVID O. MCKAY'S 1921 VISIT

During the fall of 1920, Elder David O. McKay of the Council of the Twelve received a surprising and significant assignment to tour the missions of the Pacific with the possibility of going on to Africa and Europe, thus "entirely encircling the globe." An announcement on 15 October indicated that he would "obtain general information in order that there may be someone in the deliberations of the First Presidency and Council of the Twelve thoroughly familiar with actual conditions."[7] He was also to "observe the operation of the Church in remote areas while strengthening and motivating the members and leaders alike; to study the administration of the Church school system in the Pacific; and, if he felt inspired to do so, to dedicate the formidable land of China for the preaching of the gospel."[8] At the same time he would make valuable contacts with government officials and enhance the Church's image among the people generally. Hugh J. Cannon, the editor of the *Improvement Era* and a stake president in Salt Lake City, was appointed to be his traveling companion. They were set apart as "missionaries" on 2 December 1920 in the regular weekly meeting of the First Presidency and the Twelve in the Salt Lake Temple.

After visiting Japan and China, Elders McKay and Cannon traveled halfway back across the Pacific to Hawaii, reaching the islands in February 1921. They visited the temple, the plantation, and the elementary school at Laie, where they attended a flag-raising ceremony at the school. As Elder McKay looked at the group of youngsters representing many nationalities, he was deeply moved by the potential of education to unite and bless them.

With these thoughts in his mind, Elder McKay, together with Elder Cannon and mission president E. Wesley Smith, traveled by boat to Maui, arriving there the next morning. On this occasion Elder McKay was informed of the need many Church leaders felt for a Church college in Hawaii, the first time that this idea was considered. It was on this day, after many hours of meetings and discussions among the visitors and the Maui-based missionaries, that Elder McKay made a decision to recommend the founding of a new college to be built at Laie for the young Saints of Hawaii.

This day also brought the spiritual highlight of the Hawaiian visit, one in which only a few people participated. While on the island of Maui, Elder McKay and his party visited Pulehu in the Kula district, where George Q. Cannon (Hugh J. Cannon's father) had baptized his first converts in 1851 and organized the first branch of the Church in Hawaii the same year. This was sacred ground to Elder McKay and the others present—Hugh J. Cannon, President E. Wesley Smith, Elder Samuel H. Hurst, and a Hawaiian elder, David Kailimai. President E. Wesley Smith recounted the event in these words: "While there Elder McKay felt impressed with a desire to offer a prayer to the Lord in the spirit of thanksgiving for the privilege they had of being there, and for the many . . . who had embraced the Gospel. We bowed in prayer, Elder McKay being mouth. It was a moment never to be forgotten, for indeed the spot is sacred. Elder McKay said, 'I felt certain that President Cannon and President [Joseph F.] Smith [E. Wesley Smith's father] are near, for the veil was very thin.' Elder [Hugh J.] Cannon was deeply impressed, and with tears filling his eyes and in a choked voice said, 'There was no veil.'"[9]

While Elder McKay was praying, Elder Kailimai saw in vision two hands clasped in the form of greeting. He thought Cannon and Hurst were shaking hands, but when he opened his eyes he could see that they were not. Those who heard about this supposed that the hands seen in vision were those of George Q. Cannon and his son, Hugh J. When David O. McKay visited Hawaii again in 1936, however, he clarified, "Those hands were the hands of the two fathers, George Q. Cannon and Joseph F. Smith, in the presence of the two sons, Hugh J. Cannon and E. Wesley Smith."[10]

After briefly returning to the U.S. mainland, Elders McKay and Cannon sailed south to Tahiti, arriving at Papeete on 11 April 1921. This was the first visit of a General Authority to these islands. Because Mission President Leonidas Kennard had no advance knowledge of when Elder McKay would arrive, he was away on Tubuai for a conference. Elders McKay and Cannon therefore did not stay but decided to go on to New Zealand on their steamer, the *Marama*. After arriving in New Zealand, Elder McKay was joined by President Kennard, who spent two weeks there to discuss the condition of the Tahitian Mission in detail.

Elder McKay's visit to New Zealand was an answer to long-unfulfilled requests for a General Authority visit. In New Zealand, an annual meeting of the country's Latter-day Saints had come to be known as *hui tau* and was quite the event. The *hui tau* committee delayed this significant meeting until April

23–25, to correspond with Elder McKay's arrival. Every member of the Church who had the means to attend traveled to Huntly, in the Waikato area. When Elders McKay and Cannon arrived there, they found a typical, although large, *hui tau* setup. Two large tents—one for meetings and one for eating—were the main features of the landscape. A playing field, or *marae,* had been prepared for athletic activities. The nearby chapel also served as a meeting hall for smaller sessions of the conference.

When Elder McKay stepped from the automobile, he was greeted with enthusiastic cries and received a traditional Maori *haka,* a warlike greeting. Two hundred or more Saints then formed a line, and even though the Saints had been told to shake hands in the *pakeha* (European) way, Elder McKay insisted on shaking hands and *hongi-ing,* rubbing noses and foreheads, with every person in the line. As later groups arrived, this ritual was repeated a number of times.[11]

The *hui tau* began at 10 in the morning of April 23. Elder McKay spoke at least seven times during the three days of meetings. Many wonderful things happened during the *hui tau* and also during the remainder of Elder McKay's visit in New Zealand, but the most remembered incident was his first talk at the conference. As he began speaking he said: "O, how I wish I could speak to you in your own language to tell you what is in my heart, but since I cannot, I am going to pray that while I speak in my own tongue you may have the gift of interpretation and discernment. While you may not understand my words, the Spirit of the Lord will bear witness to you of my words that I give to you under the inspiration of the Lord." Gordon C. Young, one of the missionaries who was there, later described what happened as Elder McKay continued to talk:

> He spoke several sentences and then Stuart [Meha] would interpret into Maori. Then he'd make another statement in English and Stuart would interpret. All at once everything was quiet, and all over the congregation the Maoris—not the Europeans but the Maoris—called out, "Stuart, sit down, don't interpret; we can understand what the Apostle is saying." They didn't [all] speak English, and they didn't understand anything President McKay was saying before, but now they were calling out to Stuart to sit down. He was rather disconcerted. . . . Stuart didn't know what to do so he started to interpret again. The calls came again, "Stuart, sit down. Don't interpret." So Stuart just sat down, and President McKay went on and gave one of the most beautiful talks I have ever heard in my life, and those people all understood what he was saying.[12]

From New Zealand the travelers headed to Tonga. When they arrived at Nuku'alofa on 8 May 1921, Elder McKay's ship, the *Tofua*, was quarantined. This was strange because there were no epidemics in either New Zealand or Fiji at the time. The best decision seemed to be to sail on to Samoa. The missionaries and Saints made elaborate preparations for Elder McKay's arrival. On 3 May 1921, a telegram came from him, informing the Saints that he would be at Apia harbor in one week. Mission president John Q. Adams sent messengers to all branches on Upolu and Savai'i. When the honored guests disembarked at 9 A.M. on May 11 and were rowed ashore in two Samoan longboats, they were greeted by one of the most excited groups of Saints ever assembled, as well as a great many people who were not in the Church but who knew who Elder McKay was. Members and nonmembers alike crowded around

Elders Hugh J. Cannon (left) and David O. McKay (right) spent many days on board ship as they traveled between islands of the Pacific during their 1921 world tour. © by Intellectual Reserve, Inc.)

the guests, the Sauniatu band played, and a grand parade proceeded past the shops and business houses of Apia. Almost everything came to a standstill as the first Apostle to visit Samoa greeted the people.

When the guests arrived at Pesega they were formally welcomed by an assembly of thirty high chiefs. The Saints and guests held a great feast in the afternoon and presented special entertainments in the evening. For the next four days conference meetings were held during the days, and programs of various kinds at night.

The sojourners were in these islands for twenty-eight days. During that time they sailed to American Samoa, where they held a series of meetings and visited with the Saints of Pago

Pago and Mapusaga. They also visited a number of schools and branches on Upolu.

But the most important event happened at the gathering place, Sauniatu. Elders McKay and Cannon and President Adams spent most of May 31 studying the school and plantation. During the afternoon Elder McKay and his companions administered to and blessed a number of children and others. Then, realizing they had to cover twenty-five miles of difficult terrain on horseback before nightfall if they were to be back at Pesega on schedule, the group of leaders made a hasty retreat toward Apia and Pesega. But the Saints of the village desired to shake hands with the Apostle of the Lord. The Relief Society sisters crowded the room and the porch. As Elder McKay left the mission home, the Sauniatu band began playing "Goodbye, My Feleni," which is equivalent to Hawaii's "Aloha Oe." Everyone wept as they clasped Elder McKay and Elder Cannon. As the visitors walked to their horses, the people gathered again, and the scene was reenacted. President Adams recounted the concluding events in these words: "Once more we set out, on our horses this time, and looking back we saw that they were following us slowly, the band playing their touching air. Framed and over-arched in the vista of a tunnel-like tropical lane of greenery, and rhythmically advancing to the softened tone of the faraway instruments—was ever such a picture presented to mortal eyes? And we all knew that in both parties not a dry eye could be found."[13]

At this, feeling the devotion of the Sauniatu Saints, Elder McKay said, "Let us return and hold prayer with them under the trees." He dismounted and hung his umbrella on a kapok tree. Then, raising his arms in prayer, he gave the people a blessing. He blessed them for their faith and love. He prayed for their health, for their prosperity, and for the righteousness of their leaders. He prayed for peace and harmony in the village: "Our Father, may they have clear understanding of the truth and make rapid progress in gaining a knowledge of thee and thy divine work."[14] He sealed these blessings upon the people by the authority of the "holy apostleship." Quickly turning away, he and the others lost sight of the group who lingered for one last look at their Apostle.

Before the day was over, the Saints of Sauniatu erected a lava-rock marker on the spot where Elder McKay gave the blessing. A year later they constructed a monument near the village in commemoration of the apostolic visit. Each year for many years thereafter a special service was held at Sauniatu on May 31, McKay Day.

Following their visit to Samoa, Elder McKay and his company sailed back to Tonga on the *Tofua* and were placed under quarantine again by the local health officials. Elder McKay had to wait from June 11 to 22 on the small island of Makaha'a off the coast of Tongatapu.

During the wait, Mission President M. Vernon Coombs explained the local political, social, and religious situation to Elder McKay in some detail. Shortly before this time, Brother Coombs had applied for a land lease for a new boarding school. But this and other lease applications had been denied. It appeared to him that the government had turned hostile to the Church. He even believed the quarantine was part of a Tongan Free Church plan to keep the illustrious Mormon leader out of the country.

After being released from quarantine, Elder McKay met with the Saints in several conference sessions. President Coombs arranged for him to meet with Prince Uiliami Tungi, minister of lands and consort to the queen. To Elder McKay's inquiry about his attitude toward the Church, Tungi said, "I have nothing against your efforts here, but the Wesleyan and the Tongan Free Church feel that you are taking away too many of their members."[15]

Elder McKay visited not only Tongatapu but also Ha'apai and Vava'u. The small sailing ship, *Tarawa,* left Nuku'alofa harbor at 4 P.M. The passengers sought to get as comfortable as possible on the crowded deck. As night fell and the wind fiercely whipped the seas, Elder McKay was offered a bunk in the captain's cabin. "The sea was rough, and the boat rolled and pitched as if it were a shell. I could hear the waters swishing above me and feel the waves strike the sides with blows that made the craft quiver."[16] In the midst of these harrowing conditions, Elder McKay was shocked to discover that the captain was drunk. "When he threw himself on the seat alongside the berth I occupied, I offered him my place, but he refused. Then it was that I fancied I smelled whiskey. The thought that his unsteady movement was due to drink almost chilled my blood. But I couldn't believe any man would run such a risk as to become intoxicated on a wild night with seventy men and women and children packed on the deck like cargo." Elder McKay went on: I did not know what was going on above, but the way the boat plunged and rolled, and the waters beat above us, the sea seemed to be mad. Another sudden lurch, and again off rolled the skipper. This time he lay where he fell. Then I saw for the first time that he was holding a quart bottle of whiskey! I've been in a number of serious predicaments; I've faced a few dangers, and have met with serious accidents, but I've never experienced such forebodings in my life as came over me as I lay there trying to decide what could be done. . . . I decided at once that he would drink no more from that bottle, so reached down, and slid it unseen or unfelt by him, under my pillow!" Several times the captain came back to the bunk looking for his whiskey bottle but couldn't find it. Elder McKay worried that the captain might yet have another bottle hidden someplace. "I also knew that he wouldn't drink while I watched him," Elder McKay continued. "And that is what I did all night! Not a wink of sleep from 11:30 p.m. until 6 a.m.! And oh, what a night!"[17]

The voyage continued all the following day, and the *Tarawa* and its passengers did not reach Ha'apai until six in the evening, "a bedraggled, but grateful crowd—thankful to the Lord for our lives and power to walk once again on land."[18] After changing clothes, shaving, and eating his first food in more than twenty-four hours, Elder McKay conducted a conference meeting for the 116 Saints who gathered for that purpose at 9 P.M.

Elder McKay sailed from Vava'u to New Zealand on 4 July 1921. After spending a few additional days there, the travelers continued on to Australia. During their visit in August and September, they traveled over four thousand miles and visited all of the conferences but Perth, Western Australia. Elder McKay then sailed for southeast Asia.

The magnitude of Elder David O. McKay's months-long visit is difficult for readers almost a century later to grasp. But this was without question the supreme moment in Pacific LDS history to that time. Elder McKay was the first General Authority to visit the South Pacific islands. After his visit, almost twenty more years passed before another General Authority came to this area.

RELATIONS WITH GOVERNMENTS

Although the Church has tried to be apolitical, it was not possible to avoid involvement with governments in any country of the Pacific. Since the first missionaries in French Polynesia ran into difficulties with the French, LDS missionaries have never been completely at peace with the governments of every country where they were teaching the gospel. Almost all of the governments have imposed quotas on the number of missionaries the Church could bring into their countries. As a rule, the local Pacific Isle governments reflected the attitude of one of the major powers—Great Britain or Germany, for example—toward the Church.

The problems LDS missionaries had in French Polynesia were such that they eventually led to the closing of the mission in 1852. Only in one other country in the Pacific did the local government attempt to drive the Church out. That country—surprisingly, in view of developments since World War II—was Tonga. In 1922, the legislative assembly of Tonga decided that the Mormons were undesirable and passed a law making it unlawful for Latter-day Saints to enter the country. The law did not demand that missionaries who were already in the country leave, but it did spell the eventual death of the mission when the last missionaries returned home because of natural attrition. Mission President M. Vernon Coombs saw his mission force drop from a dozen to five during the next two years. Fortunately, in 1924, the legislative assembly repealed the anti-Mormon law and the mission was saved. President Coombs had spent countless hours working on petitions, meeting with the governmental officials, British and Tongan, and trying to convince anyone with influence that the law was improper.

Coombs's efforts made a difference, but it was local factional disagreements that ultimately brought a change in the law.

Mormon missionaries were allowed into Tonga after 1924, but the government remained generally unfriendly to the Church until the 1950s. Over the years the Church had been restricted to only a handful of missionaries at any time. The small number of foreign missionaries caused the Tongan Saints to take on a larger share of the missionary responsibility than in any other island nation. Local missionary work strengthened the Church in Tonga to a remarkable degree. In the early 1980s, more than 2 percent of the Tongan Saints would be on missions. (President Spencer W. Kimball had set a goal of one percent for the stakes of Zion.) It is correct to conclude that in Tonga strength has come out of adversity.

In summary, it may be said that the Church has remained outside of politics and has not used its influence to obtain political objectives in the countries of the Pacific. Nevertheless, the Church has not been able to avoid confrontations with the island governments or their protective powers. Whereas Latter-day Saint missionaries have interpreted constitutional guarantees of religious toleration as their license to deliver their message freely, the local governments have more than once interpreted their laws of religious toleration to mean that they as a nation were free to decide who could and could not have a right to hold opinions on religious matters.

CHURCH EDUCATION IN THE PACIFIC

The missionaries to the Pacific peoples were no doubt convinced that "the glory of God is intelligence" (D&C 93:36) and that their education, particularly in regard to spiritual matters, is vital for salvation. But the obvious need the people had for education was the real motivating force behind the establishing of the early elementary schools in the Pacific. Louisa Barnes Pratt, Addison Pratt's wife, taught her children and others in Hawaii and on the island of Tubuai in French Polynesia. During the 1850s, Latter-day Saint missionaries taught school in many parts of Hawaii, and when the Laie plantation became the center of the Church there, it was not long before an elementary school was founded. That school went through various developmental stages before it was finally turned over to the Hawaiian Board of Education in 1927. Before that time, it must be noted, numerous sister missionaries had taught at the Laie Elementary School.

Elementary schools were organized in New Zealand in 1886 and in Samoa during the early 1890s. In Samoa several of these were boarding schools.

Through the early years, Church schools played a vital role in the history of the Church in the Pacific. The word *school* referred to different kinds of efforts, ranging from three or four small children learning the alphabet in their own vernacular beneath a palm tree, to German language schools in Samoa, to fairly well-developed English schools that offered a reasonably wide curriculum.

The number of schools in operation varied greatly over the years. For example, in Samoa in 1904, there were four "advanced" schools and ten smaller elementary schools. But by 1913 or 1914, the number of schools had grown to twenty-six, with 628 pupils. During the early 1900s the Church operated ten schools in New Zealand. Elementary schools were opened in Tonga almost as soon as the missionaries returned there in 1907, and by 1922 there were ten LDS primary schools there. From the 1920s through the 1940s, the Church supported more than a dozen elementary schools that met in *fales*.

The first LDS high school in the Pacific was the Maori Agricultural College in Hastings, New Zealand. Dedicated in 1913, the MAC served the educational needs of Maori boys, whether members of the Church or not, until 1931. The thirty or more boys who yearly attended the school received a standard education with emphasis on religion and agricultural and mechanical training. Although the school had regular financial problems as well as difficulties with the New Zealand Board of Education—specifically, the school was not accredited until its last year of operation—the "Old Boys," that is, the MAC alumni, provided some of the best Maori leaders in the Church. The decision had already been made to close the MAC at the end of the school year when a destructive earthquake made the buildings unusable in February 1931. The reasons given by the First Presidency for closing the school were the Church's decision to retreat from the education field and the ability of the New Zealand government to provide sound education for all the youth of the nation.

In 1925–26, President M. Vernon Coombs, several other missionaries, and a number of Tongan Saints constructed a residential coeducational school on the island of Tongatapu. Makeke College (really a secondary school) was but a small school that offered only a basic curriculum, but it became the foundation for later enlargements of the LDS schools in Tonga. No other major schools were started by the Church in the Pacific until after World War II.

IMPACT OF WORLD WAR II IN THE PACIFIC

As the decade of the Great Depression drew to a close and the number of missionaries serving in the Pacific reached new levels, the work of the Church was about to take off there.

When Nazi Germany's 1939 invasion of Poland plunged Europe into war, however, the Pacific countries in the European powers' spheres of influence were dragged in as well. The Australian prime minister, for example, announced to his people that Australia was at war. The fall of France threw the people of French Polynesia into a state of political turmoil. They had to decide whether to support the Allies or the German forces. At a special election in September 1940 the Free French received 5,564 votes and the German–supported Vichy government only 18.

As early as May 1940, the First Presidency informed mission presidents in the Pacific that no new young elders would be sent for the time being, and the load would need to be carried by sisters and older couples. "Every minute is precious and must be used to the best of advantage," President Matthew Cowley admonished his missionaries in New Zealand. "We must prepare for any emergency. A call may come at any time for all of us to return home."[19] He also instructed them to carefully record names and addresses of friends and investigators and to help the Saints perfect their local organizations. President Cowley calculated that with completion of normal mission terms, by June 1941 there would be only four missionaries from Zion in New Zealand, in addition to the president and his family. Hence, the withdrawal of the missionaries was already underway.

By the fall of 1940, Church leaders in America became increasingly concerned about the safety of missionaries in the Pacific. Therefore, on 14 October the First Presidency sent telegrams instructing mission presidents to return all elders as soon as possible, to use American ships if they were available, and to install local officers in the branches. Missionaries who had served at least two years were given honorable releases while others were notified that they would be reassigned to missions in the United States. Unlike the evacuation in Europe, the evacuation in the Pacific allowed mission presidents and their families to remain in the Pacific. When the queen of Tonga asked mission president Emile Dunn why the missionaries were being removed, he explained that the Church believes in living prophets and that President Heber J. Grant had been inspired to call them back.

Missionaries were on the cruise ship SS *Mariposa* when it sailed from Sydney 19 October 1940, only days after the First Presidency's telegram had been received. Later, additional missionaries from New Zealand boarded as the ship stopped in Auckland; missionaries from Tonga as well as Samoa joined the group at Pago Pago. The Saints all over the Pacific were deeply saddened. Nevertheless, in Tonga, for example, as they had done many times before when the elders had been transferred or released, local members prepared a feast and celebrated, though sorrowfully, the departure of the Zion elders.

Things were more complicated in Tahiti because no commercial ship was expected there for six months. The mission president therefore chartered a large, diesel-powered sailing ship, the *Benicia,* to transport the missionaries to Hawaii. As the schooner left Papeete on 19 November 1940, a thousand Saints and others bade a tearful good-bye to their beloved friends and leaders.

Although there was generally no fighting in areas covered by the Pacific missions, military personnel became increasingly evident throughout the area. Often Mormon servicemen became goodwill ambassadors for the Church. The impact of the military was mixed in some areas. Although Western

Samoa got its first airport during World War II, military personnel were also responsible for introducing such bad habits as smoking and corrupting vices, including prostitution.

In some cases Church property was requisitioned for military use, disrupting normal activities. During April 1942, the chapel and other mission buildings at Pago Pago in American Samoa were taken over by the military. By May, the entire Pesega complex in Western Samoa was occupied by hundreds of servicemen. It was necessary to close the Pesega school for a number of months because of the presence of the military. Saints living in one village were even forced to relocate.

Although most Church activities continued, they were sometimes hampered by wartime conditions. In New Zealand no large gatherings, such as the *hui tau*, were allowed during the war. For a time, evening activities were hampered by a curfew in Hawaii. When the Tongan government imposed blackouts, the Church canceled their regular night meetings, and missionary cottage meetings were difficult to conduct without light.

With the departure of the missionaries, responsibility for Church organizations and activities was shifted increasingly to local members. As more and more priesthood bearers joined or were conscripted into military service, leadership ranks became depleted. Still, the Australian government exempted three brethren per branch, enabling them to serve missions. Investigators were lost; new leaders were inexperienced. Members sometimes felt they were like sheep without a shepherd. Mission presidents felt the need to strengthen these new local leaders, but were hampered in doing so because of gas shortages and travel restrictions.

Some interesting organizational innovations accompanied

Mission president Matthew Cowley did much to further missionary work in the Pacific. He served both before and after World War II to strengthen branches throughout the islands. He is shown here in 1948 with a group of Maori boys. (LDS Church Archives)

mission presidents' efforts to share responsibility for Church programs. For example, the president of the Australian Mission called counselors. This would not become a standard practice Churchwide until 1947. Fearing that he could be pulled out at a moment's notice, the Samoan mission president appointed a local member to take his place should that become necessary. In Tonga, a single capable secretary was appointed to keep all the records in each district.

As the local Saints caught hold of their duties, they gained new confidence. Many people grew because they were given new or greater responsibilities. Although some of the mission presidents after the war were tied to their old habits and concepts of leadership and continued to place missionaries in some positions in which local leaders should have been asked to serve, the Church in many Pacific areas was ready to assume independent leadership.

During the war, local members served as missionaries throughout the Pacific. They were able to keep the work alive on all the scattered island groups of most missions. In Samoa, the local missionaries actually increased the number of converts being baptized.

The Church was able to enhance its status and image as it provided help during the war. Elders in Hawaii made a significant contribution to the civil defense effort. Relief Society sisters in Australia volunteered many hours to the Red Cross. A special fast in New Zealand raised money for that country's patriotic fund. Contributions of the Church's welfare program were especially appreciated. Despite general problems with shipping, the Church in America was able to send relief supplies to Tahiti, twenty-two crates of food arriving in 1942 and thirty-four more crates the following year. Similarly in Tonga, the Church sent food to an isolated island following a 1943 volcanic eruption and consequent drought; food was also sent to another island following a devastating hurricane.

This improved goodwill, together with the strength the Church was able to maintain during the war, provided a foundation on which to build when the conflict came to an end.

CHAPTER 11

EXPANSION IN THE PACIFIC SINCE WORLD WAR II

R. LANIER BRITSCH

1935	Oahu Stake dedicated, first outside of North America
1952	Building missionaries construct Liahona high school in Tonga
1953	Elementary, junior high, and high school open in Samoa
1954	Missionary work begins in Fiji
1955	Church College of Hawaii (now BYU-Hawaii) founded
	David O. McKay visits Pacific missions
	Joseph Fielding Smith dedicates Guam
1958	New Zealand Temple dedicated
	Auckland Stake created, first international stake
1963	Polynesian Cultural Center opens
1972	First stake in Tahiti
1975	Missionaries sent to Saipan in the Mariana Islands
1978	Early-morning seminary classes introduced in Tonga and Samoa
1980	Four new temples announced for the Pacific
1983	Papua New Guinea dedicated by L. Tom Perry for the preaching of the gospel
2000	First "small temple" dedicated in Pacific in Kona, Hawaii

During the second half of the twentieth century, the Church expanded into many new areas of the Pacific, including Fiji, Micronesia, and other areas. In addition to significant geographical growth, the Church also witnessed a substantial expansion of its educational program, the formation of many new stakes, and a multiplication in the number of Pacific area temples during this time.

CHURCH EDUCATION

Following World War II the Church expanded its schools extensively. Between 1952 and 1960 the Church opened the Liahona High School in Tonga; Pesega and Mapusaga high schools in Samoa; and the Church College of New Zealand (also a high school, despite its name). The Fiji Technical College opened at Suva in 1975. Elementary schools also opened in Fiji, Samoa, and Tahiti.

When David O. McKay became president of the Church, he was in a position to follow up on the vision he had in 1921 of a Church-sponsored college in Hawaii. When he broke ground for the Church College of Hawaii in 1955, President McKay made it clear that the school was created to serve the educational, missionary, and spiritual needs of all the people of the Pacific and Asia. Opening its door in temporary quarters later that same year, CCH became a four-year accredited university. In 1958, President McKay returned to dedicate the beautiful new campus at Laie. Sixteen years later the school officially became known as Brigham Young University–Hawaii Campus.

The Polynesian Cultural Center (PCC), adjacent to the Church's college campus in Laie, opened in 1963—a living museum of Polynesian culture and entertainment. Initially, the center consisted of clusters of huts with a lagoon winding among them. Six different villages—Hawaii, Samoa, Tonga, Fiji, Maori, and Tahiti—were re-created for visitors to explore

Chinese Premier Zhao Ziyang visited the Polynesian Cultural Center on 7 January 1984. Here, he is shown thanking the cast of "This Is Polynesia" and Ralph G. Rodgers Jr., then general manager of the Polynesian Cultural Center, for the reception given him at the center. (LDS Church Archives)

and learn about. The complex covered more than sixteen acres of land. Although there were many skeptics, the PCC has become the number-one paid attraction in Hawaii. Today, the village of Marquesas and a new Easter Island exhibit are part of the center, which now encompasses forty-two acres of land. Native craftsmen continue to ensure that the buildings in each village are authentically constructed; the landscaping, too, is as authentic as possible. An energetic canoe pageant and an elaborate and authentic luau are part of the attraction. Millions of people have visited the center, and many of them have toured the BYU–Hawaii Campus and the nearby temple grounds and information center. Hundreds of Polynesian students are employed at the PCC; while they share their respective cultures with the tourists they are able to earn income that enables them to stay in school. In 2003, the center celebrated its

fortieth anniversary, opening a new theater—the Hale Aloha—
in which to hold its large and successful luau and an Easter
Island exhibit.[1] Laie remains an important part of the Church
in the islands.

In the early years, a major purpose of building Church
schools in the Pacific was to use them to draw nonmember
children into the Church. Since the 1950s, however, the main
reason for the schools has been to provide education for young
Latter-day Saints who otherwise would receive little or no
schooling. Although it is difficult to measure, there is no question that the Church schools in the Pacific have been and
remain a vital force and influence in the lives of thousands of
members of the Church and a significant number of nonmembers. A high percentage of the Church's leaders in the
islands are graduates of LDS schools.

Religion classes have always been part of the Church school
system in the Pacific. Until 1978, Church educational leaders
in the Pacific and in Salt Lake City assumed that the religion
classes in Church schools were sufficient to meet the needs of
the island people. In 1978, however, early morning seminary
classes were introduced in Tonga and Samoa. A total of 830
students enrolled in Tonga and 226 in Samoa. This was in
addition to a large number of home-study seminary students.
The expansion of the Church's educational activity was made
possible by the introduction of a new program, "Building
Missionaries."

THE BUILDING MISSIONARY PROGRAM

In September 1947, Emile C. and Evelyn Dunn arrived in
Tonga to supervise the construction of a new high school. The
Dunns were not new to Tonga. Emile had served his first mis-

sion there during the 1920s, and together the couple had led the mission from 1936 until 1946. They had been home for only eighteen months when President David O. McKay asked them to return to Tonga to help with the new school. At the time of their arrival, plans had not yet been prepared for the new institution. All that was certain was that the old Makeke College was in need of replacement and that the First Presidency had granted approval for the new school.

It was not until 5 November 1948 that ground was broken for what was called Liahona High School. In the meantime, Emile Dunn had been recalled as mission president and had taught one of the local Saints how to make concrete blocks, a rather technical operation. Soon after construction began, other Tongan priesthood bearers were at work on the project. Before the school was completed, the mission president called almost all of the local missionaries to work full-time as builders at Liahona. In addition, Saints came not only from Tongatapu but also from the Ha'apai and Vava'u island groups. They stayed for a month or two at a time and brought their own food. This was the beginning of what came to be called the Building Missionary Program. Although the Tongan Saints were not called as building missionaries at this time, they functioned in that way.

The next stage in development of the Building Missionary Program came in New Zealand. Elder Matthew Cowley, who had served as mission president there from 1938 until 1945, had deep respect for the graduates of the Maori Agricultural College and envisioned the day when a new school—a school that would include not only Maori boys but also girls and *pakehas*—would be constructed by the Church. In May 1949, the Church purchased a large tract of land upon which to build the new school. No one knew then that nine years later President McKay would dedicate not only a seven-million-dollar campus, the Church College of New Zealand, but also a village of homes for the faculty and staff, and, most important, the New Zealand Temple. Construction began on the school in 1951, but because of labor shortages, little was accomplished until Church leaders asked for volunteer help in April 1952. Church members then voted to support volunteer laborers with food and money until the school was completed. As it turned out, all of the above-mentioned buildings would be constructed through volunteer labor.

Many Church leaders were involved in the formulation of the Building Missionary Program, but Wendell B. Mendenhall deserves special credit for his contribution to it. It was he who saw the need to import skilled volunteer Latter-day Saint craftsmen from the United States to teach and supervise the local workers. They trained Maoris, Samoans, Tongans, and others to be carpenters, brick masons, cabinet makers, electricians, concrete workers, and so forth. By 1954, the school was well enough along to host New Zealand's annual *hui tau* conference.

But the school was only the beginning. In 1955, Church leaders extended the programs to other parts of the Pacific and eventually to other parts of the world. Building missionaries ultimately constructed hundreds of chapels, a number of schools, and many homes throughout the South Pacific and Hawaii. Hundreds of building missionaries learned trades on the job, trades that they subsequently used to support themselves and their families.

The Building Missionary Program helped change the image of the Church in Samoa from that of a backward, poor

Members of the Church in New Zealand in the 1930s stand in front of a traditional Maori building. (LDS Church Archives)

church to that of a modern, prosperous, well-organized institution.

Before the period of rapid development, when so many chapels were built between 1955 and 1965, most Latter-day Saint units met in *fale* chapels. Hawaii was more advanced, but even there many branches on the outer islands met in small one-, two-, or three-room chapels. J. Phillip Hanks, who served as a missionary, as a schoolteacher at Pesega, and finally as mission president in Samoa between 1953 and 1965, saw the difference the new chapels made there. He wrote:

> [The Building Missionary] program was a blessing to the people in many ways: First, it provided buildings which they could be proud of. Second, it provides a great deal of on-the-job training for many, many young men who put it into use for a life's occupation. Third, the personality of the Church and Church members changed during those years.

For many decades the Church was looked down upon by the local populace as a poor church. This resulted in slow progress, persecution, and shame on the part of the weaker members. . . . But with the newer buildings being built, the Church began to take upon itself more prestige . . . The effect upon the local members was one of pride and confidence. No longer did the members have to walk ashamed of their poverty. Now they could walk with head erect, look people in the eye, and actually have the envy of other denominations. This brought faster growth. Thousands were baptized during this period of time.[2]

This change which the Building Missionary Program brought to the Church in Samoa occurred to some degree in all of the Pacific missions.

THE CREATION OF STAKES

Until the 1930s, there were no stakes of the Church outside North America. The first was created in 1935, when President Heber J. Grant organized the Oahu Stake at Honolulu. Today this may seem a small matter, considering the present rapid growth of the Church and the constant division and creation of stakes; however, in the 1930s it was a matter of some weight and concern in the highest councils of the Church.

The most serious question was whether the Hawaiian Mission and the proposed stake would each have enough workers to succeed separately. The Brethren found a precedent in California, where there were both stakes and a mission, and decided to give the proposal support in Hawaii.

Much effort had been made on the local level to prepare the Oahu Saints for a stake. Mission presidents organized an auxiliary board there in 1927 and a district council four years later. By 1934, the Oahu Saints were functioning on a stake-like basis.

On 20 June 1935, President Heber J. Grant and his first counselor, President J. Reuben Clark Jr., along with a number of other Church authorities, arrived in Hawaii. Ten days later, President Grant organized the Oahu Stake and presented Ralph E. Woolley, a son of former mission president Samuel E. Woolley, as stake president. President Grant and President Clark believed that after eighty-five years of experience in the Church, "the Hawaiians had earned the right to the gift of a greater power and fuller local responsibility in the administration of the Church activities upon the islands."[3] It was a source of deep satisfaction to Presidents Grant and Clark that the distribution of Church offices in the new stake between the Hawaiians and the other racial groups in the Church "was essentially proportionate to their relative numbers."[4]

After the organization of the stake in Hawaii, almost another quarter century passed before the First Presidency and Council of the Twelve saw fit to organize a second stake in the Pacific. The year 1958 was extremely important for the Saints in New Zealand. During April and May, General Authorities dedicated the new college and temple, divided the mission, and organized the Auckland Stake.

Since 1950, the successive mission presidents in New Zealand had worked to pattern district organizations after stakes and to train local leaders through leadership seminars, training classes, and personal teaching sessions with priesthood and auxiliary leaders throughout the country. President Ariel S. Ballif, particularly, worked to remove almost all missionaries from branch and district positions and placed the burden of authority on the local people. He organized elders quorums and district councils and did everything else he could to prepare for stakes. Shortly before his release, President Ballif saw the fruits of his efforts when Elder Marion G. Romney organized the Auckland Stake from the Auckland and Waikato Districts on 18 May 1958. George R. Biesinger, a Church construction supervisor from America, was called as stake president.

By following approximately the same developmental pattern, Church leaders in the Pacific have created stakes at an almost explosive rate since the early 1960s. The first stake in Australia was organized at Sydney in 1960, the first in Samoa at Apia two years later, the first in Tonga at Nuku'alofa in 1968, and the first in Tahiti by 1972. By April 1980, there were fifty-two stakes in the Pacific. By the early years of the twenty-first century, this total had more than doubled.

TEMPLES IN THE PACIFIC SINCE WORLD WAR II

In January 1955, President David O. McKay visited all of the island missions and Australia. His trip was meant to encourage the Pacific Saints in their work and faith—and it was a chance to select a site for a new temple somewhere in the islands. Before arriving in New Zealand, President McKay told Church members in Tonga and Samoa that it would not be long before they would have a temple close by. When he visited the construction site for the Church College of New Zealand, he also looked at some land that was contiguous to the site but not owned by the Church. Wendell Mendenhall drove him to the place where the temple now stands. President McKay immediately knew he had found what he was looking for. "After we stepped from the car," wrote Mendenhall, "and we were looking around, President McKay called me to one side.

By the way he was looking at the hill, I could tell immediately what was on his mind. . . . He asked: 'What do you think?' I knew what the question implied and I simply asked in return: 'What do you think, President McKay?' And then in an almost prophetic tone he pronounced: 'This is the place to build a temple.'"[5] The land was purchased, and before long the announcement was made at Church headquarters that the second temple in the Pacific, and the first in the Southern Hemisphere, would be built in Hamilton, New Zealand.

Once the building was under construction, more than two years of devoted work were required of the labor missionaries to complete the sacred structure. As the job was nearing completion, it appeared to the construction supervisors that the building would not be finished in time for the scheduled dedication services in April 1958. The volunteer workers now labored even longer and were joined by many short-term helpers from throughout the mission. At the peak of the building program, over four hundred building missionaries were engaged simultaneously at the college and temple. Through cooperation and sacrifice they completed the project on time.

At the dedication ceremonies, choirs from the various island groups performed, as did other choirs from New Zealand. Session by session, members of varied racial and linguistic groups—Samoan, Tahitian, Tongan, English—gathered in the temple. In his dedicatory prayer, President McKay "expressed gratitude that the descendants of Father Lehi were guided to these islands, to become associated with other leading and influential Nations of the world."[6]

After the temple's dedication in 1958, thousands of Saints from French Polynesia, Samoa, and Tonga, as well as from

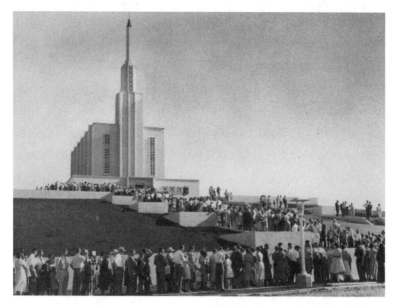

Throngs of people line up to visit the Hamilton New Zealand Temple open house. Labor missionaries provided much of the work on the structure, which was dedicated 20 April 1958 by President David O. McKay. (LDS Church Archives)

Australia, flocked to the Hamilton New Zealand Temple, often at great sacrifice.

For example, Donald Cummings and his family from Perth, Australia, sold their car and furniture to finance the trip. Just one week before they were to leave, they were still two hundred pounds short; two unexpected gifts, however, provided exactly this amount just in time. Because Brother Cummings couldn't get time off, he quit his job. To reach the temple, they first had to travel by train across the Australian continent, a distance greater than from San Francisco to New York. They were among the first to be endowed in the New Zealand Temple. When they returned to Perth, Brother Cummings was able to get a better job than the one he had left. Significantly, when a stake was organized at Perth, Donald Cummings became its first president, and when a temple was dedicated there a third of a century later, he became its first president as well.[7]

Polynesian Saints also traveled long distances to attend the temple. One sister in Tahiti often ate no more than three sardines and a piece of bread each day so she could save money from her work as a custodian in order to make the trip to New Zealand.[8] Another group of sixty-four Tahitian Saints similarly sacrificed; knowing of this group's lack of finances, Saints in New Zealand arranged to pick them up from the airport and house and feed them near the temple at no cost.[9]

While such groups were making these sacrifices, they dreamed of the day when temples would be built closer to their own homes.

The latter years of the twentieth century saw fulfillment of those dreams. On 15 October 1977, the First Presidency announced that a small temple would be built in American Samoa, at Mapusaga. Because the temple would serve members in Tonga and French Polynesia, and because travel connections were much better in American Samoa than Western Samoa, this site was selected instead of one in Western Samoa. In April 1980, however, the First Presidency announced an exciting change to this plan: temples would be built not only in Samoa but also in French Polynesia, Tonga, and Sydney, Australia. The site of the Samoan temple was moved to Apia, in Western Samoa, because many more Samoan members live in Western Samoa. The Samoan temple was completed in 1983, as were the temples in Tonga and Tahiti.

As each temple was toured during open houses and later dedicated to the Lord, the outpouring of the Spirit was evident in numerous ways. Elder John H. Groberg of the First Quorum of the Seventy, for example, personally conducted members of Tonga's royal family through the temple at Nuku'alofa during the open house. In the celestial room, the queen turned to Sister Groberg and said: "I want you to know that I have a feeling of peace here."[10]

In recent years, the Pacific area has greatly benefited from President Gordon B. Hinckley's massive temple-building plan. Hawaii received a small second temple at the city of Kailua-Kona in 2000. Three other temples have been dedicated in Australia—the Sydney temple in 1984, Perth in 2001, and Brisbane two years later.

GROWTH OF THE CHURCH IN FIJI AND OTHER NEW PACIFIC FRONTIERS

Apart from the larger or longer-established mission areas in the Pacific, there are a number of separate islands and island groups that make up an interesting and important part of international Church history. Some of these areas, such as Niue, are very small; others, like the Cook Islands, have been part of a number of missions; and yet other areas, particularly Fiji, are relatively new to LDS proselyting efforts and do not have a long history to relate. Other new areas include New Calendonia, Marquesas, the Gilberts, Kiribati, the New Hebrides, Vanuatu, the Marshalls, and the Carolines. The following text will briefly cover the Fiji Suva Mission area, with comments on the Micronesia Mission.

Fiji

There are many similarities between the Fiji Islands and the Hawaiian Islands. The climates are almost identical, the largest islands in the two groups are close to the same size, the economies both depend on sugar and tourists, and the populations of both are mixed because laborers were imported to each during the nineteenth and early twentieth centuries. Fiji was Christianized later than Hawaii, but non-Christian immigrants have made it so both areas are only around 50 percent Christian.

For the first 110 years that Latter-day Saints were in the Pacific, missionary work was limited to the peoples of Polynesia and Australia. It was not until 1954 that missionary work began in Fiji among the Melanesian people. Perhaps the reason for the long delay was that the Church did not grant the priesthood to people of African descent. Anthropologists generally classified the peoples of Fiji, New Caledonia, the New Hebrides, the Solomons, and New Guinea as Pacific Negroid. Until the mid to late 1950s, however, no one with high ecclesiastical authority in the Church had seriously looked into the question of the eligibility of Melanesians holding the priesthood. It was President David O. McKay who was satisfied that the people of the Pacific were of non-African lineage and authorized Church leaders to ordain Fijians to the priesthood.

Latter-day Saint missionary work in Fiji began officially in 1954, when the First Presidency assigned this area to the Samoan Mission. When the first two missionaries arrived in Suva, they almost immediately organized a branch on 5 September 1954. It was possible to create a branch because two or three Latter-day Saint families had been holding limited church meetings there for several decades. These families, headed by Mary Ashley and Cecil B. Smith, were both Tongan.

In January 1955, President David O. McKay stopped over in Suva, and while there he met the elders. He was not aware until then that the Church had missionaries in Fiji. On the following Sunday, President and Sister McKay and Elder Franklin D. Murdock met with a group of twenty-eight Church members in Cecil Smith's home. As he worshipped with this little branch, President McKay felt inspired to tell them that it was time to begin building up the kingdom of God in Fiji.

As a result of this visit, President McKay asked the Church Building Committee to buy land in Suva and build a large chapel. When the building was completed in 1958, the little branch hardly filled the first two or three rows. But President McKay told the Saints to live the gospel and teach their friends, and the time would come before long when not only the chapel but also the cultural hall would be filled with Church members.

In January 1958, responsibility for Fiji was transferred to the Tonga Mission. It remained under that jurisdiction until 1971, when the First Presidency authorized the formation of the Fiji Mission, which would also include Niue and the Cook Islands. The Church had grown to seven branches in Fiji. In 1972 President McKay's promise that the Suva chapel would be filled was realized. At every conference that year the building was filled with Latter-day Saints—Fijians, Indians, Rotumans, Tongans, Samoans, Europeans, and Americans.

The Fiji Mission has played the role of caretaker and pioneer during the years since 1972. This dual responsibility strained the first three presidents who directed it. After his first year in office, Ebbie L. Davis, the first mission president, wrote:

> As we have slowed down to look around, it has become increasingly clear that there is so much to do here that we are going to get very little done. There are so many

programs—construction, real estate, translation, leadership training, increasing [numbers of] missionaries, Church schools, localization of leadership, new areas to open, etc.— that we will only be able to push all of them forward a little way, rather than pushing a few [programs] a long way. . . . With our six separate national governments to deal with, five kinds of money, ten major languages, and the great distances between our areas in the mission, at times it seems like an impossible task. Half of the mission president's time is usually spent away from the office and home. We have all three major South Pacific ethnic groups in our mission. There are Polynesians in Rarotonga and Niue; Melanesians in Fiji, the New Hebrides, and the Solomons; and Micronesians in the Gilberts and Nauru. Variations and adaptations are required in the missionary program and the leadership training program for all of these distinct peoples. It seems quite clear that this is a Mission of Missions.[11]

The Fiji Mission truly is a "Mission of Missions." By the early years of the twenty-first century, more than twelve thousand members of the Church lived within its mission boundaries.

MICRONESIA

In the 1970s, Guam and the United States Trust Territory of Micronesia became a productive missionary field. During World War II, the names of many Micronesian islands were forever engrained on the minds of many Americans. Today these tiny dots in the Pacific—the Marshall, Caroline, and Mariana Islands, with their tiny atolls of Majuro, Kwajalein, Ponape, Truk, Yap, and larger Saipan—are no longer battle-fields for military gains, but for men's souls.

Latter-day Saint presence on the island of Guam has been evident since 1945, when the first servicemen's group was organized. On 25 August 1955, President Joseph Fielding Smith visited Guam and dedicated it to the preaching of the gospel. In January 1957, the first full-time missionaries arrived, and the first chapel was dedicated a year later. But until the 1970s the missionaries confined their efforts almost entirely to Americans who were interested in the Church.

During the 1950s and 1960s, Guam was part of three different Asian missions. By the end of the century, Guam and Micronesia comprised an independent mission within which nearly forty-five hundred members of the Church resided.

In January 1975, the Hawaii Mission sent elders to Saipan in the Mariana Islands. Since that time, missionaries have been sent into all seven districts of the U.S. Trust Territory. Papua New Guinea was dedicated for the preaching of the gospel in April 1983 by Elder L. Tom Perry of the Quorum of the Twelve. By the end of that year, the Church had 750 members and a chapel was under construction. In February 1992, the Papua New Guinea Port Moresby Mission was created. Although its missionary numbers remained relatively modest, Church growth was such that a stake was created in 1995 with 2,200 members in six wards and one branch. Church membership in Papua New Guinea was just over ten thousand in the early years of the twenty-first century.

Thus, since 1960 the Church has opened missionary work in a number of parts of Melanesia and Micronesia, and the work is moving forward in these areas. Most difficulties have been related to growing nationalism and the instability of some of the newer states. Great Britain has controlled or protected many island areas, and that nation's policies have frequently made it difficult for the Church to move into its areas.

THE CHURCH IN THE PACIFIC: AN APPRAISAL

In conclusion, it is good to raise the question, How well does the restored gospel fit with the peoples of the Pacific? Considering the generally underdeveloped state of island economies and the limited level of education in many island groups, are the island peoples able to adapt well to the highly structured Church of the twenty-first century? First, let the statistics speak to the question. Numerically, the Church is doing well on a percentage basis. More than 71,000 Samoans in the two Samoas are now members of the Church, or approximately 10 percent of the populace. All of both Samoas are encompassed in stakes. Samoa was the first country in the world where its members could make such a claim. In Tonga, Church growth has been explosive. Today, nearly one of every two Tongans is a member of the Church.

But what of the effectiveness of the Church among the people? In 1964, J. J. Mol, of Australia National University at Canberra, studied the religious affiliations of the Maoris. He concluded that the Latter-day Saints have done a better job of integrating the various races of New Zealand, particularly Maoris and *pakehas,* than any other Church. Mol concluded: "The Mormons are the most successful of all churches in the implementation of a policy of integration. Although in some areas nearly all its members are Maori (in such a situation one cannot very well speak of a successful policy of integration), the fact that 50% of its members go to services every Sunday, which have many non-Maori overtones, and feel at home in this environment, is certainly an achievement of the first order. This applies to the absolute numbers of Maoris who are in meaningful interaction with pakehas in face-to-face religious groups."[12]

I have already discussed (see chapter 9) some of the reasons why the Church was attractive to the Maoris during the 1880s. Some of those reasons, notably a feeling among the Maoris that they are of the house of Israel and that the teachings of the Church sustain some of their native traditions, are also attractions for other Polynesian groups. But certainly the Maoris, as all peoples of the Pacific, join the Church for essentially the same reasons people join everywhere: because they believe that Joseph Smith did see and speak to God the Father and his son Jesus Christ, that Joseph Smith did translate the Book of Mormon by the gift and power of God, that it is truly a record of an ancient people who inhabited the Americas, and that the Church has been and is led by a prophet of God.

But some people have questioned the suitability of the applied gospel, that is, its programs, to the temperament and needs of the Polynesian people. Can the Maoris adjust to a *pakeha* church? Can the Hawaiians be comfortable in a *haole* church? Can the people of Samoa accommodate to a *paalangi* church? The answer is definitely yes. The reason the Church fits so well among the Polynesians is that their traditional customs are closer to the gospel of Jesus Christ, to its actual application, than are the individualistic ways of Western man. The system of communal sharing and family concern found among the Polynesians is much closer to the Savior's way than is the aggressive way of living found among most Americans.

Further, the peoples of Tonga, Samoa, New Zealand, Tahiti, Fiji, and elsewhere are not opposed to the elements of modernity that are useful to them. People generally want to be modern. The island Saints are eager to conform to the latest

The family of Vilai Kupu holds family home evening in Tonga. (Photo courtesy Richard O. Cowan)

programs of the Church. They desire modern chapels, schools, and recreation facilities. They also believe in the Welfare Services Program of the Church. Home teaching, too, receives appropriate attention. In fact, the Church leaders in the South Pacific cannot understand why leaders in other parts of the Church would ever set a goal for monthly home teaching that is less than 100 percent.

If the disproportionately large number of missionaries the Church has sent to the islands from an early date and the large number of temples the Church has built for the Pacific peoples are an indication of God's concern for a special people, we must conclude that God's eye has been upon, and God's hand has been involved in, the history of the Church in the Pacific Islands.

CHURCH STATUS IN THE PACIFIC*

Geographical Areas	Members	Stakes	Missions	Temples**
American Samoa	13,406	4	—	—
Australia	105,087	32	7	5
Cook Islands	1,369	—	—	—
Fiji	13,228	4	1	1
French Polynesia	20,383	6	1	1
Guam	1,653	—	1	—
Hawaii	60,143	14	1	2
Johnston Atoll	25	—	—	—
Kiribati	10,019	1	—	—
Marshall Islands	3,843	—	—	—
Micronesia Federated States	3,341	—	—	—
Nauru	116	—	—	—
New Caledonia	1,631	—	—	—
New Zealand	92,631	25	2	1
Niue	260	—	—	—
Northern Mariana Islands	932	—	—	—
Palau (Belau)	399	—	—	—
Papua New Guinea	11,775	1	1	—
Samoa	61,094	16	1	1
Solomon Islands	186	—	—	—
Tonga	49,719	16	1	1
Tuvalu	94	—	—	—
Vanuatu	2,042	—	—	—
Pacific Totals:	**453,376**	**119**	**16**	**12**

* Numbers are for year's end 2002

** These numbers represent operating temples and those that had been announced or were under construction at press time.

PART III

❧

THE CHURCH IN
LATIN AMERICA

The lands to the south of the United States and Canada are commonly known as Latin America. This area includes Mexico, Central America, and South America. The designation is based on the fact that the peoples in this region speak a Latin-based language— Portuguese in Brazil and Spanish almost everywhere else.

Latin America is of special significance to Latter-day Saints for several reasons. It is the region geographically located closest to the major concentration of Church membership in the United States. Because of a high birth rate, together with particularly successful missionary efforts, Latin America is the most rapidly growing area of the Church. Latin America could well comprise a majority of all Latter-day Saints worldwide during the lifetime of many individuals now living.

Latter-day Saints also have an interest in Latin America because they identify this area with the history recorded in the Book of Mormon. Like the Polynesians, many of the Saints in Latin American consider themselves heirs to the great promises recorded in this sacred volume (see, for example, 2 Nephi 30:4–6). This is especially true of the native and mixed-blood, or "mestizo," peoples of Mexico, Central America, and the western portion of South America, who think of themselves as descendants of the Book of Mormon Lamanites. Only along the eastern seaboard of South America is the population of more purely European origin. The Book of Mormon taught that "gentiles" would cross the "many waters" to America where they would be instrumental in restoring a knowledge of the gospel of Jesus Christ to latter-day Lamanites (read 1 Nephi 13:12–14, 38–39, and 22:7–8). Hence, Church members of European descent feel a special responsibility to assist the Lamanites to "blossom as a rose" (D&C 49:24). Surely this Book of Mormon connection enhances the appeal of the gospel message to Latin Americans.

The Latin American culture is strongly family oriented. Close relationships are typically maintained even with members of extended families. Therefore, the Latter-day Saints' emphasis on the family is another appealing feature of the gospel for Latin Americans.

Those choosing to join the Church, however, have needed to overcome a significant challenge. In many areas, 95 percent of the population belongs to a single church that is supported by the governments and has immense influence. Geographical names, holidays, and even individuals' given names reflect this dominant faith. Hence, the decision to convert to another religion may seem like repudiating one's culture, and often attracts ostracism and even persecution.

Latin America was the third major area in the world to receive the restored gospel. Even though an attempt was made in 1851 to open a mission in Chile, the first successful beginning of the Church in Latin America occurred a quarter of a century later in Mexico. Despite these early beginnings, however, the real growth of the Church in Latin America came only during the closing decades of the twentieth century. Meeting the challenges and opportunities posed by this expansion has provided valuable experience for the international Church.

CHAPTER 12

MEXICO RECEIVES THE GOSPEL

RICHARD O. COWAN

1875	Porfirio Diaz restores stability to Mexico
1876	LDS missionaries in Chihuahua—the first in Mexico
1879	Elder Moses Thatcher opens mission in Mexico City
1885	Mormon colonies established in Northern Mexico
1889–1901	Mission in Mexico closed
1907–31	Rey L. Pratt presides over Mexican Mission
1912	Colonists evacuated amid revolutions
1915	Two martyrs killed at San Marcos
1917	Mexican Constitution restricts clergy and ownership of lands
1930–33	J. Reuben Clark named United States ambassador to Mexico
1936	"Third Convention" protests Anglo mission president
1946	President George Albert Smith visits Mexico City

The commitment of Latter-day Saints to work among the Lamanites was evident from the beginning days of the Church. Soon after the Church was organized in 1830, the Lord directed the Saints to "go unto the Lamanites and preach my gospel unto them; and inasmuch as they receive thy teachings thou shalt cause my church to be established among them"

233

(D&C 28:8). Thus one of the earliest official missions of the Church was to the Indians.

The Saints' expulsion to the West was of great significance in unfolding this work. Joseph Smith had prophesied that "there will be tens of thousands of Latter-day Saints who will be gathered in the Rocky Mountains, and there they will open the door for the establishing of the Gospel among the Lamanites."[1] Elder Spencer W. Kimball declared: "The Lord could not have devised a better plan than to put us where we are in order to accomplish that very thing of educating and teaching the Lamanites. Our ancestors came thousands of miles across the desert, under terrific persecutions and hardships, to locate where the Gentiles had scattered the Lamanites."[2]

As Mormon colonization pushed southward into Arizona during the 1870s, the Saints were increasingly brought into contact with another group of Lamanites—the Spanish-speaking peoples of mixed European and Indian ancestry.

A MISSION TO MEXICO, 1876

In June 1875, President Brigham Young called Daniel Webster Jones (who had lived in Mexico a number of years earlier) and Henry Brizzee to prepare for a mission to Mexico. Jones was born in Missouri in 1830 and should not be confused with the Dan Jones who had been prominent in Britain and Nauvoo. At age seventeen, he joined the army and studied Spanish in order to serve as an interpreter for the United Sates forces. In Mexico, he not only learned the language but also became thoroughly acquainted with the customs of the people. Later, during 1850, while en route to the gold mines in California, he was injured in an accident at Provo, Utah, so he remained among the Mormon people there. When he was baptized the following January, a foot of ice had to be chopped from the surface of the water. In 1851, Brigham Young personally directed that Jones be ordained a seventy so that he might preach wherever he went, particularly among Spanish-speaking people. Thus, when he received the 1875 appointment to Mexico, Elder Jones reflected: "I had expected this call to come some time. I had both desired and dreaded the mission." He wanted to do his duty but was concerned over the power of the clergy in that land. He recorded: "I felt a dread that tried me severely while on my way to the office; but before arriving I had formed the resolution to 'face the music.' My reflections were: This mission has to be commenced by someone and if it is necessary for the extreme sacrifice to be made, just as well to be me as anyone else."[3]

President Young instructed the missionaries to brush up on their Spanish and to begin translating the Book of Mormon. The two elders soon concluded that their knowledge of Spanish was not adequate for the important assignment of translating the scriptures. They therefore regarded the unexpected arrival of Meliton G. Trejo as a blessing from the Lord.

Trejo had been born in 1843 in western Spain. He became an officer and received a doctor's degree from the University of Bordeaux, France. In spite of his military life, Meliton often thought seriously about religion but was unable to find any faith that satisfied him. After hearing a fellow officer comment about "a group of 'Saints' in the Rocky Mountains who were led there by a prophet of God," Trejo felt "an urgent desire" to meet these people. Some time later, while serving in the Philippines, he "asked the Lord in fervent prayer to help him in his quest for truth and to make His will known concerning him. That night Meliton had a dream which satisfied him completely and which he always considered exceedingly sacred."[4]

He promptly began preparing to leave for America. After sewing two thousand dollars into his vest, he boarded a ship for San Francisco. Arriving there on 4 July 1874, he immediately set out for Utah. Though well-educated, Meliton could read but not speak English. He wondered how he was to receive the truth which he sought in an English-speaking community. Nevertheless, he donned his Spanish officer's uniform and strolled around Salt Lake City, hoping to find someone with whom he could communicate. A language teacher who knew Spanish met Trejo, taught him the gospel, and introduced him to Church leaders. When Meliton described his background and sacred dream to Brigham Young, he insisted that "his most fervent desire was to translate the Book of Mormon into the Spanish language and to carry the gospel to his people."[5] Trejo was put in touch with Elders Jones and Brizzee, and with his help the project of translating the Book of Mormon moved toward completion.

Another problem facing the prospective missionaries was their lack of finances. Brigham Young could not appropriate Church funds for their support, but did authorize them to solicit contributions and promised to help them from his own pocket if necessary. Raising five hundred dollars, the missionaries were able to publish fifteen hundred copies of *Trozos Selectos del Libro de Mormon* (*Selected Passages from the Book of Mormon*).

In August 1875, Helaman Pratt, Ammon M. Tenney, and Anthony W. Ivins joined Jones and Brizzee, who were preparing to depart. All three of these new missionaries figured prominently in subsequent Latter-day Saint history in Mexico. At this same time, President Young felt the need to expand the territory of Mormon colonization, perhaps even beyond the borders of the United States. He therefore commissioned the elders to look out for suitable sites in Mexico as well as Arizona. The group left their homes in Utah during September, and by the end of the year were preparing to cross the border into Mexico.

The missionaries entered Mexico at a particularly favorable time. For centuries, the Catholic Church had dominated Mexican political and economic affairs, but under the leadership of Benito Juarez, the Mexican constitution of 1857 and related laws provided for the separation of church and state and for equal protection of all beliefs. It also eliminated the Catholic Church's role in such civil functions as marriage and public education, restricted the Catholic Church's right to own real estate, and greatly curtailed the power and influence of monastic orders. Unfortunately, however, these reforms resulted in two decades of revolution, confusion, and even foreign intervention. Then in 1876, the year the missionaries arrived, Porfirio Diaz seized power. His thirty-five-year rule retained most of the reform laws and, significantly, restored economic stability and progress. He continued the liberals' policy of encouraging foreign investment and even colonization in Mexico.

Elder Jones and his companions crossed the border from El Paso, Texas, to Ciudad Juarez, Mexico, on 7 January 1876. They immediately encountered opposition from the Catholic clergy but nevertheless were able to make some friends. Near the end of March, the elders journeyed 250 miles further south to the city of Chihuahua, the state capital, where they were cordially received by the governor, who gave them valuable advice concerning possible future colonization in the area. The first public Latter-day Saint meeting in Mexico was held in a cock-fighting arena and was attended by some five hundred persons. Elder Jones recalled:

> In the evening, at the time of meeting, quite a respectable congregation had gathered. The cock fighting was still going on, but soon closed. Many persons there at their national sport remained to hear us.
>
> As I was the only one who could speak Spanish, . . . I had to do the preaching. It was quite a task but I knew the native politeness. No Mexican will ever jeer a foreigner if he tries to speak their language. They will listen intently and try to understand. I understand Spanish quite well, but had never spoken in public and, no doubt, made many blunders. However, our audience seemed pleased.
>
> When the meeting was over, many came and shook hands with us and said they liked what had been preached.[6]

Soon afterwards, a local newspaper published its own version of this first Latter-day Saint meeting in Mexico:

> A few days ago a remarkable event attracted the attention of the public of this place. Daniel W. Jones, a prominent Mormon Apostle [he was not a member of the Twelve], had printed and distributed handbills announcing that he would preach a sermon on Mormonism at the Zaragoza Theatre. Rumors that Mr. Jones and his colaborers would be stoned . . . incited us to attend the meeting. The audience present was very large and at first complete order reigned. The preaching commenced in the midst of profound silence, which was an evidence that the audience was interested. After a little while a few discontented persons commenced to initiate disorder by throwing small stones and pieces of wood at where the speaker stood, but

Juarez Academy has been in operation since 1880, but was officially organized as a stake academy in 1895. It has become one of Mexico's premier preparatory schools. (Photo courtesy Donald Q. Cannon)

they had few imitators and were frowned down by good judgment of the majority. The lecture was not very interesting, the audience diverted itself principally by contemplating the constant struggle of the orator with the difficulties of the Spanish language. The performance concluded with a heterogeneous mixture of applause and hisses.[7]

While in the city, the missionaries mailed five hundred copies of *Trozos Selectos* to the leaders of more than one hundred communities throughout the Republic of Mexico. Some of these pamphlets would become instrumental in opening missionary work in Mexico City within a few years.

After a three-week stay in Chihuahua City, the missionaries traveled by horseback west to the foothills of the Sierra Madre Mountains. Here they were received warmly by the Indians and other inhabitants of several small villages. These people expressed the strongest interest in the elders' message. Turning toward the north, the missionaries arrived at Casas Grandes on May 12. Elder Jones was especially impressed by the small valley of the Piedras Verdes River. After checking on water rights and land titles, he concluded that of all the country he passed through, this area appeared to be the most desirable for colonization. This recommendation would result in the establishing of Mormon colonies in the area only nine years later. By July, Elder Jones and his companion were back in Utah. During their ten-month absence, they had traveled about four thousand miles and had been instrumental in laying the foundations for future Latter-day Saint missionary work and colonizing in Mexico.

Latter-day Saint missionaries returned to Mexico during the fall of that same year, 1876, this time to the state of Sonora. Helaman Pratt and Meliton Trejo went to Hermosillo, the state capital, where they baptized five persons. Other missionaries went to the warlike Yaqui Indians but had no success and were fortunate to escape with their lives.

ELDER THATCHER'S MISSION
TO MEXICO CITY, 1879

There were at least two responses to the Book of Mormon pamphlets that Daniel W. Jones had mailed throughout Mexico. Both came from intellectual leaders—Ignacio Manuel Altamirano, an outstanding figure in nineteenth-century Mexican literature; and Plotino Rhodakanaty, an exponent of socialist ideas. Additional literature was mailed to them, and Dr. Rhodakanaty was instrumental in sharing the gospel with at least twenty other individuals. President John Taylor, who succeeded Brigham Young in 1877, continued the Church's interest in Mexico. In 1879, he called missionaries to take the gospel to the Mexican capital. The importance of this mission was evidenced by the fact that it was to be headed personally by Elder Moses Thatcher of the Council of the Twelve. Upon arriving in Mexico City on November 16, 1879, the elders immediately contacted Dr. Rhodakanaty, whom they baptized four days later. On 23 November, just one week after the missionaries' arrival, he became president of the first branch of the Church organized in Mexico. As verbal attacks against the Mormons in Mexico City mounted, some, including Rhodakanaty, became disaffected.

The elders turned their attention to the smaller villages in the environs of the capital. Just as Daniel Jones and his companions had found a warmer reception in the smaller villages than in the cities, so also did these missionaries find greater success in outlying communities. Several families were converted who would remain faithful to the Church through the years. The Church's second branch in Mexico was organized at Ozumba, located at the foot of the famed volcano Popocatepetl, about forty miles southeast of Mexico City. Together with a group of missionaries and converts, Elder Thatcher climbed the slopes of this mountain and on 6 April 1881 held a special conference. "Fervent prayers were raised to God, imploring his blessings on this Mission, and the country was blessed and dedicated to the Lord for the preaching of the gospel."[8]

By 1889, a year in which the persecution of the Saints in Utah was reaching a climax, the mission was temporarily closed. Much had been accomplished during the decade—18 missionaries had served, 241 converts had been baptized, and 10 small

branches were organized. Several missionary tracts were translated and published in Spanish. A complete translation of the
Book of Mormon made by Elders Meliton G. Trejo and James
Z. Stewart was published in 1886. Even though there would be
no Mormon missionaries in central Mexico for over a decade,
Latter-day Saint colonies had already been established in the
northern state of Chihuahua, and these would subsequently
provide the means of reopening the Mexico Mission.

MORMON COLONIES IN NORTHERN MEXICO

The practice of plural marriage had become the target of
intensified persecution in the United States during the 1880s.
Consequently, President John Taylor directed the Saints in
Arizona to consider possible locations across the Mexican border where the persecuted members might find refuge. In 1885,
Elder Moses Thatcher headed a group who established a colony
at the site recommended by Elder Jones nine years earlier.
Located about 180 miles southwest of El Paso, Texas, this
colony was named Juarez in honor of Mexico's national hero.
A particularly serious problem in the area was the lack of badly
needed irrigation water. For several months in the year, there
was only a trickle in the otherwise dry riverbed. One afternoon, a sharp earthquake hit the area. The following morning,
the colonists were amazed to discover that the trickle had
become a large stream. The quake had opened hot springs further up the canyon, creating a source of water which has continued to the present.[9]

Soon, seven other colonies were founded, with a total population of about four thousand. As numerous hardships were
overcome, prosperity gradually came to the colonies, and in
1895, the Juarez Stake, the first in Latin America, was organ-

ized. In coming decades, these colonies would make a significant contribution to the Church and Mexico.

MISSION WORK RESUMED, 1901

By the turn of the century, conditions seemed right for reopening the mission in Mexico. The Latter-day Saint colonies had become well established and were prospering; their young people, who by this time could speak Spanish fluently and were well acquainted with the Mexican culture, were now available for proselytizing duties. In 1901, with the approval of the First Presidency and under the immediate supervision of the Juarez Stake, the mission in Mexico City was reopened.

When the missionaries had left some twelve years earlier, most of the Saints had been in the Church for only a very short time. "With no one to teach them the gospel and Church discipline," one writer explained, "they were, as it were, like as sheep without a shepherd, and soon drifted into error."[10] Most of the branches had become disorganized and their members scattered. A few reverted to their former religion. Nevertheless, when the missionaries returned, they were able to win back most of these early Saints to the faith.

During the next ten years, the work prospered. The missionary force increased to twenty. President Anthony W. Ivins of the Juarez Stake made frequent visits to the mission, as did a total of six members of the Quorum of the Twelve Apostles from Salt Lake City. Local men and women were called and trained to be effective leaders. They received great strength from Rey L. Pratt (son of Helaman Pratt and grandson of Elder Parley P. Pratt), who became mission president in 1907 and would preside for nearly a quarter century.

Mormon colonists flee their homes in northern Mexico in 1912. Revolution throughout Mexico made the second decade of the twentieth century difficult for Saints in the area. Many were left without leadership or direction from Church Headquarters. (LDS Church Archives)

Many new converts were added, so that by 1911, the mission's membership exceeded one thousand. In that year, President Pratt observed that "prospects were never brighter for the spreading of the gospel in this land."[11] But the whirlwind of revolution had again been unleashed, and within a very short time it would disrupt the Church's progress in Mexico.

REVOLUTION AND EXODUS, 1910 TO 1917

As revolutions and counterrevolutions swept the country, missionary work became increasingly difficult. Elder W. Ernest Young, the mission secretary, described conditions in Mexico City during February 1913: "Bullets rained over most of the city. The mission home was hit many times. One bullet penetrated through the ceiling and fell on the floor while we were eating. Cannons roared most of the nights, keeping us awake. Food became scarce. One day I walked two blocks south to a store and before arriving, bullets whistled over my head so close that I fell flat on the sidewalk and crawled into a drug store to await a calm."[12]

These conditions were complicated by a growing nationalistic, anti-American sentiment. By August of 1913, it was necessary to evacuate the missionaries once again.

The Mexican Saints were left alone to take care of themselves. In San Marcos, about fifty miles northwest of Mexico City, for example, Rafael Monroy, a comparatively recent convert, was given the responsibility of serving as branch president. Just two years after the missionaries' departure, however, the brutal forces of revolutionary conflict and religious prejudice resulted in the murders of President Monroy and his cousin, Vincente Morales. As an excuse to persecute these new Mormon converts, Monroy had falsely been accused of being a colonel in a rival revolutionary faction. When he and his cousin were taken to the center of town to be shot, one of the executioners said: "Now, as one last chance, we tell you if you will renounce your religion and confess before the Virgin Mary, we will forgive you and we will spare your lives."[13]

> President Monroy, drawing himself to his full height, said: "Gentleman, I cannot for I know that what I have taught and what I have accepted is the Gospel of Jesus Christ."
>
> The spokesman for the revolutionaries said: "All right then prepare yourself, but have you anything to say before you are executed?"
>
> President Monroy said he did have and that was permission to kneel and pray.

The request was granted, and President Monroy asked in his prayer that his widowed mother be blessed, and that his widow and children be cared for. He then prayed for the members of the branch, and said, "Lord, bless this little flock that they may not go astray, but that someone will be raised up to lead them.

"Lord, forgive these men, for they know not what they do."[14]

These tragic deaths did not mark the end of the work in San Marcos; but in coming decades the small branch grew in numbers and influence. Here the Saints built their own school, a forerunner of the Church's extensive educational system in Mexico. Members of this branch, including descendants of the martyrs, would occupy positions of responsibility in the Mexican Mission during later years.

In 1912, the same forces which disrupted missionary work also brought trouble to the colonists in northern Mexico. When rebels confiscated the Saints' arms, Mormon leaders ordered an evacuation of women and children by special train to El Paso on 26 July. The men followed a few days later, coming out in a mile-long wagon caravan. Most thought they would be returning to their homes within a short time, but as conditions did not improve, they had to do the best they could while living in tents provided by the U.S. Army. By February 1913, some began returning while others remained permanently in the United States. The revolutions raged for several more years, and on repeated occasions, the Mormon colonists felt they had been protected by divine power.

In March 1916, for example, Pancho Villa's revolutionary forces crossed the U.S. border and sacked the town of Columbus, New Mexico, before heading back south into Mexico. The colonists were directly in his path and feared for their lives and property. W. Ernest Young, then a counselor in the Colonia Dublan Ward bishopric, recorded how divine intervention protected the colonists:

> It was a very serious matter, and we were in great fear. Bishop [Anson B.] Call met most of the men in Dublan in the street in the center of town near the stores. His counselors, Nephi Thayne and I, stood near him. Two opinions were voiced, to make an exodus to the mountains or to go to the small garrison at Nuevo Casas Grandes for protection. Bishop Call as our leader had the right for inspiration, and he finally told us to go to our homes, turn out all lights, and retire with a trusting faith that the Lord would answer our prayers.
>
> Villa and his army must have left the Coralitos ranch near midnight. They arrived at the north end of Dublan about 3 A.M. and stopped. Villa remarked that Carranza must have sent more soldiers to defend the place. His subalterns said they saw no reason for this. Villa persisted and swore that the place was occupied by a force of men and that there were lights, etc. . . .
>
> Bible history gives testimony of divine intervention, and Villa at this time was diverted in his course when he ordered his men to turn left and beat a new road over the prairie and travel on to the Chocolate Pass some fifteen miles to the southeast. No doubt, Villa's soldiers would like to have continued their pillage and murderous acts.[15]

In the midst of these difficulties, Stake President Joseph C. Bentley counseled the Colonia Juarez Ward: "Political conditions have taken an unhoped-for turn. Perilous times no doubt lie ahead. But let us not lose faith in the power of the Lord to protect us or ever cease striving to be worthy of that protection. . . . Though they may despoil us, deprive us of our property and misuse us in many ways, let us not forget that the despoilers . . .

are still God's children, and that our mission in this land is to be a link in the chain of their salvation."[16]

During coming years, the colonists' superior education programs and advanced agricultural methods attracted favorable attention for the Church. Furthermore, in the 1920s, the Mexican government began enforcing laws prohibiting foreign clergy from functioning. Hence, in later years, most of the missionaries in Mexico, almost all of the mission presidents, and the majority of leaders in the Church's growing school system came from among the colonists who were Mexican citizens. In this way, the Mormon colonies provided the strength that enabled the Church in later years to grow throughout Mexico and elsewhere in Latin America.

The difficulties in Mexico had a positive byproduct even beyond the borders of that nation. They led to Church expansion in the southwestern United States. Many exiled families provided new vitality and leadership to Latter-day Saint congregations in Arizona, New Mexico, and Texas. Furthermore, in 1915, the First Presidency assigned Rey L. Pratt to take charge of proselytizing among the Spanish-speaking people in the American southwest. President Pratt recognized that throughout California, Arizona, Colorado, New Mexico, and Texas there were "hundreds of thousands of Mexican people, many of them living in towns and communities by themselves" who "never had the gospel taken to them."[17] Now was his opportunity to do so. By 1919, the headquarters of this "Mexican Mission" were established at El Paso.

DIFFICULT YEARS, 1921 TO 1946

In 1921, missionaries were able to return to the Mexico City area. They found that the Saints during the elders' absence had grown in faith and testimony. Through the missionary efforts of local members, many had been converted and baptized. President Pratt dedicated a chapel at San Marcos which the members of that small branch had built themselves. But when anti-clerical agitation mounted in 1926, the forty-three elders serving in Mexico had to be withdrawn again. This new influx of missionaries into the United States enabled proselyting to be opened among Spanish-speaking people in Los Angeles, San Diego, and in most of the communities along the Mexican border. Once again, President Pratt kept in contact with the Saints in Mexico by correspondence as he had done for so many years before.

During these years the respected service of J. Reuben Clark Jr. exerted a far-reaching influence for good on the relations between the Mexican government and the Latter-day Saints. Clark, a native of Utah, had served as the United States solicitor general and as under-secretary of state. The climax of his diplomatic career was his service in Mexico—twice acting as the legal advisor to Dwight W. Morrow, the highly respected U. S. ambassador, and then succeeding him in that position in 1930. The new ambassador was already well known and respected because of his role in successfully resolving claims related to the ownership of oil reserves in Mexico. The First Presidency was pleased with Clark's appointment and personally blessed him that he might "do great good among the descendants of Lehi in that country." The Presidency declared that "there is perhaps no other place in all the world that should be of the same interest and importance to the Latter-day Saints as Mexico, where the majority of the people are of Lamanitish descent."[18] While in Mexico City, J. Reuben Clark often attended sacrament meetings with "the humble Mexican

J. Reuben Clark Jr., U.S. Ambassador to Mexico and later a counselor in the First Presidency, was well-respected for his writings about Mormonism.(© by Intellectual Reserve,Inc.)

Saints, who barefooted and meagerly clothed, met in a small, dirt-floored, adobe house, furnished only with rough-hewn logs for benches."[19] Ambassador Clark developed an unusual rapport with government officials as well as with the people in general. When he left his post in March 1933, an experienced diplomatic observer reported that no departing representative had "ever received such a remarkable expression of esteem from all classes of officials and private individuals" as had Clark.[20]

Meanwhile, President Rey L. Pratt had died unexpectedly in Salt Lake City on 14 April 1931. News of the death of their beloved president shocked the Saints in Mexico. He had presided over the mission for more than two decades, giving inspired leadership during periods of great stress. It would be difficult to find anyone who could take his place in the hearts of the people. In September, a group of local members met in Mexico City to consider the lack of missionaries and of Church literature in Spanish; while convened, they also requested a mission president of their own nationality. This action reflected the intense spirit of nationalism that dominated Mexico during and following its early twentieth-century revolutions.

In February 1934, Harold W. Pratt, a brother of Rey, became mission president. During this same year, Mexico elected a new president, General Lazaro Cardenas, who adopted a more conciliatory attitude toward religious institutions. In this improved climate, Pratt, a Mexican citizen and a legally registered minister of religion, worked to clarify the legal status of The Church of Jesus Christ of Latter-day Saints, its schools, and other institutions in Mexico. He received the cooperation of government officials who recalled very positively their associations with Ambassador J. Reuben Clark, who by now had become a member of the First Presidency. Arrangements were made for the schools in the colonies to adjust their curriculum to more closely follow the government's pattern and for the Mormon colonists to become Mexican citizens, thereby being better able to participate more fully in local government. These improved conditions also made it possible to assign more missionaries to proselyte in Mexico. With the expansion of the work, the First Presidency approved Pratt's recommendation that the Mexican Mission be divided along the international frontier. Consequently, in 1936, a separate "Spanish-American Mission" was organized north of the border.

When plans to divide the mission were first made known in Mexico, many members revived their hopes that a native Mexican might be named to preside over that part of the mission. When Church leaders announced that Harold W. Pratt would continue to preside in Mexico, these members immediately called a convention to urge for a third time that one of their own nationality be called to preside. About 120 Saints met in this "third convention" on 26 April 1936.[21] In violation of instructions from the mission presidency, the conventionists persisted in circulating petitions bearing their demands. For more than a year, Church leaders sought to achieve a reconciliation but with no success. In May 1836, a few third convention leaders were excommunicated on the grounds of rebellion and apostasy. About a third of the Mexican Mission's membership affiliated with the conventionists. Even though they professed allegiance to the General Authorities of the Church in Utah, these members could not support the "Anglo" mission president in Mexico. Hence, they found themselves out of harmony with the regular Church organization. For nearly a decade, these dissenting Saints retained control of several chapels and related property.

Arwell L. Pierce, who became president of the Mexican Mission in 1942, devoted his major effort to bringing the conventionists back into full harmony with the Church. He skillfully defused long-standing feelings of mistrust as he repeatedly demonstrated genuine love and a spirit of helpfulness toward the disaffected members. He held out the goal of eventually having a stake in Mexico under local leadership and appealed to the people to unite in working toward that end.

The climax came on 25–26 May 1946 at a special mission conference in Mexico City. George Albert Smith, the first Church president ever to visit Mexico, was present. At this conference, those who had been out of harmony with the Church for ten years again sustained mission and general

Church authorities, and in turn were received back into full fellowship. A choir composed of former third convention members provided music for the sessions. President Smith, the man of Christlike love, urged in a kindly way the need for harmony and unity. More than fifteen hundred attended the conference. All were proud and honored to meet their prophet and thronged around him. Though ill, he graciously received their attentions, thus helping to cement the new spirit of harmony and love that provided an optimistic outlook for the future.[22]

PANAMA

• Caracas
Venezuela
Temple

VENEZUELA

Georgetown •
GUYANA

• Paramaribo

SURINAME FRENCH
GUIANA

Atlantic

Ocean

Bogotá
Columbia
• Temple

COLOMBIA

• Quito
ECUADOR

• Guayaquil
Equador
Temple

PERU

BRAZIL

Recife Brazil Temple •

• Lima Peru
Temple

BOLIVIA

• La Paz

Sucre •

• Cochabamba
Uruguay
Temple

• Brasília

Pacific

Ocean

CHILE

PARAGUAY

Campinas Brazil
Temple •

• Rio de Janeiro

• São Paulo
Brazil Temple

• Curitiba Brazil
Temple

Asunción •
Paraguay
Temple

• Joinville

ARGENTINA

• Pôrto Alegre
Brazil Temple

Santiago Chile
Temple •

URUGUAY

Buenos Aires
Argentina Temple •

• Montevideo
Uruguay
Temple

FALKLAND ISLAND

CHAPTER 13

BEGINNINGS IN SOUTH AMERICA

RICHARD O. COWAN

1851	Elder Parley P. Pratt visits Chile
1925	Elder Melvin J. Ballard dedicates South America (Dec. 25) for the preaching of the gospel
1929	Missionary work opened in Brazil
1935	Separate Argentine and Brazilian Missions formed
1938	Brazil restricts use of German language
1943	Last missionaries depart, not replaced during war
1947	Uruguay Mission formed
1948	Branch organized at Asunción, Paraguay

More than two decades before Latter-day Saint missionaries entered Mexico, Elder Parley P. Pratt of the Council of the Twelve had become the first to carry the restored gospel to any part of Latin America. His efforts, however, did not result in the permanent establishment of the Church in South America. This would come only during the twentieth century.

ELDER PRATT'S MISSION TO CHILE

Early in 1851, Elder Parley P. Pratt was called to carry the gospel to Lower California, the Pacific Islands, and South America. This assignment was part of a general effort to carry the gospel message to all parts of the earth during the years immediately following the pioneers' arrival in the Salt Lake Valley.

Reaching San Francisco in July of that year, Elder Pratt immediately commenced studying Spanish while at the same time working to strengthen the branch of the Church there. On 5 September 1851, Elder Pratt, his wife Phoebe, and Elder Rufus Allen set sail for Chile. After a tedious voyage of over two months, during which Elder Pratt became ill, the group arrived in Valparaiso on 8 November.

The missionaries found conditions to be very unfavorable. Chile was in the midst of a revolution, so few people found time for or interest in a new religion. This was also a time of personal tragedy for the Pratts; under the most primitive conditions, Phoebe gave birth on 30 November to a baby boy who lived only five weeks. No mail from home came to give comfort or courage. Shortly after the baby's death, the missionaries moved from Valparaiso to the small town of Quillota, forty miles further inland, hoping that a change in scenery might also bring a change in their fortunes.

Elder Pratt studied schoolbooks and perused local newspapers in order to gain a general insight into the "manners, customs, laws, constitutions, institutions—civil, and religious" of "Spanish America."[1] He attempted to learn Spanish by reading the New Testament in that language. He copied some of the more important passages and memorized them by reading them over and over. After several weeks Parley had to confess that his progress in learning the language had been discouragingly slow and that he still could not understand even general conversations. Without having made a single convert, the missionaries sadly left Chile on 2 March 1852, and arrived in San Francisco on 20 May.

Parley P. Pratt, a member of the original Quorum of the Twelve, served as a missionary to Chile in the 1850s. (LDS Church Archives)

A series of letters written to Brigham Young during the return voyage explained Elder Pratt's efforts and the discouraging circumstances, that had frustrated his work: "The civil wars, and my own pecuniary circumstances, but more particularly the want of language, prevented my travelling much in the country, or even visiting the Arraucanian [Indians]."[2] Parley keenly lamented that he had lacked "a sufficiency of the language to turn the keys of the Gospel as yet to these nations."[3] He was especially concerned over the religious conditions existing among the Chileans: "The Bible is not in general use among them, being prohibited by their religion; but I found many who had read it, and all, so far as I tried the experiment, seemed willing to hear it read. . . . I spoke freely to many against their priestcraft and errors; showed them the true mode of baptism, etc., which very seldom gave offense."[4]

Elder Pratt observed that the Chilean constitution established only one religion and prohibited all others. Still, he
noted, there were an Anglican and an American Congrega-
tional Church in Valparaiso. He decried the clergy's charging
for the ordinances they performed.

He had also hoped to go to Peru, but "an empty purse and
imperfect tongue, which has only barely begun to stammer in
that language, together with the want of books or the means
to print them, with other circumstances, all combined to cause
me to wait a little till I could study the language more fully."[5]

Elder Pratt outlined what he believed must be done to
ensure future success:

> I feel as though the Book of Mormon and some cheap
> publications should be translated into Spanish and printed,
> and then the key be turned to these nations while a living
> Priesthood is accompanied by something for them to
> read. . . .
>
> It is in my heart to translate the Book of Mormon and
> some other works, and to print the same in Spanish as soon
> as I have the language sufficiently perfect. . . .
>
> . . . I feel to labor with patience, and to take time to
> prepare the way before me and before those who will, in due
> time, be sent unto them in power. . . .
>
> If the Twelve Apostles will divide the European lan-
> guages between them, and each become thoroughly versed
> in one, so as to translate the fulness of the Gospel and turn
> the keys of the same, it will be one great step towards the
> consummation; for a host of fellow laborers would soon be
> raised up in each to cooperate with them, and these lan-
> guages command the influence and keys of communication
> with most of the nations, tribes and languages of the earth.[6]

Elder Pratt realized that these obstacles would have to be
overcome and that the gospel would eventually be taken to the

southern continent. This, however, would not take place for nearly three quarters of a century, and would begin on the Atlantic rather than on the Pacific coast. Furthermore, conditions facing the later missionaries would be much more favorable than those encountered by Elder Parley P. Pratt.

MODERN BEGINNINGS IN ARGENTINA

The history of the restored Church in South America had its real beginning in Argentina during the early 1920s. The first seeds were sown not by missionaries from North America but by emmigrants from Europe, and not among the Spanish-speaking majority but among a German-speaking minority.

Following the close of World War I, a large number of Germans left Europe in quest of a better future in South America, particularly in Argentina and southern Brazil. Wilhelm Friedrichs, a Latter-day Saint convert, and his family arrived in 1923. Emile Hoppe, whom Friedrichs had converted in Germany, followed soon afterwards. Both were eager to share the gospel with the German community in their new homeland.

In a series of letters to Church leaders in Utah, Brother Friedrichs reported his missionary activities and requested additional help. He explained that proselytizing was complicated because prevailing customs made it difficult to meet people in their homes. "About the things which concern the mission here, it is going very hard because we cannot go from house to house, but can only work through newspapers and at the work places, because one must not go in the houses, but remain standing on the street and make a noise with his hands, and then somebody will come out and take a tract. In such cases it is well, but in most cases they will not accept."

He therefore prepared articles for newspapers, explaining

the Church's teachings and announcing public meetings in his or Hoppe's home.

"In our dwelling here, we have arranged a meeting room, but it is not perfect," Friedrichs wrote. "We have no organ, but when we have been here another three months, I will buy one. We have now joined or agreed with Brother Hoppe so that on Thursday evenings, at 7:00 we will have Bible class in his dwelling. He lives outside of the city, and they must ride two hours with the streetcars in order to get to him, but I will gladly do that if only somebody comes in order to hear the gospel. However, I have full trust in my Heavenly Father that he will send sincere friends who will accept the gospel, for I rejoice in being an instrument in the hands of God.

"The people who have come so far," he reported in March 1924, "were all of the better class, and they are always indifferent." Nevertheless, Friedrichs wrote, "I will do my best in preaching the gospel. I came into this country to prepare the way for others." By August, he was able to report that several German families were reading and believing the Book of Mormon, and that a few were ready for baptism, "but," Friedrichs lamented, "it may take a long time before elders will arrive here to baptize them. Our [daughter] Lisbeth will be eight years on August 26, and she should be baptized too. So we will have 4 or 5 ready for baptism."[7] As a deacon Friedrichs did not have the authority to baptize, so requested Church leaders to send elders. Even though he did not hold the Melchizedek Priesthood and had not received a formal missionary call, Wilhelm Friedrichs nevertheless was instrumental in opening the door in Argentina and in directing Church leaders' attention to opportunities in South America.

In the fall of 1925, the First Presidency announced that

Elder Melvin J. Ballard (center) dedicated South America for the preaching of the gospel on Christmas Day, 1925. (LDS Church Archives)

Elder Melvin J. Ballard of the Council of the Twelve was going to Argentina to open missionary work there. He would be accompanied by two members of the Seventy: Elder Rulon S. Wells, who spoke fluent German, and Elder Rey L. Pratt (grandson of Parley), whose knowledge of Spanish and of Latin American customs would prove essential. To fulfill this assignment, Elder Pratt was given temporary leave from presiding over the Mexican Mission.

They arrived in Buenos Aires on 6 December and were greeted by the Friedrichs and Hoppe families with tears of gratitude. That same afternoon the elders were taken to a cottage meeting in a nonmember's home where fifty were in attendance. Less than a week later, on 12 December 1925, the first Latter-day Saint converts in South America—six Germans—were baptized in the Rio de la Plata.

Early on Christmas morning 1925, Elder Ballard and his companions went to a secluded grove of weeping willows near the banks of the La Plata. After singing some appropriate hymns on this beautiful summer morning, the group knelt and Elder Melvin J. Ballard offered a special prayer, dedicating South America for the proclamation of the gospel:

> We are grateful that we have been chosen by thy servant, President Heber J. Grant, to come to this great land of South America, to unlock the door for the preaching of the gospel to all the peoples of the South American nations; to search out the blood of Israel that has been sifted among the Gentile nations, many of whom, influenced by the spirit of gathering, have assembled in this land. . . .
>
> And we also pray that we may see the beginning of the fulfilment of thy promises contained in the Book of Mormon to the Indian of this land, who is a descendant of Lehi, millions of whom reside in this country, who have long been downtrodden. . . . O Father, let thy Spirit work upon them, and manifest the truth of these things unto them, as we, and thy servants who shall follow us, shall bear witness of thy precious promises unto this branch of the house of Israel.[8]

After praying for blessings on political leaders that the "doors of salvation" might be opened, and that peace, righteousness, and "full liberty for the preaching of thy gospel" might prevail, Elder Ballard concluded: "And now, O Father, by authority of the blessing and appointment of thy servant, the President of the Church, and by the authority of the Holy Apostleship which I hold, I turn the key, unlock and open the door for the preaching of the gospel in all these South American nations."[9]

Elder Ballard recorded that as the brethren reflected on the importance of what they were doing, they felt that as a result of opening the mission, "many Europeans" in this land would be converted, but that, ultimately, the mission's main importance would be to the Indians—the descendants of Father Lehi. They regarded this as "a momentous day."[10]

Next, the General Authority missionaries set to work finding methods of presenting their message to the people. Elder Pratt succeeded in attracting large audiences to his slide-illustrated lectures on ancient American ruins, Latter-day Saint history, or on Salt Lake City. Typically he would deliver a gospel message before showing the slides that the people had come to see. Nevertheless, the brethren discovered that they were not making headway with the more affluent people of Buenos Aires, so they turned their attention to Liniers, a poorer section of the city. Still the missionaries found that most adults were not interested, but beginning in May 1926, they met with success in holding Sunday Schools for the children. Their first baptism came the following month.

Replacements for the original missionaries arrived in June 1926. Called to assume the presidency of the South American Mission was Reinhold Stoof, a convert from Germany. After coming to Salt Lake City, he had kept his German alive and edited a Latter-day Saint newspaper in that language. The day of his arrival in Buenos Aires was marked by a significant manifestation of divine power in the form of the gift of tongues. Elder J. Vernon Sharp, who accompanied President Stoof to Argentina, described the meeting attended by some German Saints and a few Argentine investigators. Elder Sharp was called first to give a talk in Spanish. President Pratt was to interpret the speech in English to President Stoof, who knew no Spanish, so that he, in turn, could give a German translation. As soon as Sharp began to talk, Stoof said he understood perfectly. At the conclusion of the talk, President Stoof arose and gave a word-for-word translation of the talk in German. At the end of the meeting, "great was the surprise of the Spanish-speaking persons present when they found that Brother Stoof spoke no Spanish."[11] This represented an auspicious beginning to the nearly ten years that Elder Stoof would preside over the mission.

The missionaries did not experience success immediately, but following some trying events a turning point was reached, opening the way for the real beginning of the Church in Argentina. Elder A. Theodore Tuttle, who later presided over the South American Missions, related the circumstances:

> In the suburb of Liniers, there was a little Italian girl of perhaps 6 years of age, who came to Elder Sharp one day and said that her mother and father would not let her attend Sunday School. When asked how it was that she was always in attendance, she answered that she and her younger brother would go to her aunt's home and from there attend Sunday School with her cousins. She was advised that she should first obey her parents, which she agreed to do.
>
> A short time thereafter she became violently ill with a combination of measles and small-pox. She became so ill on a Tuesday that she lost consciousness. On Friday, she returned to consciousness long enough to recognize her mother and to say, "What day is today?" Upon finding that it was Friday she said to her mother, "On Friday the missionaries hold a meeting at the home of Sister Molares and if I do not take flowers there, the missionaries will wonder what is wrong." Those were the last words uttered by Rosa before she passed away. Needless to say, this made a profound impression upon all of the family and neighbors to think that the last thoughts of this little girl should be of the missionaries and their work. . . .

Because the family could not afford to pay their church for a funeral, the missionaries offered to conduct the service.

Among those who were touched by Rosa's example of faith

were two Italian men, Donato Gianfelice and Domingo Guicci, and their families. Because neither of the men could read, Mrs. Gianfelice read a Mormon tract to them. As their interest grew, they received visits by the missionaries. Soon afterward, however, they began investigating another church. Elder Tuttle's account continues:

> The pastor of the other church demanded a debate between himself and Elder Sharp. After much reluctance and conversation the debate was agreed upon. When Brother Gianfelice took word back to the pastor, the pastor said, "I'll bet you $10.00 that we win, for I am a native of the country and Elder Sharp cannot have the knowledge of the language that I have." Brother Gianfelice said, "There will be no debate, for there can only be one church, and we do not wager about something as sacred as which is the right church." Subsequently these people and their children were baptized. [12]

The Gianfelice family became a real source of strength in the Church, two daughters eventually serving as missionaries and a son becoming a counselor in the mission presidency.

Elders Ballard and Pratt had remained in Buenos Aires for about a month after the arrival of President Stoof and the other new missionaries. En route home, the two General Authorities visited other countries in South America. Before their departure, Elder Ballard made this prophetic statement to the small group of Saints, then numbering twenty: "Work will go slowly for a time just as an oak grows slowly from an acorn—not shoot up in a day as does the sunflower that grows quickly and thus dies. Thousands will join here; it will be divided into more than one mission and will be one of the strongest in the Church. The work here is the smallest that it will ever be. The day will come when the Lamanites here will get the chance. The South American Mission is to be a power in the Church."[13]

A PERIOD OF SLOW GROWTH

Under the leadership of President Stoof, emphasis continued to be placed on the German minority in Argentina. Of the ninety-six converts baptized during the first five years, fifty were German immigrants, thirty-two were Spanish-speaking, and eleven were Italians. This focus developed a firm foundation, but it inevitably limited the scope of the mission's success. Not until 1930 did Rosario become the second Argentine city to receive the missionaries.

In the meantime President Stoof had extended missionary work into Brazil, but here again the emphasis was on German-speaking immigrants. As had been the case in Argentina, a faithful family played a key role in the Church's expansion to Brazil. In Hamburg, Germany, the oldest son of Roberto Lippelt became critically ill. Just before he died, he related a dream in which his grandparents had appeared to him, told him of the true church, and directed him to contact it at a nearby address. Following the boy's death, other family members followed these instructions and found the missionaries. Roberto Lippelt's wife, Augusta, and his remaining three children joined the Church, but he was not interested. He increasingly resented his family's activity in the Church. He eventually decided to join the German migration to Brazil as a means "to rid himself of contact with the Mormons and start a new life with his family in another land."[14] In 1923 the family reached Ipomeia, a small farming community in southern Brazil. "Here the Mormons will not find me," Lippelt imagined. But, to the contrary, his family was the means of bringing the Church there. Wanting to hold religious services with her

children, Augusta wrote Church headquarters in America asking for literature. Her request was relayed to President
Reinhold Stoof in Buenos Aires.[15] In December 1927, he traveled to Brazil to personally investigate conditions there. In São
Paulo he found the Germans to be quite scattered. He believed
the missionaries would have greater success in the southern
part of the country, where large groups of European immigrants had been settled in colonies by the Brazilian government. President Stoof visited the Lippelt family in Ipomeia,
where he was warmly received. Roberto Lippelt eventually
joined the Church, and some of his descendants became leaders of the Church in Brazil.

At Joinville, where 90 percent of the twelve thousand residents were Germans, President Stoof's public meetings were
well attended. He therefore sent missionaries the following
year. This area became the heart of Brazilian missionary work
during the next decade. In 1933 missionaries carried the gospel
to Pôrto Alegre, a large and mostly German city.

When Reinhold Stoof was released as president in 1935,
the South American Mission was divided to form the separate
Argentine and Brazilian Missions. In 1930 there had been 135
members. By the time of the division the total had reached
329, and this growth continued despite the problems associated with the coming of World War II.

MEMBERS IN SOUTH AMERICAN MISSIONS

Year	Argentine	Brazilian	Uruguayan
1935	192	137	—
1940	597	249	—
1945	801	399	—
1950	1,135	724	467

Missionaries in Rio de Janeiro in December 1939. During 1938 and 1939, the government in Brazil passed a number of decrees promoting use of the Portuguese language. Missionaries, therefore, had to change the focus of their studies from German to Portuguese. (LDS Church Archives)

In Argentina the emphasis had shifted from German to Spanish, but in Brazil Church activities were still concentrated in the large German colonies. As the Brazilian Mission president observed, "we are foreigners preaching in a foreign language (German) which is yet 'foreign' to this country."[16] Actions by the Brazilian government, however, helped to bring about a change. At the time of Hitler's rise to power, some Germans in South America sought to introduce Nazism there. The Brazilian government saw this as a threat to national unity. Therefore during 1938 and 1939 a series of decrees greatly restricted the use of languages other than Portuguese in Brazil. All public meetings in German were forbidden. Literature could not be printed in a foreign language unless a Portuguese translation was also included.

By the end of 1938, more and more members were speaking Portuguese to the exclusion of German. The following year the mission president in Brazil believed the foremost development in the mission was "the rapid change of the work from German to Portuguese . . . necessitated by the effect of decree laws of the Brazilian government." He concluded that these developments had diverted the mission's focus to the younger and more progressive element of the population, where the greatest potential for future growth was to be found.[17]

The actual outbreak of war had a marked impact on the Church in South America. While there was no mass evacuation of missionaries as there had been in Europe and the Pacific, no new elders were sent to South America after 1941. By the end of 1943 the last of the regular full-time missionaries had left for home. W. Ernest Young, who assumed the presidency of the Argentine Mission in 1944, recalled that it was a strange experience to preside over a mission with no missionaries. He traveled extensively to keep in touch with the scattered branches. The local Saints had to assume more responsibility for Church programs. Even though the Church was relatively new, having been in most cities of Argentina and Brazil for less than ten years, capable leaders in most branches were able to keep activity from lagging. The varied ethnic backgrounds of the Argentine and Brazilian populations posed a unique wartime challenge. "We have to be careful what we say," mission president Young acknowledged. "The [Argentine] government has been pro-Axis with a strong German and Italian influence, but the people in general are pro-British and American. There is a conflict of ideologies among our members of several nationalities."[18]

As the war ended, new challenges faced the South American missions. Twenty-nine new missionaries were sent to Argentina in a single group early in 1947. In addition to facing the clergy's opposition to the admission of so many elders at once, the mission president did not have enough experienced elders to become senior companions and had great difficulty locating housing. Nevertheless, most of these postwar missionaries were former servicemen and were particularly mature, disciplined, and fearless.

EXPANSION INTO URUGUAY AND PARAGUAY

During World War II, the door had been opened for the expansion of missionary work into a new area of South America. In 1940, Elder Rolf R. Larson, a missionary serving in Argentina, played in the South American basketball championship in Montevideo, Uruguay; in repeated interviews he consistently identified himself as a Latter-day Saint. Three years later, Frederick S. Williams, former president of the Argentine Mission, moved with his family to Montevideo to fill a United States government post there. The following year a Church branch was organized. Because the Latter-day Saints in Uruguay were all government or business representatives, the Church and its members made a very favorable impression on local Uruguayan officials. In 1947, the First Presidency formed a separate Uruguayan mission with Frederick Williams as its president. The people of that country were friendly and received the missionaries well, and the number of members began to multiply. By the end of 1948, six small branches were functioning in Montevideo with eight others elsewhere in the country.[19]

At about this same time, the gospel was similarly introduced into neighboring Paraguay. Samuel J. Skousen, a former Argentine missionary employed at the U.S. Embassy at Asunción, shared the gospel with Carlos Alberto Rodriguez and his wife, Mafalda, who eventually were baptized. The Asunción Branch was organized on 26 July 1948, and the following year missionary work was opened in Paraguay, under the direction of the Uruguayan Mission.[20]

The formation of this new mission, the arrival of dozens of capable missionaries, and the accelerated rate of convert baptisms represented important steps toward the fulfillment of Elder Ballard's prophetic vision of South America's destiny. Despite these advances, however, Latter-day Saint activities during the later 1940s were still confined to the continent's eastern section. Expansion into the western and predominantly Lamanite regions would come in the following decades. At mid-twentieth century, South America, like Mexico, stood poised on the threshold of an era of unprecedented progress and growth.

CHAPTER 14

GROWTH AND EXPANSION
IN LATIN AMERICA

RICHARD O. COWAN

By the midpoint of the twentieth century, foundations had been laid and the Church was poised for growth in Mexico and South America. This would include an unimaginable increase in total membership and expansion into new areas.

ELDER KIMBALL'S VISION OF THE
LAMANITES' DESTINY

In 1946, Elder Spencer W. Kimball was called to head the Church's Indian Committee, with the assignment to work with

MEXICO AND CENTRAL AMERICA

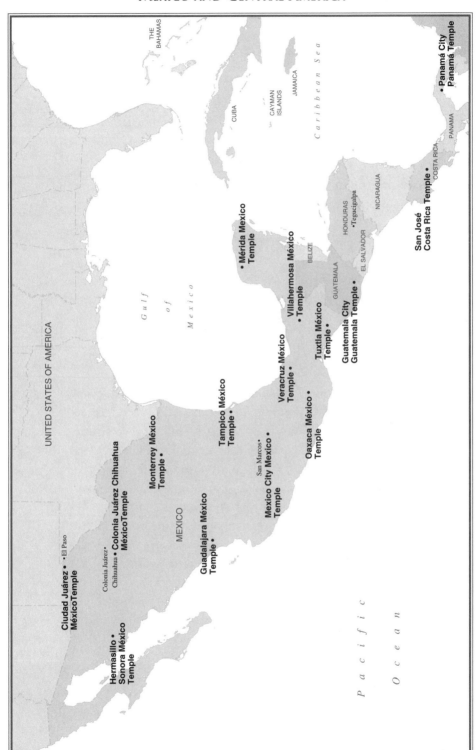

THE BAHAMAS

CUBA

CAYMAN ISLANDS

JAMAICA

Caribbean Sea

• **Panamá City
Panamá Temple**

PANAMA

COSTA RICA

San José •
Costa Rica Temple •

NICARAGUA

HONDURAS
•Tegucigalpa

EL SALVADOR

BELIZE

GUATEMALA

• **Mérida Mexico
Temple**

Villahermosa México
• **Temple**

Tuxtla México •
Temple

Guatemala City
Guatemala Temple •

Gulf
of
Mexico

Veracruz México
Temple •

UNITED STATES OF AMERICA

Tampico México
Temple •

Monterrey México
Temple •

San Marcos •

Oaxaca México •
Temple

Mexico City Mexico •
Temple

MEXICO

**Colonia Juárez Chihuahua
México**Temple

Chihuahua •
Colonia Juárez•

**Guadalajara México
Temple** •

**Ciudad Juárez •
México**Temple

•El Paso

**Hermosillo •
Sonora México
Temple**

Pacific

Ocean

the native Americans of the United States and Canada while taking a special interest in the Lamanites in Latin America and Polynesia. While touring the Mexican Mission the following year, Elder Kimball envisioned a great and glorious future for the descendants of Lehi. He shared this experience with the Lamanites gathered at their annual conference in Mesa in November of that year. Some thirty years later, as president of the Church, he conducted an area conference in Mexico City. As he addressed the large audience, he again told them of his 1947 vision, which he could then see was well on its way to fulfillment:

> Maybe the Lord was showing to me what great things this people would accomplish. . . . I could see you children of Lehi with your herds and flocks on thousands of hills. . . . In my dream I no longer saw you the servant of other people, but I saw you as the employer, the owner of banks and businesses. I saw the people of Lehi as engineers and builders building lofty bridges and great edifices. I saw you in great political positions and functioning as administrators of the land. I saw many of you as heads of government and of the counties, states and cities. I saw you in legislative positions where as good legislators and good Latter-day Saints you were able to make the best laws for your brothers and sisters. I saw many of your sons become attorneys. I saw doctors, as well as lawyers, looking after the health of the people. . . . I saw you as owners of newspapers with great influence in public affairs. I saw great artists among you. Many of you I saw writing books and magazines and articles and having a powerful influence on the thoughts of the people of the country. . . . I saw the Church growing in rapid strides and I saw wards and stakes organized. I saw stakes by the hundreds. I saw a temple.[1]

In 1948 Elder Kimball had further declared: "The new day is dawning. The day of the Lamanites is here. . . . No one else in all the world can satisfy [their] requirements. We [the Latter-day Saints] must teach them the restored Gospel. Our responsibility in this matter is almost frightening. We must not fail."[2]

Events during the second half of the twentieth century represent a substantial fulfillment of these prophecies.

REMARKABLE GROWTH

During the quarter century from 1950 to 1975 no other area of the Church experienced greater growth than did Latin America. Church membership increased from just over 8,800 to 336,657. This nearly forty-fold increase may be compared to the three-fold increase of Church membership worldwide during the same years. While only 0.8 percent of all Latter-day Saints lived in Latin America in 1950, this proportion increased to 10.9 percent during the next twenty-five years. This rapid growth would continue during the last quarter of the twentieth century.

The growing importance of this area was recognized when David O. McKay in 1954 became the first president of the Church to visit South America. The friendly reception accorded him augured well for the Church's progress in that region. Argentina's President Juan Peron invited the Church to hold its conference meetings in Buenos Aires's prestigious thousand-seat Cervantes Theater.[3]

CHURCH MEMBERS IN LATIN AMERICA

Geographical Areas	1925	1950	1975	2000
Mexico	2,500	6,400	141,768	884,071
Central America	—	100	35,851	472,038
Eastern South America	15	2,324	97,244	1,198,301
Western South America	—	—	61,794	1,350,678
Latin America Totals:	**2,515**	**8,824**	**336,657**	**3,905,088**

EXPANSION INTO CENTRAL AMERICA

Developments in Latin America have been characterized not only by an increase in the number of members, but also by an expansion into new geographical areas. Although Central America did not receive its first regular missionaries until the later 1940s, the story began much earlier. In 1935 eighteen-year-old John O'Donnal, who lived in the Mormon colonies of northern Mexico, received his patriarchal blessing. He was promised that "one day he would perform a great work among the Lamanite people in the countries farther south."[4] Six years later he was sent to Central America to work for the United States Department of Agriculture on an experimental rubber plantation. He took advantage of every opportunity to share the gospel and found the people to be quite receptive.

In September of 1946, President Arwell Pierce of the Mexican Mission visited the countries of Central America to investigate the possibility of placing missionaries there. In December of that same year O'Donnal visited Church headquarters in Salt Lake City and urged President George Albert Smith to send missionaries to Central America. The first elders were assigned to Guatemala and Costa Rica the following year. At a private swimming pool surrounded by tropical greenery, the first four converts, including O'Donnal's wife Carmen, were baptized on 25 November 1948.

Missionary work was also progressing in Costa Rica, where the first branch was organized at San José in 1950. The first native missionaries from this country were Sisters Alicia Arrendonda and Cristina Peralta, who were called in 1952.[5]

Meanwhile, in 1949, two elders were sent from the Mexican Mission to begin the work in El Salvador. On 2

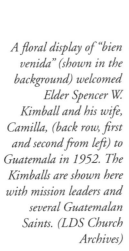

A floral display of "bien venida" (shown in the background) welcomed Elder Spencer W. Kimball and his wife, Camilla, (back row, first and second from left) to Guatemala in 1952. The Kimballs are shown here with mission leaders and several Guatemalan Saints. (LDS Church Archives)

March 1951 the initial twelve converts were baptized in this country, Ana Villaseñor being the first.[6]

The work in Central America remained part of the Mexican Mission until 1952, when a separate unit was created. On this occasion, Elder Spencer W. Kimball pronounced a blessing on the Saints, missionaries, and people of that land to the end that the gospel might go forth in power and be a source of blessing to all.[7]

Soon after the formation of a separate Central American Mission, proselyting was extended into two more countries of the region. In December of 1952, missionaries arrived in the capital city of Tegucigalpa, Honduras. The first five converts were baptized on 21 March 1953 and the first branch was organized the following day. One of these original converts was Jose Ortega, a hotel waiter with whom Elders Spencer W.

Kimball and Marion G. Romney had shared a pamphlet at the time they had come to Central America to organize the new mission there.[8]

The first missionaries arrived in Nicaragua in 1953, one of them being Manuel Arias, a native elder from Costa Rica. The first convert, Jose D. Guzman, was baptized on 11 April of the following year.

From these beginnings, missionary work spread throughout Central America. Emphasis was placed on teaching the large number of Lamanites living in the area. When missionaries began teaching the Indians of the Guatemalan highlands, they found the native languages to be unwritten. With the help of linguists at BYU, written dictionaries and grammars were developed for Quiche and other key Indian languages. This not only helped the missionaries who had to learn these tongues but also paved the way for publishing the Book of Mormon and other literature. In 1966 The Church of Jesus Christ of Latter-day Saints gained the distinction of being the first new religious organization to be formally recognized under the Guatemalan constitution.[9]

Although a branch existed in Panama as early as 1941, for U.S. servicemen assigned to the Panama Canal, regular missionary work did not begin in that country until much later. The first baptism came in 1954 when some of these servicemen shared the gospel with a Cuna Indian working on the canal. Interestingly, this convert, the chief's son-in-law, was interviewed personally by President David O. McKay, who was en route home from his visit to South America. Only after the Church was officially recognized in 1965 did regular missionary work begin in Panama. In that year, the nation also gave the Church permission to work among the Cuna Indians on the numerous San Blas Islands.[10]

Missionary work would not be opened in Belize, the last Central American country to receive the gospel, until 1980. In that year, a small branch was organized, and elders from the Honduras Mission arrived to begin teaching the gospel. In retrospect, the Church's rate of growth throughout the Central America region has been one of the highest anywhere in the world.

BEGINNINGS IN WESTERN SOUTH AMERICA

While the Church was becoming established in Central America, missionaries were also carrying the gospel to the western part of South America for the first time. When President David O. McKay toured that continent in 1954, he favorably considered the possibility of this expansion. Church leaders were impressed with the opportunity of taking the gospel to the predominantly Lamanite peoples west of the Andes.

Following Mark E. Petersen's 1955 tour of South America, Elder Petersen reported: "Peru offers a remarkable opportunity for preaching the gospel to the Indians." He pointed out that over half the population in Lima was of Indian blood and that all spoke Spanish. Even in the interior the people spoke primarily one Indian language and had a higher than average literacy rate.[11]

The decision to send missionaries to Chile and Peru was made during Elder Henry D. Moyle's 1956 South America tour. In each country, a faithful Latter-day Saint family from the United States provided a nucleus for Church activity.

The first missionaries to arrive in Chile spent their initial week at the home of William Fotheringham, an employee of the Kodak Company in Santiago. At a meeting held in the Fotheringham home on 5 July 1956, Elder Moyle officially organized the Santiago Branch with Brother Fotheringham as its first president. "Never in all my experience," Elder Moyle commented, "have I felt the power of the priesthood more in me than when I told them . . . we are ushering in . . . a new era in which the Church will go forward much faster than ever before in South America."[12]

Elder Joseph C. Bentley, one of the first missionaries sent to Santiago, recalled Elder Moyle's visit as follows:

> It was a marvelous meeting. Elder Moyle spoke in what we thought were prophetic terms about the future of the mission. He said that many family units would come into the Church in this country. One of our problems in Latin America had been that it was very difficult to interest husbands, therefore many split families came into the Church.
>
> He then gave us some very interesting instructions—to go tracting in a wealthy section of town, in a middle-income section, and in the slums, and to come back at the end of the day and tell him what we found. We took a map and selected the three neighborhoods at random. We traveled to each by bus, and we never had such success, we were admitted to almost all the homes in all three neighborhoods. We came back that night elated and thrilled to tell him of our success. . . .
>
> We then began searching for a place to live and where we could meet. After two or three weeks we found a house, and as soon as we saw it, we had no doubt but that it was the place where we should be. . . . The house had a living room and dining room combination downstairs where the branch could meet and bedrooms upstairs where the missionaries could live.
>
> It is very curious that this building was just around the corner from where we had at random started tracting in the middle class neighborhood. We went back to these first families and told them we now had a place where they could come to meetings in this neighborhood. We didn't have any ideas as to who would come to our first sacrament meeting, but the place was crowded—we had sixty-five to seventy people. I never had so much missionary success in a single

area. It was as though one street in that neighborhood was unusually blessed with receptive people. In the space of five or six blocks we baptized ten or eleven families, and they were complete families just as Elder Moyle had said. They were all very close to our building so became the nucleus of the branch. In fact, the children of one family became the first native Chilean missionaries a year or two later.[13]

Three days after the meeting in Santiago, Elder Moyle also officially organized the Lima Branch at a gathering in the home of Frederick S. Williams, who was working in Peru at the time. This was the same family around which missionary work had developed in Uruguay a decade earlier.

Elder Moyle pronounced an apostolic blessing on the land and people of Peru as he had done earlier in Chile. The families from North America not only provided valuable leadership experience, but they also served as excellent role models of Latter-day–Saint living for the new converts. The missionaries found the people in these new areas to be very receptive, and in this favorable climate the Church grew rapidly.

At first, proselyting in Chile and Peru was directed by the Argentine and Uruguayan Missions respectively; but in 1959 a separate unit, the Andes Mission, was created. Under the direction of this new mission, the gospel was introduced to northwestern South America beginning in the mid-1960s. Here, again, faithful Latter-day Saint families from North America helped to lay the groundwork.

In 1963, three North Americans living in Bolivia—Duane Wilcox and Dube Thomas in La Paz, and Norval Jesperson in Cochabamba—were instrumental in the Church becoming legally recognized in that country. In November of the following year, the first elders from the Andes Mission entered Bolivia and organized the first branch there in Cochabamba. The first

Bolivian missionary was Desiderio Arce Cano, who was working in Argentina when he was called in 1967 to return to his homeland to teach the gospel. The following year Carlos Pedraja became the first missionary to be called from Bolivia; he was assigned to serve in Chile and would in later years become both a stake and mission president.[14]

At this time, Elder Spencer W. Kimball was the member of the Twelve who was supervising South America. The small Quiriza Branch in Bolivia was erecting its own chapel and was eager to have it ready for dedication by the time of Elder Kimball's visit. When the main roof beam was lifted into place, however, it was found to be two feet too short. Because it would have to bear the full weight of the roof, it could not be spliced, and there was no way a replacement could be secured in time. After a night of fervent prayer, the beam was hoisted into place again and it fit.[15]

Meanwhile, in 1965, four elders from the Andes Mission also began preaching in Quito, Ecuador. Only three weeks later, Elder Spencer W. Kimball conducted a meeting in Quito on 9 October. He earnestly prayed for the people of that land: "They have waited so long, our Father, for the gospel to come to them. . . . We ask thee to bless them, Father, that their hearts may be warmed and that they may be filled with the glorious truths of thy Gospel."[16] Within a month the first nine converts were baptized in Ecuador. Early the following year, preaching also began in Guayaquil.[17]

During 1966, missionary work officially began in the two northwestern countries of South America. For some time Latter-day Saints from North America had been meeting in Bogotá and Cali, Colombia. In May 1966 two elders initiated proselyting in that country. During that same year, Elder

An American missionary, Elder Earl L. Underwood Jr., poses with the Chonay family of Tecpán, Guatemala, on the day of their baptism, 5 March 1960. (LDS Church Archives)

Spencer W. Kimball blessed Colombia "for the preaching of the gospel of Jesus Christ and for the building of the kingdom, because this is the land of Zion, southern Zion."[18]

By 1966, a small expatriate branch was meeting in the home of Carl C. Wilcox, a financial officer of the Del Monte Corporation working in Caracas, Venezuela; on 2 November of that year, he officially became branch president. Four missionaries also arrived during the year to begin work in that country. At first, Church activity in Colombia was supervised by the Andes Mission while that in Venezuela was assigned, interestingly, to the Central American Mission. In 1968, however, a separate Colombia-Venezuela Mission was formed.

Thus, by the end of the 1960s, the Church had expanded into almost all areas of Latin America. The task now became to develop the support system essential for continuing rapid growth.

CHAPTER 15

MODERN LATIN AMERICA

RICHARD O. COWAN

1945	Temple blessings given in Spanish
1947	Missionary work begins in Central America
1954	President David O. McKay visits South America
1956	Work inaugurated in Chile and Peru
1961	Mexico City Stake organized
1964	Church opens college near Mexico City
	Missionary work extended to Bolivia
1965	Work opens in Ecuador, Colombia, and Venezuela
1977	Missionary Training Center established in São Paulo
1978	Missionaries withdrawn from Nicaragua following Revolution
	São Paulo Brazil Temple dedicated
1983	Temple dedicated in Mexico City
1989	One hundredth stake organized in Mexico
2000	Twentieth temple in Latin America dedicated
2000–2003	Eighteen temples dedicated in Latin America

During the later decades of the twentieth century, the Church continued to grow rapidly in Latin America. In the last quarter of the century, the Church added more than three million members in Latin America alone.

Progress in Chile illustrates this growth. The first nine baptisms in Chile came four months after proselyting had begun in 1956. The small group of Saints and converts met at the Prince of Wales Country Club pool on 25 November 1956 at 4 A.M. The sun was just coming up over the Andes as the service began on this beautiful spring morning. The first Chilean to be baptized, Ricardo Garcia, subsequently became a branch president. As others joined the Church, additional branches were formed in the Santiago suburbs and in other cities. When the new Andes Mission was organized in 1959, there were 7 branches, 614 members, and 34 missionaries in Chile. Following a series of devastating earthquakes in May 1960, relief supplies were sent from Utah, and Latter-day Saint missionaries provided valuable help as translators for United States medical personnel who could not speak Spanish. The Church's prompt and effective help impressed Chilean government officials who removed restrictions that had limited the number of Mormon missionaries entering the country. The following year Chile became a separate mission of its own. The first Chilean stake was organized in 1972 at Santiago. Despite political unrest during the early 1970s, the Church prospered. As thousands joined the Church, stakes and missions were divided and re-divided to meet the needs of the growing membership.

At the area conference held in Santiago in 1977, Elder Bruce R. McConkie spoke of a bright future for the Church in Chile: "The day will come when there will be a temple in Chile. I do not say when, but it surely will be. . . . I foresee the day when the seven stakes in Chile will be seven times 70. I foresee the day when the 250 native Chilean missionaries will be increased by thousands. I foresee the day when The Church of Jesus Christ of Latter-day Saints will be the most powerful influence in this nation. . . . The Lord will pour out blessings abundantly upon this nation because of the righteousness of the people who live here."[1]

In 1979, there were five missions, ten stakes, and four hundred Chileans serving full-time missions within their own country; Church membership was more than fifty thousand. In 1983 a temple was dedicated in Santiago. By the year 2000, the Church saw a tenfold increase in the number of Chilean members; they were located in 8 missions and 115 stakes, with 880 ward or branch congregations. The Latter-day Saints, numbering 509,592, represented about 3.4 percent of Chile's population—the highest proportion anywhere in Latin America.

In the face of such growth, the Church faced many challenges in the later years of the twentieth century and the early years of this century: providing an adequate administrative structure and educational opportunities, making temple blessings more widely available, and even orienting local missionaries. In the process the Church overcame a variety of internal as well as external challenges to meet its destiny.

NEW ADMINISTRATIVE UNITS FORMED

As the Church grew, the organization of stakes became a major goal of Church leaders in Latin America. Attaining stake status represents a significant achievement in terms of Church growth and stability. Mission presidents in Latin America played a key role in preparing relatively new members to reach this goal. President J. Thomas Fyans of the Uruguayan Mission, for example, gave leadership responsibility to many individuals throughout the mission's branches and districts, provided on-the-job training for them, and helped them function, as much as possible, like fully organized wards and stakes.[2]

The first truly Latin American stake was organized in 1961 at Mexico City. (The Juarez Stake of 1895 was originally composed mostly of Anglo members who had emigrated from the United States.) The first president of this stake was Harold Brown, former president of the Argentine Mission, who had recently returned to Mexico City. Other Anglos, particularly mission presidents from the Mormon colonies in Chihuahua, provided important leadership support at first. As the stake grew and was divided, however, responsibility fell increasingly on capable indigenous leaders. This posed a challenge because many of them lacked the customary years of experience.

Agricol Lozano, an attorney for the Church and one of Brown's successors as stake president, declared: "The *norteamericanos* have helped us, but we cannot lean on them forever. The Lord gave us our own feet, and we must stand on them."[3] On another occasion, President Lozano said: "A remarkable part of the Church's growth in our area is characterized by the youth who hold important positions in the Church. The average age of our high council is 24 years, and among bishops and branch presidents it is 25 years. Can anyone imagine the inspirational and leadership power these same men will have fifty years from now? Great things are happening and about to happen among our people!"[4]

The rapid growth of the Church in Latin America was the principal reason most local leaders lacked the customary years of experience. In Mexico, for example, ninety percent of Church members in 1977 had been baptized since 1960. The number of stakes in Mexico quadrupled between 1975 and 1977, from eleven to forty-four, and continued to multiply rapidly. The milestone of one hundred stakes in Mexico was reached in 1989. Hence, new converts with great faith and ability found themselves leading congregations only a few years after their own conversion. An example was President Filibert Ledezma of Mexico City's Moctezuma Stake. In 1966, when he was nineteen, two of his Mormon friends took him to a Church social. Soon he was baptized. He was a student at the Instituto Politecnico in Mexico City, overcoming obstacles of poverty to be admitted to this prestigious college. Working his way through school, he graduated with a coveted degree in accounting. He was called as a ward clerk, assistant stake clerk, stake clerk, and then in 1972 became a counselor in the stake presidency. The following year he was called as stake president. At age twenty-five, "he was probably the youngest stake president in the Church at that time," one writer commented.[5]

Guillermo Gonzales, a future stake president in Monterrey, was first contacted by two sister missionaries in 1956:

I suppose they must have considered us "golden" investigators. I was so "golden" I even locked the door of the house to be sure they did not leave before telling us all they knew about the restored gospel.

For eight hours they talked with us about the Book of Mormon, Lehi and Nephi, the brass plates, the degrees of glory, the promises of the Lord to Israel, the welfare plan, the stakes of the Church, and many other doctrines and programs related to the kingdom of God.

I was very impressed and finally asked, a little shyly, "When will we have a stake here in Monterrey?"

It was clear to me now that one of the lady missionaries was trying to obtain a response from the unending source of wisdom which, at the time, was unknown to us. Suddenly there was a change in her whole face. Then, with a smile that lightened her countenance, she spoke, "I

believe," she said, "that within fifteen or sixteen years we will
have the first stake in Monterrey."

. . . [These sister missionaries] did not know that they
had been God's instruments in bringing the gospel to a man
foreordained to become the president of the first stake in
Monterrey—just sixteen years later.[6]

To provide training for these new leaders, the Church created area presidencies beginning in 1984.[7] Of the thirteen areas
organized that year, three were in Latin America—Mexico and
Central America, South America North, and South America
South. By the end of 2002, this region would be further sub-
divided to include nine of the Church's twenty-nine areas.

The call of Latin American leaders to serve as General
Authorities was further evidence of the Church's solid progress
in that area. The first (not counting Anglos from the Mormon
Colonies in Mexico) was Angel Abrea, a certified public
accountant from Buenos Aires who was called to the Seventy
in 1981. During the remainder of the century, a dozen more
Latin Americans were called to the Seventy. One was Helvecio
Martins, a Rio de Janeiro professor who in 1990 became the
Church's first black General Authority. Others included
Church Educational System administrators from Guatemala,
Chile, Mexico, and Uruguay; business executives from Brazil,
Mexico, and Colombia; and two retired army officers from
Brazil. In these callings, these brethren from Latin America
were able to reach out and strengthen the Church worldwide.

PROVIDING EDUCATIONAL OPPORTUNITIES

Church schools have been a major source of strength to the
Saints in Latin America and have played a key role in preparing
future Church leaders there. The Mormon colonists in

Benemerito, a Church preparatory school in Mexico City, was founded in 1963 and continues to draw students from across Mexico. (Photo courtesy Richard O. Cowan)

Chihuahua had established their stake academy just before the turn of the century. Then the small but active branch in San Marcos, just north of Mexico City, opened another school in 1946. In the early 1960s these became part of an expanding system of thirty-eight LDS schools in Mexico. Thirty-four were badly needed elementary schools, usually held in buildings adjacent to branch chapels. In 1964, the Church opened its school in Mexico City and named it "Benemerito de las Americas," ("Benefactor of the Americas") in honor of Mexico's hero Benito Juarez. This campus included elementary and secondary instruction, a preparatory school for those desiring to enter the university, and a "normal" school to prepare teachers. These schools quickly earned the admiration of government officials and became an important source of appreciation of the Church and its members. During the first several years of Benemerito's operation, all but one of the school's graduates were admitted to the university, an unheard-of achievement. Undoubtedly the most important contribution of these schools was among the Saints themselves. Not only did they offer essential education but they also provided opportunities for leadership development. By the early 1970s, most of the leaders in Mexico's stakes and wards were graduates of Church schools.[8]

Meanwhile, in Chile, the Church also established a school system. The first two schools opened in March 1964 following the summer vacation there. At the end of the first year, all of the school's students passed the standardized government exams, another unheard-of record. Incredulous government inspectors went over the tests carefully. Convinced that the results were valid, they invited the LDS supervisor to conduct a seminar for Chilean educators to explain the methods used in the Church schools.

Other schools were later added in Chile and also in Bolivia. By the late 1970s and early 1980s, however, public education was becoming more widely available, so the Church decided to close most of its schools in Latin America and to concentrate on part-time religious education through seminaries and institutes.

The positive impact of the Church's educational system has not been limited to those countries with schools. Throughout Latin America, thousands of students are being enriched by seminary and institute classes. This group is not restricted to those actually attending high school or college; many adult members, eager to increase their knowledge of the gospel, have enrolled for classes as well. Benefits have affected all aspects of Church activity. In 1976, four years after seminaries and institutes had been inaugurated in Colombia, the first group of graduates from these classes noticeably added to the number of local missionaries serving. Not only did their increased understanding of the gospel help them, but their eagerness to study the scriptures carried over into their missions.

The literacy program, developed in Bolivia with the cooperation of Brigham Young University, was particularly beneficial. Through fifteen hours of one-on-one instruction, members were taught to read Spanish. For the first time they could read the scriptures, Church handbooks, lesson manuals, or even general materials needed in their daily work. One branch president said that life had always been like a closed book for him, but he was grateful that now the book of opportunity was open. Those who completed the courses often volunteered to teach others. Thus hundreds were blessed.

TEMPLE BLESSINGS

Providing temple blessings has been another important part of the Church's program in Latin America. In 1945, the temple endowment was presented for the first time in a language other than English. Even though some Latin American members spoke English, many of them did not understand the full meaning of the temple ceremonies as presented in that language. Hence, Church leaders decided to conduct a Lamanite conference and present the endowment in Spanish at the temple in Mesa, Arizona. Following the First Presidency's approval, the exacting task of translating the temple ceremonies into Spanish got under way. Working in the Salt Lake Temple, Antoine R. Ivins of the Seventy, a native of the Mormon colonies in Mexico who spoke fluent Spanish, and Eduardo Balderas, a translator for the Church, carried out this assignment during the next year. "The opportunity of translating the sacred ordinances within the confines of the Salt Lake Temple," Balderas recalled, "was, of course, a wonderful privilege and blessing."[9] He affirmed that the "influence of the Holy Spirit . . . guided them in their challenging but enjoyable labors."[10] The Spanish-speaking Saints were also making their own preparations. Some members living in the United States made trips into Mexico to trace their family genealogies.

The long-anticipated event came in November 1945. Most of the Saints had to make substantial economic sacrifices, some even giving up jobs, in order to attend the Arizona Temple; nevertheless, about two hundred gathered, coming from as far away as Mexico City. Efforts were made to keep the costs down. The local Arizona Saints provided food. Housing was to be in the large Mezona recreational hall, which was divided by temporary curtains into three sections—men's sleeping area on one side, women's on the other, and the main central area for meetings. Members who were planning to attend were not concerned with their personal comfort. A branch president in Mexico reported: "We talked this matter over with our members, and they said to tell you not to worry about it. They will be happy to sleep on the floor, just so they get to Mesa." This, however, would not be necessary. As late as a week before the Saints were due to arrive, sufficient bedding for such a large group had not been located. At that point a Church member stationed at a nearby army base unexpectedly offered the use of two hundred cots and blankets.[11]

A special "Lamanite Conference" convened on Sunday, November 4, a warm sunny day. The Spanish-American Branch chapel in Mesa was filled to overflowing during the three conference sessions. Among Church leaders who were in attendance were President David O. McKay and Sister Belle S. Spafford; their presence meant a great deal to the Spanish-speaking members, most of whom had never met a member of the First Presidency or a general Relief Society president before. President McKay expressed appreciation for being present for an "outstanding event in Church history." He pointed out that other Lamanite groups had enjoyed the temple ceremonies in Hawaii, but always in English.

All day Monday was spent checking recommends and obtaining temple clothing. The history-making Spanish temple sessions began on Tuesday, 6 November 1945. Like little children anticipating the excitement of Christmas morning, the visitors did not sleep well before their day at the temple. "The thought of loved ones waiting, of dreams about to come true, and the nervous strain of getting up early were not conducive to good sound sleep." About 4:30 A.M. "strange noises" were heard from the direction of the ladies' room. Thinking they might be teenagers, a mission president's wife, who was acting as a chaperone, went to ask them to quiet down. She was surprised to find twelve gray-haired women getting ready for the temple! "We came in here early to get us ready because this is our wedding day," said one sister in broken English, "and our husbands are waiting in heaven for this day. We must look pretty for them."

It was not easy to feed three hundred, make beds, and sweep the large hall and still have the people at the temple by 7:00 A.M. Reaching there, they conversed only in hushed tones, believing they stood on holy ground. During the next three days, sixty-nine received their own endowments and twenty-four couples were sealed for eternity. A total of 798 ordinances for the living and the dead were performed.[12]

Those who attended gained a broader view of the Church. No longer was their perspective limited to the small group with which most of them worshiped each week, and their lives seemed to take on a greater purpose and significance. In suc-

President Spencer W. Kimball greets Saints at the São Paulo area conference in 1975. The Brazilian Saints were overwhelmed by President Kimball's announcement at the conference that a temple would be built in Brazil. (LDS Church Archives)

ceeding years, these conferences and temple sessions became eagerly anticipated annual events.

The Saints in South America had to travel even farther to receive temple blessings. They longed for the time when they could have a temple of their own. A wave of emotion swept through the 1975 Brazil area conference when President Spencer W. Kimball announced that a temple would be built in São Paulo. *The Church News* reported: "'I have an important announcement,' he said, making it the first order of business even before the opening prayer. A hush came to the congregation. Every eye was on the President. 'A temple will be built in Brazil,' he said. A gasp could be heard across the congregation. 'It will be built in São Paulo,' the president continued. By now tears filled the eyes of many. They openly wept for joy. There was no hiding their feelings."[13]

The Colonia Juárez Chihuahua Temple was one of the first smaller temples built by the Church. It was dedicated by President Gordon B. Hinckley in 1999. He said it was in Northern Mexico that he first received revelation concerning the construction of smaller temples. (Photo courtesy Donald Q. Cannon)

This temple was completed and dedicated in 1978. Within a decade there would be three more temples in South America: at Santiago in 1983, and in Lima, Peru, and Buenos Aires, Argentina, three years later.

Meanwhile, plans to construct a temple in Mexico City were announced. Complicated legal obstacles had to be overcome before work could go ahead, but ground was broken for this sacred edifice in 1979. This temple, fifth largest in the Church and the largest outside of the United States, was dedicated in 1983. The following year a smaller temple was opened in Guatemala City with John O'Donnal as its first president and his wife, Carmen, as matron.

The final years of the twentieth century brought a burst of temple construction. Sixteen new temples were dedicated in

Latin America in 1999 and 2000. Together with those dedicated earlier and those still under construction, this brought the total in Latin America to twenty-nine, including five in Brazil and twelve in Mexico.

MISSIONARY ORIENTATION

The missionary program was another important source of strength to the Church in Latin America. It was, of course, the means of bringing into the Church the individuals who would become the leaders and stalwart members of the future. During the 1970s, an increasing share of the missionaries were called from within Latin America itself. The proportion of Church members in Mexico and Central America serving on missions rose from 0.12 percent in 1965 to 0.35 percent in 1979; and in South America from 0.18 percent to 0.47 percent during the same years. This nearly threefold increase was approximately double the Churchwide rate of growth.[14]

As the number of these Latin American missionaries grew, steps were taken to provide them better preparation. In Chile during the mid-1970s, for example, mission president William R. Bradford organized a training program for local elders called to serve in his mission. Then, in October 1977, a formal missionary orientation center was established in São Paulo to serve those called in Brazil. Each month, Elder W. Grant Bangerter, the General Authority area supervisor, along with local members of the Church Educational System staff, provided inspirational as well as practical instructions. With the opening of the São Paulo Brazil Temple, the length of these training sessions was expanded from three days to five, and missionaries called from other South American countries were also included.

In 1980, a similar orientation center was inaugurated in

Mexico City.[15] Additional missionary training centers were later opened at Guatemala City, Bogotá, Lima, Santiago, and Buenos Aires. In 1997, a seven-story facility was constructed to house the program at São Paulo.

These local missionaries did not have to bridge the language or culture gaps as did the missionaries from North America. Furthermore, as these indigenous missionaries returned home, they brought testimony, experience, and enthusiasm back to their respective wards and branches. This infused new vitality into Church activity.

SOME INTERNAL CHALLENGES

The Church's explosive growth in Latin America has brought some special challenges. How can so many new converts be assimilated effectively? As the number of wards and branches multiplies, where can experienced leaders be found? How can these expanding congregations be housed? Added attention has been given to fellowshiping new members and to helping them make the transition from their former way of life to becoming Latter-day Saints in every sense. Resident General Authorities and other leaders have shared their rich experience and are providing necessary training and support to new ward and stake officers. In 2002, even a member of the Twelve, Elder Jeffrey R. Holland, was asked to relocate himself and his family to Chile. Elder Holland's role: to give personal direction to the rapidly growing Church in that area. The Church's building committee devised plans for prefabricated or other temporary structures to accommodate the needs of wards or branches until they are ready to erect permanent and more adequate chapels.

A look at membership statistics reveals another challenge. In contrast to the North American Intermountain Area, where

Elder Jeffrey R. Holland, a member of the Quorum of the Twelve, moved to Chile in 2002 to better serve and supervise the growing number of Saints in South America. (© by Intellectual Reserve, Inc.)

approximately 17 percent of all Church members are men holding the Melchizedek Priesthood, in Latin America this figure is only 4 percent. Since those bearing the higher priesthood represent the group from which stake presidencies, high councils, bishoprics, and other leaders are drawn, this means that there may not be enough individuals available to staff key positions. Missionaries have worked toward conversion of complete families in order to secure a more balanced Church membership.

SOME EXTERNAL CHALLENGES

The disruptive impact of political instability poses yet another challenge in some areas. In Nicaragua, for example, a 1978 leftist revolution toppled a long-standing dictatorship. The Church withdrew its fifty missionaries but allowed eight to return briefly to train local members to carry on the work.

Fortunately, Nicaraguan Jose Boza, who had served as assistant to the mission president in Costa Rica, returned from his mission at this critical juncture and was able to provide leadership. Local Nicaraguan missionaries baptized fifty-four converts the following month. In 1982, however, the leftist government confiscated the three LDS chapels, accusing the Church of having links to the CIA. Not until 1989 were conditions normalized enough for the mission to be reopened. In some other Latin American countries, anti-U.S. sentiment has resulted in damage to Church property and even attacks on LDS missionaries. In some areas, missionaries have needed to be withdrawn temporarily, while in others only native Latin American missionaries have been assigned to serve.

Overcoming these and other challenges has strengthened the Church. Its programs are dynamic, its leaders are inspired, and its members are dedicated. The future of the Church in Latin America appears to be bright indeed.

CHURCH STATUS IN LATIN AMERICA*

Geographical Areas	Members	Stakes	Missions	Temples**
Mexico	952,947	195	19	12
Central America				
Belize	2,837	—	—	—
Costa Rica	32,563	5	1	1
El Salvador	90,926	16	2	—
Guatemala	188,531	40	4	1
Honduras	108,217	20	3	—
Nicaragua	41,224	2	1	—
Panama	39,559	7	1	1
South America				
Argentina	320,038	66	10	1

GEOGRAPHICAL AREAS	MEMBERS	STAKES	MISSIONS	TEMPLES
Bolivia	133,170	21	3	1
Brazil	842,296	184	26	5
Chile	527,972	87	8	1
Colombia	139,351	22	4	1
Ecuador	156,988	31	3	1
Falkland Islands	12	—	—	—
French Guiana	251	—	—	—
Guyana	1,251	—	—	—
Paraguay	53,420	7	2	1
Peru	368,568	80	7	1
Suriname	518	—	—	—
Uruguay	80,550	15	2	1
Venezuela	113,652	19	4	1
Latin America Totals:	**4,194,841**	**817**	**100**	**29**

* Numbers are for year's end 2002

** These numbers represent operating temples and those that had been announced or were under construction at press time.

PART IV

∾

THE CHURCH IN ASIA

The continent of Asia is extremely large, encompassing approximately one-third of the earth's land mass and two-thirds of its people. It is a land of tremendous contrasts—from the snows of Siberia to the steamy jungles of the southeast. Asia is also the home to virtually all of the world's major religions.

Latter-day Saints sometimes think of Asia as a new mission area. This is correct from an LDS point of view, but it is far from true in relation to Christianity in general. Asia is actually one of the oldest Christian mission fields. According to tradition, missionaries have taken the message of Christ to every part of Asia, beginning with the Apostle Thomas in India shortly after the time of Jesus. Particularly since the age of discovery, Roman Catholic missionaries have planted their form of Christianity in most parts of Asia. From the eighteenth century on, Protestant missionaries added their strength to the cause.

Asia has not easily yielded converts to Christ. The obstacles to missionary success have been many, including language, well-developed religious systems (Hinduism, Islam, Buddhism, Taoism, and Confucianism, to name major faiths), political traditions that have not meshed with Western thought, the problem of colonialism and imperialism, and general cultural differences. Problems of geography and climate have also been significant.

Of all the Asian countries, only the Philippines can be counted as a Christian nation (92 percent). Christian membership in

Vietnam (at least until the Communist takeover in 1975), South Korea, and Indonesia stands near 10 percent. Taiwan is 4 percent Christian. But other great Asian lands claim few people who follow the Savior: India, 2.4 percent; Thailand, 1 percent; Japan, 0.8 percent; and the People's Republic of China, less than 1 percent. The history of Christianity varies tremendously from country to country depending on politics, local religious preferences, and other cultural variants. For example, the Philippines has been Christianized for several hundred years, but Indonesia's Christian population has developed largely since World War II.

Conditions in Asia since World War II have made it possible for Latter-day Saint missionaries to operate effectively in a number of countries that were closed before. In some instances, new constitutions that guarantee religious freedom have worked to the benefit of the Church; in other nations, the Church is still working toward acceptance and recognition. The Church is today facing many of the difficulties, such as initial admittance to nations, that other Christian groups encountered one, two, or three hundred years ago. In most instances, other churches have their roots firmly planted. The presence of other Christians is sometimes construed as a deterrent to Latter-day Saint success, but in most instances such an attitude is based on a misreading of history. The Saints have gained much from other Christian groups that have translated the Bible, established schools, hospitals, and relief units, and in most cases brought a good name to Christianity. In most instances the Protestants and Roman Catholics have been helpful to our missionaries by preparing the way for them.[1]

Challenges, obstacles, and difficulties notwithstanding, Asia also offers greater opportunities for numerical success in terms of converts than any other part of the world. As will be evident from the chapters that follow, the struggles of the early missionaries were not in vain.

CHAPTER 16

INTRODUCING THE GOSPEL IN ASIA: THE FIRST CENTURY

R. LANIER BRITSCH

1851–55	Elders have little success in India, Burma, and Siam
1853	Missionaries attempt to preach in China
1901	Heber J. Grant heads mission to Japan
1909	Book of Mormon published in Japanese
1921	David O. McKay visits Asia, dedicates China to the preaching of the gospel (9 January)
1924	Japan Mission closed
1937	"Japanese Mission" opened in Hawaii
1941	Attack of Pearl Harbor brings the United States into World War II

Asia includes most of the former Soviet Union, the Near East, India, and China; however, in this chapter we will confine our attention to those few areas where Latter-day Saint missionaries taught the gospel prior to the end of World War II. Included will be brief introductions to work in India, Burma, Siam, Hong Kong, Japan, and a Pacific area—the Japanese of Hawaii.

INDIA, BURMA, AND SIAM IN THE 1850s [2]

India in the 1850s—prior to 1857 and 1858, when the British government took control and made it part of the British

305

Empire—was ruled jointly by the English East India Company and a number of Indian rulers who maintained their positions at the sufferance of the British. The Indian populace generally lived at a poverty level, with only a small part of the people controlling most of the wealth. For most people life was a cycle of sufferings that led nowhere. Society was highly stratified through the caste system. Most people were illiterate. Religion was an integral part of life—certainly it was not considered separate as is frequently thought to be true in the Western world. Whether Hindu in its many varieties or Muslim, most of the populace followed a carefully structured, patterned existence. But the British in India also followed a highly structured way of life. Those who were part of the company's military were closely supervised by the hierarchy within the forces. And those who were employed by the company were so conscious of their position and rank in society that they too had little power over their lives. It was into this kind of a socioreligious situation that the first Latter-day Saint missionaries came in 1851.

Latter-day Saint missionaries followed the British Empire wherever it went, partly because of the protection it afforded them, and partly because the elders believed the British would hear the message wherever they were. Had the British not been in India, it is doubtful that Latter-day Saint missionaries would have gone there during the 1850s. It was from Englishmen in India that leaders in Liverpool received inquiries regarding the Church.

Two English sailors who had been baptized in their own country in January of 1849 were in Calcutta for ship repairs and were the first to begin sharing the gospel with a small Protestant group in the area. The British sailors, George Barber and Benjamin Richey, were eager to share their newfound faith. Neither of them, however, had been ordained to the priesthood so they could not perform the baptisms that at least six people requested. When they arrived back in England, they carried the message that missionaries were needed in Calcutta.

G. B. Wallace, a Church leader in England, sent Elder Joseph Richards to Calcutta, where he arrived in June 1851. He could not stay long because he was under contract as a sailmaker; but before he left he baptized James Patric Meik and his wife, Mary Ann; Matthew McCune; and Maurice White. Elder Richards ordained Maurice White an elder and appointed him as branch president of the "Wanderer's Branch," the first branch of the Church in South, Southeast, or East Asia.

Six months later, in December 1851, a second missionary arrived in Calcutta. He was William Willes, who had been assigned to India by Lorenzo Snow, an Apostle who was then preaching in Italy. Elder Snow also sent Hugh Findlay to Bombay, India, at the same time. Elder Willes found six members of the Church in Calcutta; they were essentially without leadership because branch president Maurice White had left for England to learn more about the gospel. Nevertheless, with the assistance of Meik and McCune, Elder Willes reorganized the branch, established a teaching schedule, and drew up plans for the publication of a tract in the Hindi-Urdu and Bengali languages. He also taught a number of Indian people and baptized many of them. By late March 1852, there were twenty Indian and twelve European members of the branch. Church growth was rapid during the next two months; by mid-May Willes counted nineteen Europeans and 170 native farmers as Church members.

Elder Willes was elated with his evident success and wrote to President Brigham Young in Utah and to Church leaders in

England about what he saw to be a bright future. But almost as quickly as his branch had grown, it withered. The Indian farmers fell away when they learned that the Church had no financial rewards for them, and some of the European members also apostatized. When the monsoon rains came in June, the roads and pathways in and around Calcutta turned to almost impassable muck. Attendance at meetings dropped, and Elder Willes became discouraged. While he was in this state of mind, he was joined by Elder Joseph Richards, who had arrived (in August 1852) once again from England. This time he was able to remain, and he served a courageous mission.

The monsoon rains persisted until November. By that time, the two elders had decided to seek more fruitful fields farther inland. They set out on foot for Agra, Delhi, and the Punjab a thousand miles away. They walked over 620 miles before taking a ride on an ox-drawn wagon. As they traveled they preached the restored gospel. By the time they reached Agra (the site of the Taj Mahal), they had baptized sixteen people. At Agra Elder Richards' health weakened and he decided to return to Calcutta. Willes continued on northwest through Delhi and into the plains of the Punjab. His success as a missionary was limited, however, because the British chaplains notified one another of his coming and restricted his ability to preach to the enlisted troops.

Hugh Findlay had been working alone in the cities of Bombay and Poona for a year. The first half of that year passed without a single baptism. Eventually, however, six people were baptized; and by the end of 1852 Elder Findlay had established a small branch of a mixed birth, European, Eurasian, and native population. He too had many unhappy encounters with military officers and chaplains who did their best to limit his effectiveness.

Originally from Scotland, Hugh Findlay was called by Lorenzo Snow to serve in Bombay, India, in 1851. He later served as mission president in Bombay and defended the Church against unfair attacks. (LDS Church Archives)

Unknown to Elders Willes, Richards, and Findlay—but as a result of Willes's encouraging reports—President Brigham Young called nine additional missionaries to India, four to Siam, and four to China. They were called at a special conference held in Salt Lake City on 28–29 August 1852. It was at that conference that 108 missionaries were called to diverse parts of the globe, an indication of how seriously the Church responded to the commission of the Savior to take the gospel to all the world. In late October, thirty-eight missionaries, bound for different parts of the Pacific and Asia, left Salt Lake City by wagon train for Southern California, and then sailed to San Francisco. At that point the company of missionaries divided. Those bound for Australia found passage on one ship, those bound for China took another, and those assigned to India and Siam sailed together on the ship *Monsoon.* Eighty-six days passed and the devoted elders circled half the world before they arrived in Calcutta on 23 April 1853.

The Utah elders arrived with the expectation of finding a body of Saints almost two hundred strong. To their disappointment they learned that with only one exception the Indian people had all left the Church. Furthermore, because of emigration and military assignments, the European members now numbered fewer than ten; Matthew McCune, their expected host, had been sent to Burma to fight in the Anglo-Burmese War. Elders Willes and Richards were still up-country. Dampened spirits notwithstanding, the newly arrived missionaries held a conference on the next Sabbath and plotted their course of action.

During the next two years, these missionaries, with the assistance of Willes and Richards (who were yet up-country), Hugh Findlay (who was joined in Bombay by his brother Allan), and Matthew McCune (who opened Burma to the preaching of the gospel), traversed thousands of miles of dusty or muddy Indian and Burmese roads, preached in notable and humble surroundings, encountered the highborn but mostly the lowly of India and England, debated the learned and the haughty, published gospel tracts in five languages (and had the Book of Mormon translated into Urdu), and in short, bore a witness to the peoples of India that the gospel had been restored. Before the elders departed for home, most of them having left by 1855, they had crisscrossed a major portion of India. They taught in Karachi in the Indus River basin, Bombay, Goa, and many parts of the west coast, Madras and its hinterlands, Calcutta and its environs, and up the Ganges River Plain into the Punjab. Matthew McCune, Levi Savage, Nathaniel Jones, William Willes, and Elam Luddington worked in Burma. Only Luddington eventually made his way to Siam. He had no success, and the Indian elders had little. With the exception of a brief proselytizing effort in Calcutta later in the century, India remained closed to the restored gospel until the 1960s. But the few tangible results notwithstanding, the efforts of these early elders were truly heroic.

THE CHINA MISSION OF 1852 TO 1853

Although the mission to China was intertwined with the India effort to some extent (the China-bound elders traveled as far as San Francisco with the India-Siam group), this brief mission was essentially a separate experience. Hosea Stout, James Lewis, and Chapman Duncan sailed from San Francisco on 9 March 1853 and arrived in Hong Kong on 28 April, only two days after the India group reached Calcutta. But unlike the India elders, Elder Stout and his companions had no friends to greet them and a much smaller group of Europeans—English speakers—with whom to work.

China was at that moment engulfed in a great internal war, the Tai-ping Rebellion, which lasted from 1851 until 1864. It was one of the bloodiest struggles in history; twenty million people died either in direct battles or as a result of the famines that followed. As a consequence, the Mormon elders were bound to the small island of Hong Kong, which the British had acquired as a prize when the Opium War ended in 1842. The Chinese people were governed by the Manchu Ch'ing dynasty, a ruling house that virtually refused to recognize the reality of modernity or the possibility that the dynasty might be destroyed if it did not accommodate the world order. These problems within China made it almost impossible for the Latter-day Saint missionaries to succeed.

Elders Stout, Lewis, and Duncan considered themselves

sent to the Chinese people. Nevertheless, it was only through the protection of the British Empire that they remained in Hong Kong for even the six weeks that they did. During that time they could not find a Chinese person who would teach them the language (presumably Cantonese, for that is the dialect of that area) for less than thirty dollars a month. The elders had no money. In an effort to use their time wisely, therefore, they preached to the few Europeans who were available. They estimated that there were 250 European civilians, mostly business people, and between one and two thousand British soldiers in Hong Kong. The missionaries were disgusted with the morals of the soldiers and had difficulties meeting with them or teaching them due to heavy restrictions enforced by the officers. The civilians treated the elders civilly but refused to speak with them regarding religion. The Hong Kong experience was brief; it ended on 22 June 1853, after only fifty-six days. Considering the difficult circumstances under which they labored, no one could fault these early messengers for returning home when they did.

After the first attempt in the 1850s, Latter-day Saint leaders observed the rising and falling fortunes of Christianity in China. During the respite after the Boxer Rebellion in 1900, they sent Elder David O. McKay on a world tour of missions in 1920 and 1921, asking him to visit China and the surrounding countries to evaluate their potential as mission fields and to dedicate China if he felt so impressed.

Traveling with Hugh J. Cannon, Elder McKay visited first Japan, where he was impressed by its modernity, then China, where he was saddened by its poverty and starvation. Still, on 9 January 1921, he felt impressed to dedicate the land, and "placing themselves in the hands of the Lord to lead them," he and

Cannon walked through the teeming city of Peking to a tranquil grove in the Forbidden City (the imperial residence), where Elder McKay dedicated the Chinese realm for the preaching of the gospel. He prayed that stability could be restored, that the elders and sisters called on missions would have special power to approach the people effectively, and that the suffering of the Chinese people could be alleviated. "It was such a prayer and blessing as must be recognized in heaven," Elder Cannon noted, "and though the effects may not be suddenly apparent, they will be none the less real."[3]

JAPAN FROM 1901 TO 1924[4]

Almost half a century passed after the India and China efforts before the Church saw fit to venture in the Asian direction again. In February 1901, President Lorenzo Snow announced that the Church planned to open a mission in Japan, with Elder Heber J. Grant, then a member of the Quorum of the Twelve Apostles, as its organizing president. Much had changed since the pioneer days of the 1850s. Utah and the Church had passed through difficult years of persecution. But now Utah was a state and the Church was entering a new era of financial health and international expansion. President Snow was eager to carry the Church's witness into every possible land. Japan, although far from an ideal mission field, was the most suitable country in South, Southeast, or East Asia at the time. While most Asian nations languished in political and economic backwardness, Japan had moved during the previous thirty years from a seventeenth-century state to a modern nation. Of all the Asian nations only Japan had a constitution. By 1901, Japan was riding a wave of growing nationalism.

President Grant selected three companions to go with him,

two veterans of previous missions—Louis A. Kelsch and Horace S. Ensign—and a youngster of eighteen years, Alma O. Taylor. As they prepared for their departure they pondered the unknown aspects of their mission and wondered whether they would be blessed with success. Even President Snow wondered about how much they would accomplish, but he told the elders that the Lord had revealed to him that it was their duty to go. They did not need to worry about the results.

The elders left Salt Lake City on 24 July 1901 and arrived in Japan on 12 August. To their surprise, they were greeted by a hostile Christian press. It seemed that the entire Christian community had banded together to drive the Mormons from Japan's shores as soon as they landed. A newspaper battle between the new arrivals and the established denominations continued for several months, but the Mormons remained, and in time the furor died.

On 1 September 1901, President Grant led his three com-panions to a secluded place in a small grove of trees situated on a rolling hill south of Yokohama. There they sang, prayed, and sought the Spirit of the Lord. When the spirit was right, President Grant offered the dedicatory prayer upon the Japanese people, their land, and the servants of the Lord who would preach the restored gospel there. Elder Taylor wrote that "[President Grant's] tongue was loosed and the Spirit rested mightily upon him; so much that we felt the angels of God were near for our hearts burned within us as the words fell from his lips. I never experi-enced such a peaceful influence or heard such a powerful prayer before."[5] Among many major points, President Grant prayed that Israel might be gathered, that Satan would release his hold on the people, and that the hearts of the people might be prepared to recognize the truth when it was declared to them.

The Japan Sapporo Sunday School on 16 July 1916. (LDS Church Archives)

President Grant sensed that his efforts and those of his companions would bring only slow progress. Nevertheless he wrote: "I have an abiding faith that this is to be one of the most successful missions ever established in the Church. It is going to be slow work at first but the harvest is to be something great and will astonish the world in years to come."[6]

Years of sacrifice and disappointment were required in Japan before President Grant's vision of future success was even partially realized. Probably in no other country have the first Latter-day Saint missionaries had a more difficult time establishing themselves among the people. In the islands of the Pacific and in Europe the elders had reasonable success shortly after opening those areas. But in Japan the language, customs, traditions, and history seemed to be weighted against them. It was only after eighteen months of diligent language study that the first pair of elders ventured out among the Japanese people. Even then the Japanese themselves were not eager to hear the message. Aside from the first two converts, who both proved to be dishonest in their intentions, most of the converts of the "early mission," as it is often called, were slow in coming.

When President Grant was released after twenty-five months in Japan, he was disappointed with what had been accomplished and wanted to stay longer. But he had accomplished much. He wrote a number of tracts and articles, guided the younger elders in their efforts to adapt to the Japanese way of life, and established many mission procedures that gave stability and regularity to their efforts. He also developed a feeling of love for the Japanese people that prompted him to have concern for them through the remainder of his life. President Grant sailed from Japan on 8 September 1903.

Elder Horace S. Ensign was Japan's second mission president. He also authored or directed the writing of a number of tracts and a hymnal in Japanese. President Ensign, like President Grant before him, believed that the Book of Mormon would be of great worth in proselytizing the Japanese. The completed translation was published on 6 October 1909.

The period from 1910 until 1920 was generally uneventful, almost monotonous. A few converts trickled into the Church, but growth was anything but encouraging. More than twice as many Japanese join the Church every month today as joined during the first nineteen years of the mission. By 1920 total membership stood at only 127. These members were scattered in four conferences (districts) from Sapporo in the north to Osaka, southwest of Tokyo. In that year, however, there were only eight missionaries in the field, including the mission president and his wife.

By 1920 President Heber J. Grant, then the president of the Church, was harboring serious doubts about the Japanese Mission. It clearly had not produced as many converts as the other missions that were staffed with small contingents of elders. He wondered whether the missionaries would not be better off in a more receptive nation. When Elder David O. McKay toured the missions of the world in 1920 and 1921, he visited Japan with specific instructions to evaluate the mission and to make recommendations regarding its future.

Elder McKay arrived in Japan on 20 December 1920 and remained in the country for almost a month before going on to Korea and China. While in Japan Elder McKay visited all of the conferences except Sapporo. He concluded that the mission was worth continuing but believed that it needed significantly more missionaries if it was to show more impressive results. It was his suggestion to President Grant and the Council of the Twelve that couples be called to lead each conference and that several pairs of elders be assigned to work under each married couple. Between June 1921 and November 1922, four couples arrived in Japan. The first to arrive were Hilton A. and Hazel Robertson. Unfortunately, the second part of the plan was not fully implemented. Elder McKay envisioned a force of at least thirty-two missionaries, but at its height it only reached nineteen in 1923.

The missionaries followed a set but somewhat plodding course. They proselytized in the afternoon, spent most evenings in Church meetings such as Mutual Improvement Association, taught English language classes at local schools, worked on translation projects, and so forth. The number of baptisms did not markedly increase: ten in 1921, eighteen in 1922, six in 1923, and eight in 1924.

In June 1924 President Grant sent word that the mission would be closed temporarily. He directed the missionaries to return home and sent funds to cover their expenses.

Elder David O. McKay (back row, third from left) visited Church members in Japan in late 1920 and early 1921. He found that missionary efforts were moving slowly, but he wholeheartedly recommended that the mission continue. (LDS Church Archives)

This move did not come as a surprise to President Robertson and his missionaries. They had discussed the matter among themselves for many months and had pretty well concluded that their time would be better spent in other parts of the world. Two events of the past year had also brought to a head the matter of closing. On 1 September 1923, a great earthquake caused terrible destruction in Tokyo. About 120,000 people died in the fires that followed. No Latter-day Saint Japanese or missionaries were harmed, but the disaster caused alarm among the people at home. The elders and sisters spent their time helping clean up the homes of those who were less fortunate. The earthquake's main effect was to cause Church leaders to think more seriously and more frequently about the missionaries in Japan.

A second problem was more serious. This was the passage in the United States of laws forbidding the immigration of Asians, and more specifically of Japanese and Chinese, into

America. The date that the Oriental Exclusion Law went into effect—1 July 1924—was observed throughout Japan as a day of mourning and humiliation. Although the missionaries were not harmed, during the months after the law's passage they were threatened and found signs posted to their doors telling them to go home. Some scholars date the rise of ultranationalism in Japan from this event in 1924. The exclusion law had the effect of turning public sentiment against all Americans in Japan. The result was an even greater difficulty in carrying on proselytizing work. The day of humiliation, July 1, came after President Grant's telegram arrived in Tokyo. The anti-American protests of the day firmed up in the minds of the missionaries the futility of remaining in Japan.

The last Latter-day Saint missionaries sailed on 7 August 1924. From that date until March 1948, the mission in Japan was officially closed. When the missionaries arrived in Salt Lake City, President Grant welcomed them with a grim prophecy: "Thank God you are home because I know what is in store for the people of that land and we are glad you are safely home."[7]

The results of the mission appeared to be small; but there were some lasting contributions, especially the translation of the Book of Mormon and some tracts. Also there were a few converts who remained faithful to the Church through the dark years that followed until the end of World War II.

THE JAPANESE MISSION IN HAWAII

In June 1935, President Heber J. Grant, his first counselor, J. Reuben Clark, and a number of other dignitaries arrived in Hawaii to tour the islands and to organize the Oahu Stake. While they were there they became acquainted with the Japanese and Chinese Sunday Schools of the Oahu District and were impressed to pursue the work of teaching the restored gospel among the Japanese in Hawaii. President Grant correctly believed Hawaii could be the foundation for further work in Japan.

In November 1936, President Grant called Hilton A. Robertson and his wife to go to Hawaii and open a mission among the Japanese there. They arrived in Honolulu on 24 February 1937. Since the Robertsons had closed the Japan Mission in 1924, this new mission in Hawaii was, in a very real sense, a continuation of their earlier work. By the end of 1941, there were fifty-five missionaries serving in Hawaii's Japanese Mission, far more than had ever served at one time in Japan.

The Japanese mission in Hawaii did not produce large numbers of converts. Until 1942, when World War II changed life in the islands dramatically, the missionaries averaged fewer than one baptism each per year. The Japanese attack on Pearl Harbor caused rapid changes in the thinking of the Japanese in Hawaii. Generally called Americans of Japanese Ancestry (AJA), these young people in Hawaii found themselves faced with the seriousness of the world situation and especially with their own plight as people within America's boundaries who looked like the Japanese enemy. They, like many others of that era, turned more seriously to religion. More AJAs—156— joined the Church in 1942 than in any other year of the mission's history. This growth brought the number of members to 302—126 more than the 176 people who had been baptized in Japan during the twenty-three years of that mission.

World War II brought not only rapid growth in membership, but also a rapid decline in the number of missionaries serving. The military draft dropped the missionary force in the Japanese Mission to only four in 1945. Another significant change was the name of the mission. Because the label

"Japanese" was held in derision, in 1943 the name was changed to the Central Pacific Mission (CPM). It retained that title until 1950, when it was combined with the Hawaiian Mission.

Following the war the mission force in the CPM grew rapidly to a high of eighty-nine in 1948. Unfortunately, interest in Christian religions dropped among the AJAs almost as rapidly as it had risen just a few years before. Again, the missionaries averaged fewer than one convert a year. By the end of 1949, there were 671 members on the rolls of the Central Pacific Mission.

The Japanese/CPM accomplished at least two major purposes. First, the mission successfully introduced the gospel to the Japanese people of Hawaii. Since that time many of their number have affiliated with the Church. In fact, the AJAs became extremely visible in the wards of Hawaii, where they have held thousands of responsible positions. The integration of the AJAs into the Church in Hawaii would have come with time, but not as quickly as it did. Second, the Japanese/CPM provided a disproportionate share of the missionaries and mission presidents in Japan after the country was reopened to Latter-day Saint missionary work in 1948. The Japanese/CPM also brought into the Church Elder Adney Y. Komatsu (the first person of Japanese ancestry to be called as a General Authority), Sister Chieko Okazaki (formerly of the general Relief Society presidency), and Sam Shimabukuro (formerly of the Seventy).

The first century of Latter-day Saint missionary work in Asia was not as productive as Church leaders and members would have hoped. Nevertheless, the Church did heed the commandment of the Lord to carry the gospel there. Of the countries discussed in this chapter, Japan would prove to be the most successful mission field during the postwar era.

CHAPTER 17

CHURCH GROWTH IN POSTWAR JAPAN AND KOREA

R. LANIER BRITSCH

1945	World War II ends
1948	Japan Mission reopened
1950–53	Latter-day Saint servicemen share gospel during Korean War
1951	Korean Kim Ho Jik baptized in America
1955	Joseph Fielding Smith dedicates South Korea, Okinawa, and other lands
	Northern Far East Mission formed
1962	Separate Korean Mission created
1965	First Japanese temple excursion to Hawaii
1967	Book of Mormon published in Korean
1970	Mormon pavilion at Expo in Osaka
	Tokyo Stake organized, first in Asia
1975	Elder Adney Komatsu called as first non-Caucasian General Authority
1980	Tokyo Temple dedicated
1985	Seoul Korea Temple dedicated, first on Asian mainland

JAPAN

Following the closing of its first Latter-day Saint mission in 1924, Japan moved steadily into a period of ultranational-

322

ism that eventually resulted in the Sino-Japanese War and World War II. One element of this nationalism was compulsory attendance at Shinto shrines and emperor worship. Officials defined both activities as "devoid of religious significance," while also systematically suppressing foreign Christianity by not permitting the missionaries and priests who went home on furlough during the late 1930s to return.

Despite these problems, the First Presidency was hopeful that work would again proceed in Japan. In 1939 they directed President Hilton A. Robertson of the Japanese mission in Hawaii to visit the Saints in Japan and assure them that missionaries would return as soon as conditions were right. Unfortunately he did not have accurate and up-to-date addresses for any of the Saints he was to contact. He believed that Sister Nami Suzuki, who had been a cook in the mission home when he was president in Tokyo in 1924, would likely have kept in touch with other Church members, so he set out to search for her. Of all the millions of people on the crowded streets in Tokyo-Yokohama, a particular young girl noticed this foreigner. When she asked him if he needed some help, he named the woman he was hoping to find. "That's my mother," the young lady surprisingly responded. She immediately took President Robertson to see Sister Suzuki, from whom he was able to get the needed addresses. "He visited the Tokyo, Sapporo, and Osaka Saints, and assured them that they had not been forgotten and that missionaries would return some day."[1]

As World War II began, things again looked dim for the Saints in Japan, who were restricted from attending any meetings or worship services of any kind. The handful of Japanese

Saints simply had to sit out the war, with the hope that the mission would be reopened in time.

When World War II ended, both sides braced themselves for a bitter occupation; but the Japanese generally found the Allied forces fair and honest, and the Allies in turn found the hard-fighting Japanese to be cooperative citizens. As one of the acts of the occupation, freedom of religion was declared. Even more important, on 1 January 1946, the emperor announced by proclamation that he was not divine and that the Japanese people were not superior to other races. The psychological vacuum left by this retreat, coupled with general popularity of Americans, produced perfect conditions for proselyting.[2]

Edward L. Clissold was one of the key figures in the reestablishment of the Church in Japan. A navy officer in Hawaii, he was simultaneously serving as president of the Hawaii Temple, president of the Central Pacific Mission proselyting among Japanese Hawaiians, and as a member of the Oahu Stake presidency. In 1944, he was trained as a government administrator and sent to Japan at the close of hostilities, where he began working with education and religion departments in the Occupation government. His tour of duty lasted only two months, but he became acquainted with key Occupation officials and several Latter-day Saint servicemen's groups in Japan. In the spring of 1947, the First Presidency assigned him to go to Japan and reopen the mission. His previous association with the Occupation officers proved invaluable as he engaged in the extremely complex negotiations required to obtain entry visas for missionaries and to purchase a mission home, an old mansion that had taken three direct hits during the war but still had solid ferro-concrete walls standing.[3] (This structure was subsequently razed to make way for the Tokyo Temple.)

*Elder Boyd K. Packer
baptizes one of the first
converts in postwar
Japan. (Photo courtesy
Boyd K. Packer)*

The first group of missionaries arrived in Japan on 26 June 1948, after three months of language training in Hawaii. By the end of 1948 there were seven Caucasian elders, six *nisei* (second-generation Americans of Japanese ancestry) elders, and two *nisei* sister missionaries. Their first assignment was to find any former members who were still alive. A few had already contacted the mission. Two elders found some members in the Yokohama area who had been out of touch with the Church since 1924, but who had nevertheless remained faithful.

The new missionaries had several advantages over their 1924 counterparts. The Japanese were much more interested in religion and were searching for a new value system. They also had translated materials: the Book of Mormon, a collection of hymns, and a few tracts. A third advantage was the good example and excellent teaching of Latter-day Saint servicemen. The first Japanese man to join the Church—even before the mission was officially opened in March 1948—was Sato Tatsui, who was introduced to the gospel when on a cold wintry night he offered a group of three Latter-day Saint servicemen a cup of tea. They declined, taking the opportunity to explain the health code by which they lived as part of their religion. Other gospel conversations followed, and eventually the family joined the Church. Boyd K. Packer, one of the young serviceman and a future member of the Council of the Twelve, baptized Sister Sato.[4] Brother Sato organized a Sunday School in Nagoya in 1946 and operated it almost single-handedly until missionaries arrived in October 1948. He later became the Church's official translator and translated the Doctrine and Covenants and Pearl of Great Price, and retranslated the Book of Mormon.[5]

By the time of President Clissold's departure in August 1949, missionaries were proselytizing in at least ten major cities including Tokyo, the world's largest city. In June before he left, he heard Elder Matthew Cowley of the Quorum of the Twelve prophetically promise that there would be "many Church buildings and even temples in this land."[6]

The next mission president was Vinal G. Mauss, a former Japanese missionary, who served from 1949 to 1953. In those four years, Japanese membership grew from 211 to more than 800; four new districts were organized, and the twelve Sunday Schools expanded to twenty-five branches while the little handful of missionaries reached a high of eighty-four. As these statistics indicate, President Mauss introduced solid branch organization to the mission. In addition to dealing with a drop in the number of missionaries at the outbreak of the Korean War, he also supervised the hundreds of Latter-day Saint servicemen and women organized into groups in Japan, Guam, Okinawa, and the Philippines.

But in later years, he felt that his chief contribution was calling local members on full-time missions.[7] By mid-1953, there were twenty young Japanese men and women serving. Almost all of them were supported by the contributions of Latter-day Saint service personnel. Most of these local missionaries later became leaders of the Church in Japan.

Hilton A. Robertson, a man with impressive experience in Asia, succeeded Vinal G. Mauss as mission president. As President McKay set Brother Robertson apart, he told him to preside over both the Japanese and Chinese Missions, and instructed him to make them "expand in excellency, in permanency," specifically charging him to take care of the little group of Chinese Saints in Hong Kong.[8]

Japan was a full-time job in itself; but in 1954, when President McKay sent Elder Harold B. Lee of the Council of the Twelve to Asia, the five Latter-day Saint chaplains and hundreds of servicemen urged Church leaders to send missionaries to Korea. The following year, President Joseph Fielding Smith, then president of the Quorum of the Twelve, visited Asia. Undoubtedly as a result of Elder Lee's recommendations, he reorganized to include Japan, Korea, and Okinawa in the Northern Far East Mission; Hong Kong, Taiwan, the Philippines, and Guam became a second mission under the presidency of H. Grant Heaton. Elder Smith also dedicated South Korea, Okinawa, the Philippines, and Guam for the preaching of the gospel and spent many hours explaining difficult passages to Sato Tatsui, the Church's Japanese translator.[9] At that time, Latter-day Saint servicemen and women outnumbered Asian members (1,600 in 34 groups, as compared to 1,050 in 25 branches), but the signal was clear: Church leaders had a vision of significant growth in Asia.

In 1955, Paul C. Andrus and his wife, Frances, of Honolulu, both of whom had formerly served as missionaries in Japan, were called to lead the Northern Far East Mission. They were struck by the Church's progress in just five years, and their enthusiasm fueled even more rapid growth.

During President Andrus's six-year administration, membership grew from just over one thousand to more than sixty-six hundred. He had his mission adopt a six-lesson teaching plan, where there had previously been none. By converting investigators directly to the restored gospel, using the new translation of the Book of Mormon, missionaries saw convert baptisms jump from 129 in 1956 to 616 in 1957, an average of 5.8 baptisms per missionary.[10]

President Andrus concentrated proselytizing efforts in large cities and soon saw five branches each in Tokyo, Japan; Osaka-Kobe, Japan; and Seoul, Korea. These branches became the nuclei for stakes in all three cities. He also set up a two-year program for priesthood advancement that brought the number of Japanese and Korean Melchizedek Priesthood holders to more than 350, making it possible to place local members in 75 to 80 percent of all branch and district positions—freeing many missionaries for proselytizing.

Indefatigable, President Andrus poured his efforts into making Church materials available to members. He purchased twenty-three chapel sites to house the growing local units— thirty-seven branches in Japan and Okinawa by 1962, and seven in Korea. These properties, obtained with real effort and considerable expenditure of time, later became the basis for a large building program.

President Andrus was particularly anxious to obtain a suitable site as a showplace to represent the Church well in Tokyo, the largest city in the world. He found a 30,000-square-foot property adjacent to the well-known Meiji shrine, but it was selling for more than $670,000. Elder Gordon B. Hinckley, on his first tour of Asia, was concerned about the price, but promised to seek approval for the purchase. This property became the meeting place for the Central Branch, but also proved to be an excellent investment. The Church would sell it in 1973 for $24,150,943.40.[11]

In 1961, the new mission president was Dwayne N. Andersen, a former missionary in Japan. It was a time of transition. Korea became a separate mission, and a uniform, Churchwide proselytizing plan had just been introduced. Chapels were badly needed. By the next spring, the First Presidency and the Council of the Twelve approved the construction of five buildings—two of them in Tokyo—using building missionaries.[12]

Here President Andersen ran into a problem. Japanese society held manual labor in low esteem, and many members were reluctant to accept calls as building missionaries. Again the Latter-day Saint servicemen and women set an inspiring example, colonels and privates working side by side on the sites. Furthermore, since the time of President Mauss, they had selflessly poured thousands of dollars into the mission building fund for chapels that would not be built until long after they left the area. This fund was the financial foundation of a building program that produced, in President Andersen's time alone, nine new chapels, two more remodeled, and seven building sites purchased.

President Andersen worked hard to train local leaders. He

selected two members, Watanabe Kan and Yamada Goro, as his counselors, and took them with him on his tours of the mission, explaining Church policies, procedures, and organizations. Both men have since served as mission presidents and in other assignments. In 1962 there were 355 Melchizedek Priesthood holders in Japan; in 1965, there were 584.[13]

Perhaps the most significant event of President Andersen's administration was the first temple excursion to Hawaii. One hundred seventy people pledged themselves to prepare financially and spiritually for the trip, planned for the summer of 1965. Japan Air Lines agreed to charter a jetliner for $273 per person, round trip.

As the jetliner flew over Pearl Harbor in July 1965, one of the 166 participants wondered how these people who had been bombed by his countrymen would receive them. He need not have worried. The Hawaiian Saints turned out en masse to greet them, piling their necks high with leis and embracing them warmly. Elder Gordon B. Hinckley, the member of the Twelve assigned to supervise Asia, joined them in the temple and sealed some of the couples.[14] The spiritual experiences and the leadership training sent a soberly committed group of Saints back to Japan, the first of almost yearly charter groups that continued to travel to Hawaii until July 1979, the last charter trip before completion of the Tokyo temple.

The next president, Adney Yoshio Komatsu, focused on intensifying, deepening, and training the members to be capable of providing the leadership necessary to function as a stake. Japan got its own translation and distribution services, with Watanabe Kan hired as the full-time manager in 1967. His highly motivated employees produced more than four thousand pages of newly translated materials in the first five months of production.[15] President Komatsu also laid the groundwork for the division of Japan into two missions, which would come in 1968 upon his release.

Since 1960, Elder Hinckley had handled Asia alone. Elder Marion D. Hanks was assigned to help supervise the missions in 1965. And in April 1967, Hugh B. Brown, first counselor in the First Presidency, visited Japan. He was thrilled with the devotion and number of members, and as he dedicated the Abeno Branch chapel in Osaka on 21 April, he prophesied "in the name of the Lord" that "some of you who are listening to me tonight will live to see the day when there will be a Japanese man in the Council of the Twelve Apostles of the Church."[16]

That prophecy may have been partially fulfilled in 1975 when President Komatsu was called as an General Authority, to be joined in 1977 by Yoshihiko Kikuchi, then serving as president of the Tokyo Stake; although neither was a member of the Council of the Twelve, both traveled as assistants to that body.

For President Komatsu, his call as a General Authority was another event in a series of significant "firsts" in his life. He was the first *nisei* (second-generation Americans of Japanese ancestry) to serve as an Asian mission president and the first product of the Japanese-Central Pacific Mission in Hawaii so to serve. He was the first mission president in Japan who had not served a full-time mission as a young man. A convert, he had encountered the Church through a basketball program directed by the CPM missionaries and had joined the Church in 1941 over the opposition of his widowed Buddhist mother. He promised that if she let him join, he would stop going immediately if she ever heard that he was "playing around and not doing anything good . . . and . . . bringing embarrassment upon you."[17] After the war, he served as a counterintelligence officer with the United States Occupation Forces in Japan and gained fluency in Japanese. He was serving as a bishop in Honolulu when he was called as mission president. When he was called as an Assistant to the Quorum of the Twelve in 1975, he became the first American of Japanese ancestry and the first non-Caucasian to be so called.

Another mission highlight came in February 1968 when Elder Spencer W. Kimball arrived on a non-official visit just when the mission leaders in Tokyo needed encouragement in adapting their organization to the stake model. Meeting with all district and branch presidencies in Tokyo, Elder Kimball was impressed to say, "Ninety-five percent of you have been to the temple. This is better than many stakes of Zion that I know of within comparable distance of a temple." Then to President Komatsu, he said, "Let's talk stake now, not a year from now."[18] He urged them to follow stake procedures as closely as possible. Two years later, the first Japanese stake was organized in Tokyo.

As President Komatsu prepared to end his term of service, Japan had nearly twelve thousand members in fifty-one branches and ten districts. On 1 September 1968, the Northern Far East Mission was divided to become the Japan Mission with headquarters in Tokyo, and the Japan-Okinawa Mission with headquarters in Osaka. Since then, missions and stakes have divided at an accelerating pace.

The decade of the 1970s began with a flourish with the Church's sponsoring an exhibit at Expo '70, the World's Fair, in Osaka. At Elder Hinckley's insistence, the Church's pavilion was constructed among the Japanese exhibits, not in the American section. It was a modern, two-story building topped with an eight-foot fiberglass replica of the Salt Lake Temple's angel Moroni. Strategically placed near the Japanese, Russian, and United States exhibits, it drew over 6.5 million visitors in six months; 780,000 left their names and addresses for missionaries. Elder Bernard P. Brockbank, Assistant to the Twelve and director of the pavilion, noted that the missionaries, courteous and fluent in Japanese, Chinese, and Korean, impressed the people with their love.[19]

The Tokyo Stake was organized on 15 March 1970, the same week the pavilion at the Expo was dedicated. The Japan East Mission, headquartered at Sapporo, was created on 16 March, followed by the Japan West Mission headquartered at Fukuoka on 18 March. From then on, almost all of the mission and stake leaders called have been Japanese or Americans of Japanese ancestry. Russell N. Horiuchi, first president of the Japan East Mission and a professor of geography at BYU, came from Lahaina, Maui. Many other *niseis* followed as presidents of the various missions.

But the stake leadership showed that Japanese members had come of age. Breaking the pattern of American leadership, the leadership of the Tokyo Stake was entirely Japanese. Tanaka Kenji, who had joined the Church in 1952 and would later serve as president of the Japan Nagoya Mission, was sustained president with Kikuchi Yoshihiko, later the first Asian-born General Authority in the Church, as first counselor and Sagara Kenichi as second counselor. Watanabe Kan, called as the Japan West Mission's first president, was the first native Japanese mission president.

President Komatsu retained his ties with Japan by serving as Regional Representative for Japan and Hawaii from 1970 to 1975, then returned to Japan as Asia's resident supervising

*The Tokyo Japan Temple
was the first built in Asia.
Dedicated in 1980 by
President Spencer W.
Kimball, it was said to be
the most earthquake-
proof building in Tokyo.
(Photo courtesy Donald
Q. Cannon)*

General Authority. Elder Komatsu was replaced in this assignment by Elder Kikuchi in the summer of 1978.

On 8–10 August 1975, thousands of members and friends
gathered in Tokyo's Budokan, a large cultural facility constructed for the Olympics, for the worldwide Church's seventh
area conference. President Kimball announced the proposal for
a Tokyo temple to serve the Asian Saints, an announcement
that was greeted by spontaneous applause, unusual in any
Church meeting and particularly from the restrained and deco-
rous Japanese people. Many wept with joy. The stake and mission presidents had, on the day before, accepted the challenge
to raise 20 percent of the estimated nine million dollar cost.
Elder Gordon B. Hinckley, chairman of the Church temple
committee, had begun the contributions by presenting
President Kimball with a $100 bill. At the conclusion of the

last session, with 12,300 people in attendance, many wept as they spontaneously sang, "We Thank Thee, O God, for a Prophet."[20]

The faithful Saints contributed many thousands of dollars above the assigned quota for the Tokyo temple.

At the dedication, only thirty-five Church members could sing in the choir because the celestial room was so small. Elder Mark E. Petersen of the Council of the Twelve recorded that "it seemed that there was a far larger choir singing than was present, and various people thought there must have been an angelic choir singing with our little choir because of the beauty of the music and the volume that was heard. The Spirit was so strong that everybody burst into tears, including the members of the choir, who literally sang through their tears."[21]

The temple was dedicated by President Spencer W. Kimball in October 1980.

Dwayne N. Andersen, former missionary and mission president in Japan, was called to be the temple's first president. Since his release in 1982, the temple has been presided over only by presidents of Japanese heritage, including Elder Kikuchi. On 11 June 2000, a second Japanese temple was dedicated in Fukuoka in southern Japan.

By the end of the twentieth century, Japan had far surpassed the milestone of being home to 100,000 members.

THE CHURCH IN KOREA

Korea first encountered Christianity when a book written by a Jesuit missionary in China arrived in 1631. A century later, the first Catholic priest to enter Korea was astonished to find an established Catholic community numbering more than four thousand. Protestants tried to establish missions in 1832 and again, this time successfully, in 1886. They translated the New Testament in 1889.

In 1910, Japan annexed Korea. Thus, Christian missionaries—who were despised throughout the rest of Asia—had some success in Korea because they were identified with Korea's struggle for nationalism rather than with western colonialists. This remained true in the brief period between Korea's liberation from Japan at the end of World War II in 1945 and the outbreak of the Korean War in 1950, when Communists from North Korea invaded the south. Because the Christians were persecuted by the Communists, they were again identified with nationalism. Ironically, it was war with all its horrors and misery that first introduced the restored gospel to Korea. Latter-day Saint servicemen were respected both as Americans and as Christians.

As the war went on in his homeland, Kim Ho Jik, a high-ranking government official of unusual talent, was attending Cornell University in New York. A fellow student, Oliver Wayman, befriended him and asked him to attend Latter-day Saint meetings. Brother Wayman gave Dr. Kim a copy of James E. Talmage's *Articles of Faith*. Dr. Kim read it in a week and asked for more information. The Book of Mormon followed. For some weeks he attended both Presbyterian and Latter-day Saint services on Sunday. Then, on the day Brother Wayman was leaving Cornell, he met Dr. Kim in the corridor and "felt impelled to ask [him] if he knew why he had left his home, family, and a good position in Korea to come to the U.S. . . . I then bore my testimony of the gospel and told him that it was my opinion that the Lord had moved upon him to come to America . . . that he might receive the gospel and take it back to his people."[22]

Dr. Kim reread the Book of Mormon and received a very strong confirmation of its truthfulness. In the summer of 1951, he was baptized in the Susquehanna River near the site of Joseph Smith's own baptism. As he emerged from the water, he heard a voice: "Feed my sheep. Feed my sheep."

After receiving his Ph.D. in nutritional science, he returned home to Korea in September 1951. From that time, he never hesitated to use his influence on the Church's behalf. As a university president and vice-minister of education, he held the highest government rank of any Church member in Asia.[23]

The first baptisms in Korea took place on 3 August 1952. By the next September, more than twenty other Koreans joined the Church at Pusan. In May 1953, Dr. Kim was ordained an elder and set apart as a special counselor in the Korea servicemen's group presidency.[24]

When the cease-fire in 1953 permitted refugees to return to their homes, most of the members of the Church returned to Seoul. After meeting for a few months with servicemen, they created the first truly Korean Sunday School in February 1954, with Brother Kim as superintendent. By April more than sixty people were attending regularly.[25]

In 1954 the Republic of Korea (South Korea) was only one of the countries in the Far East (Japanese) Mission. As mentioned earlier, in July and August 1955, President Joseph Fielding Smith toured East Asia and divided the mission. Korea became part of the Northern Far East Mission, with President Hilton A. Robertson continuing to serve. On the morning of 2 August 1955, in Seoul, President Smith told President Robertson and Colonel Robert H. Slover, servicemen's coordinator, that he felt it was time to dedicate the land of Korea for the preaching of the gospel. Brother Kim and several servicemen joined President Smith in prayer on a hill overlooking the city and heard him as he "literally commanded Satan to free the land from his chains that it might become choice through the preaching of the gospel of Jesus Christ."[26] (The first area conference in Korea would be held in a building at the foot of this hill in 1975.)

Although the Church had no legal status or ecclesiastical organization in Korea, President Smith set Brother Kim apart as president of the Korea District of the Northern Far East Mission. He also directed the organization of branches in Seoul and Pusan and gave guidelines in preparation for the coming of full-time missionaries—a remarkable vision considering that there were only sixty Korean Saints in the country.

When Paul C. Andrus began serving as mission president in Tokyo in December 1955, he visited Korea almost immediately. With Brother Kim's help, the obstacles of legally incorporating the Church, finding housing for the missionaries, and obtaining visas melted away.[27] The first two elders arrived in April 1956 and began work in Seoul.

Learning the difficult Korean language proved to be one of the greatest challenges facing the missionaries. They had no translated materials for over a year. Brother Kim translated the Articles of Faith and the sacrament prayers, and finally, in September 1957, the first Korean pamphlets came off the press, replacing the Japanese tracts that the elders had been using. Nevertheless, President Andrus reported a baptismal rate of eighteen converts per missionary per year. "If Korea had been a separate mission at the time," remembers President Andrus, "they would have had the highest rate of conversion of any mission in the world."[28] By the time a separate Korean

Spencer J. Palmer signs his book for a few Korean Saints. He served as chaplain, mission president, and temple president in Seoul and was beloved by the Korean Saints. (Photo courtesy Donald Q. Cannon)

mission was organized in 1962, it had more than sixteen hundred members.

Surprisingly, four out of five of those baptized were men—many of them young—and, in the late 1970s, the ratio of converts was still 55 percent male to 45 percent female. The explanation is probably a combination of Korea's male-oriented society and the deliberate efforts of the missionaries to reach potential priesthood holders.

The first president of the Korean Mission was Gail E. Carr, who had served a mission in the country just three years earlier. Its five branches were staffed almost entirely by Korean members, an unusual level of maturity for an infant mission. President Carr purchased land only ten minutes from the business and government district, which would house a mission home and office, a chapel, a translation and distribution building, and a missionary dormitory. He purchased land for other chapels, organized two new branches, and authorized the translation of a hymnal. He also assigned Chung Tai Pan to translate the Book of Mormon in 1963; he later appointed Han In Sang, one of the first converts and the second Korean to serve a mission, to revise and complete it in 1964. Han finished his work after his release from his full-time mission, and the Book of Mormon was published in Seoul in March 1967.

Spencer J. Palmer, a specialist in Korea studies and world religions, followed President Carr in July 1965.[29] President Palmer participated in the Korean Branch of the Royal Asiatic Society, hosted numerous social gatherings for government officials, academicians, and diplomats at the mission home, and introduced weekly broadcasts of the Mormon Tabernacle Choir program with translations of Richard L. Evans's "Spoken Word." All of these endeavors provided good publicity for the Church. The number of converts dropped from its previous climb—at least partly because of Korea's growing affluence—but the average age of new converts rose by more than five years between 1965 and 1968. This occurred as families came into the Church, giving it a solid image rather than the youthful one it had previously presented.[30] By 1968, the Church was established in every major Korean city and in all provincial capitals.

Robert H. Slover, the Latter-day Saint servicemen's coordinator who had set up President Smith's visit, accepted a call as the next president of the Korean mission. During his term, the number of missionaries increased from 75 to approximately 125. Also, the rate of converts per missionary rose again, partly because the Language Training Mission at the Church College

This chapel in Seoul, Korea, was built in the late 1980s and reflects the steady growth of the Church in Korea. (Photo courtesy Donald Q. Cannon)

of Hawaii provided elders and sisters with some exposure to Korean. President Slover also personally reached out to the community, speaking to many civic and social groups.

One of the most important projects was translating Church materials. The Korean Doctrine and Covenants and Pearl of Great Price, largely retranslated from a 1961 version begun by Chung Tai Pan, came off the press at the beginning of President Slover's term in 1968. In 1967, Han In Sang took charge of the Translation Services Department, which began producing the standard manuals of the Church and other materials in Korean.[31]

Housing the growing branches was a constant challenge, as Korea ranked right behind densely populated Japan and Hong Kong in terms of the difficulty of acquiring property. Each mission president made some purchases and supervised some construction, but money was still scarce. Until 1971, the few chapels constructed owed their existence mostly to the generosity of the Latter-day Saint servicemen. In fact, into the 1980s they continued to contribute significant amounts toward building projects.

Under President Slover's direction, the first Korean Saints were able to go to the temple, a process fraught with almost unbelievable challenges. Money and spiritual preparation were problems, but the biggest difficulty was the emigration policy that forbade couples to leave the country. For over a year, President Slover and a Church legal advisor, Koo Joong Shik, met with virtually everyone of influence to beg permission for the six temple-bound couples to leave the country. Finally, the policy was relaxed and the couples flew to Hawaii on 31 July 1971. The second group left about a year later, again after much negotiation. To get permission for a third group, the next mission president, L. Edward Brown, had to agree to stop applying for passports.

President Brown welcomed the opportunity to begin seminary and institute classes. Brown had the same strong academic qualifications as his predecessors and, as a former Korean missionary, understood the importance of education to Korean members. Thanks to his background, he successfully insisted that the first institute director be Korean rather than American; and Rhee Ho Nam, one of the earliest members of the Church, counselor to four mission presidents and professor of English and Spanish at a university in Seoul, was appointed as such. The first class brought more than a hundred students, rather than the five or ten that might have been expected. The Mormon Institute, respectably housed in a downtown building, almost immediately became a prestigious educational program.[32]

President Brown's great contribution was his emphasis on family unity and priesthood organization. Determined to make the gospel a natural part of the Korean Saints' lives, he saw it as a "third" culture, neither American nor Korean. Into the natural strength of the Korean family tradition he built a love and respect that had sometimes been lacking among customarily dictatorial fathers. President Brown also successfully taught respect among priesthood bearers.

All of these developments were preparations for stakes being organized, a goal established by President Slover, who maintained his tie with Korea by serving as its Regional Representative in 1972. In February 1973, President Brown received word that the president of the Council of the Twelve, then Spencer W. Kimball, would organize a stake at Seoul in March. He called Rhee Ho Nam as the first president.

The next month, President Brown received word that the mission would be divided; but because the consulate in San Francisco refused to allow visas to thirty missionaries at once, the plan was suspended until after Eugene P. Till became president in July 1974. President Till worked hard to promote the image of the Church as a "family" organization. This concept appealed to the government and, along with some personnel changes in San Francisco, dissolved the visa problems. In the spring of 1975, Han In Sang was called as the first president of the soon-to-be created Korea Pusan Mission, the first native Korean to so serve.

At the area conference in Seoul on 15–17 August 1975, the seven thousand Saints who attended had mixed feelings when President Kimball announced the Tokyo Temple. If the

Dedicated by President Gordon B. Hinckley in 1985, the Seoul Korea Temple was the first temple built on the Asian mainland. (© by Intellectual Reserve, Inc.)

government would not let couples leave the country, their financial sacrifices in contributing to that temple would be for naught.

President Kimball, knowing of this policy, promised the Saints that the Lord would provide a way for them to go to the temple when it was completed if they would keep the commandments. Many Korean Saints followed President Kimball's counsel by donating to the Tokyo Temple, paying their tithes and offerings, sending their children on missions, and carrying out their callings in the Church. Their faithfulness was rewarded as the prophet's words were fulfilled two years later. In the summer of 1977, Park Chung-Hee, president of the Republic of Korea, announced that couples would be able to leave Korea as tourists beginning in 1980—the year in which the temple was scheduled to be completed.

344

The dedication of the Tokyo Temple in 1980 left the Korean Saints anxious for a temple of their own. The Lord soon heard their prayers. On 1 April 1981, President Kimball announced plans for the Seoul Korea Temple. Deeply grateful, the Saints of Korea contributed four times the amount of their share of the building costs within a few months. The temple was dedicated in 1985, with Robert H. Slover as the first temple president and his wife, Rosemarie, as its first matron.

Church administration in Korea had long been closely tied to Japan. But after 1978, Korea had its own Regional Representatives. Since 1995, when Area Authorities were instituted in place of Regional Representatives, Koreans have held these positions. On 1 June 1991, Han In Sang became the first Korean to serve as a General Authority when he was called to the Second Quorum of the Seventy.

Enthusiasm for the new temple helped Church membership to grow from around eleven thousand in 1977 to more than forty thousand in 1985. Church membership in Korea has continued to grow at a promising rate since that time. By the end of the century, Korea had seventeen stakes, four missions, and more than seventy thousand members. Expectations for continued growth are positive.

CHAPTER 18

POSTWAR DEVELOPMENTS IN THE CHINESE REALM AND THE PHILIPPINES

R. LANIER BRITSCH

THE CHINESE REALM

Almost one hundred years passed between Hosea Stout's departure from Hong Kong in 1853 and the arrival of the next

Elder Gordon B. Hinckley (back row, second from left) with a group of servicemen from the USS Kitty Hawk *in Hong Kong on 15 April 1964. Elder Hinckley supervised the missions of Asia from 1960 until 1968. (LDS Church Archives)*

group of Latter-day Saint missionaries in 1949. From the 1840s until 1949, China was in almost continual war and tumult.

Protestant missionaries had "followed the flag" into China in 1842 as Western nations expanded business interests there. Of them, 188 were killed during the Boxer Rebellion in 1900, but others came to China after the rebellion; possibly sixteen thousand Protestant and Catholic missionaries were working there in 1925. Many were forced out by the Sino-Japanese War of 1937–45, but began to return afterwards. Before they could become fully organized, however, the Communists took over in 1949. By 1953, most missionaries were out of the country. They left behind them around 4 million Christian Chinese;

that number has since expanded manyfold, to over 65 million by the beginning of the twenty-first century.

On 14 July 1949, Elder Matthew Cowley, then president of the Asian and Pacific Missions, offered a second prayer (Elder McKay having dedicated China in 1921), to open missionary work in China. The prayer was offered on Victoria Peak on Hong Kong Island.[1] Ironically, this event happened in the same year as the Communist takeover of mainland China, which would come to be know as the People's Republic of China. The first young missionaries arrived in Hong Kong in 1950.

World War II had seen Hong Kong's population jump from six hundred thousand to almost two and one-half million. Many of the newcomers were refugees from Mainland China. The crowding made it almost impossible to find hotel rooms, let alone permanent housing. Eighteen months later (6 February 1951), the mission was closed because of the Korean War and the threat of a Communist takeover in Hong Kong. Nine missionaries had served and fourteen Chinese had joined the Church before the mission's closure.

After the end of the Korean conflict, when missionary strength had built up again, Church leaders reopened the Chinese area. H. Grant Heaton, who had been one of the first two missionaries to arrive in 1950, accompanied President Joseph Fielding Smith of the Council of the Twelve to Hong Kong, where in August 1955 he was appointed to preside over the Church's third and most successful effort to take the gospel to China.[2] President Heaton headed the Southern Far East Mission, consisting of Hong Kong, Taiwan, the Philippines, Guam, Southeast Asia, and the

People's Republic of China, even though the latter was closed to missionary work.

President Heaton instigated an intensive language and culture program for the new missionaries. By September, he had organized a Sunday School, located most of the earlier converts, and even had some investigators, largely attracted by English classes that used the Bible and the Book of Mormon as texts. By 18 September, the elders were tracting two days a week, working among English-speakers until their Chinese was better.

As they had found in other countries, the misery and suffering of war had made people receptive to religious values. Before the year ended, President Heaton had sent his missionaries into the field, created one district and three branches, and purchased a mission home. He also made significant progress on a lengthy set of missionary discussions designed especially for the Chinese, and hired Wang Kai An out of more than a hundred well-educated applicants as Church translator. During the next few years, Mr. Wang, who later became a member of the Church, translated many tracts and lesson materials for the mission.[3] These lessons took an enormous amount of time not only to memorize but also to teach. President Heaton, by this method, was trying to make sure that the Chinese were converted to the gospel and were not simply joining the Church in hopes of furthering their economic status like many Christian converts in that crowded, poverty-stricken city did.

The first eleven Chinese converts, five of whom were refugees from the People's Republic of China, were baptized on 31 May 1956. In 1957, the pace quickened. Sacrament meetings began in January. By the end of June there were forty missionaries and three hundred members. The annual report for 1957 said that the missionaries had so many investigators—most of them referred by members—that they were meeting in classes of 15 to 150 people at night, then trying to meet each investigator at home during the day. This procedure did not work well and was soon suspended.

President Heaton also worked tirelessly to acquire property—usually space in apartment buildings because the densely populated city made the land prohibitively expensive. The first Church-constructed chapel on the Asian mainland since the 1850s was probably the modest chapel at Tui King Ling. It was begun in March 1959 and dedicated during Elder Mark E. Petersen's mission tour in May and June of the same year, along with five other apartment-chapels in the Hong Kong area.

By the fall of 1959, a translation of the Book of Mormon was well underway, a monthly mission magazine was being published, sacrament meeting attendance was 53 percent—much better than Church average—and almost 80 percent of the members could be considered active or semi-active. Membership was approaching fifteen hundred and included 188 college graduates, 3 former provincial governors, 7 former generals, 5 Ph.D.s, and many skilled people. The local Chinese missionaries were very effective; Chen Hsiao Hsin (also called David) baptized 114 during this first year while his close friend Tang Ching Nan (Jonathan) baptized 78. Clearly the work was moving well in Hong Kong.

But Hong Kong was not the only responsibility of the mission; Taiwan was also included within its boundaries. After several visits to this economically, socially, and politically unsettled land, the first missionaries were assigned there on 4 June 1956. By October, the Taipei Branch included thirty-five missionaries, military personnel, and local Chinese investigators attending regularly. The missionaries held their first baptism on 27 April 1957.

By mid-1958 there were 286 members in Taiwan, 184 of whom were in Taipei. As in Hong Kong, a high percentage of converts were former Christians, even though most of the Taiwan populace were Buddhist, Taoist, or animist.[4] Thus, Latter-day Saints have built on the efforts of the hundreds of devoted Christian missionaries who first introduced the teachings of Christ to Asia.

A highlight in Taiwan's history was the visit of Elder Mark E. Petersen in 1959, the first General Authority to visit the country. On 1 June, Elder Petersen offered a prayer of dedication, mentioning Elder McKay's dedication of the entire Chinese realm, and praying "for all the freedoms that are necessary for the carrying on of the gospel."[5]

Beginning in April 1960, Elder Gordon B. Hinckley was appointed supervisor of the Asian missions. He, along with mission presidents there, pursued a number of development and expansion projects. Before Elder Hinckley was assigned to other duties in 1968, chapels had been built or acquired in Taiwan and Hong Kong, the Book of Mormon had been published in Chinese (1965), and missionary work had been initiated in the Philippines (which became a separate mission in 1967).

During the 1960s, the United States became involved in the Vietnam War. Initially only a few Latter-day Saint service people were involved, but by the later part of the decade, thousands of men and women were stationed in Vietnam, the Philippines, Thailand, and other Southeast Asian nations. As a result, these Saints in the military strengthened existing

Church organizations in some countries, notably the Philippines, and planted the Church in Vietnam and Thailand.

In 1969, Singapore, Indonesia, Thailand, and South Vietnam became the new Southeast Asia Mission. South Vietnam was returned a little later to the Hong Kong Mission, and Taiwan became a separate mission in January 1971. From this point, Hong Kong and Taiwan have separate stories.

HONG KONG

Leaders of the separate Hong Kong Mission sought to improve the Saints' lives by promoting various Church programs. Notable was the introduction during the 1970s of home-study seminary and institute. Soon, these two activities were reaching more than five hundred young people. Mission President Jerry D. Wheat worked hard to improve the Church's image by inviting media coverage of the first area conference in August 1975.

Elder Hinckley recorded in his journal: "We have had more favorable publicity in the last few days than I think we have had in all the years of the mission put together."[6]

A new mission home was soon constructed, as was a new chapel at Kowloon, which became the headquarters for the new Hong Kong Stake, organized on 25 April 1976. Mission leaders had helped prepare for stakehood as they trained members for leadership. Elder Hinckley called Poon Shiu-tat (Sheldon), age thirty, to preside over 3,410 members in six wards and two branches.

Macao, a Portuguese colony on a small peninsula on the south coast of China, two hours away from Hong Kong by boat, was a logical next place for the preaching of the gospel.

One of the several LDS meetinghouses in Hong Kong, this building was the residence of Sir Robert Tong, a noted Chinese merchant. It has a beautiful red brick face and a balcony with a commanding view of Hong Kong harbor. (Photo courtesy Donald Q. Cannon)

Encouraged by Elder Hinckley, President Wheat sent four elders there on 6 September 1976, and they began proselytizing the same day. A branch of more than one hundred Chinese members soon developed.

A visitors' center was opened in the Tsuen Wan chapel in the Hong Kong suburb of Kowloon during the administration of President David H. H. Chen. He was one of the first Hong Kong Chinese to serve as a missionary, the first native-born Chinese mission president, and a professor of political science at BYU–Hawaii. Chen had the four-story structure remodeled. Over two thousand people toured it in the first month after it was dedicated in September 1976. Between March and August 1977, forty-six people were baptized after

President Gordon B. Hinckley, who had supervised the missions of Asia for eight years in the 1960s, returned to Hong Kong to dedicate the temple in May 1996. (LDS Church Archives)

going through the center on their own, and another sixty-eight were baptized after they visited it with a member missionary.

Hong Kong faced some serious challenges in the subsequent decades. Materialism grew with the country's economy and made missionary work difficult. Traditional Chinese values were unfamiliar to Western missionaries, making proselyting difficult. Many of the best-qualified Church leaders chose to emigrate before Hong Kong once again became a part of China in 1997.

The Church in Hong Kong prospered despite these obstacles. Plans for a temple in Hong Kong were announced in the October 1992 general conference. President Hinckley's vision for the building was multipurpose, with the top three floors and the basement being the actual temple and the other floors being apartments and offices for Church leaders. At the temple's dedication in May 1996, President Hinckley said, "If ever in my life I felt the inspiration of the Lord, it was with this building."[7]

Foremost in everyone's minds after the dedication was the question of what might happen after Hong Kong came under Chinese control in 1997. President James E. Faust, second counselor in the First Presidency, met with the chief executive of the Hong Kong special administrative region of the People's Republic, Mr. Tung Chee-hwa, and was assured that religious freedom would continue in Hong Kong under the Chinese government. With this assurance, missionary and other Latter-day Saint activities in Hong Kong continued without restriction in the twenty-first century. By the early years of the twenty-first century, Church membership in Hong Kong was more than twenty-one thousand strong, with five organized stakes, one mission, and the Hong Kong Temple.

TAIWAN

The Church's work in Taiwan began more slowly than it did in Hong Kong. In 1971, however, a number of local missionaries were called—ten elders and eighteen sisters in 1971—who greatly helped in the work. In 1972, the first health services (later welfare) missionary arrived in Taiwan, followed by others within a few months in Hong Kong. The lessons taught on health care and preventative medicine were extremely successful in both locations. By the late 1970s, Church membership in Taiwan had surpassed that in Hong Kong.

Like the Hong Kong Saints, the Taiwan members responded to the presence of President Kimball and eleven other General Authorities who came to Taiwan for an area

The Taipei Taiwan Temple is located in the heart of downtown Taipei. It was the first temple built in the Chinese Realm. (Photo courtesy Donald Q. Cannon)

conference in August 1975, packing the Dr. Sun Yat-sen Memorial Hall with more than twenty-five hundred members and friends. Major administrative changes came the following year. The Taipei Taiwan Stake was created in April 1976 with the first native Chinese stake president, Chang I-ch'ing; it had six wards and five branches (4,497 members). In July the mission was divided, with the second headquarters in Kaohsiung.

Today, Taiwan has a strong and stable economy; its people are generally satisfied, and the Church has attracted many families as well as young single people. The United States' recognition of the Communist People's Republic of China in December 1978 had only a temporary negative effect on missionary work, as the Taiwanese resented this shift of diplomatic relations to what they regarded as a rival government. By the

following year, Taiwan's feelings of animosity toward the United States had died down.

Taiwan became the first country in the Chinese realm to receive a temple. On 17 November 1984, President Gordon B. Hinckley (then second counselor to President Spencer W. Kimball) and Elder Howard W. Hunter conducted five dedicatory sessions at the temple in Taipei. President Hinckley, referring to the temple's location, said, "This house, built on what was once prison property, will open the prison doors of the veil of death."[8]

Materialism and traditional values continued to impair Church growth in Taiwan, but the work still slowly progressed. Despite time-consuming economic demands, more than ninety percent of eligible students were enrolled in the Church's institute program in 1998. As the twenty-first century opened up, more than 33,500 Taiwan Saints were members of the nation's seven stakes.

MONGOLIA

Mongolia was dominated by the Communists of the Soviet Union until its breakup in 1989. Following this, a number of reforms were introduced in the country, including the government's guaranteeing of religious freedom. This provided the setting for the Church's first official contact with Mongolia.

The newly appointed Mongolian ambassador to the United States accepted an invitation to speak on the Brigham Young University campus. While he was in Utah during March 1991, he also met with Gordon B. Hinckley and other Church leaders who discussed the possibility of sending representatives to Mongolia. As a result of these contacts, the

Church sent several missionary couples into Mongolia the following year to help build its higher education system. Although these representatives were not to proselyte, they were able to answer questions about the Church.[9]

Conversions to the gospel began almost immediately. In April 1993, Elder Neal A. Maxwell visited Ulaanbaatar, the capital city, and dedicated the country for the preaching of the gospel. By the end of that year, 110 members and investigators were meeting together for sacrament meeting.

Expansion in Mongolia has not been easy. The Church and its members have suffered persecutions of many kinds. But as a legally registered organization after 1994, it managed to keep its foothold within the country and increase its membership. The Mongolia Ulaanbaatar Mission was opened in July 1995. The first Latter-day Saint meetinghouse was dedicated in June 1999. By the end of 2000 there were nine active branches in the country, comprising more than twenty-six hundred members. It is expected that the Church will continue to steadily grow in this distant land.

The Church has made giant strides in Hong Kong and Taiwan. Nevertheless, the present Chinese Saints are but a tiny fraction of the billion Chinese who are yet to be taught the gospel. Hong Kong and Taiwan are perhaps best considered training grounds for missionaries who may someday enter the People's Republic of China.

THE PEOPLE'S REPUBLIC OF CHINA

One quarter of the world's population lives within China's borders. Yet, at the time of this printing, the doors of this vast country remain closed to the preaching of the gospel. However, diplomacy and humanitarian aid are helping the Church establish a foundation of goodwill and trust with the Chinese government.

In 1978, President Spencer W. Kimball asked that Chinese experts at Brigham Young University investigate the possibility of opening missionary work in China.

The report was not encouraging because at that time the United States did not have diplomatic relations with China. In December of that year, however, U.S. President Jimmy Carter unexpectedly announced that the United States would exchange ambassadors with the mainland Chinese government. This change in diplomatic relations opened the way for Brigham Young University to send its Young Ambassadors performing group to China the following summer.

Other BYU groups followed in the ensuing years, each one accompanied by General Authorities and BYU administrators who established many contacts among China's highest officials. Chinese officials have also visited Salt Lake City, Brigham Young University, and the Polynesian Cultural Center in Hawaii since that time. In 1996, President Gordon B. Hinckley became the first president of the Church to visit China.

Humanitarian aid and disaster relief have also been provided by the Church on various occasions. In 1998, the China Teachers Program of the David M. Kennedy Center for International Studies at Brigham Young University was established. Through the program, teachers of English are placed at universities and institutes in China. Although they cannot teach about their religion, they serve to provide humanitarian service and establish a Latter-day Saint presence in China.

The Church of Jesus Christ of Latter-day Saints maintains the same missionary policy with China as it has had with all other countries—not to use devious or illegal means to enter. As Elder Dallin H. Oaks said in 1991: "As we become friends of China, and as we learn from them, our Father in Heaven, who has made 'all nations of men . . . and [has] determined . . . the bounds of their habitation' (Acts 17:26), will bring His purpose to pass in that great nation 'in his own time, and in his own way, and according to his own will' (D&C 88:68)."[10] Until that time, the Church will continue to build bridges of friendship through service.

THE PHILIPPINES

Latter-day Saint servicemen were important in the establishment of the restored gospel in the Philippines, serving there in great numbers during World War II and again during the Korean War in 1950. In 1953, a servicemen's district was organized with groups at Manila-Sangley Point, Subic Bay, and Clark Air Force Base. The Clark group had the first Relief Society in the Philippines.[11]

In 1955, President Joseph Fielding Smith of the Council of the Twelve dedicated the Philippines[12] for the preaching of the gospel and it became a part of the new Southern Far East Mission. Missionary work officially began in the Philippines when Elder Gordon B. Hinckley rededicated the land for the preaching of the gospel on 28 April 1961.When he first visited Manila the year before, there was only one known Filipino member. Elder Hinckley, however, prophesied, "What we begin here will affect the lives of thousands upon thousands of people in this island republic, and its effects will go from generation to generation for great and everlasting good."[13] Five

President Spencer W. Kimball shakes hands with Philippines President Ferdinand Marcos on 18 October 1980. The two met over breakfast at the presidential palace. (LDS Church Archives)

weeks later, four missionaries arrived in Manila from Hong Kong.

The missionaries did not meet with immediate success; by the end of 1961 they had baptized only eight people. In the first quarter of 1965, on the other hand, they baptized 115—virtually all of them in the small swimming pool of E. M. and Maxine Grimm, Americans living in Manila for business reasons. Sister Grimm particularly was a mainstay of the mission.

In 1967 the Philippines became a separate mission. By the end of that year there were 3,198 members, 631 of whom had been converted that year alone. By 1973, membership had climbed to almost 13,000 members. On 20 May of that year, Elder Ezra Taft Benson organized the Manila Philippines Stake with Augusto A. Lim as its president.

When the Philippine Saints hosted President Spencer W. Kimball and the other General Authorities 11–12 August 1975 during the first area conference in Asia, more than eighteen thousand people filled the Araneta Coliseum in Manila— more than 90 percent of the almost twenty thousand Latter-day Saints then in the country. Although the Saints received the announcement of a temple in Tokyo warmly, they undoubtedly looked forward to having one of their own. In conjunction with the conference, President Kimball was invited to breakfast with President Ferdinand Marcos at his palace in Manila. On this occasion, Elder Gordon B. Hinckley also returned to the spot where he had dedicated the land and "offered a prayer of thanksgiving to the Lord, expressing gratitude for the marvelous manner in which he had blessed us and brought a fulfillment of the prayer offered 14 years earlier."[14]

Less than a decade later, the dream of a temple in the Philippines was realized. Dedicated in September 1984, the Manila temple stands as a symbol of the maturity of the gospel in the Philippines. Gordon B. Hinckley, who had become a member of the First Presidency, testified in 1984, "I do not know of any place in the world where the harvest has been so great in such a short period. The Lord has touched this land in a miraculous and wonderful way.[15]

The Lord's hand had certainly prepared the way for the gospel to succeed in the Philippines in many ways. The Church there benefitted from its association with the United States, which provided fair government from 1898 until the Japanese invasion at the beginning of World War II, and then liberated the islands at the end of the conflict. Although nominal Catholicism was the legacy of many years of Spanish rule, Filipinos enjoyed religious freedom. Furthermore, Filipino culture worked to the Church's advantage, cooperation and friendliness being the typical response to strangers. Like all Asian societies, the Filipinos prize the family, but the emphasis is less on the veneration of ancestors than on affection and solidarity. Almost 50 percent of the Saints have brothers and sisters who are also members; over 35 percent of those who are married have a member spouse.[16]

More than half of the people speak some English, making the Philippines the third largest English-speaking country in the world. The leadership of Latter-day Saint American servicemen has been very beneficial. Because there was not an extensive language barrier, members could learn how to administer the Church from these experienced leaders rather than young missionaries. This was aided by dissolving the separate servicemen's organization and integrating them into the local districts and branches. Still, a survey revealed that only 25 percent of the members were able to communicate "effectively" in English. Unfortunately, from the 1960s until the late 1980s, Church materials were available to the Filipino Saints only in English. But in 1988, selections from the Book of Mormon became available in Tagalog for the first time. Translations in other native languages soon followed, as did translations of the Doctrine and Covenants and the Pearl of Great Price.

The various challenges accompanying this exciting growth have been enormous; poverty may be the greatest one. In 1975, the average monthly income of a Filipino Latter-day Saint was estimated to be $60.[17] About 65 percent of the average family's income went for food, 25 percent for housing, and the remaining 10 percent then had to cover transportation, clothing, tithing, recreation, budget, building fund, temple fund, fast offerings, books, manuals, and so on.

Another challenge was the Saints' lack of experience in church activity. According to a 1972 survey, 81 percent of the members had been in the Church less than five years. Because there were relatively few male members, there was a lack of priesthood leadership, although a missionary emphasis on whole families since 1970 has brought the region into better balance.

Natural disasters have also provided much tribulation. On 16 July 1990, a huge earthquake near Luzon Island destroyed nearly two thousand buildings and killed more than fifteen hundred people. Less than a year later, on 9 June 1991, Mount Pinatubo erupted, displacing millions of people. In both circumstances the Church offered financial and physical relief to the victims of the incidents.

A bright spot in the picture has been missionary service rendered by the Filipino Saints themselves. As early as 1965, two Filipino elders accepted calls to serve full-time missions. Soon, local missionaries were making up well over one-fourth of the total force in the country. Many of these were welfare services missionaries who taught useful health concepts to the people. Missionaries also participated in unique programs such as providing relief in refugee camps and experimenting with Church meetings in the home. A number of self-reliance projects have also been undertaken to help Church members become financially stable.

Gordon B. Hinckley returned to the Philippines in 1996, this time as the president of the Church, to address an audience of more than thirty-five thousand dedicated Saints. He spoke of having been asked by the media earlier why the Church was growing so much in the Philippines. "The answer," he responded, "is simply this: This Church and this gospel fill a need in the lives of the people. . . . this Church stands as an anchor, a solid anchor of truth in a world of shifting values."[18] By the end of 2000 there were nearly a half million members, located in a phenomenal total of seventy-seven stakes. The first, single Philippines Mission had been divided into an astounding thirteen separate missions.

ASIA

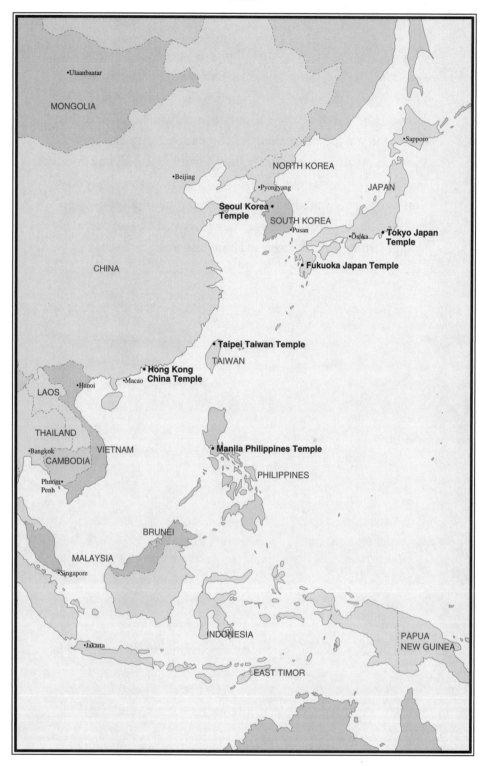

•Ulaanbaatar

MONGOLIA

•Sapporo

NORTH KOREA

•Beijing

JAPAN

•Pyongyang

**Seoul Korea
Temple** •

SOUTH KOREA

•Pusan

•Ōsaka

**Tokyo Japan
Temple**

CHINA

•**Fukuoka Japan Temple**

•**Taipei Taiwan Temple**

TAIWAN

•**Hong Kong
China Temple**

•Macao

•Hanoi

LAOS

THAILAND

•Bangkok

VIETNAM

CAMBODIA

Phnom•
Penh

•**Manila Philippines Temple**

PHILIPPINES

BRUNEI

MALAYSIA

•Singapore

INDONESIA

PAPUA
NEW GUINEA

•Jakarta

EAST TIMOR

CHAPTER 19

EXPANSION INTO SOUTHEAST AND SOUTH ASIA

R. LANIER BRITSCH

1954	Finding a tract leads to opening work in India
1955	Southern Far East Mission formed
1968	Missionaries begin teaching in Singapore
	Vietnam War reaches its peak
1969	Southeast Asia Mission formed, includes Singapore, Indonesia, Thailand, and South Vietnam
1976	Book of Mormon published in Thai
1977	Elementary school opened in Jakarta, Indonesia
1979	Sri Lanka dedicated by Elder James E. Faust
1980	Malaysia District organized
1988	First native Thai serves as mission president in his own country
1995	First stakes in Thailand and Singapore

Originally, southeast Asia was part of the Southern Far East Mission. When the separate Southeast Asia Mission was organized in 1969, with headquarters at Singapore, it was responsible for teaching 975 million people in Vietnam, Thailand, Laos, Cambodia, Singapore, Indonesia, Malaysia, Burma, Nepal, India, Ceylon, and Pakistan. The Thailand Bangkok Mission was split off in July 1973 and the Indonesia Jakarta Mission followed in July 1975. Singapore became its

367

own mission in 1980. India and Cambodia also became their own missions in the 1990s. At the beginning of 1980, only 3,800 of those millions of people were members of the Church. But by the end of the century, Church membership in South and Southeast Asia had grown to approximately 113,000; projections for the future are promising.

Even though war has caused problems for preaching the gospel in these countries, it was the Vietnam conflict that brought Latter-day Saints to the area in large numbers and gave impetus to missionary work in South Asia.

THAILAND AND CAMBODIA

Missionaries in Thailand face a society where devotion to king, country, tradition, and religion form a seamless whole. The Thais have a culture strikingly different from that of the Christian world. Though Catholic and Protestant missionaries have proselytized the country for more than three centuries, only .005 percent of the population is Christian. Over 94 percent are Theravada Buddhists. The rest follow Islamic or Chinese traditions. Most Thais feel that conversion to another religion would also be a rejection of their nation.

Formal Latter-day Saint activities began in Bangkok in 1961. In November 1963, an official group was organized that had, within a year, a Sunday School and MIA (the organization for youth and young adults). In December 1964, Elder Gordon B. Hinckley visited Thailand and noted the stable economy and government, the devotion of the members, and the general demeanor of the Thais—all positive indications for missionary success.[1] In 1965, a district with eight part-time missionaries was set up. In 1966, at least three American servicemen were baptized; so was Sister Nangnoi Thitapoora, the first native Thai to join the Church. The first branch, a servicemen's organization, was formed in July 1966 with more than two hundred members.

In November 1966, Elders Hinckley and Marion D. Hanks arrived in Bangkok after touring the rest of the mission. They met with 145 members and investigators in the district conference, and the next morning, 2 November, Elder Hinckley dedicated Thailand for the preaching of the gospel. That same day, they called on Colonel Pin Muthukanta, director general of the Ministry of Religions, who explained how to register the Church and offered to help them accomplish it.

A year later, in the fall of 1967, the Church was officially incorporated and registered; in addition, a chapel site was purchased. Two or three months after that, the first missionaries received their visas, even though they were plagued until 1978 by a regulation requiring foreigners to leave the country every seventy-five days to renew their visas. Those first six elders concentrated on learning Thai, hired a translator, published the missionary discussions and then, in November 1978, the Joseph Smith pamphlet. By then, two Thais had joined the Church and Thai groups had been organized at Bangkok and Korat.

During that same month, Elder Ezra Taft Benson of the Quorum of the Twelve visited Thailand on his first official tour as supervisor of the Asian area. He met with the king, Bhumibol Adulyadej, an audience that went nearly half an hour over the allotted time. The elders later learned that the king had kept a stadium full of people waiting while he visited with Elder Benson.[2]

By the end of 1969, the missionary force had crept up to twenty-five; after 1970, missionaries arrived with language training, first from the center in Laie, Hawaii, and then from the Language Training Mission at BYU.

When the distinct Southeast Asia Mission was organized in 1969, mission presidents were able to give more time to Thailand's needs. In December 1969, translation of the Book of Mormon began—a project that was not finished until 1976. About thirty different tracts were also translated and printed.

The first chapel was dedicated in 1974, and by 1976 fourteen new cities were opened to missionary work. The missionaries sponsored a variety of public relations efforts, including a popular missionary basketball team, open houses, and broadcasts of "Music and the Spoken Word."

Much of the good image was erased when one elder had a companion photograph him atop a statue of Buddha in Thailand's ancient capital, now a city of ruins, in 1972. Since the head is the most sacred part of the body to the Thais, this incident was highly offensive; the technician who processed the film sent the picture to a local newspaper. It quickly became a national issue. The elders were arrested, tried, found guilty of desecration of a Buddhist image and of insulting the Buddhist religion, and sentenced to six months in jail, which they served.

As a result the city in which the photograph was printed had to be closed to missionary work for two years, and the number of baptisms throughout the mission dropped. Even when the area was reopened, the mission president was still reminding elders of the consequences of "our total foolishness in that serious insult to the Thai people and their religious beliefs."[3]

Mission leaders recognized the need to counteract the negative image of the Church that had been created by the Buddha-head incident. After receiving permission from

Mission President Harvey Brown presents a Book of Mormon to the king of Thailand, King Bhumibol Adulyadej. (LDS Church Archives)

Church headquarters, the mission president organized a singing group of excellent missionary musicians. They created a great amount of attention not only with their renditions of Western songs but also with their versions of popular Thai music. No group of non-Thais had ever before been able to sing the complicated tones required by the Thai language. During the twenty-eight months while the Sidthichon Uk Sud Tai, the "Latter-day Saints," were performing, they appeared on television more than seventy times, recorded five albums, gave three performances before the king and queen of Thailand, and gave more than five hundred live performances in every major city, eventually performing for more than one million people. The results of these efforts were exactly what missionaries had hoped for. The rate of baptisms began to climb. The image of the Church having been improved, the singing group was discontinued in July 1979.

In 1980, Elder Marion D. Hanks of the First Quorum of the Seventy, then executive administrator over southeast Asia, established the refugee welfare services missionaries in Thailand to help thousands of war refugees. Not only was much suffering alleviated, but some refugees were also converted to the gospel after reaching their destination countries. The image of the Church as a welfare organization was therefore enhanced in southeast Asia.

In 1988, Anan Eldredge became the first Thai to preside over the mission. His presidency began a period of remarkable Church growth that continued through the end of the twentieth century. President Anan worked hard to see many members travel to the Manila Philippines Temple to receive their endowments and especially emphasized the need to fellowship and retain new converts and to reactivate less active members. Conversion rates were such during this time that by 1995, the Thai Saints were ready to be organized into a stake for the first time. In June, Elder Neal A. Maxwell of the Twelve called Thipparat Kitsaward, previously Bangkok District President, to be the first president of the Bangkok Thailand Stake.

Thus, the final years of the twentieth century witnessed substantial progress in Thailand. At the beginning of 1980, membership had been approximately fourteen hundred; but by 2000 it had reached over eleven thousand.[4]

In 1997, the Cambodia Phnom Penh Mission was split off from the Bangkok Thailand Mission. The Church had first been officially recognized by the government in Cambodia in 1994. Welfare missionaries there were allowed to serve but not proselyte.

The first district in Cambodia, the Phnom Penh District of the Church, was organized in January 1996, and by the end of the decade encompassed five branches and more than two thousand members. President Gordon B. Hinckley visited Phnom Penh in May 1996 and spoke at a fireside of 439 members and investigators. Before leaving Cambodia the following morning, he offered a dedicatory prayer on a hillside overlooking the Mekong River, for the peace and prosperity of the Church in Cambodia.

SINGAPORE

The Republic of Singapore, a small island at the end of the Malay Peninsula, is mostly city. Two-thirds of its people live in its 37-square-mile city boundaries; yet despite one of the highest density rates in Asia, Singapore is stable, prosperous, literate, and diverse. Its people are Chinese (74 percent), Malay (14 percent), Indian and Pakistani (8 percent), and other, including Caucasians (4 percent). Singapore has no state religion, and the principal religions of Asia are all represented: Buddhism, Taoism, Confucianism, Animism, Hinduism, Sikhism, Islam, and Christianity (about 8 percent).

The Church came to Singapore in the early 1960s. By December 1964, there were three member families who were holding regular Sunday services. No native Singaporeans joined the Church until missionaries began proselyting in 1968. The first native, Alice Tan, was baptized 4 May of that year.[5]

Evidently, the General Authorities saw Singapore at the forefront of some far-reaching plans. Soon afterwards, they made it the headquarters of the new Southeast Asia Mission. Baptisms increased significantly and by the end of 1969, converts numbered 118.

The other Christian churches in the country reacted negatively, perhaps because an estimated 90 percent of the converts were already Christian.[6] Leaders and newspaper editors of the Christian community revived the polygamy issue and conducted a smear campaign against the Church. The government, unwilling to allow any kind of religious unrest, expelled twenty-nine Latter-day Saint missionaries in March 1970, refused to grant new visas or renew old ones, and prohibited tracting. Missionary work was seriously affected. Only fifteen converts were baptized in 1974. The members drew closer together, however, and a number of young men and women served either local or full-time missions. In 1977, sixty-one new members were baptized.

Nevertheless, during these difficult years, some progress had been made. In 1970, the Church acquired property on which a chapel was built. That same year, the Church received a license to perform marriages.

In 1971, Soren Cox, a BYU English professor teaching at Nanyang University, became district president. He and his wife, Fern, who led the combined Relief Societies of the two branches, helped the local members assume the roles so suddenly given to them when the missionaries left.

In July 1975, Brother Cox returned to Singapore as mission president. During those first years, as the baptisms began once again to increase, ninety percent of the converts came from member referrals. He completed the organization of the districts and the auxiliaries and supervised the seminary and institute programs.

In 1980, India and Sri Lanka were also placed under supervision of the Singapore Mission. Soon, the mission in

Indonesia was discontinued and that country also added to the boundaries of the Singapore Mission.

Church growth continued to suffer under restrictive government policies until March 1988, when Elder M. Russell Ballard, Jon M. Huntsman Sr.—an industrial leader in Utah—and Utah Senator Jake Garn met with Prime Minister Lee Kuan Yew and were able to gain greater missionary privileges for the Church.[7]

The first stake in Singapore was created by Elder Neal A. Maxwell on 26 February 1995. Although the stake consisted of only 1,650 members, Church leaders felt that the membership was mature enough for added leadership responsibility. By the end of the century, the stake had grown to include more than twenty-one hundred members.

MALAYSIA

Just as in Singapore, the first Latter-day Saints in Malaysia were American and Australian businessmen and military personnel in the early 1960s. The first native Malaysian members were converted outside of the country and, upon returning to Malaysia, began meeting with other members in one another's homes. In 1977, the Church was granted legal recognition by the government, and three years later, in 1980, the Malaysia District was created as part of the Singapore Mission.[8]

Malaysia's government is headed by a Muslim king, and Islam is the state religion, but there is freedom of worship. However, Christians are strictly forbidden to proselytize Muslims, and foreign missionaries from any church are not allowed into Malaysia.[9] Because of this, the work there has been primarily dependent upon native elders and sisters. They have experienced much success among their own people.

Elders Bruce R. McConkie and Ezra Taft Benson with their wives in Indonesia. Elder Benson dedicated the land on 26 October 1969. (LDS Church Archives)

Church membership had grown to more than thirteen hundred by the end of the century and was divided into two districts and fifteen branches. Eleven Church leaders in Malaysia were even invited to dine with the king and queen in 1994 during the royal couple's coronation events.

INDONESIA

Indonesia's thirteen thousand islands and surrounding ocean cover almost as much map space as the contiguous United States. Though separated by different languages, the people are united by a strong feeling of nationalism. A large majority of the people are Muslim. Christianity, however, grew rapidly during the 1960s and includes about 10 percent of the population.

Church leaders considered the possibilities of Latter-day

Saint missionary work in Indonesia as early as 1965; but it was not until 1969 that Elder Ezra Taft Benson included this country on his tour of Asia. In Jakarta, the capital city, he met a small group of Canadian, Dutch, and American Latter-day Saints. On the same visit Elder Benson offered a dedicatory prayer on a hill outside Bogor, about an hour and a half away from Jakarta, on the morning of 26 October 1969. Elder Bruce R. McConkie, who was accompanying Elder Benson, explained to the twenty-three Saints and friends who were present that dedication meant "dedicating the resources of the Church and the talents and abilities of the members of the Church to spread the gospel in that nation."[10]

Six missionaries were sent into Indonesia a few months later on 5 January 1970. The first converts were baptized in March. The missionaries were limited by their lack of fluency in the Bahasa Indonesia tongue and by the lack of printed materials. ("Joseph Smith's Testimony," the first tract translated, was not published until April 1971.) Furthermore, the missionaries had to get permission to proselyte in each city where they worked, despite the government's official recognition of the Church in April 1970. By the end of 1974, there were 770 Indonesian members and six branches.[11]

In April 1975, Indonesia became a separate mission, with Hendrick Gout—a retired major in the Dutch Royal Army and a fourth-generation Indonesian—as the first president. He had joined the Church in the Netherlands, where he had served as branch and district president and, after his retirement from the military in 1969, as head of Church translation services. As mission president, he enthusiastically encouraged member missionary work, organized several new branches, saw the Book of Mormon published in Indonesian, and integrated welfare services

missionaries into the mission. Most important, he set up an elementary school in Jakarta in 1976 under the direction of the
Church Educational System; he obtained formal government
approval with the assistance of Saing Sililahih, a former BYU student who was not a member of the Church.[12]

Staffed completely by Indonesians, the school opened in
January 1977 with about 130 students, most of whom were
not Latter-day Saints. Thus, the school made it clear to the
government that the Church was interested in helping the
people in Indonesia. This desire was further underscored by the
work of the Welfare Services missionaries, who taught good
health and nutrition, along with doctrinal priciples; they were
given impetus by Mary Ellen Edmunds, who had inaugurated
similar work in the Philippines and Hong Kong. Struggling
with poverty, malnutrition, and disease, the members
responded to the mental and physical health skills taught by
the missionaries. Led by the Spirit, they were often already living the principles of mutual assistance. One Relief Society
president told Sister Edmunds, "Oh, Sister . . . we don't have
telephones. We have to ask the Spirit if someone needs help."
The Relief Society president regularly rode her bicycle to the
homes of members when the Spirit prompted her.[13]

Although there was a ban on door-to-door tracting, the
missionaries were able to make contacts by using English language classes, television and radio interviews, direct gospel discussion, and meeting people in such public places as soccer
games, shops, and buses.

Another obstacle was understaffing. There were only fifty-
two missionaries in the country at the end of 1978; ten or
twelve were local. After that the government severely restricted
missionary visas. This situation frustrated President Gout, but

This chapel is in Yogyakarta on the south side of the island of Java in Indonesia. (Photo courtesy Donald Q. Cannon)

there were still almost fourteen hundred members, and the Church was established in all of Java's major cities by the end of 1979. Unfortunately, in late 1980, because the Indonesian government would not allow any more missionary visas, the Indonesia Mission was combined with the Singapore Mission. From that point on, the work in Indonesia rested solely upon members and local missionaries supervised by a mission president in Singapore. A mini-MTC was established to train local missionaries. Seminary and institute were expanded to help prepare young people to serve missions.[14] The native missionaries experienced much success despite their small numbers—the Church continued to grow.

In 1993, Dean and Elan Belnap were called as Church welfare missionaries to work at the medical school in Jakarta and to help supervise the local branches. Their service enhanced the

379

perception of the Church held by some leaders of the Indonesian government. As a result, the Church was able to reopen the Indonesia Jakarta Mission in July 1995, with three districts. By the end of the century, those districts included twenty branches and over fifty-three hundred members of the Church.

President Gordon B. Hinckley met with the president of Indonesia at the presidential palace in Jakarta in January 2000. The following day, President Hinckley spoke to eighteen hundred members at a fireside, the largest congregation of Church members in Indonesia to date. As friendly relations continue between Church leaders and Indonesian political officials, it is hoped that more opportunities will be available for Church growth within Indonesia.

VIETNAM

The first Latter-day Saints to arrive in the country of Vietnam did so under decidedly unhappy circumstances, as advisors to the South Vietnam forces during the early 1960s. The first servicemen's group was organized in Saigon on 30 June 1963. In December 1965, Vietnam became part of the Southern Far East Mission with three districts to serve the fifteen hundred Latter-day Saint servicemen there. Six of them were called as district missionaries, and by February 1966, several servicemen and thirty Vietnamese were baptized.

Most of these Vietnamese converts were women, who were employed as secretaries, receptionists, cooks, maids, and so on by the Americans. The first Vietnamese elder, Nguyen Cao Minh, was ordained in 1966; somewhat surprisingly, he had been baptized in Biloxi, Mississippi, where he was training for a military assignment.

In that same month, Elders Gordon B. Hinckley and Marion D. Hanks met with 206 servicemen in downtown Saigon and, during the conference, dedicated the land of South Vietnam for the preaching of the gospel.[15] Unusual though it was for the Church to dedicate a country in the throes of war, there was a strong feeling that this was a different situation. In 1966, most Americans believed that South Vietnam would win the war. The success of the servicemen in preaching the gospel to that point was encouraging. Compared to other Asian nations, a large proportion of the people—10 or 11 percent— were already Christian, thanks to the long-time efforts of Catholic and Protestant missionaries. And, lastly, under assignment from President David O. McKay, Elder Hinckley had felt inspired to perform the dedication.

Elder Hinckley returned to Vietnam in 1967 and 1968. Speaking in general conference in April 1968, he deplored the misery of war but characterized the infant Church organization as "that silver thread, small but radiant with hope, shining through the dark tapestry of war," and bore his testimony that from it would "spring forth a great work affecting the lives of large numbers of our Father's children who live in that part of the world."[16]

American involvement in Vietnam reached its peak in 1968. Five thousand of its personnel were Latter-day Saints, making up sixty groups and branches served by six chaplains. The mission presidents visited the war zone often, usually every month. The men saw films of conference sessions and a special Christmas message from the First Presidency, held family home evenings, made home teaching visits to each other, and held church services. Except for a few months as part of the

Southeast Asia Mission, Vietnam remained under the supervision of the Hong Kong-Taiwan Mission.

In 1971, American troops began leaving Vietnam and, warned by the withdrawal, Vietnamese elders were called to lead the Saigon Branch. Mission leaders began working immediately to have full-time missionaries called to fill the proselyting void left by the departing servicemen. Work was already under way on a Vietnamese translation of the Book of Mormon, and several tracts and pamphlets had been translated in 1970. When permission finally came from Church headquarters to send four elders to Vietnam in March 1973, the mission president "literally shouted for joy."[17] The arrangements for housing and missionary security seemed satisfactory and, with letters of permission from the parents of the elders, they flew to Saigon on 6 April.

The branch was small—ninety-five members including only four active Melchizedek Priesthood bearers—but Nguyen Van The was set apart as branch president with Dang Thong Nhat and an American doctor, Lester Bush, as counselors. The missionaries quickly learned Vietnamese and were soon teaching the many referrals from local members and servicemen and the people they met in public places. They did not tract.

The first portions of the Book of Mormon translation, photocopied manuscripts, were distributed in May 1974. When mission leaders visited Saigon in July of that year, there were 150 members at the conference. Significantly, adults outnumbered youths, and the male/female ratio was nearly equal.

During the fall of 1974, tensions mounted, and the U.S. embassy warned Americans to keep off the streets. By mid-

January 1975, the missionary force was up to fifteen. Despite the tension, new converts joined the Church regularly, and by the end of March there were close to three hundred members. In that month, heartsick at interrupting the work but concerned for the safety of the missionaries, the mission president ordered the elders back to Hong Kong.

The members kept in touch with each other and with mission leaders who, under orders not to discuss evacuation, were working night and day with American officials to get some of the members out of the country. About a hundred members were evacuated on American planes before Saigon fell to the Communists on 30 April. Others managed to escape after the takeover. An estimated 90 percent of the active Vietnamese Saints resettled in the United States. By 1985, all but eighteen Latter-day Saint families had escaped from Vietnam. Some were aided by the Veterans Association for Service Abroad (VASA), which helped many Vietnamese members emigrate and find jobs and homes in the United States, where they were then able to receive temple ordinances.[18]

All Church representatives were denied entrance into Vietnam until November 1991, when Elder Merlin R. Lybbert, a member of the Second Quorum of the Seventy who was serving as Asia Area president, visited Hanoi with a group of surgeons who were part of Operation Smile (a humanitarian organization of surgeons who visited Vietnam twice a year to perform reconstructive surgery). Elder Lybbert presented a state-of-the-art surgical microscope to the Tran Hung Dao Hospital on behalf of the Church. His visit established contact with many leading officials, and he was invited to return and to bring volunteers to Hanoi to teach English.

Beginning in April 1992, the Vietnam constitution granted

freedom of religion, although proselyting missionaries were still not allowed. Two Latter-day Saint couples were brought into Hanoi to teach English and there experienced much success in making friends. Other humanitarian efforts continued as well, such as disaster relief and medical training to promote better health.

In 1993, expatriate members of the Church were authorized to organize a branch in Hanoi. By 1999, there were one hundred members meeting in two branches.

President Gordon B. Hinckley visited Hanoi and Ho Chi Minh City on 29 May 1996. While meeting with some Vietnamese Saints in a member's home, President Hinckley offered an "addendum" to his dedicatory prayer of thirty years earlier, dedicating the entire country of Vietnam for the preaching of the gospel.[19] Certainly, the promises of the dedicatory blessing may yet be fulfilled on the Lord's timetable.

INDIA

With the exception of Muslim Pakistan, all of the countries of South Asia have laws or immigration policies that prevent new missionary churches from entering their borders. Such anti-missionary attitudes have inhibited the work of spreading the restored gospel to the more than one billion people who live in this realm. The Church has long eyed this important part of the world with the sincere intention of planting the restored gospel there. The local political, cultural, and religious frameworks, however, have made open, straightforward missionary work difficult.

In spite of these problems, some progress has been made in India and Sri Lanka during the past few years. More than in any other part of Asia, the efforts of individuals working almost alone have accounted for the small toehold the Church has gained.

By 1980, there was a community of 225 Latter-day Saints living in and around the south Indian city of Coimbatore. All of these converts were brought into the Church as a result of one man's dedication and faith. That man was S. Paul Thiruthuvadoss. Brother Paul, as he was known, was born a Christian, but he was not satisfied with the denominations he found and joined during the earlier years of his life. In 1954, when he was on the verge of turning to Hinduism, he found a Latter-day Saint tract inside of a used book. He was impressed with its contents and wrote to Church headquarters in Salt Lake City for more information. By 1957 he had read the standard works of the Church and much other Latter-day Saint literature. He requested baptism. At about the same time, he started preaching the gospel and even founded a Sunday School.

Years passed before Paul met an LDS Church leader—Elder Richard L. Evans of the Council of the Twelve Apostles, who was traveling in India on behalf of Rotary International. Elder Evans did not want to baptize Paul and then leave him without the support of the Saints. Two years later the president of the Southern Far East Mission—which included India within its bounds—visited Paul for three days. His investigation started matters moving at a quicker pace. In December 1964 the mission president returned again, this time with Elder Gordon B. Hinckley. Together they decided to send two representatives of the Church to live in Coimbatore, to baptize Paul and some of his associates, and to teach the new members the doctrine and order of the Church. On 5 February 1965, Elders John Aki and Gilbert Mantano arrived in India. Two days later they baptized

Paul and his wife, Paul's ninety-six-year-old father, and another man. The elders remained in India for six months on tourist visas. During that time they visited with prospective members in Madukarai, Rathanapuri, Sumedu, Sawadi, and other villages in and near (within forty miles) Coimbatore. They gained some fluency in the Tamil language and ultimately baptized six other Indians. Most of their contacts were with extremely poor farmers, most of whom were illiterate.

In 1968 Paul was visited by mission leaders in Southeast Asia, and a new phase of closer contact and supervision was begun. Twenty-four more Indian converts were baptized at that time. During the next eight years, mission presidents made two or three trips to India each year. They supervised baptisms almost every time. Two pairs of elders were also sent to Coimbatore during 1973 and again in 1974. These men, George Groberg and Arn Hallam, and then Arn Hallam and Wayne A. Jones, worked under very restricted circumstances but helped the fledgling group find its way and gain stability. Their work might have been easier if the members had not been situated in four different villages, making it difficult to create one strong branch of the Church.

Considering the unlikely circumstances, the Church in Coimbatore became surprisingly strong. By the end of the twentieth century, three of the groups had humble chapels, there were five local elders and thirteen Aaronic Priesthood holders, and the groups were continuing to grow gradually. All church services were conducted in Tamil.[20]

But the young branch of the Church in Coimbatore was not the only fresh growth in India. In addition to some teaching missions that have involved several couple missionaries in the region near Goa, another small group of Saints has been planted in Hyderabad, the capital city of Andhra Pradesh.

In December 1977, Brother and Sister Edwin Dharmaraju, who had recently been converted to the Church in Western Samoa, returned to their native India for the wedding of a daughter. While they were there they spoke freely with their relatives concerning the restored gospel. It was fortunate that most of their relatives were already Christians. The response to their newfound religion was warm and positive.

After Brother and Sister Edwin returned to Samoa—they traveled by way of Salt Lake City—they received letters asking for more information about the Church. After a series of discussions among the General Authorities concerning who could go to India to teach the gospel, it was decided that the Edwins were the logical choice to be assigned to that mission. In October 1978 they were set apart in Samoa as short-term missionaries to India. On 9 December, they departed with five hundred pounds of Church materials—books, tracts, sacrament trays and cups, Church tapes, and so on. When they reached Hyderabad, family members gathered to hear the gospel message. Soon, 27 December was appointed as the day for baptisms. Brother Edwin baptized and confirmed eighteen people that day, including his father, mother, and a number of brothers and sisters. The next day the Edwins traveled to Vijayawada, several hours' train ride away, and baptized twenty-two people, ordained four men to the Aaronic Priesthood, and organized a group of the Church.

Brother Edwin described another important part of their mission:

> From Hyderabad we went to see my wife's parents, who live in a place called Bheemunipatnam, which is about 16

hours by train. Sister Edwin's father, the Reverend P. Sreenivasam, is engaged, since the last 14 months, in the translation of the Book of Mormon into local language of Hyderabad State called "Telugu." This language is spoken by nearly 50 million. Reverend Sreenivasam is an ordained Baptist minister.

Reverend Sreenivasam showed us more than 500 neatly handwritten sheets of the translation. We were taken back by the amount of work he has already accomplished. He is now at the rate of a little more than a page per day. . . . Arrangements will be made with the Church to print the translated version of the Book of Mormon in India as soon as it is ready. At this moment of time, we just cannot visualize the impact this book will have on the more than 40 million people living in Hyderabad State. We consider this our greatest, single humble contribution to the Church of Jesus Christ of Latter-day Saints in India.[21]

Near the end of his report, Brother Edwin wrote that whatever he and his wife had accomplished on their mission was "just a minute droplet in the ocean." He was speaking of India's vast population of nearly 700 million people then (1 billion now) and the many nations and kindred and languages that coexist within that land. Truly, whatever Brother Paul and Brother and Sister Edwin started was but a crack in the door of India. But it was a beginning.

The Church in India existed as little more than a series of small, isolated groups of members in 1978. But in 1981, President J. Talmage Jones of the Singapore Mission discovered that couples from British Commonwealth nations could enter the country without visas and work as Church representatives. The Church began making significant progress once these couples began to arrive. Membership jumped from two hundred in 1981 to seven hundred in 1987.[22] Church growth was also largely due to individual members such as Michael Antony, who almost single-handedly founded the Bangalore Branch. Missionary work also became more effective in 1985 when the Church began calling native Indian members to serve exclusively in their own country. These elders and sisters not only already understood the culture, beliefs, and language of their own people, but they also had the legal right to actively proselyte among their own people, a privilege denied to outsiders.

In 1993, the India Bangalore Mission was created with Gurcharan Singh Gill as its first president. President Gill was a native Indian and professor of mathematics at BYU who had joined the Church when in college in California. India had 1,150 members attending thirteen branches at that time. By the end of the century, membership had grown to over twenty-eight hundred in twenty-one branches. President Gill also helped the Church expand from India into Nepal, where a branch of nearly fifty members was meeting at his release in 1995.[23]

SRI LANKA

Sri Lanka (formerly known as Ceylon) seems to hang like a pendant off the south tip of India. This beautiful island is about the size of Utah, but has a population of over 18 million. The flora looks much like Hawaii, but the climate is somewhat hotter. The people are divided among Singhalese and Tamils. Unfortunately, for over twenty years these two cultural groups—Buddhists and Hindus, respectively—have been at war, and serious destruction and tension has troubled what should be a paradise.

Latter-day Saints have lived in Sri Lanka since World War II, but only since the 1970s have Church leaders made more concerted efforts to grow the Church there. The first two couples served in Colombo from about 1977 to 1980. They were able to obtain official recognition for the Church in March 1979 and to guide various translation projects. In 1979, Elder James E. Faust of the Quorum of the Twelve dedicated Sri Lanka for the preaching of the gospel.

In January 1980, the Young Ambassadors from Brigham Young University performed in Colombo. Again in 1982 and 1986, the Young Ambassadors shared their talents and friendship with the gracious people of Sri Lanka.

In 1982, the Church began sending sister missionaries to Sri Lanka to teach English as a foreign language. That project produced many friends for the Church, but few baptisms resulted before that program was discontinued later in the decade.

Sri Lanka has been supervised by the Singapore Mission since the 1970s. A number of couples and single missionaries have represented the Church there for brief periods of time. Proselyting is not allowed, so regular missionary work is not possible. The single branch that was established in August 1977 grew very slowly. By the end of the century there were more than thirty Latter-day Saints in Sri Lanka.

CONCLUSION

Billions of people live in the countries of South, Southeast, and East Asia. Most of these people have never heard the name Jesus Christ, much less the name Mormon or The Church of Jesus Christ of Latter-day Saints. The relatively small group of people who make up the Church can be justly proud of their missionary success in Asia. What has been done is only a beginning, but it is a solid start. Only since World War II has the Church been numerically and financially strong enough to seriously take on the task of teaching the restored gospel to the peoples of this vast realm. Promising success notwithstanding, at the end of the year 2000 there were still a number of political entities that had no Latter-day Saint missionaries within their borders; for example, Burma, Bangladesh, the People's Republic of China, and the Communist states of Vietnam and Laos. In a biblical sense, the commission to take the gospel to all nations still seems far from completed.

CHURCH STATUS IN ASIA*

COUNTRIES	MEMBERS	STAKES	MISSIONS	TEMPLES**
Cambodia (Kampuchea)	5,072	—	1	—
Hong Kong	21,302	5	1	1
India	4,013	—	1	—
Indonesia	5,604	—	1	—
Japan	118,508	30	7	2
Macao (Macau)	992	—	—	—
Malaysia	1,922	—	—	—
Mongolia	4,358	—	1	—
Pakistan	1,200	—	—	—
Philippines	517,374	81	13	1
Singapore	2,265	1	1	—
South Korea	74,360	17	4	1
Sri Lanka	663	—	—	—
Taiwan	36,598	7	3	1
Thailand	13,032	1	1	—
Asia Totals:	**807,263**	**142**	**34**	**6**

* Numbers are for year's end 2002

** These numbers represent operating temples and those that had been announced or were under construction at press time.

PART V

❧

THE CHURCH IN
OTHER AREAS

This section treats developments in parts of the world that do not fit neatly into the broader areas discussed earlier. Africa and the Caribbean region have at least one thing in common: there has been a remarkable expansion and the beginning of significant growth in recent years. The Near East is important, not just as a region in the present world, but also because of the great events that occurred in the past and are prophesied for the future in the Holy Land.

Some may wonder why a chapter on North America has been included in a book dealing with taking the gospel to the nations of the world. Is it really part of "the international Church"? The Church of Jesus Christ of Latter-day Saints is not just a North American church. While members in the Unites States and Canada may think of other areas as "foreign," members in Europe or Latin America, for example, would regard the U.S. and Canadian Saints in the same way. Furthermore, there are sections of North America where the Church has faced the same challenges and passed through the same stages as in areas overseas. Understanding these similarities can be instructive.

AFRICA

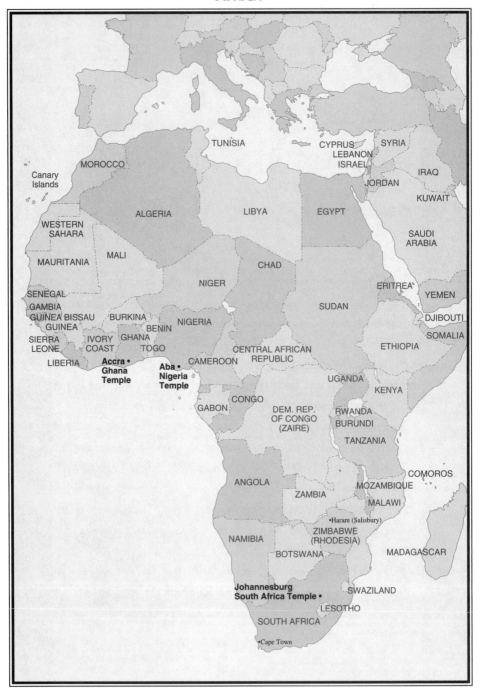

Canary Islands

MOROCCO

WESTERN SAHARA

MAURITANIA

MALI

ALGERIA

LIBYA

TUNISIA

CYPRUS
LEBANON
ISRAEL
JORDAN

SYRIA

IRAQ

KUWAIT

EGYPT

SAUDI ARABIA

NIGER

CHAD

SUDAN

ERITREA

YEMEN

DJIBOUTI

SENEGAL

GAMBIA

GUINEA BISSAU

GUINEA

SIERRA LEONE

LIBERIA

BURKINA

BENIN

IVORY COAST

GHANA

TOGO

NIGERIA

CENTRAL AFRICAN REPUBLIC

ETHIOPIA

SOMALIA

**Accra •
Ghana
Temple**

**Aba •
Nigeria
Temple**

CAMEROON

UGANDA

KENYA

CONGO

GABON

DEM. REP.
OF CONGO
(ZAIRE)

RWANDA
BURUNDI

TANZANIA

COMOROS

ANGOLA

ZAMBIA

MOZAMBIQUE

MALAWI

•Harare (Salisbury)

NAMIBIA

ZIMBABWE
(RHODESIA)

BOTSWANA

MADAGASCAR

**Johannesburg
South Africa Temple •**

SWAZILAND

LESOTHO

SOUTH AFRICA

•Cape Town

CHAPTER 20

THE CHURCH IN AFRICA

DAVID F. BOONE AND RICHARD O. COWAN

1853	First missionaries arrive in South Africa
1865	Last missionaries depart
1903	Mission reopened in South Africa
1915–21	South African government bars Mormon missionaries
1950	First missionaries preach in Rhodesia (now Zimbabwe)
1951	Missionaries begin learning Afrikaans
1954	President David O. McKay visits South Africa
1970	Stake organized at Johannesburg
1973	Southern Africa rededicated by President Spencer W. Kimball (2 December)
1978	Revelation extends priesthood to all races
	Missionary couples open work in Ghana and Nigeria
	President Kimball speaks at area conference in Johannesburg
1980	Africa West Mission organized
1985	Johannesburg South Africa Temple dedicated (24–25 August)
1988	Aba Nigeria Stake created, first in Church with all black leaders (15 May)
1998	President Gordon B. Hinckley visits Africa, announces temple for Accra, Ghana
2000	Temple announced for Aba, Nigeria

By the mid-nineteenth century, when Latter-day Saint missionaries first arrived in South Africa, European colonies had already been established in the area for nearly two hundred years. Originally a stopover point for ships going to and from the Orient, the Cape of Good Hope became a place of settlement for Dutch, English, and French colonists. Early in the 1700s, Dutch farmers and French Huguenot refugees began settling the interior; intensely patriotic to their new homeland, these people came to be known as "Afrikaaners." Between 1835 and 1837, less than two decades before the arrival of Latter-day Saint missionaries, about ten thousand "Boers" (or Dutch farmers) made their "Great Trek" northward into the Transvaal region, seeking new land and freedom from interference by the British, who had taken control of the Cape in 1795.

Perhaps no other mission field presented such religious and racial diversity as did South Africa. Only 18 percent of the population were white or of predominantly Protestant European origin; 3 percent were Asiatic, mostly from India. Several tribes of blacks constituted 70 percent of the total, and among them the indigenous or "primitive" African religions flourished. Finally, an additional 9 percent were "Cape Colored," a people of mixed racial background.

LATTER-DAY SAINT BEGINNINGS IN SOUTH AFRICA

The first three Latter-day Saint missionaries to South Africa were called at a special conference held in Salt Lake City in August 1852; they were part of a group of 106 elders who were sent to widely scattered places around the world. They left Utah the following month, traveled by way of England, and arrived in Cape Town on 18 April 1853.[1] The day after their arrival they climbed Lion's Head, a prominent hill overlooking Table Bay, and offered a prayer of dedication for the preaching of the gospel. Elder Jesse Haven prophesied that the work of the Lord would meet with great success in the colony. Unfortunately, this prophecy did not reach early fulfillment.

Despite great expectations, the three elders faced much opposition. They scheduled the town hall for a series of lectures on Mormonism. "As soon as Joseph Smith was mentioned as prophet," one missionary recalled, "they began to hoot and holler 'Old Joe Smith.' A mob broke up the meeting in an uproar."[2] On subsequent occasions the missionaries were assailed with rocks, rotten eggs, and turnips. At the encouragement of local ministers, most residents combined to withhold food and lodging from the missionaries. The elders' few friends advised them to leave the country rather than endure such persecution. Nevertheless the missionaries chose to remain.

The elders officially organized the Church in the Cape of Good Hope on 23 May 1853. Their first baptism came three days later, and within six months, forty-five persons had been brought into the Church. The first branch was organized on 16 August 1853, in Mowbray. When the first two missionaries departed from South Africa in late 1855, there were three conferences, six branches, and 126 members in the Church in South Africa.

The Church in South Africa, however, was faced with a number of challenges. Opposition to polygamy was the greatest of these. Ministers and the public press continued to print and circulate false charges regarding plural marriage that the elders publicly answered. Jesse Haven was an ardent pamphleteer. During Haven's two-year term of service in South Africa, he was responsible for preparing eleven items of printed literature defending the Church, including a work entitled "Celestial Marriage, and the Plurality of Wives."[3]

Another challenge resulted from the Church's policy of not ordaining blacks to the priesthood. Latter-day Saint missionaries, therefore, limited their proselyting to members of the European community.

The Afrikaans language imposed yet another limitation. A derivative of high Dutch, it had become a distinct language in South Africa by 1800. It was the mother tongue of about 60 percent of the whites; half again as many as spoke English. It was spoken almost exclusively in some of the Western provinces of the country. None of the early Mormon missionaries knew Afrikaans, and the first elders to speak Dutch did not arrive until 1861. Furthermore, Church literature in Dutch, which would have been of at least some value in South Africa, was in short supply. Hence, the missionaries were able to teach only an extremely small minority of the total population.

A final factor that seemed to discourage the establishment of more permanent branches of the Church in South Africa was the encouragement to physically gather with the Saints in America. Many converts, usually the strongest or more committed, left South Africa with their families to settle in Utah. The last of the early missionaries departed in 1865 with a large company of emigrating Saints, leaving the work in South Africa in the hands of local elders.

LAYING A NEW FOUNDATION IN THE TWENTIETH CENTURY

After a lapse of thirty-eight years, the Church reopened its mission in South Africa. There had been almost continual

Elders Earl Spafford and James H. Oakey with Kaffi natives in South Africa around 1915. (LDS Church Archives)

political strife during this period, climaxed by the English-Boer War, which ended just the year before the elders returned. Only a remnant of the original members had remained faithful.

During the early decades of the twentieth century, South Africa continued to be a difficult field of labor, and progress was slow. By 1917, the total number of Latter-day Saints in the country stood at only 339. Membership grew to one thousand by 1933, and reached two thousand some twenty-two years later.

A serious problem developed from 1915 to 1921 when the South African government refused to admit any Mormon missionaries into the country. A few weaker branches that had depended on the elders' leadership were forced to close. Others had to depend on local leaders—a blessing in the long run. A new mission president was permitted to enter South Africa in 1921, but only after twenty months of negotiations. Shortly after his arrival, a new government was elected, and the mission president was able to secure clearance for up to twenty-five missionaries. Even though this quota was increased in later years, the limited number of missionaries from America led to a greater emphasis on training local elders to preach the word. In 1930, the five full-time and three part-time local missionaries were enjoying greater success than their counterparts from America. Even though the Church was granted full legal status in 1936, the quota remained, and relations with the South African government continued to be a delicate matter.

Another problem arose with a lack of adequate meeting places. The first chapel in Johannesburg was not dedicated until 1924; other branches simply had to do the best they could by meeting in rented halls or remodeled homes.

Furthermore, as had been the case in the previous century, the elders still did not learn Afrikaans, and there was no Church literature available in that language. Proselyting, therefore, was still restricted mainly to the English sector of South African society. The Afrikaaners were largely neglected until 1951, when elders were instructed to learn their language. South Africa was officially designated as a foreign language mission in 1963, and missionaries going there were required to learn Afrikaans at the Church's Language Training Mission.

Continued Church policy against ordaining blacks to the priesthood remained a challenge. Some converts, especially in Cape Province, were of mixed racial ancestry, so intermarriage was a big source of concern. Before receiving the priesthood, every male member was required to trace his genealogy off the African continent to prove that he did not have Negro blood. Because this was often very difficult to accomplish, the potential number of local priesthood leaders was thereby diminished.

Worthy men who because of lineage could not receive the priesthood were nevertheless encouraged to participate in Church activity.[4] David O. McKay, the first Church president to visit the African continent, made a significant change in policy when he came to South Africa in 1954. He stipulated that a man could receive the priesthood unless there was clear evidence, such as official records, that he had Negro blood; hence, the responsibility for proof or disproof was laid upon the Church rather than on the individual. This issue would later be resolved with a revelation received in 1978.

President McKay's visit in 1954 also did much to encourage the Saints in South Africa in other ways. He was the first General Authority at any level to visit the mission. He determined that these Saints, who lived farther away from Church headquarters than members in any other mission, needed closer contact with Church leaders and consequently sent other General Authorities to visit and assist in the work.

The next year, 1955, was a time of racial unrest in the country, and for a time visas were denied to missionaries of many denominations from most foreign countries. Thereafter the work had to be carried on by local missionaries and missionaries from other British commonwealth countries, mainly Canada.

EXPANSION INTO RHODESIA

The 1950s also laid the groundwork for future growth on the African continent. During this decade, as a number of old problems were resolved, missionary work spread into new areas. Twenty years of occasional missionary visits to the scattered Saints in Southern Rhodesia (later named Zimbabwe) paid off in the fall of 1950, when the government gave permission for proselyting to begin in the area. Latter-day Saint elders were assigned to the towns of Salisbury and Bulawayo. The first Rhodesian convert, Hugh H. Hodgkiss, was baptized 1 February 1951 at beautiful Mermaid Pool, an hour's drive from Salisbury in Africa's lion country. Brother Hodgkiss later became a leader of the Church in the area. At first, only a Sunday School was conducted in Salisbury, and it met in a rented school. The missionaries capitalized on the opportunity to gain favorable attention through teaching square dancing, which was very popular in the country. In 1952, missionary work was extended to Northern Rhodesia (later called Zambia), especially in the Copper Belt mining district. Church members living in this area were some two thousand miles from mission headquarters in Cape Town. Membership in the mission had doubled to nearly four thousand in the years between 1955 and 1961.

The 1960s brought even faster growth to the Church. Membership increased to more than six thousand. This growth was stimulated when mission headquarters were moved from Cape Town to Johannesburg, the largest population center in South Africa.

By 1970, the Church had been firmly established, with an emphasis on local leadership, and the gospel had been extended to the entire European community. The area was now ready for greater work that was poised to take place.

AN ERA OF PROMISING GROWTH

The first stake of Zion on the African continent was created at Johannesburg on 22 March 1970. The creation of the Transvaal Stake marked the beginning of a new period of growth and expansion and provided greater responsibilities and blessings for local members and leaders.

Another critically needed improvement in meeting the needs of the members and missionaries of South Africa was an accelerated effort to make Church literature available in Afrikaans. Under the direction of Bishop Johannes P. Brummer, who headed the Church's translation effort, the Book of Mormon became available to the majority of the population in their native tongue.

On Sunday, 2 December 1973, President Spencer W. Kimball of the Quorum of the Twelve met with local leaders and missionaries at the mission home in Johannesburg to officially rededicate South Africa "to a great cause . . . that will bring greater numbers and greater devotion to the people of this land." He prayed that "numerous thousands may be convinced, comforted and converted," that "stakes and branches may dot this land," and that even a temple might provide "endowments and blessings."[5]

Many members in South Africa regarded President Kimball's prayer as one of the most significant events in the Church's 120-year history there. Mission President E. Dale LeBaron, who had earlier served in South Africa as a missionary and then as a Church Educational System supervisor, reported that previously there had been "an unsettled feeling among the members of the Church. President Kimball's visit had a calming effect. His prayer told them they have a future, and that the kingdom is going to grow. There is a different spirit here now."[6]

Steady growth continued during the 1970s. Introduction of home study seminary and institute in 1973 brought new opportunities for gospel learning and an immediate increase in the number of local missionaries and temple marriages, even though the closest temple was in London, England, some five thousand miles away. Some couples told their parents they would forego having a wedding reception if instead their way to the temple could be paid. Visits by Brigham Young University performing groups and the Church's microfilming of vital records attracted favorable publicity. By 1978, there were two stakes of approximately two thousand members each and a total Church membership of 6,831 in South Africa, with an additional 778 in Rhodesia.

When the first area conference convened at Johannesburg in October of that year, Saints sacrificed much to be present. Members in Johannesburg opened their homes to those who had to travel as many as eight hundred miles. Many homes were lined wall to wall with sleeping bags, and meals were provided by the host families. Because of civil war and unrest in neighboring Rhodesia, members traveling through its bush country had to take special precautions against terrorist attacks. The Glen Gifford family of Salisbury carried a machine gun in their family car during the eight-hundred-mile drive to Johannesburg. Some members traveled in convoys accompanied by armed government vehicles. Once, a chartered bus broke down soon after leaving a Rhodesian chapel, causing some of the members to miss the convoy that departed only twice a day at specified times. After a prayer offered by the branch president, the group decided to go on alone, armed with three automatic weapons and the power of faith. "The Lord asked us to come to Johannesburg, and so here we are," said one of the passengers, Sister Pauline Wainwright, after the delayed bus arrived safely for the conference. Brother Gifford spoke with similar faith: "I believe the prophet has a message for the people of Rhodesia in South Africa, and we wanted to be here to hear it."[7]

The area conference provided a great reassurance for the members in South Africa and Rhodesia and was regarded as a manifestation of God's love and as a promise of future growth and success. By this time other events had already begun that would profoundly affect the direction of Church growth in Africa.

BEGINNINGS IN WEST AFRICA

The Church's almost instant growth among the blacks of West Africa is unique in the annals of Latter-day Saint history. Many people, especially in Nigeria and Ghana, were prepared to accept the restored gospel even before missionaries could be sent to them from Church headquarters in the United States.

The Church's involvement in Nigeria, Africa's most populous nation, which is richly endowed with oil and other natural resources, began as early as the 1940s when individuals wrote to Church headquarters in Salt Lake City asking for information. For example, Honesty John Ekong, a Nigerian, requested information on the beliefs of the Mormon people. His letter was answered by LaMar S. Williams, the secretary to the Church missionary committee. As Ekong received Latter-day Saint literature, he distributed it freely in his local village. Williams began receiving many letters of inquiry from other villages and towns of Nigeria. Later, a pleading letter from Adeqole Ogunmokum, a Nigerian news reporter, prompted President David O. McKay to have Williams visit Nigeria. President McKay and his counselors were impressed with Williams's reports of the Nigerians' desire to have the gospel. Following this first visit, Williams, his wife, and four other couples were called to serve as missionaries to Nigeria, and he was set apart as the presiding elder. However, because of unfavorable publicity regarding blacks and the Mormon priesthood, the couples were denied visas and could not serve. Nevertheless, individual Nigerians who were interested in the Church were more determined than ever to join. Williams continued to correspond with them.[8]

Elder N. Eldon Tanner, West European Mission president, visited Nigeria in 1962 and discovered four different groups— the largest having four thousand members—that identified themselves with The Church of Jesus Christ of Latter-day Saints. They seemed to understand the teachings of the gospel and were sincere in their faith. They "realized black African men couldn't hold the priesthood until President McKay said they could," and "they were trying to live worthy of that privilege."[9] Nevertheless, President McKay felt impressed to discontinue efforts to establish missionary work in western Africa. Almost immediately following this decision, a vicious civil war broke out in the very areas of Nigeria where missionaries would have been working.

Although the Church did not send any official representatives to Nigeria, some members visited the country on education, legal, and business assignments. Homer Austin was set apart as a group leader and coordinator for Nigeria in 1971 by Church authorities in Utah. While in Nigeria, he contacted leaders of the congregations calling themselves by the name of the Church. These people urged him to have missionaries sent so they could be baptized and officially become members of the Church. Nigeria and Ghana were placed under the jurisdiction of the president of the Switzerland Mission until 1978 when the revelation was received.

Emmanuel Abu Kissi and his wife joined the Church in Manchester, England, where he was working in a hospital as a medical doctor. The Kissis returned to Ghana, where Emmanuel began operating the Deseret Hospital. Brother Kissi was called to serve as an Area Authority Seventy in 2002. (Photo courtesy Richard O. Cowan)

Lorry Rytting, while living in Nigeria as a teacher on a Fulbright fellowship, was set apart as a group leader there in 1974. Rytting's last act in 1975 before leaving the country was to assist the Nigerians in organizing a coalition of leaders of the various local congregations.

Inspired individuals also played a key role in introducing the gospel to the neighboring nation of Ghana. R.A.F. Mensah first came in contact with the Church while visiting California. Later, in England, he happened to mention the Church to a woman named Lilian Emily Clark. Clark had met with LDS missionaries before and, although she chose not to be baptized, was interested in their message. She had retained a copy of the Book of Mormon and several pamphlets, including "Joseph Smith's Testimony." Upon hearing of Mensah's interest in the Church, Clark shared these materials with him.

He became "a zealous teacher of the gospel. [And] it was only a matter of a few months before he had persuaded friends and others to join him in organizing a group of the Church at Bubiuashi, a suburb of Accra," Ghana's capital. In 1964 Mensah shared the gospel message, along with the Book of Mormon, with a fellow pastor, thirty-year-old Joseph W. B. Johnson, who then became the greatest driving force in gaining converts and establishing congregations in Ghana—particularly in the Cape Coast area, about seventy miles from Accra. Although Brother Johnson and his associates did not have priesthood authority, they baptized over a thousand Ghanians, giving many of them a "very interesting certificate of baptism. This certificate contained quotations from the Bible, and the Book of Mormon, as well as a listing of the Church's thirteen articles of faith." This group met in a building identified as "The Church of Jesus Christ of Latter-day Saints." Hence, many of the early members of the Church in Ghana "either directly or indirectly trace their activity" back to these brethren.[10]

IMPACT OF THE 1978 REVELATION ON PRIESTHOOD

The possibility of extending priesthood blessings to people of all nations had weighed heavily on President Spencer W. Kimball, as it had on Presidents David O. McKay and Harold B. Lee before him. "I remember very vividly," recounted President Kimball in the 1978 Johannesburg area conference, "that day after day I walked over to the temple and ascended to the fourth floor where we have our solemn assemblies and where we have our meetings of the Twelve and the First Presidency. After everybody had gone out of the temple, I knelt and prayed. I prayed with much fervency. I knew that something was before us that was extremely important to many of the children of God. I knew that we could receive the revelations of the Lord only by being worthy and ready for them and ready to accept them and to put them into place."[11]

Elder Gordon B. Hinckley remembered that in a special meeting with the First Presidency and the Quorum of the Twelve in the Salt Lake Temple on 1 June 1978, "there was a hallowed and sanctified atmosphere in the room. For me, it felt as if a conduit opened between the heavenly throne and the kneeling, pleading prophet of God who was joined by his Brethren. The Spirit of God was there. And by the power of the Holy Ghost there came to that prophet an assurance that the thing for which he prayed was right, that the time had come, and that now the wondrous blessings of the priesthood should be extended to worthy men everywhere regardless of lineage. Every man in that circle, by the power of the Holy Ghost, knew the same thing."[12]

The news of this revelation traveled rapidly around the world, the reaction being especially poignant in Africa. The revelation received by President Spencer W. Kimball in 1978 was of special interest and significance to members and missionaries in South Africa. It meant that racial lineage would no longer be a concern in bestowing the priesthood, so missionary work among blacks and mixed-blood "coloreds" could now go forward in earnest—at least as far as the apartheid laws and policies of the South African government would permit.

The impact of this revelation was most clearly seen in the lives of individuals that were significantly changed because they could now be ordained and receive the blessings of the priesthood. Joseph Johnson, the Church's pioneer in Ghana, remembered that he had tuned in his radio to the British Broadcasting station (BBC) about midnight. Although it had been years since he had listened to the station, the first thing he heard was a news report about the priesthood revelation. "I burst into tears of joy, because I knew the priesthood would come to Africa," Brother Johnson recounted.[13] He would later become Ghana's first official branch president and would be ordained as the first stake patriarch in that country.[14]

Alice Johanna Okkers, a long-time Church member from Cape Town, South Africa, dreamed of the day she could attend the temple. She was seventy-eight years old when the revelation made this possible. In the Salt Lake Temple she was able to receive her own endowments and do the work for her parents, siblings, and for her deceased husband. During the sealings, she was so moved she was unable to speak. "The temple was so wonderful," she said, "I thought that if I should close my eyes, I could be with the Lord."[15]

Although the Church had been first duly registered as a legal corporate body in Nigeria on 29 September 1964 and in Ghana on 26 July 1969 by native citizens of these two countries, the full organization and programs of the Church were first made available to the people of West Africa only following the momentous 1978 revelation on priesthood. It marked the beginning of a great new day for the Church among the blacks of Ghana and Nigeria.

On 21 July 1978, Edwin Q. Cannon Jr. and Merrill J. Bateman were called and set apart to carry out a fact-finding trip to Ghana and Nigeria. They were to determine conditions there and make recommendations on how best to proceed in carrying the full blessings of the Church to the people of West Africa. Brother Bateman recalled:

> Toward the end of the trip, we arrived in Calabar, Nigeria, on a Friday afternoon, needing the services of a previously identified member to help us find approximately fifteen congregations in the southeastern part of the country. . . .
>
> The member, Ime Eduok, was not at the airport or at the hotel. Brother Cannon and I checked in and went to our room not knowing where or how to find Brother Eduok in a city of one million. The next two days were a critical part of the trip, and Brother Eduok was the only one who could help us. We knelt in prayer and asked the Lord to guide us to him. We returned to the lobby and asked the desk clerk if she knew Mr. Eduok. She did not. Within a few minutes a large number of Nigerians had gathered around us discussing our plight but lacking the information needed. Suddenly, I felt a hand on my shoulder. I turned to see a large man standing next to me who said: 'Did I hear you say Ime Eduok? He is my employee. I just entered the hotel to buy a newspaper on my way home from work. Ime will be leaving the firm in fifteen minutes. I do not know where he lives. If he leaves the office before you arrive, it is unlikely that you will find him before Monday.' The man hurriedly put us in a taxi and gave the driver directions. We arrived at the business just as Ime Eduok was locking the door. Brother Eduok guided us to each congregation during the Saturday and Sunday that followed. Many people in those congregations are now members of the Church, and information gleaned from them formed an important part of the report given to the First Presidency upon our return.[16]

In October, the First Presidency announced the assignments of Rendell and Rachel Mabey of Bountiful, Utah, and Edwin and Janath Cannon of Salt Lake City as "special representatives of the Church's International Mission" to serve in Ghana and Nigeria. Other couples followed later. All were seasoned and highly qualified Church workers.

The Church's representatives were counseled to move cautiously. A unique legal challenge was posed by the fact that local groups had already incorporated under the name "Church of Jesus Christ of Latter-day Saints." The missionaries wondered if they could use the official title of the Church since it had already been adopted by these other groups. "So we made an effort to get acquainted with those who were the trustees of these churches," Elder Mabey recalled, "because some of them had written to Church headquarters [in Salt Lake City] and were very desirous of joining the Church."[17] In this way the Church was able to assimilate these groups and to use the corporate identities already established.

The missionaries found hundreds of people who had been waiting patiently for as many as fifteen years for authorized representatives to come and establish the Church among them. Brother Johnson even had a ten-year-old son named Brigham after President Young. There were several independent groups operating under the Church's name; many groups were not acquainted with one another. Upon hearing of the restored gospel through a variety of means, each had organized on its own. Not having any knowledge of proper Church government and policies, some different practices crept in. "They just didn't know the procedures . . . ," Elder Mabey observed, "but they said to us, 'Tell us what to do and we'll do it!' There were no arguments. They wanted to do what was right."[18]

The Mabeys and Cannons spent one year in Nigeria and Ghana. The fruits of their labors were truly inspirational and

Workers hoist an angel Moroni statue atop the Johannesburg South Africa Temple. The temple was dedicated 24–25 August 1985 and today serves sixty-nine stakes and districts in Africa, south of the Sahara. (LDS Church Archives)

dramatic. The time had fully come for the prospering of the Church in West Africa. In December 1979, *The Church News* featured a large photograph showing scores of West Africans being baptized in a single service. Seeds sown over a period of several years were now taking root.

These new converts were progressing noticeably. They studied and restudied the gospel literature and were very well prepared when called on to teach or speak. The missionaries believed the talks and lessons they heard in Africa were better organized than many they heard back home. An outstanding example was Emmanuel Abu Kissi. Brother Kissi, a medical doctor, had come into contact with the Church in England. After his baptism, he returned to Ghana, where he opened a small medical facility called Deseret Hospital. He would later serve in numerous leadership positions in the Church and help convert many of his fellow countrymen and women.[19] By the end of 1979, Church membership in Ghana and Nigeria exceeded seventeen hundred.[20] A regular mission of the Church was organized in that area in 1980. Although the cultural background of the West African Saints was quite different than that of most Church members in North America, perhaps nowhere was there any greater faith manifest than among these new converts.

UNPRECEDENTED EXPANSION IN AFRICA

In 1981, the Church announced that the first temple in Africa would be built at Johannesburg. Members and missionaries in that area were exhibiting greater optimism than at any previous time in history. They had adopted a new phrase: "We're as far from Salt Lake City as any Mormon on earth, but we're just as close to heaven." President Gordon B. Hinckley dedicated the temple in 1985.

At the other end of the continent the first Nigerian Stake was organized in 1988. It was the first stake in the Church in which all leaders were black.

During the 1980s and 1990s the Church expanded into at least twenty-eight more African nations, including such well-known countries as Republic of the Congo, Ivory Coast, Kenya, Uganda, and Zaire (later Democratic Republic of the Congo). In some cases families from abroad became the Church's first presence in the area. In several, the Church's first members were local citizens who had accepted the gospel while living overseas, particularly in Europe. In each country, the establishing of branches and even stakes and the securing of legal recognition have constituted significant milestones.

A Nigerian Primary class meets ca. 1985. Three years later, in 1988, the first Nigerian stake was organized. By the year 2000, Nigeria was home to more than 55,000 Church members, and a temple had been announced for Aba, Nigeria. (LDS Church Archives)

Additional missions have been formed to aid the gospel's spread.

Several of these countries benefited from substantial contributions by the Church to varied humanitarian projects particularly aimed at combating drought and famine. In Kenya, for example, one Church project in 1989 brought water to fifteen villages, and another project five years later provided personal "water taps" for hundreds of families. Latter-day Saint agronomists also worked with families to help them raise more nutritious or profitable crops. Tons of clothing were sent to Uganda and other countries. Millions of dollars for these projects came from special fast offerings and other donations.[21]

Civil wars and other fighting have disrupted the work in some of these nations. Even in Ghana, where the Church had thousands of members, the government in 1989 unexpectedly expelled the missionaries and banned Church operations and services there; fortunately the government reversed this action the following year.[22] Within a few months, Ghana's first two stakes were organized at Accra and Cape Coast. When the Church contacted the seventy-two local Ghanaian missionaries who had been released at the time the ban had been imposed, more than three-fourths of them chose to resume their missions; one elder had kept himself ready by reading the Book of Mormon twenty times and studying several other church works during his enforced furlough.[23]

Brighter days were ahead for the Saints in West Africa. In February 1998 President Gordon B. Hinckley became the first Church president to visit that area. One leader pointed out that when children were taught about the Lord's living prophet, he seemed as remote to them as prophets in the Old Testament. "Now," he exclaimed, "they will see his face with their own eyes."[24] In Nigeria, President Hinckley visited 1,150 priesthood leaders in a special meeting and 12,417 people in a general session. In Accra, Ghana, his announcement of the first temple in West Africa was received with joyous applause. In Kenya, faithful Saints from neighboring countries traveled hundreds of miles to see their prophet. He then continued to Zimbabwe and South Africa. During this trip President Hinckley traveled nearly 25,000 miles, almost the distance around the earth.

Two years later, at the April general conference of the Church, President Hinckley further announced a new temple to be constructed in Aba, Nigeria. With previous growth as a pattern, the future holds promise of even greater progress for the Church in this heretofore sleeping giant.

CHURCH STATUS IN AFRICA*

Countries	Members	Stakes	Missions	Temples**
Angola	563	—	—	—
Botswana	1,001	—	—	—
Cameroon	181	—	—	—
Cape Verde Islands	5,759	—	1	—
Central African Republic	127	—	—	—
Democratic Rep of Congo	13,637	3	1	—
Egypt	114	—	—	—
Ethiopia	507	—	—	—
Ghana	22,164	5	1	1
Ivory Coast (Cote d'Ivoire)	7,840	2	1	—
Kenya	5,680	1	1	—
Lesotho	485	—	—	—
Liberia	3,871	1	—	—
Madagascar	2,634	1	1	—
Malawi	377	—	—	—
Mauritius	341	—	—	—
Mozambique	1,352	—	—	—
Namibia (South West Africa)	336	—	—	—
Nigeria	60,087	13	5	1
Republic of Congo	2,958	—	—	—
Réunion	740	—	—	—
Sierra Leone	4,782	—	—	—
South Africa	36,297	10	3	1
Swaziland	856	—	—	—
Tanzania	540	—	—	—
Togo	361	—	—	—
Uganda	3,089	—	—	—
Zambia	951	—	—	—
Zimbabwe	10,655	1	1	—
Africa Totals:	**188,285**	**37**	**15**	**3**

* Numbers are for year's end 2002

** These numbers represent operating temples and those that had been announced or were under construction at press time.

CHAPTER 21

THE CHURCH IN THE MIDDLE EAST

RICHARD O. COWAN

1841	Elder Orson Hyde offers prayer of dedication on Mount of Olives (24 October)
1873	President George A. Smith and others rededicate the Holy Land (2 March)
1884	Jacob Spori opens missionary work in Constantinople
1886	Spori teaches Germans in Haifa
1887	Work opens among Armenians in Turkey and Syria
1921	Elder David O. McKay offers prayer on Mount of Olives (3 November)
	Armenians Saints evacuated from Aintab to Aleppo
1927	First Presidency decides not to establish colony in the Near East
1928	Joseph Booth dies in Aleppo
1950	Near East Mission closed
1968	First BYU Study Abroad program opens in Israel
1972	Jerusalem Branch organized by President Harold B. Lee
1974	Cairo Branch organized
1979	Orson Hyde Memorial Garden dedicated by President Spencer W. Kimball (24 October)
1989	BYU Jerusalem Center dedicated by Elder Howard W. Hunter (16 May)
	Center in Amman opened
1998	Islamic texts translation series launched

MIDDLE EAST

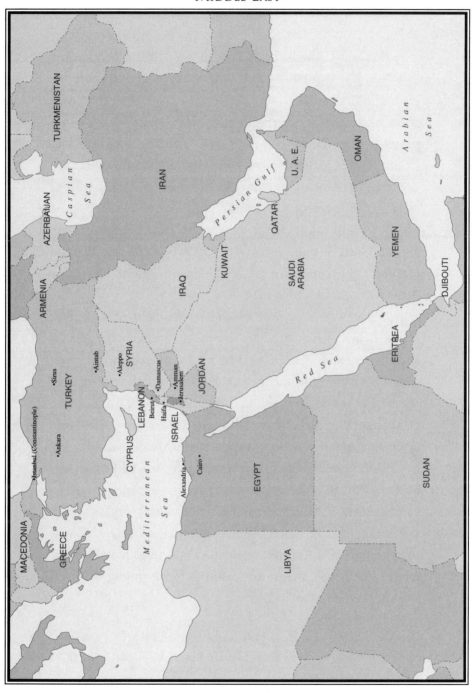

Of all the Church's international areas, this is perhaps the most unique. It includes the lands where God dealt with his people during Old Testament dispensations and where the Savior of the world spent his earthly ministry. Here, too, great events are prophesied to transpire in the future. Furthermore, the Holy Land has received more apostolic dedications than any other area.

In earlier times, the term *Near East* was commonly used to identify the countries around the eastern end of the Mediterranean, while *Middle East* referred to areas closer to the Persian Gulf. In more recent years, however, *Middle East* has become the preferred name for the entire region. This latter usage will be followed here.

Unlike most other areas, missionary work in the Middle East has been disrupted many times because of turmoil in the area. In addition, mission headquarters have been moved several times, creating further instability and challenges. Still, there have been remarkable examples of faithful commitment to the work despite great difficulties; probably no other area has seen more deaths per capita than among the elders serving in the Middle East.

The restored Church's early interest in the Middle East was evidenced in 1841 when one of the Twelve Apostles arrived to offer a prayer of dedication. Actual missionary work, however, did not commence in the region for more than forty years—at first among small European colonies and then later among an ethnic minority. For various reasons, efforts among the Arab majority have had to be limited.

EARLY APOSTOLIC DEDICATIONS
OF THE HOLY LAND

For centuries, travel in the Holy Land was so dangerous that pilgrims from the west generally stayed away. In 1831,

Orson Hyde, one of the original Twelve Apostles, traveled to Jerusalem and ascended the Mount of Olives in October 1841, where he dedicated the Holy Land for the gathering of the children of Abraham. (LDS Church Archives)

however, a rebellion led by Mohammed Ali brought significant reforms. "For the first time in centuries, the rights to life and property were guaranteed to all inhabitants of the region."[1] Thus the window was opened for a representative of the restored Church to visit the Holy Land.

In March 1840, Elder Orson Hyde, one of the original Twelve Apostles, had a very significant dream: "I retired to my bed one night as usual; and while meditating and contemplating the field of my future labors, the vision of the Lord, like clouds of light, burst into my view. (See Joel 2:28). The cities of London, Amsterdam, Constantinople and Jerusalem, all appeared in succession before me, and the Spirit said unto me, 'Here are many of the children of Abraham whom I will gather to the land that I gave to their fathers; and here also is the field of your labors.'"[2]

At the general conference held in Nauvoo the following month, "by the counsel of the Holy Spirit," Church leaders appointed Elder Hyde to fulfill this mission.[3]

By spring of 1841 Elder Hyde was in England where he briefly joined eight of his fellow Apostles before spending a few months in Holland and Germany. By fall, he was in the Holy Land. Elder Hyde's ship arrived at Jaffa in the middle of the night. "Elder Hyde and others saw a bright glistening sword with a beautiful hilt etched in the sky, grasped by an extended arm and hand." Elder Hyde believed that this was one of the "signs in heavens" that he had been promised.[4] Upon arriving in Jerusalem he was able to report that the city appeared "precisely according to the vision which I had."[5]

On Sunday morning, 24 October 1841, "a good while before day," Orson Hyde "arose from sleep, and went out of the city as soon as the gates were opened, crossed the brook Kedron, and went upon the Mount of Olives." There, he offered his prayer of dedication. "Thy servant has been obedient to the heavenly vision which Thou gavest him in his native land; and under the shadow of Thine outstretched arm, he has safely arrived in this place to dedicate and consecrate this land unto Thee, for the gathering together of Judah's scattered remnants, according to the predictions of the holy Prophets—for the building up of Jerusalem again after it has been trodden down by the Gentiles so long, and for rearing a Temple in honor of thy name." He also petitioned the Lord to "remove the barrenness and sterility of this land, and let springs of living water break forth to water its thirsty soil. Let the vine and olive produce in their strength, and the fig-tree bloom and flourish. Let the land become abundantly fruitful."[6] At the conclusion of his prayer, Elder Hyde erected a pile of stones as a witness according to ancient custom. He then left the Holy Land, stopping once again in Europe en route back to America.

Following Elder Hyde's visit, such challenges as the martyrdom of Joseph Smith, the westward trek of the pioneers, and the need to eke out a living in the deserts of the Rocky Mountains all kept the Church from following up in that area. Finally, in 1872, President Brigham Young appointed his first counselor, George A. Smith, to visit Palestine and offer a second dedicatory prayer there. Lorenzo Snow and Albert Carrington of the Twelve, Elder Snow's sister Eliza, and four others accompanied him.

The group left Utah in November 1872 and arrived at Jerusalem nearly four months later. On Sunday, 2 March 1873, they ascended the Mount of Olives (as Elder Hyde had done over three decades before) where they set up a tent to shield them from the cool wind and afford some privacy. In his prayer of rededication, President George A. Smith petitioned that the land "might become fertile" and that "the prophecies and promises unto Abraham and the prophets be fulfilled here in the own due time of the Lord."[7]

MISSION OPENED IN CONSTANTINOPLE AND PALESTINE

Actual missionary work commenced in the Middle East just over ten years later, not in Palestine but rather in Turkey. Hagop Vartooguian, an Armenian living in Constantinople (later renamed Istanbul), had heard about the Church and began corresponding with European Mission headquarters in England and requested that a missionary be sent to begin preaching in person. Jacob Spori, a missionary from Switzerland, was sent to fill this request. He arrived in Constantinople on the last day of 1884 and soon found Hagop. After teaching the gospel to him and his family, Elder

Spori baptized them on 4 January 1885. Unfortunately, however, when no others joined the Church immediately, the Vartooguian family's interest diminished and within a short time they had fallen away. Still, the first baptisms had been performed—interestingly among the same ethnic minority that would subsequently provide the largest number of converts in the Middle East.

Elder Spori's arrival in Constantinople marked the opening of what became known as the Turkish Mission. At that time, the Ottoman Turkish Empire ruled most of the Middle East plus the Balkans region of Europe. During most of the year 1885, Jacob Spori worked alone, seeking any opportunity to share the gospel. He held public meetings and wrote missionary tracts and articles for newspapers, reaching primarily a German audience. He sought to learn the various languages spoken in this cosmopolitan city, yet there were no further converts to reward his diligent, lonely efforts.

Finally, Elder Spori received a companion near the end of 1885 with the arrival of Joseph Tanner in Constantinople in December of that year. They worked together for the next several weeks. Although they obtained a room where they could hold meetings, their efforts were hindered by a lack of language fluency.

Francis M. Lyman Jr., son of the recently appointed Apostle, arrived in Constantinople intending to travel through the Middle East. He asked Elder Tanner to accompany him, once again leaving Jacob Spori alone. During March and April of 1886, Lyman and Tanner visited Athens, Corinth, Alexandria, Cairo, Jerusalem, Haifa (in Israel), Damascus, and Beirut. Their objective was not to proselyte but rather to gain a broader understanding of the diverse peoples of this region.

They were particularly interested in visiting groups of German Christians living around the port city of Haifa. Believing that Christ's second coming was at hand, these "Templers" had established their colonies in Palestine to be present for the anticipated glorious event. In June, Elder Tanner wrote to the European Mission president recommending that missionaries be sent to these colonies. Elder Spori soon received the assignment.

The night before his departure, Jacob Spori had a remarkable and comforting dream. "I had a vision in the night," he related, "and was told to begin my labors in the town of Haifa. In this vision I saw a man with a short coal-black beard. He was a blacksmith and as I passed his shop he came out to meet me. I was further told that he would be notified of my coming and that he and his family should be prepared to receive me and to receive the message I had for them. I shall know of the man if I ever see him."[8]

Elder Spori sailed from Constantinople for the Holy Land on 29 July 1886. His ship made its first stop in Palestine at Jaffa, the port serving Jerusalem. Even though most of the other passengers got off there, Jacob stayed on board until the next stop, at Haifa. Upon landing, he found his way to the street he had seen in his dream: "Some distance before he reached George Grau's blacksmith's shop he heard the ring of the anvil. He kept the middle of the road, as he was commanded to do, until he reached a spot directly in front of the door of the blacksmith's shop. Mr. George Grau, the blacksmith, upon seeing Elder Spori immediately dropped his hammer, tongs, and iron and ran out into the road, calling to Elder Spori. He told this Elder that he had seen him the night before in a dream and was told that this stranger had a divine message for him. Thereupon Elder Spori was invited into the man's home and treated to a repast. Grau's family was called together and Elder Spori delivered his message."⁹

Elder Spori baptized Johan George Grau in Haifa Bay on 29 August 1886 and ordained him an elder the following week. Grau baptized his wife, Magdalena, two weeks later. The Graus remained in Haifa for the rest of their lives, sharing the gospel and providing leadership to the small branch and to the scattered Saints in surrounding areas.

Elder Spori remained in Palestine several months, working primarily among German groups in Haifa and Jerusalem. In the spring of 1887 he returned to Constantinople, trading places with Elder Tanner, who went to Palestine. Tanner spent five months there, preaching in Haifa and Joppa, and baptized seven people: four Russians, two Germans, and one Arab.¹⁰

Elder Tanner was released in September 1887 and Spori early the following year. Eventually seven of their German converts from Palestine immigrated to Utah and settled in Provo, the first members of the Church to gather to the new Zion from the land of the old Zion. The two missionaries' meager success had been among immigrant groups rather than with the native peoples of Turkey and Palestine. Still, they had laid foundations for future growth in the area.

WORK AMONG THE ARMENIANS

Ferdinand F. Hintze, who had arrived in 1887, was the only missionary remaining following the departures of Elders Spori and Tanner. For ten months he lived with an Armenian family at Constantinople, making a diligent effort to learn their language. At length, he was able to teach the gospel to Dekran Shahabian, a visitor from Sivas, a small town in eastern Turkey. Evidently interested in the missionary's message, Shahabian invited Hintze to visit Sivas and teach him further. In the summer of 1888, the European Mission president directed Hintze to visit the recent converts in Palestine. He decided to stop in Sivas on the way. He remained there a few weeks and was able to baptize several converts, including Shahabian and his wife. He stopped at other towns along his route, again finding people who were interested in his message; at Aintab, for example, he preached to several hundred listeners. These contacts opened the door for teaching the large Armenian population living in southeastern Turkey. He was convinced that the mission's future growth would be here in the interior rather than among the Europeans in the larger cities.

He later reflected that the Greeks "were mostly indifferent" and that there were restrictions against teaching Muslims. The government, on the other hand, allowed the Mormons to teach the Armenians, believing that this would "break up Armenian unity and thus make it easier to govern them."[11]

With this unexpected cooperation from government officials, Elder Hintze and his recently arrived companion doubled their efforts to teach the Armenians. By 1888 the missionary force was increased to ten: seven Americans and three natives. The conditions these missionaries faced, however, were extremely difficult. Communications and transportation were primitive; missionaries were frequently robbed as they traveled between towns. They were often arrested for trumped-up violations of travel regulations. Illness was almost a constant challenge. In fact, Edgar Simmons, an elder laboring in Aintab,

*Joseph Wilford Booth
served for thirty years in
the Turkish and
Armenian regions of the
Middle East. (LDS
Church Archives)*

died of smallpox on 4 February 1890. Because of all these
problems, the missionary force was cut back to only three
within a year.

Elder Simmons was only the first of several missionaries to
pay the ultimate price while serving in the Middle East. In
1892 Adolph Haag died of typhus fever, and three years later
John A. Clark died of smallpox; both were working in Haifa
and were buried in the German cemetery there. In 1908 Emil
Huber died of typhus and was buried at Aleppo.

THE MISSIONARY SERVICE OF
JOSEPH WILFORD BOOTH

"No man contributed more to the missionary program of
the Church in the Near East than did Joseph Wilford Booth,"

one scholar has asserted.[12] Booth's service extended off and on for three decades. A schoolteacher from Utah, he left his wife behind when he accepted his call to the Turkish mission in 1898. Soon he was assigned to work with the Armenians in Aintab, Turkey.

Although the largest branch in the mission was located at Aintab, opposition was persistent and often violent. On one holiday in 1899, for example, Elder Booth and his companion, Philip Maycock, went to an area where a large number of people were picnicking, hoping for an "opportunity of bearing testimony of the Gospel." One group did ask the elders to tell them something about Mormonism. The elders moved with this group to a more secluded area, and, sitting on some rocky ledges, began their discussion. "A huge crowd soon gathered and made such a disturbance that conversation could not be heard, so a formal address was begun by a local member. Stones started falling around him and then he was pushed from his rock rostrum." The missionaries had to be rescued by the police, who at first dispersed the crowd but then learned the meeting was peaceable and encouraged the elders to continue. A large group of dissenters returned and caused such a commotion that the police were required to escort the missionaries home. The rumor spread among the Armenian Latter-day Saints, however, that the missionaries were being carried off to jail: "Our brethren were excited on hearing these rumors; and one, quickly arming himself with a sword, rushed out, determined to defend us, as Brother Peter once wanted to defend his Master. The occasion was past, however, on his arrival, for we were already out of all danger."[13]

As was true in other parts of the world, opposition was

often led by Protestant missionaries. These men had helped prepare the way for Latter-day Saint missionaries by having introduced Christianity but now resented the Mormons' success. Latter-day Saint children who had attended the Protestant schools before their conversion were excluded or harassed to the point that they withdrew. At the suggestion of Elder Anthon H. Lund, a member of the Quorum of the Twelve who visited Turkey in 1898, the Church opened its own school. The faculty consisted of Elder Booth (who taught English) and two local teachers. With some interruptions, the school functioned for ten years. It not only provided needed education but also created some goodwill for the Church, especially among the more educated people.

During this time, two Apostles visited the Holy Land. In 1898, while visiting Palestine with Ferdinand Hintze, Elder Anthon H. Lund offered a prayer of dedication at the Mount of Olives. Four years later, Elder Francis M. Lyman offered prayers at three locations: in Jerusalem, on the Mount of Olives, and in Haifa on Mount Carmel.

When Elder Booth began presiding over the mission in 1904, his wife, Reba, joined him. However, political turmoil mounted in the Ottoman Empire prior to World War I, and the mission was closed in 1909. During World War I the Armenians generally sided with Russia against Turkey. Those who remained within the boundaries of Turkey following the war therefore had reason to fear for their lives. They felt safe as long as the French armies were present to keep order, but the French mandate was due to expire at the end of 1921. Most Armenians, including the hundred or so Saints who remained in Aintab, were desperate to evacuate before the anticipated genocide. (An estimated 600,000

Hugh J. Cannon and Elder David O. McKay (on camels) visited several areas of the Holy Land, including the Sphinx, on their world tour of missions in 1912. (LDS Church Archives)

to 1.5 million Armenians were massacred during the years between 1915 and 1923.)

Church members in America had collected money for the relief of the suffering Armenian Saints. In 1921 the First Presidency determined that someone who had lived in the area should meet Elder David O. McKay, who was then on an around-the-world tour of missions, to distribute these funds. To help meet the Armenians' needs and to resume proselyting in the area, Church leaders reappointed Wilford Booth to once again preside over the newly renamed "Armenian Mission." The First Presidency thus instructed Booth and McKay to rendezvous, visit the Armenians, and determine how to best meet their needs.

431

Neither President Booth nor Elder McKay knew where to find one another. After visiting the pyramids and other sights in Egypt, Booth took a train from Alexandria along the coast to Haifa. At this same time, Elder McKay and his traveling companion, Hugh J. Cannon, were visiting points of interest in the Holy Land. On 3 November, they ascended the Mount of Olives and sought out a secluded place where they might meditate and pray. They petitioned God's blessings upon his church worldwide and upon the city and land that lay at their feet.[14] They prayed that they might be led by inspiration on their way to the Armenian mission and specifically, that they might find Brother Booth.[15] "It was an impressive occasion," Cannon reflected. "The veil separating the brethren from the presence of the Lord seemed very thin.[16]

Although they had originally planned to drive by car through the Holy Land, when they returned to the hotel, both brethren felt that they should take the train to Haifa. They were keenly aware of the need to meet Brother Booth, who could speak the Turkish language and who knew something about where the scattered Saints might be located. Their anxiety was heightened when both the American and British consuls advised them against going to Aintab in Turkey. Upon arriving in Haifa, Elder Cannon remained on the station platform with their luggage while Elder McKay took a few minutes to inquire about a suitable hotel where they might stay. "The delay caused by seeking information about hotels brought us to the station office door just at the same moment that another traveler reached it," Elder McKay recalled. "He touched me on the shoulder saying, 'Isn't this Brother McKay?' Astonished beyond expression to be thus addressed in so strange a town, I turned, and recognized Elder Wilford

Booth, the one man above all others whom we were most desirous of meeting." President Booth was in the process of determining if there was a ship in the harbor that he could take directly to Beirut. "We had met, too, at the most opportune time and place," Elder McKay continued. "Having known nothing of our whereabouts he had come from the western part of the world, hoping in his heart to meet us. Knowing from the cablegram, only that he was en route to Syria, we had come from the eastern part of the world, traveling westward, praying that we might meet him; and there we had met at the very time and place best suited to our convenience and to the success of our mission to the Armenians. It could not have been better had we been planning it for weeks."[17]

Elder McKay and President Booth visited the frightened Armenian Saints to assess what needed to be done for them. Only about one-third of the prewar members could be located. Booth regarded it a miracle that he could get the needed passports for all fifty-eight Saints remaining in Aintab. The plan was to move them eighty miles to Aleppo, another Armenian center just across the border in Syria. He hired nine wagons to carry the Saints and their few belongings to safety. This curious wagon train headed out on 13 December 1921 and reached the new home three days later. The members likened their exodus to the honored 1847 trek of the Mormon pioneers to the Rocky Mountains.

The idea of a Latter-day Saint colony in the Middle East had been proposed as early as 1889. Converts had already typically grouped together for mutual support and protection. Some had "gathered" to Zion in America. But most were prevented from doing so because of poverty or government regulations. As isolated Saints tended to fall away, the idea of gathering gained popularity. President Booth kept the idea alive, investigating the possibility of renting or purchasing land as a gathering site. However, following a thorough review of the idea and a visit to the area by Franklin S. Harris, then president of Brigham Young University, the First Presidency in 1927 decided not to pursue the idea any further. Acting on another recommendation by Harris, mission headquarters were moved to Haifa in 1928.

On 5 December 1928, overworked and disappointed by the conduct of some of the members, President Joseph Wilford Booth died at Aleppo and was buried there among the people for whom he had worked so long. Upon his death, his wife returned to America and the mission was closed.

MISSIONARY WORK AMID INCREASING TENSIONS

In 1927, the year before President Booth's death, Elder James E. Talmage visited the Armenian Mission. While in Jerusalem, he ascended the Mount of Olives as others had done before and offered yet another prayer of dedication.

In 1933, Elder John A. Widtsoe, then serving as president of the European Mission, visited the Holy Land. He offered prayers of dedication at Haifa and on the Mount of Olives. At this time, five years following President Booth's death, the mission was reopened. Badwagan Piranian, of Armenian descent, was called to preside.

For the next two years, President Piranian carried on the work with the help of only his family and one other missionary. The new name, "Palestine-Syrian Mission," reflected a broadening scope of the work. Unfortunately, the English and German-speaking people in the area proved to be indifferent, so the mission's membership remained completely Armenian.[18] In 1935 headquarters were moved to Beirut, Lebanon, and soon missionary work in Palestine was completely discontinued because of dangerous conditions there.[19] The mission was closed once again in 1939 with the outbreak of World War II.

Following the end of the war, the mission was reopened in 1947 with Badwagan Piranian again serving as its president. The mission had about seventy members with organized branches in Aleppo, Syria, and Beirut, Lebanon, and a few Saints in Damascus, Syria, and Jerusalem in Israel. The missionary force grew to seventeen by 1950. A basketball team led by one of these elders, Carlos E. Asay (a future General Authority), made many friends for the Church.

In 1950 the name was changed once again—this time to the "Near East Mission"—but it was closed in December of that same year because of the increasingly turbulent conditions in the region. Most of the missionaries were reassigned to the British Mission, but President Piranian was transferred to Fresno, California, where there was a large Armenian population. Because most of the faithful Armenian Saints also emigrated to America, most Church activities in the Middle East area ceased.[20] For a time during the 1960s, elders from the Swiss Mission worked in Beirut, primarily among Armenians living there.

MORE RECENT DEVELOPMENTS IN THE HOLY LAND

During most of the 1950s and 1960s there was only a handful of Latter-day Saints in the Holy Land, usually expatriate graduate students or individuals filling government and

*With the hills of Jerusalem in the background, President Spencer W. Kimball
confers with Jerusalem mayor Teddy Kollek at the dedication of the Orson Hyde
Memorial Garden. (LDS Church Archives)*

business assignments. The Church assumed a much greater
presence in the area beginning in 1968 when Brigham Young
University sent groups of students and teachers to study
there.

In September 1972, Church President Harold B. Lee
became the first living prophet to visit the Holy Land in nearly
2000 years. At a meeting in the Garden Tomb, believed to be
the place where the Savior's body was laid between his cruci-
fixion and resurrection, President Lee officially organized the
few resident Latter-day Saints into the Jerusalem Branch. They
asked about the possibility of holding Church meetings on
Saturday, the day on which the Sabbath was observed in that
land; a short time later the First Presidency gave their approval.
While in Jerusalem, President Lee directed local Church lead-

ers to look for a place where a monument might honor the 1841 visit of Elder Orson Hyde, and also to seek a site for a Church building there. "President Lee's visit to Jerusalem is a landmark in Church history there," latter-day historians have concluded. "Most developments related to the Church in the Holy Land have their foundation in his visit."[21]

When the Church applied for legal recognition in the country, it was required to provide proof that it had been "actively established in that land prior to the partition of Palestine and organization of Israel." The graves of Elders Haag and Clark at Haifa were presented as evidence. The desired legal status was granted in 1977.[22] During that same year, the Israel District was formed to supervise branches not only at Jerusalem but also in Tel Aviv, Haifa, and the Galilee area.

Development moved forward on the Orson Hyde Memorial Garden, a five-acre plot on the slopes of the Mount of Olives just above the Garden of Gethsemane. Church members around the world donated more than a million dollars for this project, which was the largest single unit in an extensive beautification program for the city of Jerusalem. On 24 October 1979, the 138th anniversary of Elder Hyde's dedicatory prayer, President Spencer W. Kimball dedicated this beautiful garden with its amphitheater overlooking the Old City of Jerusalem. Many local government and other leaders attended, which brought extensive favorable publicity for the Church. On this occasion, plans were also announced to construct a center to house Brigham Young University's study abroad programs.

Planning for the BYU Jerusalem Center for Near Eastern Studies moved forward under the direct supervision of the First

Presidency and with the active encouragement of Jerusalem's mayor, Teddy Kollek. The plan was to construct a building that would serve the Church's ecclesiastical and educational needs.

Many miracles led to the Church's finally obtaining property and permits to build on one of the most prominent sites in Jerusalem—the north end of the Mount of Olives. Although surrounding areas had been built up, remarkably, this prime site had remained undeveloped. In the face of vocal opposition, primarily from orthodox Jews, the Church signed a pledge that the new center would not be used for any proselytizing activities. Construction began in 1984 and three years later students moved into the nearly completed facility. Dedicated by Elder Howard W. Hunter of the Council of the Twelve in May 1989, it accommodated two hundred students and staff and included classrooms, a library, two auditoriums, dining facilities, and a gymnasium.[23] Its beautiful gardens and large windows afforded magnificent views of historic Jerusalem.

The Church has tried to remain impartial in the Israeli-Palestinian conflict. Elder Hunter affirmed: "Both the Jews and the Arabs are children of our Father. They are both children of promise, and as a church we do not take sides. We have love for and an interest in each."[24] Unfortunately, as tensions increased between the Arabs and Jews in the year 2000, BYU chose not to send any students to Jerusalem for the time being.

LATTER-DAY SAINT ACTIVITIES IN OTHER PARTS OF THE MIDDLE EAST

Since the mid-twentieth century there have been individual Latter-day Saints or small groups of members scattered throughout much of the Middle East. Many of them were educators, petroleum engineers, businessmen, diplomatic officials, or military advisors and their families. As their numbers grew, several Arab countries granted permission for such non-Muslim groups to meet for fellowship or worship. During the 1950s, for example, small expatriate branches were established at Ankara, Istanbul, and other locations in Turkey. A branch at Beirut, Lebanon, opened in 1965 but was closed from 1975 through 1990 because of the civil war in that land. The Cairo Branch was organized in 1974 by three Latter-day Saints living there; as membership climbed to as high as 150, a villa was leased for religious services. Because branch membership fluctuated widely, mature couples were assigned to Egypt beginning in 1980 to help with fellowshipping and related activities. Religious services, primarily for expatriates, were also held at various locations in Jordan. In 1997 a Latter-day Saint branch was organized in Damascus, Syria.

Middle Eastern governments typically have "allowed foreign residents to hold religious services on condition that these activities remain low-key and that Islamic laws and traditions, including the restriction against proselyting, be respected."[25] Despite the Latter-day Saints' reputation for extensive missionary activity elsewhere in the world, "the Church has observed religious restrictions in the Middle East by making nonproselyting commitments to government leaders and by issuing strict instructions for members to honor these commitments."[26]

In Jordan, cordial relations over the years between Jordanian government officials and leaders of the Church and Brigham Young University led to a 1989 agreement that allowed for the Church to lease property and establish the Center for Cultural and Educational Affairs in the capital city

The Jerusalem Center for Near Eastern Studies was dedicated by President Howard W. Hunter in 1989. It houses students and faculty and hosts concerts for the public. (Photo courtesy Donald Q. Cannon)

of Amman. The Church leased and remodeled a villa, formerly the Swiss embassy, to house the center. It became the the only Latter-day Saint building in the Middle East that publicly displayed the name of the Church. The center has paved the way for greater cooperation between the Church and Jordan. It has facilitated academic agreements and cultural interactions between BYU and Jordanian universities. The center has also channeled humanitarian and charitable assistance and sponsored community health programs.[27]

Coordinating a project to translate ancient Islamic texts has provided Brigham Young University another opportunity to build bridges in the Middle East. The first two volumes to appear in the Islamic Translation Series were works written by al-Ghazali, a twelfth-century Muslim philosopher, considered by many to be the greatest after Mohammed. This was the first time these works had appeared in any Western language. Daniel C. Peterson, a BYU professor of Asian and Near Eastern studies and managing editor of the project, believed that these translations would allow people in the West to become better acquainted with some sacred writings of Islam. Diplomats from thirty-five Muslim nations attended a 1993 reception at the Waldorf-Astoria hotel in New York City honoring this project; this was the first contact many of them have had with members and teachings of The Church of Jesus Christ of Latter-day Saints. Dr. Parviz Morewedge, a Muslim professor at State University of New York, praised the Church and BYU for their involvement with this project: "This university, this Church, these scholars are the grace of not only Christianity and American values, but also of the entire globe. Their brotherly love and compassion make them the hope of peace, the path of peace for our children and grandchildren of the 21st century."[28]

Latter-day Saint scriptures have been translated into several Middle Eastern languages. The Book of Mormon has appeared in Arabic, Hebrew, Farsi, Turkish, Urdu, and Armenian. The Doctrine and Covenants and Pearl of Great Price have been translated into Arabic and Armenian. Pamphlets and other Church publications have also been issued in several of these same languages.

Church activities in the Middle East have been interrupted from time to time because of wars or other sources of tension. Still, Latter-day Saints maintain a high interest in this prophetically significant part of the world.

CHURCH STATUS IN THE MIDDLE EAST

COUNTRIES	MEMBERS	STAKES	MISSIONS	TEMPLES
Armenia	1,265	—	1	—
Bahrain (Bahrein)	59	—	—	—
Cyprus	184	—	—	—
Israel*	235	—	—	—
Jordan*	227	—	—	—
Lebanon*	142	—	—	—
Qatar*	34	—	—	—
Syria*	58	—	—	—
Turkey	178	—	—	—
United Arab Emirates*	160	—	—	—
Middle East Totals:	**2,542**	—	**1**	—

* Numbers are for year's end 2000. All other numbers are for year's end 2002.

CHAPTER 22

The Church in North America

David F. Boone and Richard O. Cowan

1830	Church organized in western New York (6 April)
1830s	Northeast becomes important missionary field
1833	Joseph Smith preaches restored gospel in Canada
1842	South becomes flourishing missionary field
1844	Prophet Joseph Smith martyred (27 June)
1846	Saints aboard the *Brooklyn* arrive in San Francisco (31 July)
1847	Brigham Young and pioneers enter Salt Lake Valley (24 July)
	Removal of Saints to the West hampers missionary work
1857	Missions close as hostile army approaches Utah
1875	Missionary work reopens in South
1879	Joseph Standing murdered in Georgia
1890s	Missions expand during era of goodwill
1895	Alberta Stake organized, first in Canada
1923	Los Angeles Stake created, first outside of Intermountain West
	First Canadian temple dedicated in Cardston
1934	New York Stake organized, first in eastern United States
1941–45	World War II leads to growth in many new areas

443

1956	Los Angeles Temple dedicated, the Church's largest temple to date
1974	Washington D.C. Temple dedicated
1998	Monticello Utah Temple dedicated, the first of more than three dozen smaller temples
1999	Temples dedicated at Halifax and Regina, Canada—both on 14 November
2000	Palmyra New York Temple dedicated (6 April)
	100th functioning temple dedicated in Boston, Massachusetts (1 October)
	Conference Center dedicated adjacent to Temple Square (8 October)
2002	Rebuilt Nauvoo Illinois Temple dedicated (27 June)

Throughout much of the Church's existence, North America, specifically the United States and Canada, has provided a strong base for international growth. In western New York, the Father and the Son visited Joseph Smith in 1820, and the restored Church was organized there ten years later. Despite rapid growth in other areas, there were still more members in the United States and Canada than all the rest of the world combined as late as 1998. From Ohio, the first Latter-day Saint missionaries crossed the Atlantic to preach in Britain in 1837, and since then hundreds of thousands of North American missionaries have carried the gospel message to the four corners of the earth. The Saints in these scattered lands have continued to be benefited by the inspired guidance, leaders, and varied materials coming from Church headquarters in America.

Prophecy indicates that the key role of North America is to continue. The City of Zion, or the New Jerusalem, will be built in Jackson County, Missouri, and to its glorious temple the Lord will come at the time of his Second Advent. From here his law will go forth to bless the whole earth.

For most Latter-day Saints, the study of Church history in North America has amounted to a consideration of what might be called the mainstream. Beginning in New England, New York, and Pennsylvania, they have traced the Church's history to Ohio, Missouri, and Illinois, and then accompanied the pioneer wagons and handcarts to the valley of the Great Salt Lake. Nevertheless, the Church was and is growing in other parts of North America as well. Developments in these areas often followed patterns like those observed in other areas of the world and can profitably be compared or contrasted with the experience abroad. At the same time, progress of the Church in the United States and Canada both influences and is influenced by developments overseas. A consideration of North America is, therefore, vital to a complete understanding of the international Church.

EARLY BEGINNINGS

Less than a year after the Church of Jesus Christ was organized on 6 April 1830, persecution forced the early Saints to leave their homes in New York and Pennsylvania and to settle around Kirtland in northeastern Ohio. In the summer of 1831, the Prophet Joseph Smith identified Independence, Missouri, as the center place of Zion, and this area soon became a second focus of Church activity. In this same year, the first missionaries preached in Kentucky and South Carolina. As Church officials and members made frequent trips between these two centers they took advantage of opportunities to spread the gospel along the way. Missionary work also pushed slowly into adjoining states. As early as 1832, a branch was established in what is now West Virginia. In 1834, missionaries traveled eastward from Missouri through Kentucky and Tennessee.

The most important missionary field during the 1830s, however, was the Northeast. Latter-day Saints naturally wanted to return to their homes in New England or in the Middle Atlantic States to share the gospel with friends and relatives. Many were converted and immediately began sharing their newfound faith. Through the mid-1830s, the bulk of Latter-day Saint converts came from this area. During this same period missionary work was also extended into eastern Canada.

Most groups were small and scattered. Branches were, in some places, farther apart than fifty miles. For example, in 1835, the ten "branches" in Kentucky and Tennessee had only nine to twenty-four members per branch. These isolated Saints longed to associate with other Church members, so the spirit of gathering was strong among them. Sometimes a complete branch would move en masse to join the main body of the Saints. This gathering inevitably slowed growth of Church membership and the development of stable institutions in the outlying areas.

A period of persecution and apostasy during the later 1830s generally disrupted missionary work, although difficulties in Kirtland did give rise to the first mission to Great Britain, and missionaries were called to go to the Lamanites in 1830 (see D&C 28:8). Faithful Latter-day Saints were forced to leave their homes in Ohio and then Missouri, and in 1839 began building their new city of Nauvoo on the banks of the Mississippi. Missionary work expanded into North Carolina in 1838 and penetrated into the deep South.[1] Proselyting began in New Orleans during 1841. In 1842, Alabama and Mississippi were flourishing missionary fields. In 1843, missionaries were sent to Texas. The tragic martyrdom of Joseph Smith in 1844 and the Saints' exodus from Illinois two years later profoundly affected the course of the Church's development in North America.

THE TREK WEST

The epic trek of the Mormon pioneers shifted the geographic center of Latter-day Saint activity some fifteen hundred miles westward to the Rocky Mountains. This exodus so occupied the Saints' attention that it hampered missionary work around the world. For example, the departure of a large company of Mississippi converts in 1846 left missionary work in the South virtually at a standstill.

Saints in the eastern states were likewise preparing to join the westward migration. On 4 February 1846, the very day that Brigham Young and the pioneers began leaving Nauvoo, the ship *Brooklyn* set sail from New York harbor. After a difficult six-month voyage around Cape Horn, it sailed into San Francisco Bay on 31 July, marking the beginning of a Latter-day Saint presence on the West Coast. About a year later the Mormon pioneers headed by Brigham Young reached the Salt Lake Valley on 24 July 1847. Five days later, Latter-day Saints from Georgia and Mississippi arrived in the Valley, and they plaed a key role in the pioneering venture. They immediately set to work to tame the wilderness and to make "the desert . . . blossom as the rose" (Isaiah 35:1). The first settlements were established in the Salt Lake and adjoining valleys along the Wasatch Mountains. An early objective was to create a chain of settlements between Salt Lake and Southern California; immigrants could travel along this "Mormon Corridor" from Pacific Ocean ports to the Great Basin. Therefore, in 1851,

San Bernardino in 1857. This settlement along the "Mormon Corridor" was patterned after those in Utah. (LDS Church Archives)

Brigham Young appointed Apostles Amasa M. Lyman and Charles C. Rich to establish the southernmost Mormon settlements in San Bernardino, about sixty miles east of Los Angeles.

A total of ninety-six colonies or settlements, including twenty-seven along the Mormon Corridor, were founded by the Saints during the first ten years after they entered the Great Basin in 1847. During this initial phase, "the pattern was one of directed settlements," historian Leonard Arrington has explained, "that is, the colonization was a community effort directed by Church authorities rather than the result of spontaneous and independent movement of individuals."[2] Another wave of colonizing took place during the 1870s in southern and eastern Idaho, southwestern Wyoming, southern and eastern Nevada, southwestern Colorado, and northern and central Arizona. "While this colonization was not called or directed in the same sense as in the 1850s, it was encouraged and supported by the central church. In most instances, the colonies were supervised and assisted by local wards and stakes located near the area being settled."³ These latter settlements fairly well defined the boundaries of what would come to be known as the predominantly Mormon Intermountain area.

Mormon colonization in the Great Basin depended on the gathering from abroad and from other areas of North America. As converts from Europe and eastern America left their homes, they looked forward to starting a new and better life for their families on land available in the West. They could easily be absorbed as scores of new communities were being founded. At the same time, these immigrants from many regions contributed essential skills and also enriched the culture of their new homeland. Scandinavian immigrants, for example, populated the Sanpete Valley of Utah near Manti, while Saints from the South settled in Colorado's San Luis Valley.

While the third quarter of the nineteenth century witnessed laudable achievements in colonizing the Intermountain West, it was a period of relative inactivity elsewhere in North America. Geographical isolation made the sending of missionaries more difficult. During an era of colonization, relatively few could be spared for missionary service, and most of these went overseas. This left almost none available to serve in the United States or Canada. In 1857 the approach of a hostile U.S. Army led Church leaders to call home missionaries serving around the world. The American Civil War of 1861–65 and its aftermath further interrupted missionary work. The Eastern States Mission did reopen in 1865, but was closed again only four years later.

Rudger Clawson and Joseph Standing faced much persecution during their 1879 mission to the Southern States. Standing was martyred during his service. (LDS Church Archives)

WORK REOPENED IN THE SOUTH

By the 1870s conditions favored the reopening of missionary work. In 1875, Latter-day Saint elders resumed formal missionary work in the South for the first time in about three decades and found that some members had remained faithful there throughout this period. A growing spirit of intolerance, however, would limit the success of these efforts for at least another quarter of a century.

A bitter anti-Mormon press dwelt on such concerns as the Mountain Meadows Massacre and the practice of plural marriage. The resulting persecution was particularly intense in isolated areas of the rural South. Two examples were particularly heinous. Elder Joseph Standing was confronted by a mob near Varnell Station, Georgia, on 21 July 1879 and was shot in the face at close range with a pistol. His assailants then turned to

Rudger Clawson, his companion (who would later serve in the Quorum of the Twelve Apostles), and shouted, "shoot that man." Elder Clawson calmly folded his arms and replied, "Shoot." His "calm, resigned dignity caught the mobsters off balance and it was perhaps this few seconds of tense courage that saved the day for Rudger Clawson for one of them spoke up, commanding 'Don't Shoot.'"[4] In Lewis County, Tennessee, near a farming community called Cane Creek, two missionaries—John H. Gibbs and William S. Berry—were killed by a mob at the home of James Condor, a local member, as they prepared for Sabbath services 10 August 1884. In addition to the missionaries, mob leader David Hinson (a local protestant minister) and the two sons of James and Malinda Condor, James Riley Hudson and Martin Condor, were also killed. Malinda was also severely wounded and never fully recovered. One scholar reported that "the Southern States Mission has been the scene of more persecution than any other LDS Mission."[5]

Unfortunately, these were not isolated events. Missionaries as well as the scattered Saints were in almost constant fear of mob attacks. On one occasion, George Albert Smith, a missionary, and J. Golden Kimball, the mission president, were sleeping in a house in southern Alabama when a hostile mob began shooting into the house. Fortunately, the mob aimed too high for the beds and nobody was hit. Elder Smith later recalled:

The men pounded on the door and used filthy language, ordering the Mormons to come out, that they were going to shoot them. President Kimball asked me if I wasn't going to get up and dress and I told him no, I was going to stay in bed, that I was sure the Lord would take care of us. In just a few seconds, the room was filled with shots. Apparently the mob had divided itself into four groups and were shooting into the corners of the house. Splinters were flying over our heads in every direction. There were a few moments of quiet, then another volley of shots was fired and more splinters flew. I felt absolutely no terror. I was very calm as I lay there, experiencing one of the most horrible events of my life, but I was sure that as long as I was preaching the word of God and following his teachings that the Lord would protect me, and he did.

Apparently the mob became discouraged and left. The next morning when we opened the door, there was a huge bundle of heavy hickory sticks such as the mob used to beat the missionaries in the South.[6]

On another occasion, Elder John T. Alexander was traveling along a road near Plainville, Georgia, when a group of three men, armed and masked, stepped out of the woods and asked him if he was "one of those 'Mormon' preachers." When he acknowledged that he was, they ordered him to walk into the woods some distance. "He supposed they intended to whip him with hickory switches," but it became apparent that they intended to kill him.

They asked him if he had anything to say before his death. He replied by asking their reason for wishing to murder him. Using a blasphemous expression, they said, "If we don't kill you you'll come back again. If you have anything to say, say it quickly."

He replied, "If I must die, I will offer a few words of prayer," which he then did, while the weapons of the men were leveled upon him.

As soon as he concluded his prayer, Brother Alexander closed his eyes and folded his arms, feeling that his last moment had arrived and was perfectly resigned to what appeared to be his inevitable fate. At the same time that he assumed this attitude, the three fired simultaneously, and he instantly fell and became insensible. When he recovered consciousness he got upon his hands and knees and looked about, but his assailants had departed, no one being near.[7]

Elder Alexander discovered that one bullet had passed through his low-crowned hat, and another had hit him in the chest near his heart, so "his escape from death was apparently by a hairsbreadth."[8]

The religious zeal that fueled this persecution also had its positive side. People in the South read the Bible and generally believed that religion was important. Hence many were prepared to recognize and accept the truths taught by the Mormon missionaries. Even though growth was slow, it was steady, and by the end of the nineteenth century the Southern States became the largest mission in North America. Stories of heroism in the midst of intense persecution became part of the heritage for later generations of Southern Saints.

EXPANSION IN OTHER AREAS

The years immediately preceding and following the turn of the century witnessed growth in other missions. While the 1880s had been a period of misrepresentation and persecution, an era of goodwill was inaugurated with the 1890 announcement that the practice of plural marriage was being suspended. This improved climate allowed missionary efforts once again to flourish throughout the United States and Canada.

During the 1890s missionary work revived in the Midwest and the East, this area being served by missions covering huge areas: Central States, headquartered in Independence, Missouri; Northern States, headquartered in Chicago, Illinois; and Eastern States (also including part of Canada), headquartered New York City. The Southern States Mission had also expanded, at one time stretching from Texas to Maryland. For many years headquarters were in Chattanooga, Tennessee, before being established in Atlanta, Georgia.

Church expansion in the western United States during this decade was actually benefited to a degree by the Church's difficulties. Many faithful Latter-day Saints fled from anti-polygamy persecution in Utah. The influx of Church members into the Golden State led to the reopening of the California Mission in 1892. Two years later Karl G. Maeser was appointed not only as mission president but also as director of an exhibit in San Francisco highlighting the Saints' educational attainments. The home of Eliza Woollacott, who had moved from Utah to Los Angeles in 1884, became the meeting place for members and missionaries and the hub of Church activities. The Los Angeles Branch was officially organized in 1895 with approximately twenty members.[9]

During this same decade two very unusual missions were formed. The Montana Mission was organized in 1896 and was placed under the jurisdiction of the Bannock Stake with headquarters at Rexburg, Idaho. The following year the Northwestern States Mission, centered in eastern Oregon, was formed under the jurisdiction of the Oneida Stake, also in southeastern Idaho. These were not stake missions in the usual sense, because their territories lay far beyond the regular stake boundaries. In 1898, however, these two units merged to form a new Northwestern States Mission, a regular full-time mission independent of any stake direction, headquartered in Portland, Oregon. In 1896 the Colorado Mission was also organized with headquarters at Denver; as proselyting expanded into neighboring states, it became known as the Western States Mission.

This expansion was reinforced by a changed understand-

Members of the Central States Mission in 1915. Spencer W. Kimball is pictured in the second row, third from left. (LDS Church Archives)

ing of the "gathering." Early revelations proclaimed the importance of gathering to one central place (see D&C 29:7–8); this was characteristic of Church history during the nineteenth century. These revelations also anticipated a second phase, more typical of the twentieth century, when there would be "other places" appointed as places of gathering that "shall be called stakes" (D&C 101:20–22). This latter phase would be more spiritual than geographical (see D&C 133:14). Though remaining in their homelands, converts would "gather" out of the wicked world and become identified with the Saints.

Church leaders began counseling against the geographical gathering during the 1890s, a decade of particularly severe economic depression. Furthermore, as historian Frederick Jackson Turner concluded, 1890 had marked the end of the frontier and of readily available free land in America. Most immigrants therefore congregated in the cities and many failed to find work, became discouraged, and wanted to return home. It was just such conditions the Church wanted to avoid. At about the turn of the century, the General Authorities began emphasizing that the need to gather into one place had passed, and that now the important task was to build up the other places around the world.

This new emphasis not only discouraged immigration to the Intermountain West but it also facilitated emigration from this traditional center of Mormon colonization. During the 1920s, and especially during the depression of the 1930s, thousands of Latter-day Saints left Utah and Idaho, whose semi-arid agriculture did not share in the general prosperity of the time. Young people in particular sought improved economic opportunities in major metropolitan centers, especially in southern California.

While most nineteenth-century migrations of the Saints had been encouraged or even sponsored by the Church, the movements during the twentieth century were the results of individual decisions. At least some of the Saints leaving the Intermountain area in the first half of the century wondered if they were doing the right thing. A group in Santa Monica, California, for example, asked President Heber J. Grant in 1921 if they were out of harmony with Church policy by living there. President Grant answered their letter in person during one of his frequent visits to the Golden State. He assured them that "at the present time the idea of a permanent Mormon settlement at Santa Monica was in full accordance with Church policies."[10]

TWENTIETH-CENTURY GROWTH

The formation of new stakes near the turn of the century was clear evidence of Latter-day Saint growth in widely scattered urban centers. In 1844 Joseph Smith had declared: "I have received instructions from the Lord that from henceforth wherever the Elders of Israel shall build up churches . . . there shall be a stake of Zion. In the great cities, as Boston, New York, etc., there shall be stakes."[11] During the 1920s, stakes were established in Los Angeles and San Francisco, and during the following decade in such key cities as New York, Chicago, Portland, Seattle, and Washington D.C.

Not all Church members leaving the Intermountain area went to large cities. Many joined the thousands already scattered in small branches throughout the United States and Canada. In the early decades of the twentieth century, providing meaningful activity for these scattered Saints was a challenge. For example, only 40 percent of members in New England during the 1930s lived close to regularly organized Church branches. Another 20 percent of New England members met with small groups in homes or rented halls. This meant that nearly half of the Church members in that area had little or no access to organized activity. Missionaries were frequently assigned to visit these members; they had to divide their time between proselyting and performing such member-related tasks as teaching classes or even presiding over a branch or district.

To reduce the number of isolated members, several missions sponsored regional colonies where the scattered Saints might gather. In 1901, for example, one such colony was laid out on land owned by the Saints at Kelsey in northeast Texas; the plan followed the familiar Mormon pattern of wide streets, square with the compass. By 1906, four hundred colonists were settled there. The mission established a school that was staffed by about ten missionaries.

The need for such colonies, however, declined over the years. As the spirit of tolerance and acceptance grew, the necessity for a separate religious community diminished.[12]

As World War II began, many defense industries were

The Atlanta Georgia Temple was dedicated in June 1983, the first in the southern United States. Today, the temple serves 13 stakes in Georgia and small portions of Tennessee and Alabama. (© by Intellectual Reserve, Inc.)

established along the West Coast. Resulting new jobs accelerated the westward migration of the United States population, especially toward the sunny climate of southern California. Many Mormons were lured from the Intermountain area to the Pacific Coast, thus accelerating the trend established in previous decades. Servicemen, impressed with the favorable climate and attractive economic opportunities in various parts of the country where they had been stationed, chose to return to these areas and to establish their families in these localities following the war.

The first stakes in the South were organized at Jacksonville, Florida, and at Columbia, South Carolina, during 1947. The first of these stakes, in Jacksonville, was organized by Elder Charles A. Callis, of the Quorum of the Twelve, who earlier had presided over the Southern States Mission for twenty-eight years. He prophesied that this stake was only the beginning, that there would be more stakes and also temples in the South. In contrast to the pattern in other outlying stakes, all the leaders in the Jacksonville unit were local southern Saints. This increasing strength enabled the Church to develop its activities more fully.

As the Church gained strength, an increasing percentage of its members lived within stakes, where they could enjoy and participate in all the programs and activities of the Church. By 1960, 95 percent of Church members along the Pacific Coast lived within the boundaries of organized stakes. Forty years earlier, in 1920, only 25 percent of members along the coast were part of stakes. In the Midwest and East—areas that have typically grown more slowly than the West Coast—58 percent of Church members lived in stakes by the year 1960. By the year 2003, nearly all areas of North America had approached the ideal of having 100 percent of their membership benefited by stake organization and programs.

Saints emigrating from the Intermountain area have made a significant contribution to the growing strength of the Church in other regions. During the 1920s and '30s, members from the Intermountain region accounted for most of the growth throughout North America, only a small share coming from convert baptisms. New stake leaders typically were successful men who had been drawn from the Intermountain area to other metropolitan centers because of greater opportunities there. To illustrate, George W. McCune, first president of the Los Angeles Stake, was a banker and businessman from Ogden, Utah. Fred G. Taylor, a former Salt Lake City businessman, was the manager of a sugar company when he was called as president of the New York Stake. Monte L. Bean, another

Utahn, was in Portland as a retail store executive. Ezra Taft Benson, a native of Idaho (and future president of the Church), was serving as the executive secretary of the National Council of Farmer Cooperatives when he became president of the Washington D.C. Stake. One of his counselors, Ernest L. Wilkinson, who was from Ogden, Utah, was practicing law in the nation's capital.

North America continued to be a source of support for developments abroad. For example, in the late 1940s, President Heber Meeks of the Southern States Mission was assigned to visit Cuba to determine the feasibility of sending missionaries there. A quarter of a century later, Glen Rudd, president of the Florida Mission, helped supervise the opening of proselyting in the Caribbean.

During unprecedented growth following World War II, about half of the members of stakes in the West or in the large metropolitan centers of the East had come from the Inter-mountain states. Because the Saints from the Intermountain area usually had longer and more varied experience in the Church, they often were called to carry the heaviest share of Church leadership and activity. Because they had come for professional or business opportunities, they represented a substantial reservoir of leadership talent. During the early 1970s, two-thirds of all North American stake presidents outside of the Intermountain area were still from Utah, Idaho, or Arizona. In educational centers such as Berkeley, Boston, or Raleigh, groups of well-informed Latter-day Saint students and faculty members brought a special dedication and depth to Church service and gospel study in the decades following World War II. In some places, such as Jacksonville, Florida, or southern California, the Church had been established long enough to have developed strong local institutions and traditions; in these stakes a higher proportion of leaders and active members were native to that particular locality.

Today, levels of participation in Church activity vary widely from one area to another. One explanation may lie in the ratio of Church members to total population. It may be that where the proportional number of Saints is greatest, travel distances to Sunday meetings and weekday activities are shorter and attendance therefore is better. No matter where they are, however, most Latter-day Saints find that they identify more with their Mormon heritage than with the prevailing lifestyle of the community, and thus turn to the Church for involvement in a smaller and more intimate community. Indeed, many Latter-day Saints who have relocated from the Intermountain West to other areas have found their group consciousness as Latter-day Saints to be even stronger than it had been in their hometowns. Some who have been indifferent have found their religious faith awakened. Others, unfortunately, who have not been fully active in the Church, still do not identify with it when moving to another city.

The erection of temples during the late twentieth century and early twenty-first century has meant that the blessings of the house of the Lord are more readily available in many, many locations. This has further strengthened Church growth in all of North America. In the eastern United States, for example, only 17 percent of Latter-day Saints were marrying in the temple in 1965. By 1975, the year following the dedication of the Washington D.C. Temple, this figure had climbed to 46 percent. The construction of many smaller temples during the closing years of the twentieth century made temple blessings available even more widely.

The presence of eight temples in the southeastern U.S. by

As commuters drive around the Beltway in Washington D.C. they are often astonished at the beauty of these white spires coming through the dark greenery of surrounding trees. The Washington D.C. Temple was dedicated in November 1974. (Photo courtesy Donald Q. Cannon)

2003 represents a fulfillment of Elder Charles A. Callis's 1947 prophecy that temples would one day bless that region. The number of temples in Canada has similarly expanded. And the 2002 dedication of the reconstructed Nauvoo Temple not only reminded the Saints of early difficulties in North America but provided an opportunity for the Church to proclaim its message at a time when Latter-day Saints had achieved widespread acceptance.

Indeed, as the Church has gained strength, it has been in a better position to be an influence for good in the country as a whole. Latter-day Saints increasingly are accepted members of North American communities, not only in predominantly Mormon areas, but in other sections of the United States and

Canada as well. Church members have come to represent a more typical cross-section of the population and include many successful individuals. In such business centers as New York, Chicago, and Toronto. Latter-day Saints have been among the top-level executives assigned to the home offices of some of North America's largest companies. Similarly, government service has attracted highly qualified Church members to Washington D.C. During the second half of the twentieth century, Elder Ezra Taft Benson, David M. Kennedy, George Romney, and T. H. Bell all served in the U.S. presidential cabinet. In Alberta, Canada, N. Eldon Tanner (who later became a member of the First Presidency) was an influential industrial and government leader.

The Church received widespread recognition during the 1930s when the press lauded the Mormon welfare plan. Church activities such as family home evenings and youth programs likewise have attracted the admiration of nonmembers in more recent years. The Saints' education attainments have been recognized as being well above the average of the population as a whole. Latter-day Saint athletes as well as government or business leaders have received national and even international prominence. Re-enactment of the pioneer trek at the time of its 1997 sesquicentennial attracted international publicity. Likewise, the 2002 Winter Olympics in Salt Lake City called widespread attention to the values and character of the Latter-day Saints. Aware of the positive benefits of such recognition, the Church has developed a Public Affairs Department, and at the local level has appointed representatives to work with the media in publicizing Latter-day Saint activities.

All these developments have helped to open the way for the Church to play an increasingly influential and beneficial role throughout North America and the world.

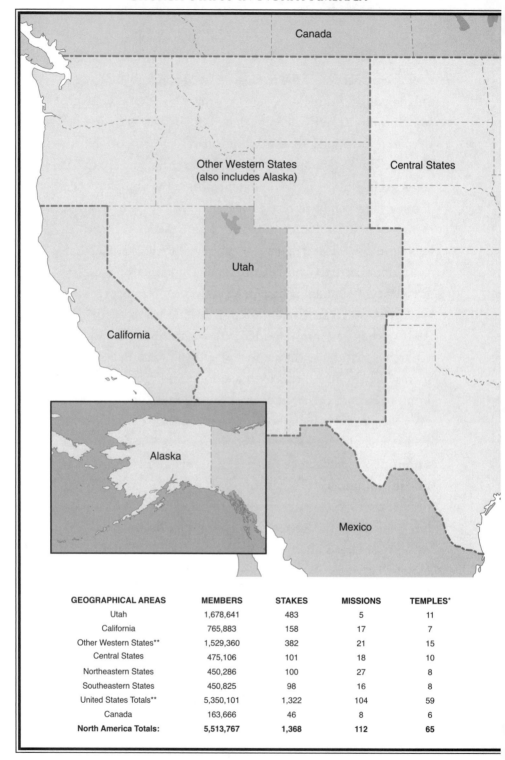

GEOGRAPHICAL AREAS	MEMBERS	STAKES	MISSIONS	TEMPLES*
Utah	1,678,641	483	5	11
California	765,883	158	17	7
Other Western States**	1,529,360	382	21	15
Central States	475,106	101	18	10
Northeastern States	450,286	100	27	8
Southeastern States	450,825	98	16	8
United States Totals**	5,350,101	1,322	104	59
Canada	163,666	46	8	6
North America Totals:	**5,513,767**	**1,368**	**112**	**65**

Northeastern States

Southeastern States

The number of stakes is approximate because many straddle political boundaries. Missions represent number of headquarters even though parts of these missions may be in different political subdivisions.

*These numbers represent operating temples and those that had been announced or were under construction at press time.

**Does not include Hawaii, which is grouped with the Pacific.

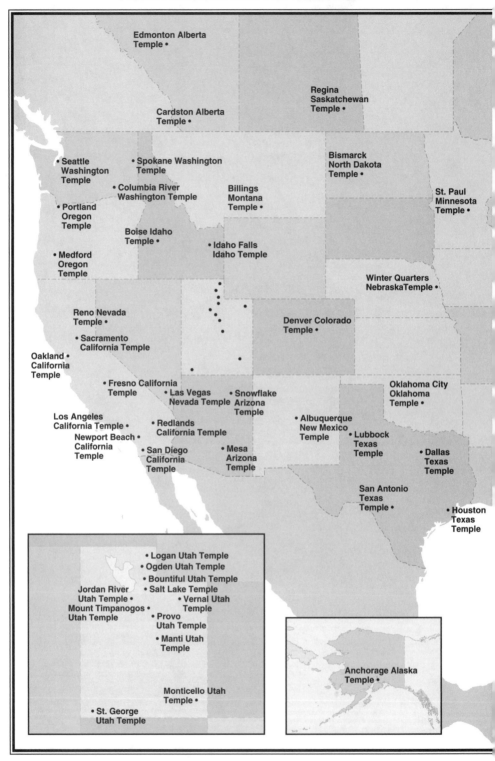

Edmonton Alberta
Temple •

Regina
Saskatchewan
Temple •

Cardston Alberta
Temple •

• Seattle
Washington
Temple

• Spokane Washington
Temple

Bismarck
North Dakota
Temple •

• Columbia River
Washington Temple

Billings
Montana
Temple •

St. Paul
Minnesota
Temple •

• Portland
Oregon
Temple

Boise Idaho
Temple •

• Idaho Falls
Idaho Temple

• Medford
Oregon
Temple

Winter Quarters
NebraskaTemple •

Reno Nevada
Temple •

Denver Colorado
Temple •

• Sacramento
California Temple

Oakland •
California
Temple

• Fresno California
Temple

• Las Vegas
Nevada Temple

• Snowflake
Arizona
Temple

Oklahoma City
Oklahoma
Temple •

Los Angeles
California Temple •

• Redlands
California Temple

• Albuquerque
New Mexico
Temple

• Lubbock
Texas
Temple

• Dallas
Texas
Temple

Newport Beach •
California
Temple

• San Diego
California
Temple

• Mesa
Arizona
Temple

San Antonio
Texas
Temple •

• Houston
Texas
Temple

• Logan Utah Temple
• Ogden Utah Temple
• Bountiful Utah Temple

Jordan River
Utah Temple •

• Salt Lake Temple

Mount Timpanogos •
Utah Temple

• Vernal Utah
Temple

• Provo
Utah Temple

• Manti Utah
Temple

Monticello Utah
Temple •

• St. George
Utah Temple

Anchorage Alaska
Temple •

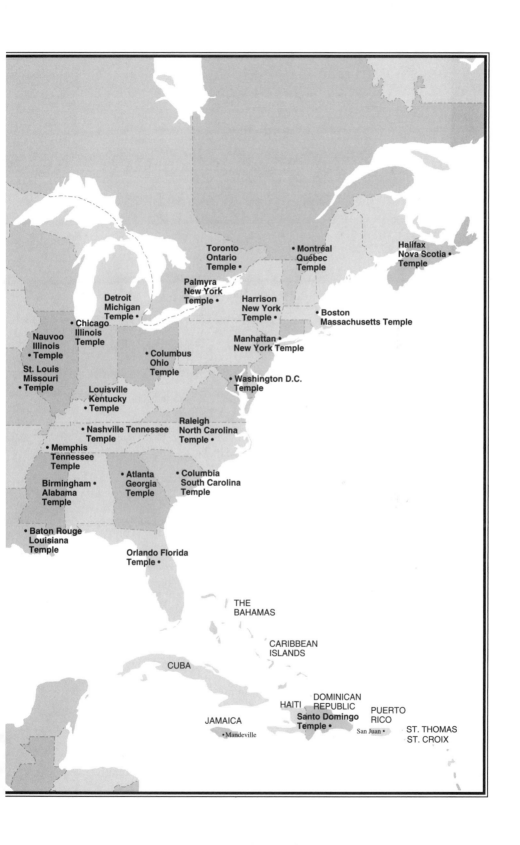

Toronto
Ontario
Temple •

• Montréal
Québec
Temple

Halifax
Nova Scotia •
Temple

Palmyra
New York
Temple •

Harrison
New York
Temple •

• Boston
Massachusetts Temple

Detroit
Michigan
Temple •

• Chicago
Illinois
Temple

Nauvoo
Illinois
• Temple

• Columbus
Ohio
Temple

Manhattan •
New York Temple

St. Louis
Missouri
• Temple

• Washington D.C.
Temple

Louisville
Kentucky
• Temple

Raleigh
North Carolina
Temple •

• Nashville Tennessee
Temple

• Memphis
Tennessee
Temple

• Atlanta
Georgia
Temple

• Columbia
South Carolina
Temple

Birmingham •
Alabama
Temple

• Baton Rouge
Louisiana
Temple

Orlando Florida
Temple •

THE
BAHAMAS

CARIBBEAN
ISLANDS

CUBA

DOMINICAN
HAITI REPUBLIC
Santo Domingo
Temple •

PUERTO
RICO

JAMAICA
• Mandeville

San Juan •

ST. THOMAS
ST. CROIX

CHAPTER 23

THE CHURCH IN THE CARIBBEAN

DAVID F. BOONE

The Caribbean region includes hundreds of islands extending nearly two thousand miles from Cuba, just below Florida, to Trinidad and other small islands off the coast of Venezuela. The more than twenty-five distinct island nations are scattered widely. Each has its own government. Some are independent, but most are satellite territories of major world powers. Most have unique languages, many being dialects of Spanish, French, Dutch, or English. These countries have distinctive cultures and traditions. Also known as the West Indies, the area's main industry is tourism; visitors are attracted by the region's tropical climate, beautiful beaches, and inexpensive shopping. The dominant religion in the area is Roman Catholic, although there are many Protestants as well. These Christian faiths are sometimes mingled with African and even East Indian religions. Communist Cuba has the highest population of the islands, with more than ten million people.

Even though the first Latter-day Saint contact with the Caribbean came early, substantial growth began only during the last quarter of the twentieth century. Several factors combined to delay the gospel's establishment in the region: the diversity of languages and cultures, long distances forming a natural barrier to transportation, many distinct governmental jurisdictions, and opposition by established religions.

EARLY CONTACTS

The earliest introduction of the gospel in the Caribbean appears to be the travel and ministry of Elder Harrison Sager, who preached briefly in Jamaica in 1841. A decade later, at a special conference held in Salt Lake City in August 1852, more than one hundred missionaries were called to carry the gospel to many lands around the world, including the Caribbean.

Four of these missionaries reached Jamaica the following year, but after only six weeks they were driven from the island by mobs. It would be nearly a century before missionaries returned to the West Indies.

In the mid-1940s Heber Meeks, president of the Southern States Mission, was directed by the First Presidency to visit Cuba "to make a survey of the situation there as to opening up Cuba for missionary work."[1] President and Sister Meeks, accompanied by other mission staff members, visited Havana and other Cuban cities with letters of introduction to Boy Scout, government, and educational executives and leaders. The Church delegation was warmly received, and the delegates were highly impressed with the country and its people. Despite anticipated favorable possibilities, missionaries were not sent to Cuba at that time due mainly to the instability of the Cuban government and economy, and World War II restrictions.[2] Another concern was that a majority of the population had African ancestors and at this time the Church's policy was to not seek out people with this lineage.[3] (See also chapter 20 of this work.)

When Fidel Castro overthrew the United States-sanctioned Batista government in the late 1950s, American-Cuban relations were strained and finally broken off. His alignment of Cuba with Russian Communism made Latter-day Saint missionary work in Cuba quite impossible.

MODERN BEGINNINGS

As early as the 1940s faithful Latter-day Saint families throughout the Caribbean, mostly military personnel and American businessmen, held church meetings in their homes and performed limited missionary work. These faithful Saints lived their religion and were good examples to their neighbors. For example, two families held church meetings in their homes at San Juan, Puerto Rico, from 1940 to 1942. A decade later, servicemen assigned to military bases were holding meetings. Two branches were organized, and in 1955 an island-wide conference was held.

Mission presidents in adjacent parts of the United States supervised Church growth in the West Indies. Ned Winder, president of the Florida Mission, visited Puerto Rico in October 1963. As a result of his visit he felt impressed to send missionaries to this U.S. commonwealth having a population of over four million people. Missionaries arrived in Puerto Rico in January 1964, and the first Latter-day Saint convert was baptized in March of that year. At this time President Winder organized the Caribbean District of the Florida Mission.

The British island of Bermuda followed a similar course. In 1953 a group of LDS servicemen's wives organized a Relief Society there. However, full-time missionaries did not arrive until April 1966, their work being supervised by the Eastern States Mission in New York City. Progress was slow.

During the late 1960s, Glen L. Rudd, President Winder's successor, had a very unusual experience that illustrated early patterns of growth in the Caribbean. President Rudd received a letter in Spanish from a young mother living in Santiago in the democratic Dominican Republic. When the letter was translated for him, President Rudd expressed surprise since he was not familiar with any local Church members in that area. The mother reported that she had joined the Church in Mexico, met and married a young man from the Dominican Republic, and now they were the parents of a year-old baby boy who had not yet been named or blessed by priesthood authority. Sister

Flavia Salazar Gomez's urgency to write President Rudd in Florida was that she had only recently been diagnosed with cancer, was not expected to live, and wanted to give her child all the benefits of the gospel before she died.

President Rudd went to see this family as soon as possible, but, upon reaching the outskirts of Santiago, suddenly realized he didn't have an address and had no idea how to contact the family. Through a series of miracles, President Rudd directed his driver to within a few feet of the home of the family, and the first person they asked directions from was the husband of the very woman he was seeking.

President Rudd and his associate interviewed Sister Gomez and found her to be worthy and as active in her religion as an isolated member could possibly be. Her son was given a name and a blessing and then she was administered to. "I felt impressed," President Rudd remembered, "to bless her that she would recover from her cancerous condition and become well."[4] Nearly a year later, President Rudd, on his way to Puerto Rico on Church business, stopped off to see the family in the Dominican Republic and found Sister Gomez "in good health, looking well and happy. She told us she had been completely cured." President Rudd concluded, "What happened was that this lovely . . . mother needed a priesthood blessing. She knew there was no way to get one except to ask the Lord to help her."[5] She and her family remained in the area for a short time.

GROWTH ACCELERATES

The decade of the 1970s brought a veritable explosion of Church activity and success in several Caribbean areas. This growth generally built on the foundations laid in earlier

472

decades by the faithful U.S. Latter-day Saint families living in the Caribbean. Unlike growth in earlier years, growth during the last three decades of the twentieth century was primarily among the local residents of the area. Most of this growth came following the 1978 revelation that extended priesthood blessings to worthy members of all races, opening the door to an expansion of Church activity among the mixed-lineage peoples of the Caribbean.

A Spanish-speaking branch in Puerto Rico was organized in 1970, and the first LDS chapel in the Caribbean was dedicated at San Juan, Puerto Rico, that same year. The Caribbean became a mission of its own in 1979 with headquarters located in San Juan. The following year the first stake in the area was established, also at San Juan.[6] Three more stakes were formed during the next five years. In 1993, however, all four stakes were dissolved with the reduction of U.S. military personnel. As converts continued to come into the Church, three of these stakes were reinstated and one new stake was formed later during the decade.[7]

Faithful Latter-day Saint families also promoted Church growth in the Dominican Republic. The Amparo and Rappleye families, the first permanent Church members in the country, arrived in June 1978, the month the priesthood revelation was received. They shared the gospel, and their first convert was baptized two months later. Full-time Spanish-speaking missionaries from the Florida Ft. Lauderdale Mission arrived in November and further assisted the growth. In January 1981 a separate Dominican Republic mission was established.

In 1981, Spencer W. Kimball became the first Church president to visit the Caribbean.[8] Approximately three thousand members attended the regional conference in San Juan,

Puerto Rico, on Sunday, March 8. The following evening some fifteen hundred Saints attended a similar gathering in a Santo Domingo hotel convention hall, three hundred having to stand because all seats were filled. "Few in either convention hall had been members of the Church more than three years," The *Church News* reported. "Now they were seeing a prophet with their own eyes, hearing him with their own ears. The experience was new, first-hand, and emotional."9

Attending these meetings represented a definite sacrifice for the generally impoverished Saints. Many had to travel long distances, in some cases even from adjacent islands. Those who had never owned traditional Sunday clothing sacrificed because they wanted to be dressed appropriately for this once-in-a-lifetime occasion.

One hundred members of the Puerto Plata Branch crowded into an old bus for the trip to Santo Domingo. Unfortunately the bus broke down, and they did not reach the conference site until 10 P.M., over an hour after the session had concluded. When they found the hall dark and empty, "many wept because they were so disappointed." President and Sister Kimball had already gone to bed. When the President's personal secretary learned of these late arrivals, he reluctantly knocked on the Kimballs' door, apologizing for disturbing them and suggesting that the president might want to dictate a statement that could be read to the group. "I felt that wouldn't be good enough," the prophet reflected, "and not fair to those who had come so far under such trying circumstances." He therefore "dressed and went downstairs to meet with the members who had made such an effort" to be there.10

When he reached the hall, President Kimball apologized for making the people wait. They couldn't imagine he was apologizing to them when they felt they had actually inconvenienced him. He spent more than an hour with these Saints, who thus enjoyed a private, intimate meeting with the prophet. After this unforgettable experience, the group boarded their bus for an overnight trip home because many had to be at work or school early the next morning.[11]

During his 1981 visit, President Spencer W. Kimball referred to recent temple dedications in other areas of the world, and the prophet challenged his listeners to prepare for their own endowments and sealings. "How would you feel if some day a temple could be built here for you?"[12] The Caribbean Saints would need to wait nearly two decades until the blessing hinted at in this question would be realized.

Following President Kimball's visit, the Dominican Republic experienced the most sustained and consistent growth in the West Indies. The Santo Domingo Stake, first in the country, was organized in 1986, and the mission was divided the following year. By the end of the following decade there were eleven stakes and three missions.

The Dominican Republic shares the island of Hispaniola with the French-speaking nation of Haiti. The first Haitian convert, Alexander Mourra, heard about the gospel and traveled to Florida in June 1977 to be taught and baptized. Fortunately, Mourra, a prominent Haitian businessman, returned to his homeland to share his newfound religion. He was able to assist missionaries who arrived in May 1980 from the France Paris Mission. The first Haitian branch of the Church was organized in October of the same year. On 17 April 1983 Elder Thomas S. Monson dedicated Haiti for the preacing of the gospel, and the following year a mission was established.

Elder Thomas S. Monson with a group of Primary children in Haiti in April 1983. (LDS Church Archives)

Unfortunately, due to a military coup, foreign missionaries were withdrawn from Haiti in 1991 and the country remained closed to all but local missionaries until July 1996. The first Haitian stake, created through the efforts of mostly local emissaries, was organized there in September 1997.[13]

By 1970 the Church also had a presence in Jamaica, the Mandeville Branch being organized to serve several American families working on the island. Victor Nugent, in 1974, was the first Jamaican to be baptized, and in 1978 was ordained an elder and became the first native branch president, under the direction of the Ft. Lauderdale Florida Mission.[14] On 5 December 1978, Elder M. Russell Ballard dedicated Jamaica for proselyting, and significant growth has thus ensued. A separate mission was established there in 1985.[15]

Missionary efforts also began in the Virgin Islands—a protected territory of Great Britain and the United States—during the late 1960s and early 1970s. The gospel was introduced on St. Thomas through several Latter-day Saint families who organized a Sunday School. After several converts joined the group, a branch was created in St. Thomas in December 1977, and the first missionaries arrived on 9 June 1978, the very day the revelation extending priesthood blessings to all worthy males was made public. Additional converts added to the strength of the branch and a meetinghouse was completed in July of the same year. In a similar move, missionaries arrived in St. Croix in January 1981. As had been the case on St. Thomas, these missionaries were greatly assisted by Latter-day Saint families already living in the area, a branch was organized, converts were baptized, and soon a meetinghouse was erected.[16]

RECENT EXPANSION

While growth continued in the larger Caribbean nations where the Church had already been established, the gospel was also taken to many of the smaller, less populated islands. In 1983 the West Indies Mission was created in areas formerly served by the Ft. Lauderdale, Florida; San Juan, Puerto Rico; and Caracas Venezuela missions.

The gospel was introduced into the Bahamas in much the same way as into other Caribbean areas. Two families, the McCombs and the Ballards, arrived in this independent commonwealth—whose citizens speak predominantly English and where the population is largely Protestant—in the summer of 1979. By December of the same year, they were joined by full-time missionaries. As happened in other Caribbean areas, these

The children of the Maypan Branch in Jamaica on 16 May 1982. (LDS Church Archives)

elders were not allowed to stay. In 1982, however, a senior missionary couple was permitted to labor in the Bahamas, and they experienced significant success. Other missionaries returned in March 1985 and a meetinghouse was dedicated in May 1988; but within weeks the facility was out grown and other arrangements for the meetings of the Saints had to be made.[17]

During the 1980s branches were organized on the free adjoining islands of Curaçao, Aruba, and Bonaire. Located just off the coast of Venezuela, all three are self-governing territories affiliated with the Netherlands. The predominately black population speaks Papiamento, a creole language blending elements of Dutch, Spanish, and Portuguese. Selections of the Book of Mormon was translated into Papiamento in 1987. By the end of the year 2000 these three island groups had a combined membership of nearly seven hundred.

Even though there are only a few Latter-day Saints in many of the small Caribbean islands, they have not been forgotten. In March 2001, for example, President Gordon B. Hinckley and Elder Dallin H. Oaks, en route to the Montevideo Uruguay Temple dedication, made an unexpected stop to meet with the Latter-day Saints living in Aruba and the neighboring islands off the coast of Venezuela. The normally talkative and joyous people were left speechless with emotion. "During the last hymn we could not sing," a branch president reported, "there was too much crying, everybody was crying."[18] President Hinckley challenged his listeners to reach out to their neighbors: "You are the pioneers of this land, and the Church will grow as you live the gospel," the Prophet admonished. "I think the time will come when there will be thousands of members here in Aruba and Curaçao."[19] Local Saints had only dreamed the prophet would ever visit them. "We are a small island," one member explained, so the president's visit "is evidence that miracles do happen."[20] The same growth may well be anticipated throughout the Caribbean as the work continues and members do their part to share the gospel with their neighbors.

A TEMPLE IN THE CARIBBEAN

A high point for the Saints in the Caribbean was the dedication of the first temple in that area, a blessing that President Spencer W. Kimball mentioned as a possibility during his visit in 1981. Plans for the temple in Santo Domingo were announced on 16 November 1993.[21] Ground was broken by Elder Richard G. Scott on 18 August 1996. As construction progressed, peoples' lives were changing. "I have witnessed

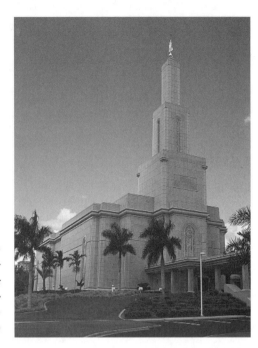

*The Santo Domingo
Dominican Republic
Temple has served Saints
in the Caribbean since
September 2000. (© by
Intellectual Reserve, Inc.)*

people working day and night for this temple," one stake president affirmed.

The new 65,000-thousand-square-foot structure was dedicated by President Gordon B. Hinckley on 17 September 2000. This was a spiritual occasion for Latter-day Saints in the Dominican Republic as well as in other neighboring countries. "There has been a history of trouble between our two countries," a Haitian member said, "but when we are in the celestial room of this temple there will be no Dominicans, no Haitians—only daughters and sons of our Heavenly Father."[22] One of the original missionaries to the Dominican Republic, who had returned for the dedication, remarked, "Christopher Columbus came here over 500 years ago and they built lighthouses in those days for protection. Now the real lighthouse has come."[23]

CHURCH STATUS IN THE CARIBBEAN*

COUNTRIES	MEMBERS	STAKES	MISSIONS	TEMPLES
Antigua	140	—	—	—
Aruba	297	—	—	—
Bahamas	622	—	—	—
Barbados	594	—	—	—
Bermuda	117	—	—	—
Bonaire	78	—	—	—
Cayman Islands	110	—	—	—
Curaçaco	342	—	—	—
Dominican Republic	84,754	11	3	1
Grenada	157	—	—	—
Guadeloupe	251	—	—	—
Haiti	11,329	1	1	—
Jamaica	4,888	—	1	—
Martinique	137	—	—	—
Puerto Rico	22,974	4	1	—
Saint Kitts-Nevis	115	—	—	—
Saint Vincent & Grenadines	366	—	—	—
Trinidad & Tobago	1,778	—	1	—
Virgin Islands, British	32	—	—	—
Virgin Islands, U.S.	395	—	—	—
Caribbean Totals:	**129,476**	**16**	**7**	**1**

* Numbers are for year's end 2002

CHAPTER 24

ADMINISTERING THE
INTERNATIONAL CHURCH

RICHARD O. COWAN

The Church's worldwide growth has presented substantial
challenges to its leaders—not the least of these being the area of
Church administration. Fortunately, divine revelation has provided sound and lasting guidelines for those who direct the
Lord's work on earth today. The Savior revealed the administrative structure of his Church in the 1830s, when the Church
had only a few hundred members. Designated officers were to
"hold the keys," or power, to give direction (D&C 124:123).
This early organizational framework continues to serve well in
a time when Latter-day Saints number in the millions and are
found around the world.

Within three years of the Church's beginnings (by 1833),
the First Presidency had been established (D&C 90:3–9). In
February 1835, the original quorums of the Twelve and
Seventy were organized. The following month, a great "revelation on priesthood" (D&C 107) explained the roles of these
three presiding quorums. Another revelation two years later
reemphasized the responsibility of the Twelve, "chosen to bear
testimony of my name and to send it abroad among all
nations, kindreds, tongues, and people" (D&C 112:1). This
work continues to date.

What follows is an overview of the Church's ability to grow

482

Elder Gordon B. Hinckley uses a world map in the late 1950s to illustrate the growth of the Church across the earth. (© by Intellectual Reserve, Inc.)

and adapt as its membership has flourished throughout the world.

WORLDWIDE SUPERVISION OF MISSIONS

In 1837 the Church's first overseas mission was opened in Great Britain. Preaching commenced in France in 1849 and in Scandinavia the following year. Within a few years the work had spread to all the major countries of Western Europe. All these missions with their respective presidents were, until the early 1900s, under the jurisdiction of the British Mission president, who almost always was a member of the Twelve. Thus Elder Franklin D. Richards, who presided in Britain at the midpoint of the nineteenth century, bore the title "President of the British Isles and Adjacent Countries." Certainly that is not a job that one man could do today. Nonetheless, for the next three-quarters of a century, British Mission presidents simultaneously supervised the European Mission as a whole. This arrangement continued until 1929 when a separate president was called to preside over the British Mission; like the presidents of the missions on the continent, he would serve under the direction of the European Mission president.[1]

World War II interrupted the work in Europe; but early in 1946, just after the end of the war, Elder Ezra Taft Benson was sent to Europe to supervise the reopening of the missions there. Later the same year Matthew Cowley was given a similar assignment in the Pacific. During the decade of the 1950s the Church entered an era of unprecedented growth worldwide. Following the first worldwide mission presidents' seminar in June 1961, the Church's missions were divided into nine groups, each group to be supervised by a General Authority, while each mission retained its own president.[2] By 1965 the number of these groupings was expanded to twelve; each group came to be designated as an "area."[3] One historian has described this move as "the genesis of an administrative structure to run an increasingly international Church, and [it] may well be seen at some future date, if not now, as one of the farthest-reaching decisions made in the twentieth-century Church."[4] This same historian further stated:

> From that date a pattern of Church administration known as area supervision has evolved to become the backbone of LDS Church governance in all lands. The result achieved by the end of the century is an expandable administrative structure that permits the Twelve and their assistants, the Seventy, to direct a membership of millions.[5]

While missions throughout the world grew in number dur-

484

ing the 1960s and following decades, the number of local congregations also continued to multiply. This posed another administrative challenge: strengthening local leaders who could take up the work in their own country.

STRENGTHENING LOCAL LEADERS

In the beginning of the Restoration, local congregations were called "churches" (see D&C 20:81, for example). As members shared the gospel with relatives and friends in neighboring communities, the resulting new congregations came to be called "branches," reflecting the manner in which the Church was spreading. From time to time, the branches in a given region met together for inspiration and to transact necessary business. Soon the term *conference* was applied not only to these meetings but also to the specific geographical area they covered. In 1927 the term *district* officially replaced *conference*.[6]

As the Church expanded, General Authorities found it necessary to delegate more responsibility to local leaders. Bishops, for example, assumed increasingly important roles as the shepherds of their flocks, as well as administrators of ward activities. The *General Handbook of Instructions* in 1968 listed thirty-eight distinct duties for which bishops were responsible. But, as Dean L. Larsen—who would be set apart as a member of the First Quorum of the Seventy in 1976—observed, many of these local leaders were "virtually without experience in administrative affairs. Most outside the stakes close to the Church headquarters have only a limited tenure of experience in Church membership and service. Every level of education is represented among these local leaders, yet they are expected to learn and to administer a code of inspired principles, procedures, and policies that are determined by the General

AREAS OF THE CHURCH

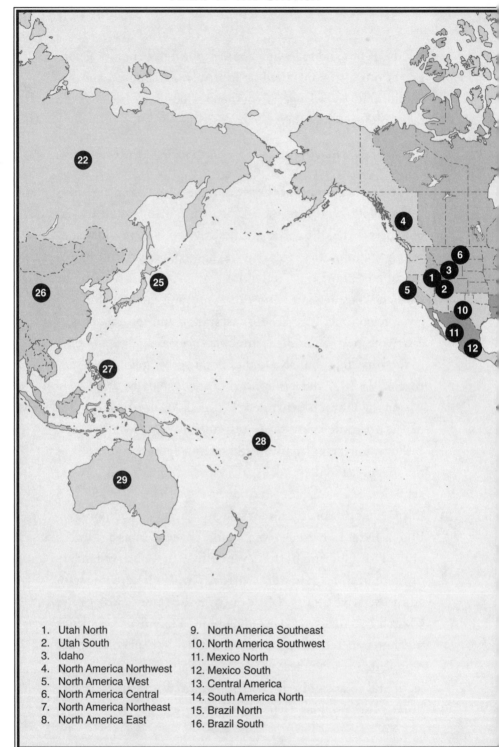

1. Utah North
2. Utah South
3. Idaho
4. North America Northwest
5. North America West
6. North America Central
7. North America Northeast
8. North America East
9. North America Southeast
10. North America Southwest
11. Mexico North
12. Mexico South
13. Central America
14. South America North
15. Brazil North
16. Brazil South

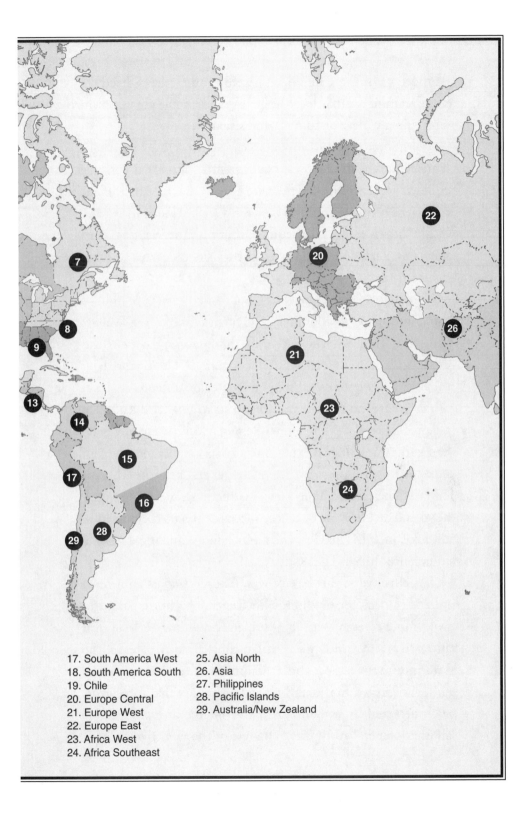

17. South America West
18. South America South
19. Chile
20. Europe Central
21. Europe West
22. Europe East
23. Africa West
24. Africa Southeast

25. Asia North
26. Asia
27. Philippines
28. Pacific Islands
29. Australia/New Zealand

Authorities of the Church." Therefore, there was a need for more training so that local bishops could apply "correct principles" in a variety of cultures and situations.[7]

Although much of this help came through printed bulletins, Church administrators consistently found that personal contacts were still more effective. During the first half of the twentieth century, contacts between General Authorities and local Church leaders had come either by supervisory assignments over missions and stakes or by visits to stake and other conferences.

Then, in 1936, *regions*—as Church administrative units— came into being to coordinate the functioning of the Welfare Program. In 1964 the scope of these *welfare regions* was expanded to serve other Church programs.[8] Three years later the First Presidency called sixty-nine "Regional Representatives of the Twelve" to provide training to stake and ward leaders at regional meetings. All Regional Representatives were men who had gained leadership experience by serving as members of stake or mission presidencies or on general priesthood committees. They received their own instruction concerning priesthood and auxiliary programs at special seminars conducted in connection with the Church's annual and semiannual general conferences in Salt Lake City.

As effective as this service was, Church leaders continued to sense a need for brethren with General Authority status to work more directly with local leaders, providing ecclesiastical authority and guidance similar to that available in the Intermountain region and at Church headquarters. To this end, the United States and Canada were divided into areas, each directed by a member of the Twelve and assisted by another General Authority. The rest of the world was placed under the supervision of Assistants to the Twelve, who were assigned to live in their designated areas.[9] The organization of the First Quorum of the Seventy during the mid-1970s enabled the Council of the Twelve to delegate many of its detailed administrative responsibilities and expand worldwide supervision by General Authorities.

QUORUMS OF THE SEVENTY

The original Quorum of the Seventy was created in 1835 under divine revelation when the *office* of seventy was given to a number of men who had participated in Zion's Camp. These seventies were "called to preach the gospel, and to be especial witnesses unto the Gentiles and in all the world" (D&C 107:25). Seven presidents were called to preside over the original Quorum of the Seventy. In a relatively short period of time, the number of men called to the office of seventy expanded. Additional quorums were subsequently created. But only the seven presidents of the First Quorum of the Seventy were General Authorities. These seven presidents were called the First Council of the Seventy and presided over all of the quorums of seventy. Over the years a number of changes and adaptations have been made to the office of Seventy and the role of the First Quorum and the First Council.

By 1904, 146 quorums of seventy with ten thousand total members were in existence. The chief function of a seventy was to serve as a missionary for the Church. Seventies quorums were organized within stakes, each being presided over by its own set of seven presidents.

As the number of stakes and missions expanded during the 1930s, Church leaders pondered the need to lighten a growing administrative load carried by the Quorum of the Twelve. In

1941, a number of high priests were called as Assistants to the Twelve to "assist the Twelve Apostles in their heavy work and to fill a role similar to that envisioned by the revelations for the First Quorum of Seventy."[10] Over the next thirty-five years, the number of these "Assistants to the Twelve" was enlarged as need dictated. In 1976, twenty-one men were serving in this capacity.

Responsibilities of the First Council of the Seventy were increased in 1961, when all its members were ordained to the office of high priest. President David O. McKay explained their responsibilities: "Under the direction of the Twelve Apostles, the First Council of Seventy go to all parts of the world to set in order the affairs of the Church. That means ordaining high priests, setting apart presidents of stakes, high councilmen, setting apart presidents of high priest quorums, etc., and doing other things necessary for the advancement of the work."[11]

In October 1975 President Spencer W. Kimball announced the formation of the First Quorum of the Seventy. Unlike the seventies quorums in each stake, all members of this quorum would be General Authorities and they would have the same authority as the Assistants to the Twelve.[12] In a short time, additional members were called into this Quorum, including the Assistants to the Twelve, who were discontinued as a distinct group in October 1976. "With this move," President Kimball emphasized, "the three governing quorums of the Church defined by the revelations, the First Presidency, the Quorum of the Twelve, and the First Quorum of Seventy, have been set in their places as revealed by the Lord [see D&C 107:22–26, 33–34]. This will make it possible to handle efficiently the heavy load and to prepare for the increasing expansion and acceleration of the work, anticipating the day when the Lord will return to take direct charge of his Church and Kingdom."[13] Additional members were called to this quorum in subsequent years.

The growing number of these seventies enabled the Church in 1984 to organize a presidency for each of thirteen large areas of the Church. With a presidency rather than a single individual heading each area, more decisions were delegated by general Church leaders to the area level. In subsequent years the number of areas increased, reaching thirty in the year 2003. Outside of the United States and Canada, members of the presidencies resided within their assigned areas and were rotated from one area to another every two or three years; this simultaneously provided immediate contact with a particular area and a broadened perspective through service in other parts of the world.

With the organization of a seventies quorum among the General Authorities, Church leaders decided in 1986 to discontinue all local seventies quorums. Their members were integrated into either elders quorums or high priests groups in their wards and branches.[14]

By 1989 the number of members in the First Quorum exceeded seventy and so a Second Quorum was formed. Those with five-year appointments became members of this quorum, while those who were called for life were thereafter assigned to the First Quorum. The Seven Presidents of the Seventy presided over both quorums (see D&C 107:95).

To administer to this growing membership, continual refinements have been made in the Church's organization. In 1995, the 284 Regional Representatives were released and replaced by 117 new "Area Authorities." These new leaders were high priests who continued in their existing employment, lived in their own homes, and served for a period of approximately six years. Unlike the Regional Representatives (who had been assigned only to stakes in a specific region), Area Authorities could serve anywhere in the broader area as assigned by the Area Presidency. Their expanded assignments included presiding at stake conferences, creating or reorganizing stakes, and in a few cases, even serving in Area presidencies.[15]

Two years later, in 1997, all Area Authorities were ordained to the office of seventy and became known as "Area Authority Seventies." Although they were not set apart as General Authorities, they became members of three new quorums of seventy: the Third Quorum, whose members serve in Europe, Africa, Asia, Australia, and the Pacific; the Fourth Quorum, whose members serve in Mexico, Central America, and South America; and the Fifth Quorum, whose members serve in the United States and Canada. President Hinckley explained that this arrangement gave Area Authorities "a quorum relationship presided over by the Presidents of the Seventy."[16]

DEVELOPMENTS IN CONFERENCE PATTERNS

For nearly three-quarters of the twentieth century, Church auxiliaries (which include the Relief Society, Primary, Sunday School, the former MIA, and the Young Men and Young Women organizations) conducted annual conferences in Salt Lake City, at which auxiliary presidencies and board members presented the coming year's programs and provided training and inspiration for local officers and teachers. In 1975, these auxiliary conferences were discontinued. Henceforth, leadership training has been provided regionally.

Also, beginning in 1977, the length of general conferences

was shortened from three to two days. General sessions would be scheduled for the first weekend of April and October, respectively. This meant that the spring conferences would not necessarily include April 6, the anniversary of the Church's organization, as a traditional general conference date. Limiting the general sessions to the weekends facilitated attendance for stake presidents and others who often could not leave employment responsibilities during weekdays.[17]

At the local end of the spectrum, beginning in 1979, the number of conferences held annually in each stake was also reduced—from four to two. This was done to ease the burdens of time and travel upon members of the Church.[18]

As the number of stakes has multiplied throughout the world, General Authorities have been able to attend stake conferences less frequently. Additionally, bringing the leaders of far-flung units to general conferences held at Church headquarters has become an ever-greater economic burden. The Church therefore inaugurated area conferences in 1971, sending a group of General Authorities to meet the Saints in given parts of the world.

A new channel of communication between Church leaders and members worldwide was opened in 1981, when the first satellite-sending-and-receiving station in the Mountain West was dedicated. This made it possible to broadcast general conference sessions and other programs from Church headquarters with both sound and picture. At the same time, stakes began installing smaller satellite dishes to receive these broadcasts.[19] Today, members of the Church in virtually every land are able to view and listen to conference via satellite or Internet transmission in fifty-six different languages.

CHURCH LITERATURE WORLDWIDE

Making the Church's program accessible to an expanding worldwide membership has created yet other formidable administrative challenges. One of the greatest needs has been to provide Church literature in the growing number of languages spoken by the Saints around the world. During the Church's first century almost all translation was done by the staff in the various overseas mission offices. It was not until 1939 that Eduardo Balderas became the first full-time translator assigned to work at Church headquarters in Salt Lake City. Just after World War II he was joined by a few others who were brought to Salt Lake City from several of the missions of Europe. In 1966 the Presiding Bishopric received the assignment to supervise the translation, publication, and distribution of Church literature worldwide. The original charge was to see that Spanish-speaking members received materials at the same time they were received by Church members elsewhere. This assignment was soon expanded to include other languages. Thousands of pages of material had to be translated yearly into each language. By 1970 a worldwide organization had been developed with publishing plants and distribution centers throughout the world. These international facilities enabled the Church to avoid the delays and expense of long-distance shipping, as well as eliminating the problems of bringing imported materials through customs.

A high-quality monthly magazine has been another important means of instructing and inspiring Church members throughout the world. Over the years most missions had developed publications of their own. The idea for a "unified magazine" for the non-English-speaking peoples of the Church was developed by Elder Howard W. Hunter of the Council of the

LANGUAGES IN WHICH THE *LIAHONA* IS PUBLISHED

Albanian	Fijian	Latvian	Slovenian
Armenian (East)	Finnish	Lithuanian	Spanish
Bulgarian	French	Malagasy	Swedish
Cambodian	German	Marshallese	Tagalog
Cebuano	Haitian	Mongolian	Tahitian
Chinese	Hungarian	Norwegian	Tamil
Croatian	Icelandic	Polish	Telugu
Czech	Indonesian	Portuguese	Thai
Danish	Italian	Romanian	Tongan
Dutch	Japanese	Russian	Ukrainian
English	Kiribati	Samoan	Vietnamese
Estonian	Korean	Sinhala	

Twelve in 1966 with the goal of saving missionary hours, cutting expenses, and at the same time upgrading the quality of the publications. Material for these international magazines was drawn largely from the Church's English-language periodicals, with some space provided for news or other features of local interest. The magazine first appeared in nine European languages in 1967. At first the international magazines retained such traditional names as *La Liahona* (Spanish), *Der Stern* (German), and *L'Etoile* (French).[20] By 2003 all international magazines were named *Liahona* and were published in forty-seven languages; nearly half of these appear monthly, while others are issued less often.

Providing the full range of Church curriculum materials has placed members that speak various languages on more of an equal footing than ever before. Members in Europe were pleased to point out that they were actually the first to commence new courses of study each year—being ahead of the Saints in Salt Lake City because of the difference in time. One mission president stated that members in his area were ready to be organized into a stake but were only waiting the necessary handbooks and other materials to be translated. The great expansion of non-English stakes has come since the Church enlarged its translation program. Because the Lord indicated that "every man shall hear the fulness of the gospel in his own tongue, and in his own language" (D&C 90:11), those involved in Church translation feel that their service is a "literal fulfillment of prophecy."[21]

SCATTERED SAINTS ABROAD

Isolated Latter-day Saints may be found in many countries around the world. Typically they are filling business or government assignments far away from their homes, facing diverse challenges and opportunities. Their experiences also show how Church programs are adapted to fit unique situations.

The family of Nyle G. Merkley, an oil-drilling rig supervisor from Vernal, Utah, discovered that a unique friendship and kinship occurs among scattered Latter-day Saints overseas. When they went to Benghazi in North Africa, they thought they were all alone. Nevertheless, Sister Merkley described meeting a couple while shopping: "I noticed a husband and wife in the little shop and I walked right past them. But the woman said 'Hello,' and I replied, 'Hi.' The woman said, 'You must be American, where are you from?' I told her we had just moved up from Tripoli. Just then our son walked up wearing one of his brother's BYU T-shirts. The woman then said, 'Brigham Young University, do you folks happen to be LDS?' I told her yes. She said, 'So are we.' I had an instant flood of tears as we embraced, shook hands and all talked at once."[22]

Wherever they are found, scattered Saints generally value

Church membership and activity. In the Church's earlier years, these members' needs were met through the nearest organized missions. The Swiss Mission, for example, had the assignment to keep in touch with Saints in the eastern Mediterranean and the Middle East. In 1972, however, a new unit, the International Mission, assumed this responsibility worldwide. Headquartered in Salt Lake City, it provided needed materials, received tithes, coordinated the issuing of temple recommends, and facilitated priesthood advancements for isolated Latter-day Saints worldwide. As Elder Bernard P. Brockbank, the mission's first president, put it, wherever these members are, "the Church is as close as the nearest mailbox."[23] When area presidencies were appointed during the 1980s, they assumed the functions performed by the International Mission, and it was eventually discontinued.

The Church developed its "small units" or "basic units" program beginning in 1978. To strengthen isolated families and to help them achieve success in teaching gospel principles to their children, the Church published a family guidebook explaining how the family should be organized, how it should function, and what meetings it should hold. A branch could be organized where two or more member families were in an area with at least one worthy priest or Melchizedek Priesthood bearer to serve as president. A guidebook was also prepared to aid those responsible for directing these small branches.

Obviously these small units could not support the full range of activities conducted in larger congregations. An isolated family could conduct a simple sacrament service on Sundays and a home evening on Mondays. Where several families could meet together and a branch be organized, they could add a priesthood meeting and a session for women and children at the same hour; home teaching could also be inaugurated. Growing groups could introduce still other activities.

By 1979 a series of four manuals containing basic and simplified lessons had been provided for use by small groups, especially in the emerging or developing areas of the Church: *Gospel Principles* (for adults), *Duties and Blessings of the Priesthood, The Latter-day Saint Woman,* and *Walk in His Ways* (for children).

When the family of Lass de Linde, an architectural consultant from Norway, moved to Tanzania in east Africa, their services were "family style," as Sister Birgitta de Linde explained. "For the sacrament service, we bring a small table in from the hall. . . . My husband presides and blesses and passes the sacrament. . . . In our 'living-meeting' room, the children are willing and able to behave as if they were in a church. They leave the 'living room' 15 minutes before our services start, and then reenter the 'chapel' quietly and reverently in time for the services."[24]

Agronomist Bernard Silver's family was authorized to hold sacrament meetings at Ferkessédougou, perhaps the first Latter-day Saint services in the Ivory Coast. He invited nonmember associates to attend. Later, three other American Latter-day Saints joined him. One of them, a less-active elder, was attracted by the novelty of attending a priesthood meeting so far from home. He became the priesthood clerk and, although shy, offered many prayers and gave some talks. He was the first in the group to share a copy of the Book of Mormon with a person he met on the train.[25]

The "small units" program, originally intended for scattered groups abroad, has also blessed Saints living in large stakes and wards but who are cut off from the majority by language or cultural barriers. Likewise, features of Church activities developed overseas have been introduced into existing units at home as a means to simplify programs and reduce travel expense.[26] The "small units" program preceded the 1980 consolidation of meetings (all meetings were now to be held on Sunday in one three-hour block) Churchwide by only two years.

HELPING TO OPEN DOORS

In 1974 President Spencer W. Kimball challenged the Saints to "lengthen their stride" and prepare to carry the gospel to all the world. An especially significant step was taken that same year with the appointment of David M. Kennedy as the Church's special consultant for diplomatic affairs. A former counselor in the Chicago Stake presidency, Brother Kennedy had also served as secretary of the treasury, United States ambassador at large, and as U.S. ambassador to the North Atlantic Treaty Organization. Previously he had headed the Continental Illinois National Bank and Trust Company, the largest bank in Chicago and eighth largest in the United States. All these assignments gave him an unusually rich background of experience in international relations and provided him with extensive contacts with government and business leaders around the world. Although Brother Kennedy reported directly to the First Presidency, he also worked in close cooperation with the Church's Missionary and Public Communications Departments and with the International Mission.[27]

One of the Church's most serious challenges was the lack of official recognition in several countries. Although specific laws varied from place to place, this generally meant that the Church could not hold property or enjoy any other legal rights in the country. Receiving recognition usually meant that restrictions on Church meetings would be lifted or relaxed. As Brother Kennedy approached government officials, he emphasized that the Church teaches its members to be good citizens and to be loyal to the country where they live. He found that government leaders appreciated the Church's emphasis on individual industry and strong families. Largely as a result of his efforts, the Church gained legal recognition in several countries, including Portugal, Malaysia, and Sri Lanka.[28] Particularly significant were his negotiations with the Polish government, culminating in official recognition and an invitation for President Kimball to visit the country.

At a banquet with the prophet in Warsaw, Communist government officials acknowledged: "At this table are people from two different lands who think differently. Some are staunch Communists and some are staunch believers in God." Nevertheless, they pledged to cooperate with the Church because "we of the government think high moral standards are very important in life as does your Church. . . . We are happy to have your Church in Poland."[29]

Beginning in the mid-1970s several experienced couples were called to represent the Church in areas where regular full-time missions were not organized. They did not do missionary work in the traditional sense, but rather were instructed to be sensitive to local customs and to carefully observe laws respecting proselyting. Their assignment was to make friends and to maintain contacts with government officials and others and to provide service in their assigned areas. In most areas they made further contributions by bolstering the faith and activity of the few Saints already living there. More than sixteen years earlier, during a tour of south Asia, President Kimball had begun formulating his ideas concerning the appropriateness of missionary methods in some areas. He said: "Yes, I'd proselyte in Burma, but not in our conventional style." He felt that mature individuals or couples prepared "to rough it" could be called to open the work in countries where circumstances might be particularly difficult.[30]

The Tabernacle Choir and performing groups from Brigham Young University and other Church organizations have had a particularly positive impact. In 1977, BYU's Young Ambassadors—a musical variety group—performed before thousands in Romania and Bulgaria. The following year they made a precedent-setting tour of Poland and Russia and appeared on Soviet national television. Then, in 1979 they were the first cultural exchange group to perform in mainland China under the Communist regime's "open door" policy.[31] Vast audiences still welcome the clean-cut appearance of these performers and the wholesome nature of their shows. The Tabernacle Choir made a favorable impression during its concert tours to the Holy Land in 1992 and in Europe and the Mediterranean six years later.

The Church's organization and programs have had to be flexible enough to respond to the varied challenges of international growth. Just as revelation through living prophets led the Saints in meeting the challenges of the past, so also is divine guidance evidenced in meeting the present-day challenges and responsibilities of growth and expansion worldwide.

HOW FAR HAVE WE COME?

RICHARD O. COWAN

As early as 1830, the Saints took seriously the Savior's injunction to go "into all the world, and preach the gospel to every creature" (Mark 16:15). From the beginning, they looked forward to the fulfilling of Daniel's prophecy that in the last days God would establish a kingdom which would "stand for ever" and eventually fill "the whole earth" (Daniel 2:26–45, particularly v. 35 and 44). In 1842, the Prophet Joseph Smith insisted that God's work would not be completed until "the truth of God . . . has penetrated every continent, visited every clime, swept every country, and sounded in every ear."[1]

Having considered the progress of the Church in various parts of the world, there are now some questions we should be able to answer. How far have we come in fulfilling the Church's divinely appointed global destiny? Just what has been accomplished? How was it done? What roles have leaders and members played? What external factors have had an impact? What challenges and opportunities has worldwide growth brought?

DIVINE HELP THROUGH CHURCH LEADERS

It is God's kingdom that is destined to roll forth and fill the whole earth. The Church bears the name of God's beloved Son, Jesus Christ. The power of the Holy Ghost is the ultimate teacher of those who seek a testimony of the truth. Hence all three members of the Godhead are directly interested and involved in the progress of their work on earth.

The Lord has called prophets, seers, and revelators to give direction to his earthly kingdom. Specifically, the Twelve were to be "special witnesses of the name of Christ in all the world." Under the direction of the First Presidency, they were charged to "build up the church, and regulate all the affairs of the same in all nations." Furthermore, they were given "the keys, to open the door by the proclamation of the gospel of Jesus Christ, and first unto the Gentiles and then unto the Jews" (D&C 107:23, 33, 35).

On 23 July 1837 the Lord reminded Thomas B. Marsh, president of the Quorum of the Twelve, that his quorum had the responsibility to "unlock the door of the kingdom in all places" where the First Presidency could not go. "Whithersoever they shall send you," the Lord continued, "go ye, and I will be with you; and in whatsoever place ye shall proclaim my name an effectual door shall be opened unto you." Furthermore, the Lord promised Brother Marsh that "whosoever ye shall send in my name, by the voice of your brethren, the Twelve, duly recommended and authorized by you, shall have power to open the door of my kingdom unto any nation whithersoever ye shall send them" (D&C 112:17, 19, 21). As has been seen, on the very day Brother Marsh received this command, Reverend James Fielding in England was prompted to open his chapel to Elders Heber C. Kimball and Orson Hyde of the Twelve and their fellow missionaries, thus opening the promised door for proclaiming the restored gospel.

The Twelve are to be assisted by the Seventy, to whom the Lord gave essentially the same responsibilities (compare verses 23 with 25, and 33 with 34, in D&C 107). Hence the formation of Quorums of the Seventy during the last quarter of the twentieth century represented a significant step in filling out God's plan for Church administration.

Although these earthly leaders direct the programs and activities of the Church, they consistently testify that Jesus Christ stands at the head of this Church and is the ultimate source of its direction. Though the church may be "built upon the foundation of the apostles and prophets," "Jesus Christ himself" is "the chief corner stone" (Ephesians 2:20).

Dr. James R. Moss spoke of a divine timetable as he wrote the concluding chapter in an earlier Brigham Young University text on the international Church.[2] God, who knows "all things" (2 Nephi 9:20), "the end from the beginning" (Abraham 2:8), understands when certain events need to occur in order to have the desired results. For example, it was not an accident that the first overseas mission was opened in England. In the middle nineteenth century the British Empire extended around the world. This made it possible for early English converts to carry the gospel to such far away places as India and Siam.

HOW CHURCH MEMBERS HAVE HELPED

Latter-day Saints, as individuals or in groups, have had an interest in sharing the precious gospel that has blessed their lives so much. Certain character traits have contributed to their success. The Saints have typically been a friendly and outgoing people. But other qualities have also been vital in teaching the gospel.

LANGUAGE ABILITY

In foreign countries, a knowledge of the language has been essential. The elders who opened the mission in England obviously had an advantage because they already knew the language and culture of the people there. Conversely, Parley P. Pratt and Hosea Stout regarded their inability to speak the local language to be an insurmountable barrier in introducing the gospel to Chile and China respectively. The first missionaries to Scandinavia were converts who had come from that same area; they knew the people, customs, and language of those whom they taught, so enjoyed great success. Sons of these missionaries returning to their ancestral homelands may have had the same ethnic background, but they had grown up in America and thus had to learn the ways and language in order to be effective.

A knowledge of the language and local culture was also a definite advantage to the missionaries who first carried the gospel to Mexico. Anglo youth who grew up in the Mormon colonies of northern Mexico became immersed in the language and culture of the area. Even though they were of a different ethnic background, they were able to become effective instruments in God's hands in establishing the gospel throughout Latin America. In like manner, members of the Japanese community in Hawaii who knew the language played a key role in opening the gospel in post-World War II Japan. The work in Portugal was opened largely by missionaries from Brazil who spoke the same language and shared similar cultures. Certainly the work will accelerate as indigenous missionaries increasingly carry the gospel to their own countrymen.

Broad Cultural Sensitivity

The ability to accept and appreciate other cultures has been another essential quality. To be effective in spreading the gospel, however, this trait had to go beyond a mere tolerance of others' ways. It had to embrace a genuine love for the people, their culture, and their language. Young George Q. Cannon was effective in the Pacific because he demonstrated a respect and love of the Hawaiian people as he ate their food and slept in their humble island homes. The more recent yet similar example of Elder John H. Groberg has become legendary, even being documented on film as a major motion picture in Walt Disney's 2001 release *The Other Side of Heaven*.

EAGERNESS TO SHARE GOSPEL

New converts have typically shared their faith with their relatives. This has sometimes enabled the Church to gain a foothold in a new area, leading to substantial success. Two examples from the opening of the British mission illustrate this point. Joseph Fielding, one of the original missionaries, introduced the elders to his brother James, the minister who opened his chapel and gave them their first opportunity to proclaim the gospel in Great Britain. Similarly, William Benbow, a convert in the Potteries, introduced the missionaries to his brother John in Herefordshire; John Benbow was the first of the six hundred United Brethren to be baptized by Elder Wilford Woodruff.

Ethnic groups have frequently played a key role in taking the gospel into new areas. In some cases, individuals receive the gospel while abroad and then carry the good news back when returning to their homeland. For example, Italians met the missionaries in West Germany while working there and then shared their new faith with family and friends back in Italy. In other cases, people who were already members shared the gospel with new neighbors after moving abroad. German immigrants to Argentina preached the gospel to other Germans in Buenos Aires; this small ethnic group provided the nucleus from which the Church soon spread into the Spanish-speaking majority. The same thing happened in southern Brazil.

Men and women in military service sometimes provide the Church's first contact in a new area. The first converts in Spain, for example, came as personnel at American military bases there shared the gospel. A similar function is played by Latter-day Saint expatriates working for businesses or in government service abroad. Families from Europe as well as from North America conducted the first Church meetings in several countries of Africa.

There have been times when there were no members or missionaries available to introduce the gospel into a particular area of the world. The Lord in such circumstances has, of course, used other means to accomplish his ends. A man in western Africa was prompted to pick up a specific scrap of paper from a cluttered gutter; written on it was the name of the Church and its headquarters city. He was moved to write for information, and later played a key role of teaching others in his area about the Restoration. Similarly, a tract found by an individual in India led him to find out more, share the gospel, and gather a group of believers. Truly, "God moves in a mysterious way His wonders to perform."[3]

EXTERNAL FACTORS
AFFECTING CHURCH GROWTH

Even though the Saints' commitment to sharing the gospel with the world has remained, results have varied. At a given time, progress in one country might be substantial, while nearby it might be blocked completely. Likewise, in a given area long periods of negligible progress can be interspersed with great success. Reasons for these fluctuations are many. In addition to the Lord's direction and the varying resources the Church could commit to sharing the gospel at different times, several external forces have had a substantial impact.

GOVERNMENT POLICIES

In New Testament times, the Roman Empire facilitated the spread of Christianity through its well-developed system of travel, trade, and communication. On the other hand, persecutions instituted and promoted by certain Roman emperors posed major obstacles to the progress of the Lord's work. Likewise, in the present dispensation, governmental policies and actions have both helped and hindered the spreading of the gospel.

The Lord affirmed that he had established the Constitution of the United States through "wise men [He] raised up unto this very purpose" (D&C 101:80). Constitutional guarantees of religious freedom and the protection of basic inalienable freedoms enabled America to become the land where the gospel and Church could be restored and the base from which it could spread throughout the world.

The enacting of laws protecting religious freedom in Denmark, Switzerland, and Holland immediately preceded the opening of missions in those countries and certainly contributed to success there during the mid-nineteenth century. In the Germanic areas, however, such guarantees were lacking; missionaries were sometimes jailed or even expelled. Obviously, under such conditions progress was slower.

Laws restricting proselyting have hampered missionary work in several areas. Therefore, securing legal recognition has become a high priority whenever the Church has entered a new land. Depending on specific regulations in different countries, having this status enables the Church to conduct religious services, perform marriages, distribute literature, own property, and in other ways support the spiritual progress of the Saints.

Nationalism has sometimes impeded spreading the gospel. This was true in Japan during the early twentieth century when a general reluctance to accept anything foreign was complicated by a resentment of U.S. immigration policies that were regarded as offensive.

Feelings about America have both benefited and hurt the Church. In areas where the United States was regarded positively, missionaries from America were well received. On the other hand, anti-American feelings have hampered the Church even in certain areas of Latin America.

Elder Orson Pratt looked forward to the time when "despotic powers" would be overthrown and be replaced with governments more friendly to allowing the Church to be established there.[4] Eastern Europe provides a good example. As Soviet Communism spread across the area following World War II, missionaries were expelled from Czechoslovakia and eastern Germany, and religious activities of the Saints in those countries were severely restricted. It seemed impossible that missionaries would ever be permitted to work in that region. When, beginning in 1989, Communist regimes toppled and were replaced by democratically elected governments, doors were opened. Missions were established in such areas as Poland, Hungary, Bulgaria, Romania, the Baltic states, and even the former Soviet Union.

THE IMPACT OF WARS AND REVOLUTIONS

The disruption of life caused by destructive revolutions or rebellions has sometimes brought missionary work to a halt. Such conditions existing in Chile and China definitely contributed to the failure of Elders Pratt and Stout in those countries. In Mexico, on the other hand, the 1850s revolution led by Benito Juarez secured the freedom of religion that enabled Latter-day Saint missionaries to enter that country just a few years later. Still, it was another revolution in Mexico that caused the evacuation of colonists and missionaries during the early twentieth century.

Major wars have likewise had a mixed impact. World Wars I and II clearly disrupted the Church's work, not only in areas where there was actual fighting, but worldwide, as young men were diverted from missionary to military service. Hundreds of Saints were killed during these conflicts, thousands lost their homes, and some chapels or other Church buildings were destroyed. Still, World War II took Latter-day Saints into new areas where they later returned, established their homes, and help to introduce or build up the Church. This war also created conditions in Japan allowing the return of missionaries, this time to enjoy substantial success. Similarly, Latter-day Saint chaplains and other servicemen set a good example and shared the gospel during the Korean conflict; as soon as fighting ended, formal missionary work started in Korea and built on the good foundation laid by the military personnel. Latter-day Saint soldiers also introduced the gospel into the Philippines and later into southeast Asia.

ECONOMIC CONDITIONS

Economic factors have also had a mixed impact on the Church's progress around the world. Financial distress during the Great Depression cut the number of missionaries almost in half and delayed construction of many badly needed chapels. Times of prosperity, on the other hand, have not necessarily resulted in more progress for the Church; during economic good times many people see no need for God or religion.

In many nations the gospel has been received first by humble people in the lower socioeconomic classes. In England, for example, success in the industrial areas surrounding Preston and Manchester was in marked contrast to the cooler reception the missionaries received in the more sophisticated climate of London. Yet extreme poverty has been a limiting factor. People who are preoccupied with where their next meal will come from sometimes think they have no time for religion. In some developing areas, Church programs have needed to be simplified or even cut back so they can be afforded by the poverty-stricken members.

THE RELIGIOUS SETTING

Over the years, Latter-day Saint missionaries have enjoyed their greatest success in areas where Christianity was already established. The people whom they taught had already accepted the Bible, so the missionaries had a shared heritage or common ground on which to build. Furthermore, those who already had faith in the Lord Jesus Christ were more likely to be spiritually prepared to recognize the added gospel light made available through the latter-day Restoration.

Religious history had a unique impact in Europe. The restored Church was first established in areas such as Great Britain, Scandinavia, Switzerland, and Holland, which had supported the Protestant Reformation. Here, people had been encouraged to study the Bible for themselves. There was already in place a tradition of being willing to change religions. Furthermore, most of these areas had also established the freedom of religion. By contrast, the missionaries initially enjoyed less success in France and southern Europe, which had remained Catholic. In the New World, on the other hand, the Church is growing rapidly throughout Catholic Latin America; this is due to a variety of factors, including the unique appeal of the Book of Mormon to the descendants of Father Lehi.

In non-Christian areas, Latter-day Saint missionaries often sought out and enjoyed their initial success among the Christian minority. The growing number of Christian converts provided a broader base from which to reach out to the non-Christian majority. Early success in Korea, for example, came among the ten percent of that country's population who were already Protestant Christians. Significantly, the Asian area where the restored Church is growing fastest is the Philippines, where more than four centuries of preaching primarily by the Catholics has made ninety percent of the people at least nominal Christians.

Still, established Christian churches often became the Latter-day Saints' most bitter opponents. Clergymen in Britain as well as on the European continent were almost always the prime movers in attacking missionaries and their converts. This problem was particularly acute in areas that had not traditionally been Christian. In the Pacific, for example, Protestant missionary organizations rightfully claimed credit for converting native populations to Christianity and therefore resented the Mormons' "stealing sheep" from their flocks.

Yet another impact of the spiritual climate was seen in England. Many people had become disillusioned with existing churches that seemed not to be teaching the gospel of Christ as recorded in the Bible. Furthermore, the working classes felt abandoned by the "absentee clergy" of the dominant churches.

Groups such as the United Brethren in England were actively seeking for something better; they presented a "field white and already to harvest" to the Latter-day Saints.

STAGES OF CHURCH GROWTH

Latter-day Saint scholar James R. Moss identified three distinct phases or stages the Church passes through as it becomes established in a given area. Using this framework, we can more easily and clearly assess progress in one region and compare it with another.

LAYING THE FOUNDATION

Typically, missionaries from abroad introduce the gospel message. During this first stage, converts often come from the lower classes of society. These humble Saints may be faithful but lack experience; hence the foreign missionaries need to provide leadership and generally assume a dominant role in activities of the local congregation. The lack of lesson materials and even scriptures translated into the local language further hampers and discourages new members from getting more involved. Without a background in the restored gospel, they sometimes struggle to weed out remnants of former religious traditions and practices and to keep doctrinal teaching pure. Facilities are inadequate, the small groups usually meeting in rented and sometimes substandard halls. As these humble people join the Church, they often turn their backs on the general society. This, plus their typically small numbers, means that they generally attract little attention other than ridicule or persecution.

BUILDING THE KINGDOM

In this second stage, members increasingly assume responsibility for the leadership and activities of their congregation. Church materials have become available in the local language. Physical facilities are more adequate. The Saints commonly meet in a remodeled home or apartment building floor or in a small Church-built or purchased meetinghouse; these facilities often have too few classrooms so programs need to be curtailed. Second- and third-generation members often move into the middle class and increasingly attract converts from this level of society. More and more they have their own local heroes or role models so do not need to depend so much on examples from abroad. Still, this is a particularly difficult time, Moss concluded, "with the weak leaving the Church and the strong becoming tempered by adversity."[5]

FLOWERING MATURITY

In this last stage, local Saints are mature in the gospel, give leadership to their own activities, and even carry the main load in missionary work within the area. Beautiful chapels include facilities to support the full range of Church activity. The organization of stakes and construction of temples make gospel blessings as available in this area as in any other part of the world. High levels of meeting attendance, tithe paying, and temple activity all reflect stability and strength. As Church members increasingly reach out in Christian service, and as they reach a "critical mass" or noticeable share of the population, the Latter-day Saints come to be appreciated by the general society, which may even look to them for leadership. Within the Church itself, leaders in this locality finally reach

514

the point that they are called to help strengthen the Saints in other areas or even worldwide.

STATUS OF THE CHURCH AROUND THE WORLD

During the closing years of the twentieth century, The Church of Jesus Christ of Latter-day Saints passed two significant milestones. For the first time, there were more members living outside of the United States than inside. In 1997, total membership worldwide surpassed the ten million mark. These accomplishments indicated that the Lord's kingdom was truly rolling forth, and that it was blessing an ever-increasing share of the world's population. But has it filled the earth? By the end of the twentieth century, Church membership was approximately eleven million, but the estimated population of the earth was about five and one-half billion. This meant there were about five hundred people for every one Latter-day Saint worldwide. Though God's kingdom has experienced remarkable growth, there is still a long way to go before Daniel's prophecy is fulfilled.

Obviously the Church is gaining strength, but is it equally strong in all the world? What stage of development has it reached in various geographical areas? Referring to the chronology at the end of this book may provide the answer. In the United States and Canada the Church clearly has reached the third stage in many areas. Yet there are some places, generally outside of the western region of North America or other large population centers, where local groups have not reached that plateau. In other parts of the world, especially Latin America and western Europe, there is an increasing number of areas where Church development clearly has reached the third stage. Typically these are in urban centers. But there are many

515

more locations where foundations are just being laid or where building the kingdom is just beginning. Of course the objective is to see all areas reach the level of gospel maturity so the Saints can enjoy the full blessings of the Church and gospel.

During the early decades of the Church's history, outlying missions strengthened the central areas of the Church as thousands of converts gathered to build Zion. Over the years this central nucleus has provided direction and strength to its branches worldwide. Finally, in more recent decades, outlying units have reached such a level of maturity that they can lend strength to the whole Church by providing qualified leaders who may be called as General Authorities to serve Churchwide.

While most of the world has received the blessings of the gospel to one degree or another, there are still large areas where the Church has no presence. Local customs, laws, prejudices, or even downright danger have prevented Church representatives from going there. These include large sections of Asia and Africa, as well as isolated spots elsewhere in the world, such as in the Middle East. Nevertheless, the Lord has commanded his Latter-day servants: "Therefore, go ye into all the world; and unto whatsoever place ye cannot go ye shall send, that the testimony may go from you into all the world unto every creature" (D&C 84:62). The Internet provides a means of keeping this commandment. When the Church established its Internet website during the 1990s, the scriptures, general conference messages, information about temples, an explanation of basic gospel doctrines, and many other items became available virtually anyplace in the world. As more and more individuals gain access to the Internet, there will be fewer people who cannot be reached by the gospel.

SOME CHALLENGES FROM
WORLDWIDE GROWTH

The global growth of the Church has presented a variety of challenges. Some are unique to particular localities or may have occurred only in the past. Others seem to be encountered in most areas where the Church is introduced and will likely continue into the future. These challenges have not been stumbling blocks, however, but rather stepping stones to further progress. Divine guidance and direction have also been evident as these challenges have been met and overcome.

RELATING THE GOSPEL TO VARIED CULTURES

As the Church has become more global, it has increasingly encountered peoples whose system of values and way of life are quite different from those familiar to the General Authorities. These differences have been in such diverse matters as the roles of men and women in society, modes of dress and grooming, types of music used in religious services, or even the necessity of adhering to fixed rules or standards. Church leaders have pondered to discern which matters were inherent in the gospel and which were merely customs followed in the western United States. Inspiration has been sought as lesson manuals are adapted to teach gospel truths as effectively in one culture as in another. For example, Primary manuals in Polynesia don't use stories about snowball fights or other climate-specific events. The Brethren have determined that the scriptures will not be adapted, but will remain a consistent standard. Even though cultural diversity enriches the Church, there must still be a "unity of the faith" (Ephesians 4:13).

TRANSLATING AND DISTRIBUTING LITERATURE

As the twenty-first century dawned, the Church was translating its leadership handbooks and basic curriculum materials into more than fifty languages. This posed a huge burden on the staff at Church headquarters. To reduce this load, Church leaders concluded that there should be a significant reduction in the volume of printed materials distributed to the Saints. This streamlining was initially intended to reduce the task of the Church's translation and publication departments, but has proved to be a blessing to Church members who find that these "leaner" materials place greater emphasis on weightier matters. Furthermore, much of the responsibility for translation and publication has been shifted to overseas centers. This has had the fringe benefit of reducing the enormous cost of shipping everything from Salt Lake City to remote parts of the world.

PROVIDING PHYSICAL FACILITIES

The rapid multiplication of local Church units has created an exploding need for places where these units can meet. Because the Church does not have unlimited financial resources, plans have needed to be devised for using existing facilities and resources more efficiently. Meeting schedules have been arranged so that two or three (and sometimes even more) congregations can use the same meetinghouse. To conserve limited funds, members have replaced paid custodians in assuming the main responsibility for cleaning Church buildings. A fringe benefit of this plan has been the fact that members have taken a greater interest in caring for the facilities in which they meet.

KEEPING IN TOUCH WITH A GLOBAL MEMBERSHIP

During the early twentieth century when most Latter-day Saints lived in Utah or the immediate surrounding areas, it was easy for General Authorities to keep in close touch with members. As the number of stakes—and consequently the number of conferences to be held—multiplied, and as distances to be traveled lengthened, the Church leaders found it ever more difficult to maintain the close association with the Saints they had enjoyed in earlier years. Modern technology has helped the Church to meet this challenge. Jet planes have enabled the General Authorities to fly from Salt Lake City to almost anywhere in the world in a matter of hours; this was in marked contrast to the situation during the Church's earliest decades when weeks or even months were required for these same trips. Furthermore, the invention of television enabled Latter-day Saints, even those living in remote areas, to both see and hear their leaders speak. This blessing has been expanded with the development of satellite transmission extending the range of television signals to virtually the entire earth. Video recording has also made it possible for Church leaders to prepare instructional and inspirational materials that can be viewed time after time by members living anywhere. At the end of the twentieth century, the Internet provided yet another means by which Church leaders and members could keep in touch worldwide.

DEVELOPING LOCAL LEADERS

As the globalization of the Church has moved forward at an ever-increasing pace, more responsibility of necessity has had to be shifted to the local or regional level. The General Authorities increasingly assume the role of training leaders at these levels and then delegating responsibility to them. Not only has this enabled the Church to adapt its programs more readily to local needs, but it has been a great blessing to those who have assumed additional leadership responsibilities.

THE OUTLOOK FOR THE FUTURE

As the twenty-first century unfolds before our eyes, what does the future hold for the Lord's work? Because God loves all his children, the scope of his kingdom must truly be global. Daniel's prophecy that it will fill the earth must be fulfilled. God's work *will* "penetrate every continent" and his word *will* "sound in every ear."

As the twenty-first century was about to dawn, President Gordon B. Hinckley declared:

> This is the focal point of all that has gone before. This is the season of restitution. These are the days of restoration. This is the time when men from over the earth come to the mountain of the Lord's house to seek and learn of His ways and to walk in His paths. This is the summation of all of the centuries of time since the birth of Christ to this present and wonderful day. . . .
>
> The centuries have passed. The latter-day work of the Almighty, that of which the ancients spoke, that of which the prophets and apostles prophesied, is come. It is here. . . . There has been a flowering of science. There has been a veritable explosion of learning. This is the greatest of all ages of human endeavor and human accomplishment. And more importantly, it is the season when God has spoken, when His Beloved Son has appeared, when the divine priesthood has been restored, when we hold in our hand another testament of the Son of God. What a glorious and wonderful day this is. . . .
>
> We stand on the summit of the ages, awed by a great and solemn sense of history. This is the last and final dispensation toward which all in the past has pointed.[6]

CHURCH STATUS WORLDWIDE*

GEOGRAPHICAL AREAS	MEMBERS	STAKES	MISSIONS	TEMPLES**
Europe	426,944	102	50	11
Pacific	453,376	119	16	12
Latin America	4,194,841	817	100	29
Asia	807,263	142	34	6
Africa	188,285	37	15	3
Middle East	2,542	—	1	—
North America	5,513,767	1,368	112	65
Caribbean	129,476	16	7	1
World Totals	**11,716,494**	**2,601**	**335**	**127**

* Numbers are for year's end 2002

** These numbers represent operating temples and those that had been announced or were under construction at press time.

Worldwide Church Chronology

Church and World	North America	Latin America
1830 Church organized 1835 Quorums of Twelve and Seventy organized 1836 Keys of gathering restored	1831 Saints settle Kirtland, Ohio, and Independence, Missouri 1832 First Canadian branch of the Church formed 1833 School of the Prophets begins in Kirtland, Ohio 1834 First stake of the Church formed, in Kirtland, Ohio 1836 Kirtland Temple dedicated 1839 Nauvoo settled; gospel preached in South	
1842 Relief Society founded; first endowments given 1844 Joseph Smith martyred; *Samuel Morse develops telegraph* 1847 Brigham Young sustained as president of the Church 1848 *Communist Manifesto drafted* 1849 Perpetual Emigrating Fund established	1846 Nauvoo Temple dedicated; Saints leave Nauvoo on trek west; the ship *Brooklyn* arrives in California 1847 Pioneers arrive in the Salt Lake Valley 1847–50 Groups of Saints settle in California	
1851 Pearl of Great Price published as pamphlet 1852 106 missionaries called to various parts of world; doctrine of plural marriage publicly announced 1857 Missionaries called back to Utah on account of Utah War	1851 Stake created in San Bernardino, California 1856 First handcart company leaves Iowa 1857 Utah War	1851 Parley P. Pratt arrives in Chile
	1861–65 *United States Civil War* 1869 *Transcontinental railroad completed*	

EUROPE	ASIA AND AFRICA	PACIFIC
1837 British Mission organized		
1840 Quorum of the Twelve teach gospel in England; *Millennial Star* started; gathering to Zion launched 1848 Religious freedom granted to citizens of France, Denmark, Holland, and Switzerland; 17,000 members attend conference of the British Mission in Manchester	1841 Orson Hyde dedicates Holy Land for the gathering of the Jews 1849 Gospel preached in India	1841 First baptism in Australia 1844 First branch organized in Australia; missionaries enter Tahiti
1850 Missions organized in Scandinavia, Italy, France, and Switzerland 1851 Book of Mormon published in Danish 1852 German mission organized	1853 South African Mission organized	1850 First LDS missionaries arrive in Hawaii 1851 Australian Mission organized 1854 Australasian Mission formed, which includes Australia and New Zealand
1861 First baptisms in the Netherlands 1862 Missionaries asked to leave Italy 1864 Netherlands mission organized 1869 Steam ships first chartered to transport Saints across Atlantic; *Der Stern* periodical inaugurated	1865 South African Mission closed	1863 Missionaries begin teaching in Samoa 1865 Laie, Hawaii, named as gathering place for Pacific Saints

CHURCH AND WORLD	NORTH AMERICA	LATIN AMERICA
1876 *Alexander Graham Bell receives patent for telephone* 1877 Brigham Young dies 1879 *Thomas Edison invents electric light*	1876 Missions resumed in southern states; Saints colonize Arizona 1877 St. George Utah Temple dedicated 1878 Mormon settlements established in Colorado 1879 Joseph Standing murdered	1876 LDS missionaries arrive in northern Mexico 1879 Moses Thatcher organizes Mexican Mission in Mexico City
1880 John Taylor sustained as third president of the Church 1889 Wilford Woodruff sustained as fourth president of the Church	1882 Edmund Anti-Polygamy bill becomes law 1884 Logan Utah Temple dedicated 1887 First Mormon settlements in Canada established 1888 Manti Utah Temple dedicated	1885 Mormon colonies established in Chihuahua, Mexico 1888 Juárez Academy built
1890 "Manifesto" ends plural marriage 1890s *First gasoline-powered automobiles available* 1898 Lorenzo Snow sustained as fifth president of the Church	1892 California Mission reorganized after closure in 1858 1893 Salt Lake Temple dedicated 1895 Alberta Stake organized, the first outside the United States 1897 Northwestern States Mission formed	1895 Juárez Stake organized in Mormon colonies
1901 Joseph F. Smith sustained as sixth president of the Church 1903 *Wright Brothers make first flight*	1907 A member of the Quorum of the Twelve (Elder Reed Smoot) elected to United States Senate	1907–31 Rey L. Pratt serves as president of Mexican Mission

EUROPE	ASIA AND AFRICA	PACIFIC
1878 Book of Mormon published in Swedish	1873 George A. Smith rededicates Palestine	
1883 First baptism in Austria	1884 Turkish Mission organized	1883–84 Rapid Church growth occurs among Maoris in New Zealand 1888 Joseph Dean officially organizes Samoan Mission
1890 Book of Mormon published in Dutch		1891 Missionaries arrive in Tonga 1892 Society Islands Mission organized (includes Tahiti) 1899 Missionary work commences in Cook Islands
1902 First chapel in Denmark built in Copenhagen 1906 Joseph F. Smith becomes first Church president to visit Europe	1901 Heber J. Grant visits Japan and organizes mission there 1903 South African Mission reorganized	1900 *Samoa divided between United States and Germany*

CHURCH AND WORLD	NORTH AMERICA	LATIN AMERICA
1914–18 *World War I* 1917 *Lenin and the Bolsheviks overthrow the Czar in Russian Revolution* 1918 Heber J. Grant sustained as seventh president of the Church		1912–13 Mormon colonists and missionaries withdrawn from Mexico during revolution 1913–21 Foreign missionaries exiled from Mexico 1915 Martyrs in San Marcos 1917 Mexico's constitution restricts churches from owning property
1920 *First commercial radio broadcast* 1920–21 David O. McKay and Hugh J. Cannon tour missions around the world 1927 *First transatlantic solo flight completed by Charles Lindbergh* 1928 100th stake of the Church organized 1929 *New York Stock Market crash begins Great Depression*	1923 Cardston Alberta Temple dedicated; Los Angeles California Stake created, the first outside the intermountain region 1927 Mesa Arizona Temple dedicated	1921 Missionaries return to Mexico City 1923 German immigrants in Argentina share gospel 1925 South America dedicated for preaching of the gospel 1926 First Argentine convert baptized 1929 Missionaries in Brazil baptize first converts
1936 Church introduces a formal welfare program 1939–45 *World War II*	1930s Many Saints leave the intermountain region during Great Depression 1934 New York Stake created, the first in the eastern United States	1935 Brazil Mission separated from South America Mission 1938 Brazil restricts use of German in public meetings
1941 Position of Assistant to the Twelve created—first five assistants called 1945 George Albert Smith sustained as eighth president of the Church 1947 Church membership reaches 1 million 1949 General conference televised in Salt Lake City	1945 Idaho Falls Idaho Temple dedicated	1940 Book of Mormon first printed in Portuguese 1945 First non-English temple ordinances given in Spanish 1947 Uruguay mission created; missionary work formally organized in Central America

EUROPE	ASIA AND AFRICA	PACIFIC
1914 Missionaries evacuated from Europe		1913 Maori Agricultural School established in New Zealand 1919 Hawaii Temple dedicated
1924 Swiss-German missions become largest in world 1929 Czechoslovak Mission organized	1920–22 David O. McKay dedicates China and visits other Asian countries 1924 Japan Mission closes for more than two decades	1921 David O. McKay visits Pacific missions 1922 Mormon Exclusion Law enacted in Tonga
1933 *Hitler rises to power in Germany* 1937 President Heber J. Grant visits Europe 1939 Missionaries evacuated from Europe as WWII starts	1937 Japanese Mission created in Hawaii for Americans of Japanese ancestry	1935 First Hawaiian stake organized in Oahu 1938 George Albert Smith visits Pacific
1946 Ezra Taft Benson reopens missions in Europe; Church sends supplies to Saints in Europe 1947 Finnish Mission organized 1949 *Berlin blockade and airlift*	1946 Servicemen baptize first postwar converts in Japan 1947–50 Missionaries begin teaching in Near East 1949 *Communists take power in mainland China*	1940 Missionaries evacuated from Pacific missions due to WWII 1946–49 Matthew Cowley presides over Pacific missions

Church and World	North America	Latin America
1950–53 *Korean War* 1951 David O. McKay sustained as ninth president of the Church 1952 *Polio vaccine invented; world's first commercial jetliner service begins in Britain* 1957 *Soviet Union puts first man-made satellite in orbit*	1956 Los Angeles Temple dedicated, largest in Church to date	1956 LDS missionaries enter Chile and Peru, first in western South America 1959 *Fidel Castro establishes Communist government in Cuba*
1961–73 *Vietnam War* 1961 *Soviet Union begins construction on Berlin Wall* 1967 Regional Representatives appointed; *Six-Day War in the Middle East* 1969 *First man walks on the moon*	1964 Oakland California Temple dedicated	1961 Mexico City Stake is organized 1966 São Paulo Stake organized, first in South America
1970 Joseph Fielding Smith sustained as tenth president of the Church 1970s *Satellites facilitate intercontinental communications* 1972 Harold B. Lee sustained as eleventh president of the Church 1973 Spencer W. Kimball sustained as twelfth president of the Church 1976 First Quorum of the Seventy established 1978 Revelation extends priesthood to all races 1979 The Church organizes its 1000th stake	1972 Temples dedicated in Provo and Ogden, Utah 1974 Washington D.C. Temple dedicated	1975 Eleven new stakes organized in Mexico City 1978 São Paulo Brazil Temple dedicated
1984 Area Presidencies appointed 1985 Ezra Taft Benson sustained as thirteenth president of the Church 1989 Second Quorum of the Seventy created	1980 Seattle Washington Temple dedicated 1981 Jordan River Utah Temple dedicated 1983 Atlanta Georgia Temple dedicated 1984 Temples dedicated in Boise, Idaho, and Dallas, Texas 1985 Chicago Illinois Temple dedicated 1986 Denver Colorado Temple dedicated 1989 Temples dedicated in Portland, Oregon, and Las Vegas, Nevada	1981 Angel Abrea is called to the First Quorum of the Seventy, the first General Authority from Latin America 1983 Temples dedicated in Mexico City, Mexico, and Santiago, Chile 1984 Guatemala City Guatemala Temple dedicated 1986 Temples dedicated in Buenos Aires, Argentina, and Lima, Peru 1988 Seven stakes created in Lima, Peru 1989 Mexico's 100th stake organized

EUROPE	ASIA AND AFRICA	PACIFIC
1955 Swiss Temple dedicated; Tabernacle Choir tours Europe 1958 London England Temple dedicated	1950 Proselyting begins in Rhodesia (Zimbabwe) 1952 Servicemen baptize converts in Korea 1956 First missionaries arrive in Taiwan	1954 First missionaries arrive in Fiji 1955 Church College of Hawaii founded (now BYU–Hawaii) 1958 Hamilton New Zealand Temple dedicated, the first in the southern hemisphere; Auckland Stake created
1961 First non-English-speaking stake of the Church organized at The Hague, Netherlands 1966 Italy Mission reopened after Italian government grants permission for LDS missionaries to enter country—first time since 1862 1969 Germany Dresden Mission organized; missionaries allowed to enter Spain	1961 Missionary work begins in Philippines 1964 First meetinghouse in Asia is dedicated in Tokyo, Japan 1968 Missionaries enter Thailand	1963 Polynesian Cultural Center established
1970 Spain Mission organized 1971 First area conference of the Church held in Manchester, England 1975 Charles Didier called to First Quorum of the Seventy 1977 President Spencer W. Kimball dedicates Poland for the preaching of the gospel	1970 First stakes created in Asia and Africa—one in Tokyo and one in Johannesburg 1972 President Harold B. Lee visits Holy Land 1977 Yoshihiko Kikuchi called to First Quorum of the Seventy, the first General Authority from Asia 1978 Missionary work begins in Nigeria and Ghana	1975 Proselyting begins in Melanesia
1985 Temples dedicated in Freiberg, Germany, and Stockholm, Sweden 1987 Frankfurt Germany Temple dedicated 1988 Church granted legal status in Hungary 1989 *Berlin Wall falls;* ground broken for first meetinghouse in Poland	1980 Tokyo Japan Temple dedicated 1984 Chinese premier visits United States, including the Polynesian Cultural Center; temples dedicated in Manila, Philippines, and Taipei, Taiwan 1985 Temples dedicated in Johannesburg, South Africa, and Seoul, Korea 1988 Aba Nigeria Stake organized, the first in West Africa 1989 BYU Jerusalem Center for Near Eastern Studies dedicated	1980 Micronesia Guam Mission created 1983 Temples dedicated in Apia, Samoa; Nuku'alofa, Tonga; and Papeete, Tahiti; Papua New Guinea dedicated for preaching of the gospel 1984 Sydney Australia Temple dedicated

CHURCH AND WORLD	NORTH AMERICA	LATIN AMERICA
1991 *Soviet Union breaks up* 1994 Howard W. Hunter sustained as fourteenth president of the Church 1995 Gordon B. Hinckley sustained as fifteenth president of the Church; Area Authorities appointed 1997 Church membership passes 10 million, more members outside the United States than inside	1990s Increased work among ethnic minorities 1990 Toronto Ontario Temple dedicated 1993 San Diego California Temple dedicated 1994 Orlando Florida Temple dedicated 1995 Bountiful Utah Temple dedicated 1996 Mount Timpanogos Utah Temple dedicated 1997 Temples dedicated in St. Louis, Missouri, and Vernal, Utah 1998 Monticello Utah Temple dedicated 1999 Temples dedicated in Anchorage, Alaska; Spokane, Washington; Columbus, Ohio; Bismarck, North Dakota; Columbia, South Carolina; Detroit, Michigan; Halifax, Nova Scotia; Regina, Saskatchewan; Billings, Montana; Edmonton, Alberta; Raleigh, North Carolina	1999 Temples dedicated in Colonia Juárez, Mexico; Bogota, Colombia; and Guayaquil, Ecuador
2000 Thirty-four temples dedicated, including the Church's one hundredth temple; 100 millionth copy of the Book of Mormon printed 2001 Perpetual Education Fund created; *World Trade Center in New York City and Pentagon in Washington D.C. attacked by terrorists* 2002 Seven new missions of the Church announced; members of the Quorum of the Twelve assigned to live outside the United States; temple recommends now valid for two years	2000 Temples dedicated in St. Paul, Minnesota; Albuquerque, New Mexico; Louisville, Kentucky; Palmyra, New York; Fresno, California; Medford, Oregon; Memphis, Tennessee; Reno, Nevada; Nashville, Tennessee; Montreal, Quebec; Baton Rouge, Louisiana; Oklahoma City, Oklahoma; Houston, Texas; Birmingham, Alabama; and Boston, Massachusetts 2001 Temples dedicated in Omaha, Nebraska (Winter Quarters) and Richland, Washington (Columbia River) 2002 *Salt Lake City hosts the 2002 Winter Olympics;* temples dedicated in Snowflake, Arizona; Lubbock, Texas; and Nauvoo, Illinois	2000 Eight temples dedicated in Mexico (in Ciudad Juárez, Hermosillo, Oaxaca, Tuxtla Gutierrez, Tampico, Villahermosa, Merida, and Veracruz); temples dedicated in Cochabamaba, Bolivia; San Jose, Costa Rica; Caracas, Venezuela; Recife, Brazil; Porto Alegre, Brazil; and Santo Domingo, Dominican Republic 2001 Temples dedicated in Montevideo, Uruguay and Guadalajara, Mexico 2002 Temples dedicated in Monterrey, Mexico; Campinas, Brazil; and Asuncion, Paraguay

EUROPE	ASIA AND AFRICA	PACIFIC
1990–93 Missions created throughout former Communist countries 1991 Tabernacle Choir tours the Soviet Union, Austria, Hungary, Poland, and Czechoslovakia 1993 Church receives legal recognition in Italy 1998 Preston England Temple dedicated; temple announced for Kiev, Ukraine 1999 Madrid Spain Temple dedicated; Copenhagen Denmark Temple announced	1990 Church receives official recognition in Kenya 1991 Church receives official recognition in Ivory Coast 1992 Church legally recognized in Tanzania; missionary couples arrive in Mongolia; Tabernacle Choir tours the Holy Land 1993 Church receives legal recognition in Madagascar, Cameroon, and Ethiopia; Church service missionaries enter Hanoi, Vietnam 1996 President Gordon B. Hinckley visits mainland China, first Church president to do so; Hong Kong Temple dedicated 1997 Church membership in Africa reaches 100,000 1998 President Gordon B. Hinckley visits West Africa, first Church president to do so; Accra Ghana Temple announced	1991 Tonga observes 100th anniversary of Church in Tonga 1997 President Gordon B. Hinckley addresses 52,500 members in eight Pacific islands
2000 Helsinki Finland Temple announced 2001 Meetinghouses dedicated in Ukraine; Sea Trek 2001 commemorates gathering of European Saints; branch created in Kazakhstan (a former state of the Soviet Union) 2002 First LDS meetinghouse in Serbia dedicated; The Hague Netherlands Temple dedicated	2000 Fukuoka Japan Temple dedicated; Aba Nigeria Temple announced 2002 Missionary Training Center opens in Africa	2000 Temples dedicated in Kona, Hawaii; Adelaide, Australia; Melbourne, Australia; and Suva, Fiji 2001 Perth Australia Temple dedicated 2003 Brisbane Australia Temple dedicated

NOTES

NOTES TO INTRODUCTION—GLOBALIZATION OF THE CHURCH

1. Joseph Smith, *History of The Church of Jesus Christ of Latter-day Saints,* 7 vols., 2d ed. rev., ed. B. H. Roberts (Salt Lake City: The Church of Jesus Christ of Latter-day Saints, 1932–51), 4:540. Hereafter cited as *HC.*

2. See Gordon Douglas Pollock, *Northern Voices: A Folk History of Mormonism among British Americans, 1830–1867* (Halifax, Nova Scotia: Kelso Associates, 1995), 1–42.

3. See Donald Q. Cannon, "The Impact of Mormonism on Great Britain," paper presented at the annual meeting of the International Society for the Comparative Study of Civilizations, Dublin, Ireland, 7–10 July 1994.

4. See ibid., 2.

5. See ibid., 2–4.

6. See *Church History in the Fulness of Times,* Church Educational System manual (Salt Lake City: The Church of Jesus Christ of Latter-day Saints, 1993), 238–39. Hereafter cited as *Fulness of Times.*

7. See Bruce A. Van Orden, *Building Zion: The Latter-day Saints in Europe* (Salt Lake City: Deseret Book, 1996), 54–64.

8. See ibid., 64–66.

9. See S. Kent Brown, Donald Q. Cannon, Richard H. Jackson, eds., *Historical Atlas of Mormonism* (New York: Simon & Schuster, 1994), 32–33. Hereafter cited as *Historical Atlas.*

10. See Shirley Taylor Robinson, "Mexico, Pioneer Settlements in," in Daniel H. Ludlow, ed., *Encyclopedia of Mormonism,* 5 vols. (New York: Macmillan Publishing Company, 1992), 2:895–97.

11. See *Fulness of Times,* 529–33.

12. See *Historical Atlas,* 122–23, 130–35.

13. See R. Lanier Britsch, *From the East* (Salt Lake City: Deseret Book, 1998), 318–24.

14. See ibid., 327–41.

15. See ibid., 342–48.

16. Gordon B. Hinckley, as quoted in Britsch, *From the East,* 348.

17. See Flavia Garcia Erbolato, "Brazil," in *Encyclopedia of Mormonism,* 3:1395.

18. See ibid., 3:1395–6.

19. See *2003 Church Almanac* (Salt Lake City: Deseret News, 2002), 288.
20. See Erbolato, "Brazil," in *Encyclopedia of Mormonism,* 3:1396. See also *2003 Church Almanac,* 288–90.
21. See Kahlile Mehr, "Kresimir Cosic of Yugoslavia: Basketball Superstar, Gospel Hero," in Bruce A. Van Orden, D. Brent Smith, and Everett Smith Jr., eds. *Pioneers in Every Land* (Salt Lake City: Bookcraft, 1997), 22–38.
22. See E. Dale LeBaron, "Emmanuel Abu Kissi: A Gospel Pioneer in Ghana," in *Pioneers in Every Land,* 210–20.
23. See Victor L. Ludlow, "The Internationalization of the Church," in *Out of Obscurity: The LDS Church in the Twentieth Century* (Salt Lake City: Deseret Book, 2000), 206.
24. Ibid., 210–12.
25. Ibid., 213–14.
26. Ibid., 218–21.
27. Ibid., 212–13.
28. Ibid., 209.
29. Ibid., 218.
30. Ibid., 216–17.
31. Ibid., 226.
32. Ibid., 215.
33. Neal A. Maxwell, from a speech given at a Brigham Young University symposium, 30 March to 9 April 1976, notes from the address in the possession of the author.
34. Based on author's examination of several LDS publications over the past twenty years.
35. See Britsch, *From the East,* 331.
36. See ibid., 335.
37. Interview with Brian Q. Cannon, associate professor of history at Brigham Young University, 23 February 1998, notes in possession of the author.

NOTES TO CHAPTER 1—OPENING THE BRITISH MISSION: 1837 TO 1841

1. Joseph Smith, *History of The Church of Jesus Christ of Latter-day Saints,* 7 vols., 2d ed. rev., ed. B. H. Roberts (Salt Lake City: The Church of Jesus Christ of Latter-day Saints, 1932–51), 2:392. Hereafter cited as *HC.*
2. Heber C. Kimball, in *Autobiography of Parley P. Pratt* (Salt Lake City: Deseret Book, 1985), 110.
3. In Smith, *HC,* 2:489.
4. Ibid., 2:490
5. Heber C. Kimball, in Orson F. Whitney, *Life of Heber C. Kimball* (Salt Lake City: Bookcraft, 1945), 104.
6. In Smith, *HC,* 2:489.
7. Heber C. Kimball, in Whitney, *Life of Heber C. Kimball,* 107.
8. See Malcolm R. Thorp, "The Setting for the Restoration in Britain: Political, Social, and Economic Conditions," in V. Ben Bloxham, James R. Moss, and Larry C. Porter, eds., *Truth Will Prevail: The Rise of The Church of Jesus Christ of Latter-day Saints in the British Isles, 1837–1987* (Cambridge: The Church of Jesus Christ of Latter-day Saints, 1987), 44–70.

9. For a more complete account of this mission, see James B. Allen, Ronald K. Esplin, and David J. Whittaker, *Men with a Mission, 1837-1841: The Quorum of the Twelve Apostles in the British Isles* (Salt Lake City: Deseret Book, 1992), chapter 2.

10. See James R. Moss, "The Gospel Restored to England," in *Truth Will Prevail*, 73.

11. See ibid.

12. See ibid.

13. Heber C. Kimball, in Whitney, *Life of Heber C. Kimball*, 125.

14. Ibid., 130.

15. Orson Hyde, as quoted in Whitney, *Life of Heber C. Kimball*, 131.

16. Joseph Smith, as quoted in Whitney, *Life of Heber C. Kimball*, 132.

17. Moss, "The Gospel Restored to England," in *Truth Will Prevail*, 80.

18. See ibid., 87.

19. Heber C. Kimball, in Whitney, *Life of Heber C. Kimball*, 138.

20. See Moss, "The Gospel Restored to England," in *Truth Will Prevail*, 90.

21. Ibid., 90–91.

22. Heber C. Kimball, in *The Latter-day Saints' Millennial Star* 26 (1 Oct 1864): 632.

23. See Moss, "The Gospel Restored to England," in *Truth Will Prevail*, 92.

24. Heber C. Kimball, in Whitney, *Life of Heber C. Kimball*, 172.

25. Ibid., 187.

26. Heber C. Kimball, in *Journal of Discourses*, 26 vols. (London: Latter-day Saints' Book Depot, 1854–86), 5:22. Hereafter referred to as *JD*.

27. Joseph Smith, in *JD*, 5:22; original spelling maintained.

28. Heber C. Kimball, in Whitney, *Life of Heber C. Kimball*, 188–89.

29. Ibid., 174.

30. Wilford Woodruff, as quoted in Matthias F. Cowley, ed., *Wilford Woodruff: History of His Life and Labors as Recorded in His Daily Journals* (Salt Lake City: Bookcraft, 1964), 109.

31. Whitney, *Life of Heber C. Kimball*, 265.

32. Heber C. Kimball, in ibid., 267

33. Brigham Young, in *Times and Seasons* 1 (November 1839–October 1840): 70–71.

34. For an excellent analysis of the Twelve's 1840 to 1841 service in Great Britain, see Allen, Esplin, and Whittaker, *Men with a Mission*, chapters 5–10.

35. In Davis Bitton, *George Q. Cannon: A Biography* (Salt Lake City: Deseret Book, 1999), 33–34.

36. George Q. Cannon, as quoted in V. Ben Bloxham, "The Apostolic Foundations, 1840–41," in *Truth Will Prevail*, 126.

37. In Cowley, *Wilford Woodruff*, 116.

38. Bloxham, "The Apostolic Foundations," in *Truth Will Prevail*, 133.

39. Wilford Woodruff, in *JD*, 15:344–45.

40. Wilford Woodruff, in Cowley, *Wilford Woodruff*, 118.

41. Ibid., 120.

42. See Bloxham, "The Apostolic Foundations," in *Truth Will Prevail*, 139.

43. Wilford Woodruff, in *JD*, 15:344–45.

44. Wilford Woodruff, in *Times and Seasons* 2 (November 1840–October 1841): 330–31.
45. See Bloxham, "The Apostolic Foundations," in *Truth Will Prevail,* 143.
46. In Smith, *HC,* 4:183–84.
47. Heber C. Kimball, in Smith, *HC,* 4:222.
48. Brigham Young, as quoted in James R. Moss, R. Lanier Britsch, James R. Christianson, Richard O. Cowan, *The International Church* (Provo, Utah: Brigham Young University, 2001), 25–26; compare Joseph Smith's tribute, in Smith, *HC,* 4:390–91.
49. Allen, Esplin, and Whittaker, *Men with a Mission,* 309. See also Ronald K. Esplin, "Brigham Young and the Transformation of the 'First' Quorum of the Twelve," in Susan Easton Black and Larry C. Porter, eds., *Lion of the Lord* (Salt Lake City: Deseret Book, 1995), 54.

NOTES TO CHAPTER 2—THE GOSPEL CARRIED TO THE CONTINENT

1. See James R. Clark, comp., *Messages of the First Presidency of The Church of Jesus Christ of Latter-day Saints,* 6 vols. (Salt Lake City: Bookcraft, 1965–75), 2:35.
2. See Brent L. Top, "Denmark," in Arnold K. Garr, Donald Q. Cannon, and Richard O. Cowan, eds., *Encyclopedia of Latter-day Saint History* (Salt Lake City: Deseret Book, 2000), 284–85. Hereafter cited as *Encyclopedia of LDS History.*
3. See ibid.
4. See ibid.
5. See Bruce A. Van Orden, "Anthon H. Lund: Gentle Danish Apostle," in Bruce A. Van Orden, D. Brent Smith, and Everett Smith Jr., eds., *Pioneers in Every Land* (Salt Lake City: Bookcraft, 1997), 163–82.
6. See John Thomas, "Sweden," in *Encyclopedia of LDS History,* 1204–5; see also Carl Erich Johansson, "History of the Swedish Mission" (master's thesis, Brigham Young University, 1973).
7. In Fred E. Woods, "Fire on Ice: The Conversion and Life of Gudmundur Gudmundsson," *BYU Studies* 39 (2000):57-60.
8. See Bruce A. Van Orden, *Building Zion: The Latter-day Saints in Europe* (Salt Lake City: Deseret Book, 1996), 57–58.
9. Ibid.
10. See Top, "Denmark," in *Encyclopedia of LDS History,* 285.
11. See William Mulder, *Homeward to Zion: The Mormon Migration from Scandinavia* (Minneapolis: University of Minnesota Press, 2000), 18–19.
12. See ibid., 102.
13. See Francis M. Gibbons, *Lorenzo Snow: Spiritual Giant, Prophet of God* (Salt Lake City: Deseret Book, 1982), 63.
14. See *The Waldensian Churches in Italy, Das Waldenser Kulturzeitraum, The Waldensian Valleys* (pamphlets obtained from the Waldensian Museum, Torre Pellice, Italy), in possession of the author.
15. See James E. Toronto, "Italy," in *Encyclopedia of LDS History,* 556–57.
16. See Gibbons, *Lorenzo Snow,* 64.
17. See Toronto, "Italy," in *Encyclopedia of LDS History,* 556–57.
18. See ibid.
19. See Van Orden, *Building Zion,* 68–69; see also Dale Z. Kirby, "History of The

Church of Jesus Christ of Latter-day Saints in Switzerland" (master's thesis, Brigham Young University, 1971).

20. See ibid.
21. See ibid.
22. In "Swiss Mission Manuscript History, 1851–1940," manuscript available at the Historical Department, The Church of Jesus Christ of Latter-day Saints, Salt Lake City, Utah. Hereafter cited as LDS Church Archives.
23. See James R. Christianson, "Jacob Spori: Nineteenth-Century Swiss Missionary, Educator, and Kingdom Builder," in Donald Q. Cannon and David J. Whittaker, eds., *Supporting Saints: Life Stories of Nineteenth-Century Mormons* (Provo: Religious Studies Center, 1985), 343–68.
24. See Gilbert Scharffs, "Germany," in *Encyclopedia of LDS History,* 421–25. See also Gilbert Scharffs, *Mormonism in Germany* (Salt Lake City: Deseret Book, 1970).
25. See Van Orden, *Building Zion,* 62-63.
26. See Scharffs, "Germany," in *Encyclopedia of LDS History,* 421–25.
27. See ibid.
28. See Catherine Britsch Frantz, "Karl G. Maeser," in *Encyclopedia of LDS History,* 692-93; see also Douglas F. Tobler, "Karl G. Maeser's German Background, 1828-1856," *BYU Studies* 16 (Winter 1977): 155–75. For more on Maeser's conversion and subsequent service in Europe, see chapter 4 of this book.
29. See Ronald D. Dennis, "William Howells: First Missionary to France," in *Supporting Saints,* 43–82.
30. John Taylor, as quoted in B.H. Roberts, *The Life of John Taylor* (Salt Lake City: Bookcraft, 1963), 232.
31. See Richard D. McClellan, "Louis Bertrand," in *Encyclopedia of LDS History,* 99–100.
32. See Camille Fronk, "France," in *Encyclopedia of LDS History,* 394–96.
33. See ibid.
34. See McClellan, "Louis Bertrand," in *Encyclopedia of LDS History,* 99–100.
35. See ibid.
36. See Ralph L. Cottrell Jr., "A History of the Mediterranean Missions" (master's thesis, Brigham Young University, 1983), 39; see also JoAn Bitton, "Malta," in *Encyclopedia of LDS History,* 697–98.
37. See Cottrell, "Mediterranean Missions," 51-66; see also Richard O. Cowan, "Gibraltar," *Encyclopedia of LDS History,* 428; Joseph Grant Stevenson, "Edward Stevenson," in *Encyclopedia of LDS History,* 1192.

NOTES TO CHAPTER 3—GATHERING TO ZION

1. Article of Faith 10 states, "We believe in the *literal gathering* of Israel and in the restoration of the Ten Tribes."
2. Joseph Smith, Jr., *Teachings of the Prophet Joseph Smith,* sel. Joseph Fielding Smith (Salt Lake City: Deseret Book, 1976), 307–8.
3. See Wallace Stegner, *The Gathering of Zion: The Story of the Mormon Trail* (New York: McGraw Hill Book Company, 1964), 8.
4. In D&C 20:2–3, Joseph Smith and Oliver Cowdery were designated by revelation as the first and second elders of the restored Church. As such, they received

the keys of the gathering. Note that both the Prophet and Oliver personally fulfilled the Lord's call to gather the house of Israel from throughout the world: Joseph Smith proselytized in Upper Canada and Oliver Cowdery among the Lamanites.

5. Authors James B. Allen and Glen M. Leonard (*The Story of the Latter-day Saints*, 2d ed. rev. and enl. [Salt Lake City: Deseret Book, 1992], 127), note that the other missionaries were Willard Richards, a dear friend of Heber C. Kimball, as well as four Canadian missionaries: Elders Fielding, Goodson, Russell, and Snyder.

6. Joseph Smith, *History of The Church of Jesus Christ of Latter-day Saints*, 7 vols., 2d ed. rev., ed. B. H. Roberts (Salt Lake City: The Church of Jesus Christ of Latter-day Saints, 1932–51), 2:492. Hereafter cited as *HC*.

7. See James B. Allen, Ronald K. Esplin, and David J. Whittaker, *Men with a Mission, 1837-1841: The Quorum of the Twelve Apostles in the British Isles* (Salt Lake City: Deseret Book, 1992), 53. Apostles Kimball and Hyde left England on 20 April 1838.

8. For more information on the mission of the Twelve to the British Isles see, James B. Allen and Malcom R. Thorp, "The Mission of the Twelve to England, 1840-41: Mormon Apostles and the Working Class," *BYU Studies* 15 (Summer 1975): 499–526; see also Allen, Esplin, and Whittaker, *Men with a Mission*.

9. See Smith, *HC*, 4:119. By this time the total membership of the Church in the British Isles was reported as 1,671, including 132 priesthood holders (see Orson F. Whitney, *Life of Heber C. Kimball* [Salt Lake City: Bookcraft, 1967], 278).

10. See Smith, *HC*, 4:134. This maiden voyage ended in New York. The migrants then traveled by rail and steamboat to Nauvoo.

11. Hugh Moon, *Autobiography of Hugh Moon*, manuscript available at BYU Special Collections, Writings of Early Latter-day Saints, 3. Similar support was also provided on subsequent voyages to Nauvoo. See, for example, the *Reminiscences and Autobiographical notes of Thomas Callister*, 8, available at the Historical Department, The Church of Jesus Christ of Latter-day Saints, Salt Lake City, Utah. Hereafter cited as LDS Church Archives. See also *Diary of William Clayton*, 73, LDS Church Archives.

12. Priscilla Staines, in Edward Tullidge, *The Women of Mormondom* (New York: Tullidge & Crandall, 1877), 288. Jane C. Robinson Hindley ("Journals 1855–1905," vol. 1, 11-14, LDS Church Archives), who experienced the challenge of leaving her home and gathering a decade later than Staines (in 1855), also seems to have experienced the magnetic pull of the gathering and therefore left England with, as she noted, "the fire of Israel's God burning in my bosom."

13. William Clayton, as quoted in Paul E. Dahl, "William Clayton: Missionary, Pioneer and Public Servant" (master's thesis, Brigham Young University, 1959), 22.

14. Francis Moon, "Letter of Francis Moon," in *The Latter-day Saints' Millennial Star* 1 (February 1841): 254–55. Hereafter cited as *Millennial Star*.

15. M. Hamlin Cannon ("Migration of English Mormons to America," *American Historical Review* 52 [April 1947]: 441), asserts that 4,733 British Saints gath-

ered to Nauvoo from 1840 to 1846. Andrew Jenson ("Church Emigration," *Contributor* 12 [October 1891]: 441), puts the figure at an even 5,000.

16. *Millennial Star* 1 (February 1841): 263.

17. See Smith, *HC*, 4:186; see also *HC*, 5:296; D&C 124:25–27.

18. First Presidency letter in *Millennial Star* 1 (April 1841): 311.

19. See Fred E. Woods, *Gathering to Nauvoo* (American Fork, Utah: Covenant Communications, 2001), 84–87.

20. First Presidency statement in Smith, *HC*, 4:272.

21. First Presidency statement in James R. Clark, comp., *Messages of the First Presidency of The Church of Jesus Christ of Latter-day Saints,* 6 vols. (Salt Lake City: Bookcraft, 1965–75), 2:108.

22. Albert L. Zobell Jr., *Under the Midnight Sun: Centennial History of Scandinavian Missions* (Salt Lake City: Deseret Book, 1950), 48–49.

23. Leonard J. Arrington, *Great Basin Kingdom: An Economic History of the Latter-day Saints 1830–1890* (Cambridge: Harvard University Press, 1958), 64. John D. Unruh Jr. (*The Plains Across: The Overland Emigrants and the Trans-Mississippi West 1840–1860* [Chicago: University of Illinois Press, 1993], 253), maintains: "At least 10,000 forty-niners detoured via the Mormon oasis."

24. See Fred E. Woods, "Perpetual Emigrating Fund," in Arnold K. Garr, Donald Q. Cannon, and Richard O. Cowan, eds., *Encyclopedia of Latter-day Saint History* (Salt Lake City: Deseret Book, 2000), 910. Hereafter cited as *Encyclopedia of LDS History.*

25. Brigham Young to Elder Franklin D. Richards, in *Millennial Star* 16 (28 October 1854): 684.

26. George Q. Cannon to Brigham Young, 23 April 1859, LDS Church Archives.

27. Thomas Taylor to Brigham Young Jr., 30 May 1866, recorded in the "New York Emigration Book," 22 March 1866 to 10 July 1866, 34, LDS Church Archives.

28. Brigham Young, in *Millennial Star* 17 (22 December 1855): 813–14.

29. See Leroy R. Hafen, "Handcarts to Zion, 1856–1860," *Utah Historical Quarterly* 24 (January 1956): 316.

30. In Davis Bitton, *George Q. Cannon: A Biography* (Salt Lake City: Deseret Book, 1999), 100.

31. See John K. Hulmston, "Mormon Immigration in the 1860s: The Story of the Church Trains," *Utah Historical Quarterly* 58 (Winter 1990): 32-48.

32. Richard L. Jensen and William G. Hartley (in "Immigration and Emigration," Daniel H. Ludlow, ed., *Encyclopedia of Mormonism,* 5 vols. [New York: Macmillian Publishing Company, 1992], 2:674) observed, "Enthusiasm for emigration was highest during periods of international unrest, with accompanying millennialist expectations of increasing troubles worldwide prior to Jesus' second coming."

33. "Civil War in America—Its Importance as a Warning to the Saints," *Millennial Star* 23 (11 May 1861): 297–300.

34. On this topic, see Fred E. Woods, "East to West through North and South: Mormon Immigration during the Civil War," *BYU Studies* 39 (2000): 7–29.

35. See Conway B. Sonne, *Saints on the High Seas: A Maritime History of Mormon Migration 1830-1890* (Salt Lake City: University of Utah Press, 1983), 69, 126.

36. For excellent studies on the story of Latter-day Saint emigration from Great

Britain and Scandinavia, see P. A. M. Taylor, *Expectations Westward: The Mormons and the Emigration of their British Converts in the Nineteenth Century* (Ithaca, New York: Cornell University Press, 1966); see also William Mulder, *Homeward to Zion: The Mormon Migration from Scandinavia* (Minneapolis: University of Minnesota Press, 1957).

37. The *Millennial Star* 69 (23 May 1907): 329 notes that the European Saints were counseled to "stay and build up the work abroad."

38. First Presidency statement in Clark, comp., *Messages of the First Presidency*, 4:222.

NOTES TO CHAPTER 4—THE EUROPEAN CHURCH BECALMED

1. See James B. Allen, Ronald K. Esplin, and David J. Whittaker, *Men with a Mission, 1837–1841: The Quorum of the Twelve Apostles in the British Isles* (Salt Lake City: Deseret Book, 1992), 118–35.

2. See Robert L. Lively, "Some Sociological Reflections on the Nineteenth-Century British Mission," in Richard L. Jensen and Malcolm L. Thorp, eds., *Mormons in Early Victorian Britain* (Salt Lake City: University of Utah Press, 1987): 25.

3. George Reynolds, in Bruce A. Van Orden, "The Decline in Convert Baptisms and Member Emigration from the British Mission after 1870," *BYU Studies* (Spring 1987): 102.

4. George Q. Cannon, in Davis Bitton, *George Q. Cannon: a Biography* (Salt Lake City: Deseret Book, 1999), 410. For other anti-Darwinian statements by George Q. Cannon, see Donald Q. Cannon, "George Q. Cannon and the British Mission," *BYU Studies* (Winter 1987): 109.

5. See Gilbert Scharffs, *Mormonism in Germany* (Salt Lake City: Deseret Book, 1970), 16-20, 26-27.

6. See Hoyt W. Brewster Jr., "Netherlands," in Arnold K. Garr, Donald Q. Cannon, and Richard O. Cowan, eds., *Encyclopedia of Latter-day Saint History* (Salt Lake City: Deseret Book, 2000), 833–34. Hereafter cited as *Encyclopedia of LDS History*. See also Keith C. Warner, "History of the Netherlands Mission" (master's thesis, Brigham Young University, 1967).

7. See Paul Y. Hoskisson, "Austria," in *Encyclopedia of LDS History*, 65-66; see also F. Enzio Busche, "The Church in Germany, Switzerland and Austria," in F. Lamond Tullis, ed., *Mormonism: a Faith for all Cultures* (Provo: Brigham Young University Press, 1978), 44–51.

8. See Arnold K. Garr, "Finland," in *Encyclopedia of LDS History*, 376–77; see also *Muistame: We Remember* (Salt Lake City: Henry A. Matis Family Society, 1997).

9. See An Burvenich and Wilfried Decoo, "Belgium," in *Encyclopedia of LDS History*, 81–84.

10. See Alan K. Parrish, "*Millennial Star*," in *Encyclopedia of LDS History*, 752.

11. See Richard D. McClellan, "Periodicals," in *Encyclopedia of LDS History*, 905–10.

12. See Robert L. Millet, "Pearl of Great Price," in *Encyclopedia of LDS History*, 900–902; see also H. Donl Peterson, *The Pearl of Great Price* (Salt Lake City: Deseret Book, 1987).

13. See Richard Neitzel Holzapfel, "Journal of Discourses," in *Encyclopedia of LDS History*, 592–93.

14. See Richard O. Cowan, "Church Growth in England, 1841–1914," in V. Ben Bloxham, James R. Moss, and Larry C. Porter, eds., *Truth Will Prevail: The Rise of The Church of Jesus Christ of Latter-day Saints in the British Isles, 1837-1987* (Salt Lake City: Deseret Book, 1987), 228–29.

15. See *Church History in the Fulness of Times,* Church Educational System manual (Salt Lake City: The Church of Jesus Christ of Latter-day Saints, 1993), 489–90.

16. See Matthew K. Heiss, ed., "Life and History of Elder Mischa Markow," in Kahlile B. Mehr, *Mormon Missionaries Enter Eastern Europe* (Provo: Brigham Young University Press, 2002), 339–84.

17. See ibid., 343.

18. For a historical sketch of Jacob Spori, see James R. Christianson, "Jacob Spori: Nineteenth-Century Swiss Missionary, Educator, and Kingdom Builder," in Donald Q. Cannon and David J. Whittaker, eds., *Supporting Saints: Life Stories of Nineteenth-Century Mormons* (Provo: Religious Studies Center, 1985), 343–68.

19 In Heiss, ed., "Life and History of Elder Mischa Markow," 351.

20. Ibid., 352.

21. Ibid., 354.

22. See ibid., 344–56.

23. Ibid., 374.

24. Heiss, in "Life and History of Elder Mischa Markow," 346. Other details retold in this book's account of Mischa Markow's life come specifically from pages 344–46, 352–56, and 374–76 of Heiss, "Life and History of Elder Mischa Markow."

Notes to Chapter 5—The Church and the World Wars

1. See Bruce A. Van Orden, *Building Zion: The Latter-day Saints in Europe* (Salt Lake City: Deseret Book, 1996), 123.

2. Quoted in *Improvement Era* 19 (February 1916): 369.

3. See Van Orden, *Building Zion,* 124–25.

4. See Donald Q. Cannon, "Gathering the Saints from Germany: The Case Study of Schneidemuehl," paper present at conference of the Mormon History Association, Tuscon, Arizona, 17 May 2002.

5. See Jeffrey L. Anderson, "Mormons and Germany, 1914–1933: A History of The Church of Jesus Christ of Latter-day Saints in Germany and Its Relationship With the German Governments from WWI to the Rise of Hitler" (master's thesis, Brigham Young University, 1991), 120–22, 129.

6. See Joseph M. Dixon, "Mormons in the Third Reich, 1933–1945," in Donald Q. Cannon and David J. Whittaker, eds., *The Exodus and Beyond: Essays in Mormon History* (Salt Lake City: Hawkes Publishing, Inc., 1980), 224–25. Hereafter cited as "Mormons in the Third Reich."

7. See ibid., 227.

8. See Richard O. Cowan, *The Latter-day Saint Century* (Salt Lake City: Deseret Book, 1999), 112–13.

9. See ibid., 118–19; see also David F. Boone, "The Evacuation of the

Czechoslovak and German Missions at the Outbreak of World War II," *BYU Studies* 40 (2001): 122–54.

10. See Martha Toronto Anderson, *A Cherry Tree Behind the Iron Curtain* (Salt Lake City: Martha Toronto Anderson, 1977), 31-32.

11. See Alan F. Keele, "Helmut G. Heubener," in Arnold K. Garr, Donald Q. Cannon, and Richard O. Cowan, eds., *Encyclopedia of Latter-day Saint History* (Salt Lake City: Deseret Book, 2000), 516–17; see also Rudi Wobbe and Jerry Borrowman, *Three Against Hitler* (American Fork, Utah: Covenant Communications, 2002).

12. See interview by Matthew K. Heiss, 1991, 16, in Walter Erich Krause Oral History, manuscript available at the Historical Department, The Church of Jesus Christ of Latter-day Saints, Salt Lake City, Utah.

13. See Robert C. Freeman and Dennis A. Wright, *Saints at War: Experiences of Latter-day Saints in World War II* (American Fork, Utah: Covenant Communications, 2001), 18–19.

14. See Cowan, *Latter-day Saint Century*, 136–37.

15. Ezra Taft Benson, in Conference Report, April 1947, 153.

16. See Cowan, *Latter-day Saint Century*, 136–38.

17. See Frederick W. Babbel, *On Wings of Faith* (Salt Lake City: Bookcraft, 1972), 7–8.

18. Ibid., 148–49.

19. See Cowan, *Latter-day Saint Century*, 138.

20. See ibid., 141.

21. See http://www.cnn.com/SPECIALS/cold.war/episodes/04/interviews/halvorsen/

NOTES TO CHAPTER 6—THE CHURCH COMES OF AGE IN EUROPE

1. Richard O. Cowan, *The Latter-day Saint Century* (Salt Lake City: Deseret Book, 1999), 165.

2. Samuel E. Bringhurst, "Acquisition of Property of the Swiss Temple," in N. B. Lundwall, *Temples of the Most High* (Salt Lake City: Bookcraft, 1993), 198–99.

3. See Richard O, Cowan, *Temples to Dot the Earth* (Springville, Utah: Cedar Fort, Inc. 1997), 160–63.

4. See ibid., 159–60.

5. See ibid., 168–170.

6. See ibid., 170.

7. See *Deseret News 2003 Church Almanac* (Salt Lake City: Deseret News, 2002), 472–75.

8. Gilbert W. Scharffs, *Mormonism in Germany* (Salt Lake City: Deseret Book, 1970), 173.

9. See Warren J. Thomas, *Salt Lake Tabernacle Choir Goes to Europe* (Salt Lake City: n.p., 1957), 89.

10. David O. McKay, in *Millennial Star* 123 (26 February 1961): 172.

11. See Scharffs, *Mormonism in Germany*, 150.

12. See mission journal of Donald Q. Cannon, 26 Dec. 1958; 13 Feb. 1959; 2 April 1959; 2 June 1959; 21 July 1959. A copy of the journal is available at the Historical Department, The Church of Jesus Christ of Latter-day Saints, Salt

Lake City, Utah. Hereafter cited as LDS Church Archives. Information comes from the author's experiences as mission secretary.

13. Statistics from The Church of Jesus Christ of Latter-day Saints, Management Information Center, Salt Lake City, Utah, 31 May 2001. Figures for Eastern Europe are found in chapter 7.

14. See *2003 Church Almanac*, 36.

15. See ibid., 89; see also Bruce A. Van Orden, *Building Zion: The Latter-day Saints in Europe* (Salt Lake City: Deseret Book, 1996), 238–39.

16. See *2003 Church Almanac*, 89; see also Derin Head Rodriguez, *From Every Nation* (Salt Lake City: Deseret Book, 1990), 30–47.

17. See *2003 Church Almanac*, 89–90; see also Rodriguez, *From Every Nation*, 64–81.

18. See *2003 Church Almanac*, 91; see also Van Orden, *Building Zion*, 247.

19. See *2003 Church Almanac*, 43.

20. "News of the Church," *Ensign*, May 1994, 109.

21. See *2003 Church Almanac*, 36; see also, Van Orden, *Building Zion*, 245.

22. See James A. Toronto, "Italy," in Arnold K. Garr, Donald Q. Cannon, and Richard O. Cowan, eds., *Encyclopedia of Latter-day Saint History* (Salt Lake City: Deseret Book, 2000), 556–58.

23. Roberto Asioli, in DeAnne Walker, "News of the Church," *Ensign*, June 1999, 78.

24. See ibid.

25. See *2003 Church Almanac*, 354.

26. See Cynthia Doxey, "Spain," in *Encyclopedia of LDS History*, 1169–70; see also *2003 Church Almanac*, 415–17.

27. See Michael Mitchell, "Madrid Spain: Just the Beginning," *Ensign*, February 1996, 78.

28. See Kyle Walker and Francesco Diaz, "Portugal," in *Encyclopedia of LDS History*, 937–38.

29. See Mark Grover, "Pioneers in a Land of Explorers," *Ensign*, April 1997, 46–47.

30. See R. Douglas Phillips, "Greece," in *Encyclopedia of LDS History*, 445; see also *2003 Church Almanac*, 342.

NOTES TO CHAPTER 7—THE CHURCH BEHIND THE IRON CURTAIN

1. Spencer W. Kimball, "When the World Will Be Converted," *Ensign*, October 1974, 7.

2. Thomas S. Monson, *Faith Rewarded: A Personal Account of Prophetic Promises to the East German Saints* (Salt Lake City: Deseret Book, 1996), 5.

3. See Garold N. Davis and Norman S. Davis, collectors and translators, *Behind the Iron Curtain: Recollections of Latter-day Saints in East Germany, 1945-1989* (Provo: BYU Studies, 1996), xiii.

4. James H. Backman, "The Two German Temples—Legal Background," paper presented at the annual conference of the Mormon History Association, July 1987, 1–2. Copy in possession of Richard O. Cowan.

5. See Garold N. Davis, "Freiberg Temple," in Arnold K. Garr, Donald Q. Cannon, and Richard O. Cowan, eds., *Encyclopedia of Latter-day Saint History*

(Salt Lake City: Deseret Book, 2000), 396–97. Hereafter cited as *Encyclopedia of LDS History.*

6. David F. Boone and Richard O. Cowan, "The Freiberg Temple: A Latter-day Miracle," *Regional Studies in LDS Church History: Europe* (in press); see also Phillip J. Bryson, "Background on the Temple in the German Democratic Republic: An Eyewitness Account," remarks given at Brigham Young University, 3 and 9 July 1985, transcript in possession of Richard O. Cowan.

7. See Edwin B. Morrell, "Czech Republic," in *Encyclopedia of LDS History*, 270.

8. See Kahlile B. Mehr, *Mormon Missionaries Enter Eastern Europe* (Provo: Brigham University Press; Salt Lake City: Deseret Book, 2002), 48–49, 93–94, 166–87. Hereafter cited as *Eastern Europe.*

9. See ibid., 186–87.

10. Statistics from The Church of Jesus Christ of Latter-day Saints, Management Information Center, Salt Lake City, Utah. Hereafter cited as LDS Statistics.

11. See Bruce A. Van Orden, *Building Zion: The Latter-day Saints in Europe* (Salt Lake City: Deseret Book, 1996), 276–78.

12. See Mehr, *Eastern Europe*, 160-161.

13. See ibid., 164, 189–90.

14. LDS Statistics.

15. See *Church News,* 17 September 1977, 3.

16. See Van Orden, *Building Zion,* 281.

17. See Mehr, *Eastern Europe,* 165, 169.

18. See ibid., 172.

19. Ibid., 191.

20. See Van Orden, *Building Zion,* 283; LDS Statistics.

21. See Carmin Clifton, *Come Lord, Come: A History of The Church of Jesus Christ of Latter-day Saints in Romania* (San Jose, Calif.: Writers Club Press, 2002), 24.

22. See ibid., 25.

23. See ibid., 28-61.

24. See ibid., 155–57.

25. See ibid., 83–96.

26. LDS Statistics.

27. See Van Orden, *Building Zion,* 286.

28. See Mehr, *Eastern Europe,* 204–13.

29. See ibid., 217.

30. See Van Orden, *Building Zion,* 280–89.

31. LDS Statistics.

32. See Van Orden, *Building Zion,* 289.

33. See ibid.

34. See ibid., 289–90.

35. LDS Statistics.

36. See Kahlile Mehr, "Kresimir Cosic of Yugoslavia: Basketball Superstar, Gospel Hero," in Bruce A. Van Orden, D. Brent Smith, and Everett Smith Jr., eds., *Pioneers in Every Land* (Salt Lake City: Bookcraft, 1997), 22–38.

37. From personal files of Donald Q. Cannon; LDS Statistics.

38. See Van Orden, *Building Zion,* 290–91.

39. Gary L. Browning, "Out of Obscurity: The Emergence of The Church of Jesus

Christ of Latter-day Saints in That Vast Empire of Russia," *BYU Studies* 33 (1993), 4:680.

40. See Van Orden, *Building Zion,* 293–96.
41. See ibid., 297–300.
42. LDS Statistics.
43. See Mehr, *Eastern Europe,* 227–28, 307–12.
44. LDS Statistics.
45. See Mehr, *Eastern Europe,* 312–13.
46. LDS Statistics.
47. See Mehr, *Eastern Europe,* 230–35, 306–7.
48. LDS Statistics.

NOTES TO CHAPTER 8—BEGINNINGS IN FRENCH POLYNESIA AND HAWAII

1. The material in this and the three following chapters is documented in the my (R. Lanier Britsch) book, *Unto the Islands of the Sea: A History of the Latter-day Saints in the Pacific* (Salt Lake City: Deseret Book, 1986).
2. See Joseph Smith, *History of The Church of Jesus Christ of Latter-day Saints,* 7 vols., 2d ed. rev., ed. B. H. Roberts (Salt Lake City: The Church of Jesus Christ of Latter-day Saints, 1932–51), 5:404–6. Hereafter cited as *HC.*
3. S. George Ellsworth, "Zion in Paradise: Early Mormons in the South Seas," (The Faculty Association: Utah State University, 1959), 13.
4. Grouard, who Pratt said was wedded to his mission field, also had a wife in Nauvoo. He wrote numerous letters to his wife in Nauvoo but received no answers. They had been emotionally disaffected from each other before his mission call. He concluded that she had left him and the Church. His first wife in Polynesia, Tearo, died not long after giving birth to a baby girl. Grouard then married a woman named Nahina, who eventually bore three sons.
5. Addison Pratt, in Andrew Jenson, *Manuscript History of the French Polynesia Mission,* 14 November 1846. Manuscript available at the Historical Department, The Church of Jesus Christ of Latter-day Saints, Salt Lake City, Utah. Hereafter cited as LDS Church Archives.
6. Addison Pratt, *Millenial Star,* 14:109.
7. See George Q. Cannon, *My First Mission,* 2d ed. (Salt Lake City: Juvenile Instructor Office, 1882), 22.
8. George Q. Cannon, as quoted in Samuel E. Woolley, Journal, 23 December 1900, LDS Church Archives.
9. In *Church News,* 10 May 1958, 2. There is an unconfirmed story which asserts that Addison Pratt convinced Joseph Smith that the Hawaiians were brothers to the American Indians. Allegedly, as a result of this discussion, Pratt was sent on his mission to the Pacific. See Nettie Hunt Rencher, *The First Pacific Missionary,* LDS Church Archives. See also Norman Douglas, "The Sons of Lehi and the Seed of Cain: Racial Myths in Mormon Scripture and their Relevance to the Pacific Islands," *Journal of Religious History* 8 (June 1974): 94–98.
10. In Britsch, *Unto the Islands of the Sea,* 108.
11. *Life of Joseph F. Smith, Sixth President of The Church of Jesus Christ of Latter-day*

Saints, comp. Joseph Fielding Smith (Salt Lake City: Deseret News Press, 1938), 170, 173, 185.

12. See R. Lanier Britsch, "The Lanai Colony: A Hawaiian Extension of the Mormon Colonial Idea," *Hawaiian Journal of History* 19 (1978): 68–83.

13. Gibson has received more attention than any other character in LDS Pacific history. Among the sources most frequently cited concerning him are R. Lanier Britsch, "Another Visit with Walter Murray Gibson," *Utah Historical Quarterly* 46 (Winter 1978): 65–78; Gavan Daws, "The Shepherd Saint," in *Shoal of Time: A History of the Hawaiian Islands* (Honolulu: University of Hawaii Press, 1968), 220–25; and James A. Michener and A. Grove Day, "Gibson, the King's Evil Angel," in *Rascals in Paradise* (London: Secker and Warburg: 1957), 120–54.

14. Brigham Young to King Kamehameha V, 24 March 1865, *Letters of Brigham Young,* LDS Church Archives.

NOTES TO CHAPTER 9—BEGINNINGS IN AUSTRALIA, NEW ZEALAND, SAMOA, AND TONGA

1. See Hirini Whaanga, "A Maori Prophet," *Juvenile Instructor* 37 (1902): 152–53. See also Matthew Cowley, "Maori Chief Predicts Coming of LDS Missionaries," *Improvement Era,* September 1950, 696.

2. Ibid.

3. For documentation regarding four other similar prophecies, see Brian W. Hunt, "History of the Church of Jesus Christ of Latter-day Saints in New Zealand," (master's thesis, Brigham Young University, 1971), 28; Stewart Meha, "The New Zealand Mission," typescript, 3–4, Mendenhall Library, Church College of New Zealand; Nolan P. Olsen, "New Zealand—Our Maori Home," *Improvement Era* 35 (May 1932): 446; Matthew Cowley, "Maori Chief Predicts Coming of L.D.S. Missionaries," *Improvement Era* 53 (September 1950): 697 and *Matthew Cowley Speaks* (Salt Lake City: Deseret Book, 1954), 200–5; William Bromley, Journal, June 16, 1881, manuscript available at the Historical Department, The Church of Jesus Christ of Latter-day Saints, Salt Lake City, Utah. Hereafter cited as LDS Church Archives.

4. Joseph H. Dean, Journals, 21 June 1888, LDS Church Archives.

NOTES TO CHAPTER 10—GROWTH AND CHALLENGES IN THE PACIFIC THROUGH WORLD WAR II

1. In Samoan Mission Historical Record, 31 December 1908. Manuscript available at the Historical Department, The Church of Jesus Christ of Latter-day Saints, Salt Lake City, Utah. Hereafter cited as LDS Church Archives.

2. George Q. Cannon, General Minutes, Hawaiian Mission Conference, 3 April 1915, LDS Church Archives.

3. Reed Smoot, in Joseph Fielding Smith, *Life of Joseph F. Smith* (Salt Lake City: Deseret Book, 1969), 421.

4. Joseph F. Smith, in Conference Report, October 1915, 8–9.

5. Heber J. Grant, "The Dedicatory Prayer in the Hawaiian Temple," *Improvement Era* 23 (February 1920).

6. Manuscript History of the Hawaiian Mission, 11 December 1919, LDS Church

Archives; see also R. Lanier Britsch, *Unto the Islands of the Sea* (Salt Lake City: Deseret Book, 1986), 158.

7. In *Deseret News,* 15 October 1920, 5.

8. In Francis M. Gibbons, *David O. McKay: Apostle to the World, Prophet of God* (Salt Lake City: Deseret Book, 1986), 100.

9. Wesley Smith, as quoted in Mission Financial and Statistical Reports, Hawaiian Mission, 1921. Manuscript available at LDS Church Archives. See also, Britsch, *Unto the Islands of the Sea,* 162.

10. David O. McKay, in J. Pia Cockett, "Visit of President David O. McKay in 1921," typescript in LDS Church Archives; see also Britsch, *Unto the Islands of the Sea,* 163; and Reuben D. Law, *The Founding and Early Development of the Church College of Hawaii* (St. George, Utah: Dixie College Press, 1972), 19–21. Law quotes a transcript of D. Arthur Haycock, president of the Hawaii Mission, in which President McKay retold this story again in 1955. President McKay also related this story in New Zealand shortly after it happened.

11. See Manuscript History of New Zealand Mission, 22 April 1921, LDS Church Archives. I have relied heavily on the "Manuscript History" and also on the Mission Financial and Statistical Reports for New Zealand, for this section and the several topics that have preceded it. Both manuscripts are available at LDS Church Archives.

12. Gordon Claridge Young Oral History, interviews by Lauritz G. Petersen, 1972, typescript, 9–10, James Moyle Oral History Program, LDS Church Archives.

13. John Q. Adams, as quoted in *Deseret News,* June 1921.

14. David O. McKay, "Sauniatu," *Improvement Era* 69 (May 1966): 366.

15. In Mark Vernon Coombs, Journal and Memoirs, 1920 to August 1926, typed copy, 60, LDS Church Archives.

16. David O. McKay, *Cherished Experiences from the Writings of President David O. McKay,* comp. Clare Middlemiss (Salt Lake City, Deseret Book, 1976), 82.

17. Ibid., 82–83.

18. Ibid., 84.

19. Matthew Cowley, in Manuscript History of the New Zealand Mission, 16 June 1940, LDS Church Archives; see also Britsch, *Unto the Islands of the Sea,* 314.

Notes to Chapter 11—Expansion in the Pacific Since World War II

1. See "Polynesian Cultural Center to celebrate 40th anniversary in 2003," Polynesian Cultural Center press release, 8 January 2003, www.polynesia.com/aloha/press/press_40year.shtml

2. J. Phillip Hanks, "Missionary Summary," 1, in possession of the author.

3. J. Reuben Clark Jr., "The Outpost in Mid-Pacific," *Improvement Era* 38 (September 1935): 535.

4. Ibid.

5. Wendall Mendenhall, as quoted in David W. Cummings, *Mighty Missionary of the Pacific* (Salt Lake City: Bookcraft, 1961), 52. See also Wendall Mendenhall, in Conference Report, April 1955, 4–5.

6. Jeanette McKay Morrell, *Highlights in the Life of President David O. McKay* (Salt Lake City: Deseret Book, 1966), 197.

7. See Thomas S. Monson, in Conference Report, April 2002, 59.

8. See John L. Hart, "At Center of Serenity: Making Journeys of Faith," *Church News,* 6 November 1983, 7, 10.

9. See John L. Hart, "Let a Temple Be Built," *Church News,* 12 May 1985, 16.

10. In "Tongan Royalty Tour Temple," *Church News,* 24 July 1983.

11. Ebbie L. Davis, Fiji Mission, Historical Record, 28 June 1973. Manuscript available at the Historical Department, The Church of Jesus Christ of Latter-day Saints, Salt Lake City, Utah. Hereafter cited as LDS Church Archives.

12. J. J. Mol, "The Religious Affiliations of the New Zealand Maoris," *Oceania* 35 (1964–65): 136–43.

NOTES TO CHAPTER 12—MEXICO RECEIVES THE GOSPEL

1. Joseph Smith, as quoted in Wilford Woodruff, in Conference Report, April 1898.

2. Spencer W. Kimball, in Conference Report, October 1950, 66.

3. Daniel W. Jones, *Forty Years among the Indians* (Salt Lake City: Juvenile Instructor Office, 1890), 219, 220.

4. K. E. Duke, "Meliton Gonzalez Trejo: Translator of the Book of Mormon into Spanish," *Improvement Era* 59 (October 1956): 714.

5. Ibid., 714, 715.

6. Jones, *Forty Years among the Indians,* 276.

7. This excerpt was published in the San Francisco *Chronicle* as translated from the *Seminario Oficial,* the official organ of the government of the State of Chihuahua, and cited in *Deseret Evening News,* 30 June 1876, 3.

8. Rey L. Pratt, "History of the Mexican Mission," *Improvement Era* 15 (April 1912): 487.

9. See E. LeRoy Hatch, "Mormon Colonies: Beacon Light in Mexico," *Ensign,* September 1972, 23–24.

10. Pratt, "History of the Mexican Mission," 493.

11. Ibid., 498.

12. W. Ernest Young, *The Diary of W. Ernest Young* (n.p.: Walter Ernest Young, 1973), 88.

13. As cited in Rey L. Pratt, in Conference Report, April 1920, 92–93.

14. In *Church News,* 3 July 1971, 11.

15. Young, *The Diary of W. Ernest Young,* 135–36.

16. Joseph C. Bentley, in Nelle S. Hatch, *Colonia Juarez: An Intimate Account of a Mormon Village* (Salt Lake City: Deseret Book, 1954), 208.

17. Rey L. Pratt, "Review of Missionary Labors among the Lamanites," *Liahona The Elders Journal,* 7 November 1916, 296.

18. Blessing given to J. Reuben Clark Jr., 6 November 1930, First Presidency Letterbooks. Manuscript available at the Historical Department, The Church of Jesus Christ of Latter-day Saints, Salt Lake City, Utah. Hereafter cited as LDS Church Archives.

19. Marion G. Romney, in *Addresses at the Ceremony Opening the J. Reuben Clark Law School,* 27 August 1973 (Provo: Brigham Young University, 1973), 21–22.

20. Aurthur Bliss Lane to the Secretary of State, quoted in Marin J. Hickman, "The Ambassadorial Years," *Brigham Young University Studies* 13 (Spring 1973): 412.

21. For a good discussion of the Third Convention Movement, see F. LaMond Tullis, *Mormons in Mexico* (Provo: Museo de Historia del Mormonismo en Mexico A. C., 1997), 137–68.
22. See Mexican Mission History in LDS Church Archives; see also *Church News,* 8 June 1946, 1; 15 June 1946, 2–3.

NOTES TO CHAPTER 13—BEGINNINGS IN SOUTH AMERICA

1. Parley P. Pratt, in *Autobiography of Parley P. Pratt* (Salt Lake City: Deseret Book, 1985), 363.
2. Ibid., 365.
3. Ibid., 365–66.
4. Ibid., 366.
5. Ibid., 368–69.
6. Ibid., 369–70
7. Wilhem Friedrichs manuscripts, available at the Historical Department, The Church of Jesus Christ of Latter-day Saints, Salt Lake City, Utah. Hereafter cited as LDS Church Archives.
8. Melvin J. Ballard, in *Improvement Era* 29 (June 1926): 575–76.
9. Ibid., 576.
10. See A. Theodore Tuttle, "South America: Land of Prophecy and Promise," *Improvement Era* 66 (May 1963): 358.
11. In ibid.
12. Ibid.
13. Melvin J. Ballard, as quoted in Tuttle, "South America," 358.
14. *Church News,* 31 May 1980, 5.
15. See ibid.
16. See Mission Annual Reports, 1936, 80; 1938, 76; and 1939, 76, in LDS Church Archives.
17. See Mission Annual Reports 1938, 76, LDS Church Archives.
18. W. Ernest Young, *The Diary of W. Ernest Young* (n.p.: Walter Ernest Young, 1973), 409.
19. See "The Church in Uruguay and Paraguay," *Ensign,* February 1975, 30; see also Frederick S. Williams, *From Acorn to Oak Tree: A Personal History of the Establishment and First Quarter Development of the South American Missions* (Fullerton, Calif.: Et Cetera, 1987).
20. See Nestor Curbelo, "Acts of Faithfulness Write Story of Church Growing in Paraguay," *Church News,* 27 May 1995, 10.

NOTES TO CHAPTER 14—GROWTH AND EXPANSION IN LATIN AMERICA

1. Spencer W. Kimball, as quoted in *Church News,* 19 February 1977, 3; compare 20 December 1947, 9.
2. Spencer W. Kimball, as quoted in *Church News,* 15 December 1948, 19.
3. See *Church News,* 13 February 1954, 3.
4. In *Church News,* 13 January 1979, 16; see also *Pioneer in Guatemala: The*

Personal History of John Forres O'Donnal (Yorba Linda, Calif.: Shumway Family History Services, 1997), 6–7.

5. See Mario Javier Jimenez Sandi, "Costa Rica," in Arnold K. Garr, Donald Q. Cannon, and Richard O. Cowan, eds. *Encyclopedia of Latter-day Saint History* (Salt Lake City: Deseret Book, 2000), 253. Hereafter cited as *Encyclopedia of LDS History.*

6. See *Deseret News 2001–2002 Church Almanac* (Salt Lake City: Deseret News, 2000), 320.

7. See Terrence L. Hansen, "The Church in Central America," *Ensign,* September 1972, 40–42.

8. See *2001–2002 Church Almanac,* 338.

9. See *Church News,* 6 November 1965, 13; see also *Church News* 30 July 1966, 6–7; 20 August 1966, 15; 19 November 1966, 7; 28 January 1967, 8–9.

10. See *2001–2002 Church Almanac,* 377.

11. Mark E. Petersen to the First Presidency, spring 1955. Letter available at the Historical Department, The Church of Jesus Christ of Latter-day Saints, Salt Lake City, Utah. Hereafter cited as LDS Church Archives..

12. Henry D. Moyle, as quoted in A. Delbert Palmer, "Establishing the LDS Church in Chile (master's thesis, Brigham Young University, 1979), 73.

13. Interview with Joseph C. Bentley, 23 December 1965.

14. See *2001–2002 Church Almanac,* 282.

15. See "Bolivia," *Ensign,* February 1977, 40.

16. Spencer W. Kimball, as quoted in "Ecuador," *Ensign,* February 1977, 34.

17. See *2001–2002 Church Almanac,* 318.

18. Spencer W. Kimball, as quoted in "Colombia," *Ensign,* February 1977, 27.

NOTES TO CHAPTER 15—MODERN LATIN AMERICA

1. Bruce R. McConkie, as quoted in *Church News,* 12 March 1977, 3.

2. See *Church News,* 26 August 1961, 13–14.

3. Agricol Lozano, as quoted in Orson Scott Card, "Mexico," *Ensign,* February 1977, 17.

4. Agricol Lozano, as quoted in Jay M. Todd, "Los Mormones," *Ensign,* September 1972, 10.

5. Card, "Mexico," *Ensign,* February 1977, 17.

6. Guillermo Gonzales, as quoted in "In the Vineyards of the Lord," *Ensign,* September 1972, 16.

7. See the discussion in chapter 24 of this book.

8. See Efrain Villalobos Vasquez, "Mormon Schools in Mexico," in LeMond Tullis, ed., *Mormonism: A Faith for All Cultures* (Provo: Brigham Young University Press, 1978), 134–35.

9. Eduardo Balderas, "Northward to Mesa," *Ensign,* September 1972, 30.

10. Ibid.

11. Ibid., 31.

12. See Papers of Ivie Huish Jones, available at the Historical Department, The Church of Jesus Christ of Latter-day Saints, Salt Lake City, Utah. Hereafter cited as LDS Church Archives.

13. *Church News,* 8 March 1975, 3.

14. Membership summaries for 1965 and 1979, LDS Church Archives; see also *Church News,* 14 June 1980, 11.
15. See *Church News,* 21 October 1978, 8. Information also came from a personal interview with Elder William R. Bradford, 6 May 1980.

NOTES TO CHAPTER 16—INTRODUCING THE GOSPEL IN ASIA: THE FIRST CENTURY

1. For further information on Christian missionary history see Stephen Neill, *A History of Christian Missions,* 2d ed. rev. (Harmondsworth, England: Penguin Books, 1992); Donald E. Hoke, ed., *The Church in Asia* (Chicago: Moody Press, 1975); R. Lanier Britsch, "Taking the Gospel to Asia," *Ensign,* June 1980, 6–10.
2. For additional reading in LDS history in these areas see R. Lanier Britsch, *From the East: The History of the Latter-day Saints in Asia, 1851–1996* (Salt Lake City: Deseret Book, 1998); R. Lanier Britsch, *Nothing More Heroic: The Compelling Story of the First Latter-day Saint Missionaries in India* (Salt Lake City: Deseret Book, 1999); R. Lanier Britsch, "The Latter-day Saint Mission to India: 1851–1856," *BYU Studies* 12 (Spring 1972): 262–78; R. Lanier Britsch, "The Early Missions to Burma and Siam," *Improvement Era* 73 (March 1970): 35–44; and R. Lanier Britsch, "Church Beginnings in China," *BYU Studies* 10 (Winter 1970): 161–72.
3. Hugh J. Cannon, "The Chinese Realm Dedicated for the Preaching of the Gospel," *Improvement Era* 24 (March 1921): 445.
4. For in-depth histories of the early mission in Japan, see R. Lanier Britsch, "Early Latter-day Saint Missions to South and East Asia," (Ph.D. diss., Claremont Graduate School and University Center, 1967); and Murray L. Nichols, "History of the Japan Mission of the Church . . . , 1901–1942," (master's thesis, Brigham Young University, 1958); R. Lanier Britsch, "The Closing of the Early Japanese Mission," *BYU Studies* 15 (Winter 1975): 171–90; and J. Christopher Conkling, "Members without a Church: Japanese Mormons in Japan From 1924 to 1948," *BYU Studies* 15 (Winter 1975): 191–214.
5. Alma O. Taylor, *Church News,* 21 October 1901; Alma O. Taylor, Journal B, 1 September 1901, in Harold B. Lee Library, Brigham Young University, Provo, Utah. See also, Britsch, *From the East,* 50.
6. Heber J. Grant, as cited in Jerry P. Cahill, "News of the Church," *Ensign,* January 1981, 74.
7. Heber J. Grant, as quoted in Andrew Jenson, "Manuscript History of the Japan Mission," 1918–1924, 22 August 1924, available at the Historical Department, The Church of Jesus Christ of Latter-day Saints, Salt Lake City, Utah. Hereafter cited as LDS Church Archives. See also Britsch, *From the East,* 68.

NOTES TO CHAPTER 17—CHURCH GROWTH IN POSTWAR JAPAN

1. J. Christopher Conkling, "Members without a Church: Japanese Mormons in Japan From 1924 to 1948," *BYU Studies* 15 (Winter 1975): 208. The majority of information in this chapter, unless otherwise noted, can also be found in R.

Lanier Britsch, *From the East: The History of the Latter-day Saints in Asia, 1851–1996* (Salt Lake City: Deseret Book, 1998).

2. See Richard H. Drummond, *A History of Christianity in Japan* (Grand Rapids: William B. Eerdmans Publishing Company, 1971), 272–73.

3. See Mission Financial and Statistical Reports, Japanese Mission, 1948, available at the Historical Department, The Church of Jesus Christ of Latter-day Saints, Salt Lake City, Utah. Hereafter cited as LDS Church Archives. See also Manuscript History of the Japanese Mission (Quarterly Historical Reports), December 1948, LDS Church Archives.

4. See Spencer J. Palmer, *The Church Encounters Asia* (Salt Lake City: Deseret Book, 1970), 67–68; see also Richard O. Cowan, *The Latter-day Saint Century* (Salt Lake City: Bookcraft, 1999), 143.

5. See Harrison T. Price, "A Cup of Tea," *Improvement Era,* March 1962, 160ff; see also Palmer, *The Church Encounters Asia,* 65–69.

6. Matthew Cowley, as quoted in Kan Watanabe, Kiyoshi Sakai, Shuichi Yaginuma, Mildred E. Handy, and Grace Vlam, "Japan: Land of the Rising Sun," *Ensign,* August 1975, 41.

7. See Vinal G. Mauss Oral History, interviews by R. Lanier Britsch, 1975, typescript, 15, 27, 28, passim, the James Moyle Oral History Program, LDS Church Archives.

8. In Hilton A. Robertson, Daily Diary, Japanese Mission 1954–1955, 2, copy in possession of the author.

9. See Joseph Fielding Smith, "Report from the Far East Mission," *Improvement Era,* December 1955, 917.

10. See Paul C. Andrus Oral History, interviews by R. Lanier Britsch, 1974, typescript, 24-25, Oral History Program, LDS Church Archives.

11. See Britsch, *From the East,* 109–10.

12. As cited in Britsch, *From the East,* 100.

13. See Dwayne N. Anderson Oral History, interviews by R. Lanier Britsch, 1973, typescript, 45–47, LDS Church Archives.

14. See Anderson Oral History, 26; see also Watanabe, et al., "Japan," *Ensign,* August 1975, 42.

15. See Adney Y. Komatsu Oral History, interviews by R. Lanier Britsch, 1974, typescript, 33–34, the James Moyle Oral History Program, LDS Church Archives; see also Don W. Marsh, *The Light of the Sun* (n.p.: n.d.), 66.

16. Marion D. Hanks, as cited in Hugh B. Brown, "Prophecies Regarding Japan," *BYU Studies* 10 (Winter 1970): 159–60.

17. See Komatsu Oral History, 4.

18. In ibid., 20, 29–30.

19. See Britsch, *From the East,* 131–35; see also Gerald Joseph Peterson, "History of Mormon Exhibits in World Expressions," (master's thesis, Brigham Young University, 1974), 144–5; and "Expo '70 Groundbreaking," *Church News,* 17 May 1969, 4.

20. See Britsch, *From the East,* 141–44; see also Cherie Campbell, in "Temple to be Built in Tokyo," *Ensign,* October 1975, 86; "Japan Area General Conference," *Church News,* 16 August 1975.

21. Mark E. Petersen, in Peggy Petersen Barton, *Mark E. Petersen: A Biography* (Salt Lake City: Deseret Book, 1985), 188.

22. Oliver Wayma, in Palmer, *The Church Encounters Asia,* 96.

23. See Palmer, *The Church Encounters Asia,* 95-96; see also Andrus Oral History, 15-16, LDS Church Archives.

24. See Calvin R. Beck, "History of the Seoul LDS Group, August 1953 to May 1954," unpublished article, LDS Church Archives.

25. See Andrus Oral History, 14, LDS Church Archives.

26. See Palmer, *The Church Encounters Asia,* 100.

27. See Andrus Oral History, 15-16, LDS Church Archives.

28. Ibid., 18.

29. Unless otherwise noted, the information regarding the organization of the Korea Pusan Mission has been derived from Spencer J. Palmer Oral History, interview by S. Brad Jenkins, 1977, tapes in possession of R. Lanier Britsch; Robert H. Slover Oral History; Korean Mission (later called the Korea Seoul Mission), Historical Reports, LDS Church Archives.

30. See Palmer, *The Church Encounters Asia,* 109.

31. See Korean Mission, *The White Field,* September 1968, 7-9, LDS Church Archives.

32. See "Church Educational System, Overview," pamphlet (Salt Lake City: The Church of Jesus Christ of Latter-day Saints, 1978), 39.

NOTES TO CHAPTER 18—POSTWAR DEVELOPMENTS IN THE CHINESE REALM AND THE PHILIPPINES

1. See Steven N. Talbot, "A History of the Chinese Mission of the Church . . . , 1949 to 1953," (unpublished paper, Brigham Young University, 1977); see also Matthew Cowley, "The Language of Sincerity," *Improvement Era* 52 (November 1949): 715.

2. See Southern Far East Mission (Hereafter cited as SFEM), Historical Reports, 30 September 1955. Manuscript available at the Historical Department, The Church of Jesus Christ of Latter-day Saints, Salt Lake City, Utah. Hereafter cited as LDS Church Archives.

3. See Diane E. Browning, "The Translation of Mormon Scriptures into Chinese," (unpublished paper, Brigham Young University, 1977), 2, in possession of the author; unless otherwise noted, the basic source for the following information is SFEM Historical Reports by date. President Heaton kept a very thorough record of mission developments and activities.

4. See SFEM, 30 September 1958, LDS Church Archives.

5. Mark E. Petersen, as quoted in SFEM, 30 June 1959, LDS Church Archives.

6. Gordon B. Hinckley, Journal, 13 August 1975; journal is in President Hinckley's possession.

7. Gordon B. Hinckley, from notes taken by the author at the Hong Kong Temple dedication, 27 May 1996, Hong Kong; see also R. Lanier Britsch, *From the East: The History of the Latter-day Saints in Asia, 1851–1996* (Salt Lake City: Deseret Book, 1998), 296.

8. Gordon B. Hinckley, as quoted in Gerry Avant, "First Temple in Chinese

Realm," *Church News,* 25 November 1984, 12; see also Britsch, *From the East,* 292.

9. See Steven C. Harper, " 'Nothing Less Than Miraculous,': The First Decade of Mormonism in Mongolia," *BYU Studies* 42 (2003):24–32.

10. Dallin H. Oaks, as quoted in "Open Minds, Hearts to People of China," *Church News,* 16 March 1991, 5. See also Britsch, *From the East,* 306.

11. See Joseph V. Cook, Ruben Lancanienta, Clifford H. Huntington, and Augusto Lim, comps., *A History of The Church of Jesus Christ of Latter-day Saints in the Philippines* (n.p., 1965), 2–3.

12. See Joseph Fielding Smith, "Report on the Far East Mission," *Improvement Era* 58 (December 1955): 917.

13. Gordon B. Hinckley, as quoted in Augusto A. Lim, "Missionary Work in the Philippines," *Ensign,* November 1992, 82.

14. Gordon B. Hinckley, Journal, 13 August 1975, in President Hinckley's possession; see also "The Saints in the Philippines," *Ensign,* January 1975, 42–49; and "Philippines: The Land of Joyous Service" *Ensign,* August 1975, 58–61. Many of the ideas for this section are derived from interviews with Augusto A. Lim and Maxine T. Grimm.

15. Gordon B. Hinckley, as quoted in Dell Van Orden, "Emotional Rites Note 'Miracle of the Philippines,'" *Church News,* 7 October 1984, 10.

16. See Spencer J. Palmer, R. Lanier Britsch, Ray C. Hillam, and Richard S. Beal, "Educational Needs of The Church of Jesus Christ of Latter-day Saints in Asia: Final Report," Church Educational System, October 1972, 83, 87, 90, LDS Church Archives.

17. See Augusto A. Lim, "The Church in the Philippines," in F. LaMond Tullis, ed., *Mormonism: A Faith for All Cultures* (Provo: Brigham Young University Press, 1978), 160.

18. Gordon B. Hinckley, in "Prophet Testifies, Reaffirms Blessings," *Church News,* 8 June 1996, 7; see also Britsch, *From the East,* 369–70.

NOTES TO CHAPTER 19—EXPANSION IN SOUTHEAST AND SOUTH ASIA

1. Gordon B. Hinckley, Journal, 9 December 1964, in President Hinckley's possession.

2. See Alan H. Hess, Journal, 30 November 1968, available at the Historical Department, The Church of Jesus Christ of Latter-day Saints, Salt Lake City, Utah. Hereafter cited as LDS Church Archives.

3. Paul D. Morris to Dale Patterson, 19 October 1974, as quoted in Dale Patterson, "One Thoughtless Moment" (research paper, Brigham Young University, 1974), 15; see also Manoth Suksabjarern, "Roman Catholic, Protestant, and Latter-day Saints Missions in Thailand: An Historical Survey" (master's thesis, Brigham Young University, 1977), 89–90. I have used Manoth's thesis as a basic reference source for writing this section.

4. See R. Lanier Britsch, *From the East: The History of the Latter-day Saints in Asia, 1851–1996* (Salt Lake City: Deseret Book, 1998), 389, 404.

5. See Spencer J. Palmer, *The Church Encounters Asia* (Salt Lake City: Deseret Book, 1970), 158.

6. See G. Carlos Smith Jr., Oral History, interviews by William G. Hartley, 1972, typescript, 41, Oral History Program, LDS Church Archives.

7. See Britsch, *From the East,* 464–5.

8. See ibid., 472.

9. See ibid., 471, 473.

10. Bruce R. McConkie, as quoted in Palmer, *The Church Encounters Asia,* 161.

11. See Southeast Asia Mission Historical Reports, by date, LDS Church Archives; see also Indonesia Jakarta Mission Historical Reports, 31 December 1974, LDS Church Archives.

12. See ibid.; and Alton L. Wade, interview by the author (R. Lanier Britsch), 5 July 1979, Salt Lake City, Utah, tape recording.

13. In an interview with Mary Ellen Edmunds by Dale S. Cox, 27 February 1979, Provo, Utah, tape recording.

14. See Britsch, *From the East,* 498.

15. See Vietnam Zone Historical Report, 1962 entry, 30 October 1966, LDS Church Archives; see also Richard C. Holloman Jr., "The Snap of Silver Thread: The LDS Church in Vietnam" (research paper, Brigham Young University, 1977), 4, copy in LDS Church Archives; this paper should be consulted for a more complete bibliography; Palmer, *The Church Encounters Asia,* 141–43; Hinckley, Journals, October 30, 1966; George L. Scott, "South Vietnam, Thailand Dedicated for Missionaries," *Church News,* 19 November 1966, 5. See also R. Lanier Britsch and Richard C. Holloman Jr., "The Church's Years in Vietnam," *Ensign,* August 1980, 25–30.

16. Gordon B. Hinckley, "A Silver Thread in the Dark Tapestry of War," *Improvement Era* 71 (June 1968): 48–50.

17. In William S. Bradshaw Oral History, interviews by R. Lanier Britsch, 1974, typescript, 55–56, James Moyle Oral History Program, LDS Church Archives.

18. See Britsch, *From the East,* 440–43.

19. See ibid., 449.

20. This section is based on the testimony of S. Paul Thiruthuvadoss, LDS Church Archives; the journals of Gilbert Mantano and Wayne A. Jones, partial copies in possession of the author; and the author's interview with George Groberg, 12 June 1974, Provo, Utah.

21. Edwin Dharmaraju, "Mission to India," 14 February 1978, typed copy in possession of R. Lanier Britsch, 5.

22. See Britsch, *From the East,* 537.

23. See ibid., 548.

NOTES TO CHAPTER 20—THE CHURCH IN AFRICA

1. For a general background see Farrell Ray Monson, "History of the South African Mission of The Church of Jesus Christ of Latter-day Saints, 1853–1970" (master's thesis, Brigham Young University, 1971); see also Lawrence E. Cummins, "The Saints in South Africa," *Ensign,* March 1973, 4–10.

2. In William Walker Holmes, *The Life Incidents and Travels of Elder William Holmes Walker and His Association with Joseph Smith, the Prophet* (Elizabeth Jane Walker Piepgrass: Salt Lake City, 1943), 23–24.

3. For an overview of this missionary's extensive output, see David J. Whittaker,

"Early Mormon Imprints in South Africa," *BYU Studies* 20 (Summer 1980): 404–16.

4. See Monson, "History of the South African Missions," 43, 44.

5. Spencer W. Kimball, Personal Journal, 2 December 1973, as quoted in James R. Moss, R. Lanier Britsch, James R. Christianson, and Richard O. Cowan, eds. *The International Church* (Provo: Brigham Young University Publications, 1982), 241.

6. E. Dale LeBaron, as quoted in Duane Cardall, *News of the Church, Ensign,* December 1978, 53.

7. In ibid., 52.

8. See LaMar S. Williams, in an interview with Spencer Palmer, November 1979, as quoted in Moss et al., *International Church,* 243.

9. N. Eldon Tanner, in Moss et al., *International Church,* 244

10. See Spencer J. Palmer, "Mormons in West Africa: New Terrain for the Sesquicentennial Church," Annual Religion Faculty Lecture, 27 September 1979, copy of transcripts in Special Collections, Harold B. Lee Library, Brigham Young University, 3–4.

11. Spencer W. Kimball, *The Teachings of Spencer W. Kimball: Twelfth President of The Church of Jesus Christ of Latter-day Saints,* ed. Edward L. Kimball (Salt Lake City: Bookcraft 1982), 450–51.

12. Gordon B. Hinckley, "Priesthood Restoration," *Ensign,* October 1988, 70.

13. Joseph W. B. Johnson, "Ghana," in E. Dale LeBaron, ed., *"All Are Alike Unto God"* (Orem, Utah: Granite Publishing, 1998), 25.

14. See E. Dale LeBaron, "Joseph W. B. Johnson," in Arnold K. Garr, Donald Q. Cannon, and Richard O. Cowan, eds., *Encyclopedia of Latter-day Saint History* (Salt Lake City: Deseret Book, 2000), 577–78. Hereafter cited as *Encyclopedia of LDS History.*

15. Alice Johanna Okkers, "South Africa," in LeBaron, ed., *"All Are Alike unto God,"* 217–18.

16. Merrill J. Bateman, "A Zion University," *Brigham Young University 1995–96 Speeches of the Year* (Provo: Brigham Young University, 1996), 124; compare *Church News,* 4 July 1992, 6.

17. Rendell Mabey, in Rendell and Rachel Mabey, "A Mission to West Africa," *This People* 2 (1980): 32.

18. Ibid., 33.

19. See E. Dale LeBaron, "A. Emmanuel Kissi," in *Encyclopedia of LDS History,* 625.

20. See *Church News,* 22 December 1979, 5.

21. See Glen L. Rudd, "Humanitarian Aid," in *Encyclopedia of LDS History,* 518; see also *Deseret News 2001–2002 Church Almanac* (Salt Lake City: Deseret News, 2000), 350–51, 407.

22. See E. Dale LeBaron, "Ghana," in *Encyclopedia of LDS History,* 426–27.

23. See ibid.; see also *Church History in the Fulness of Times,* 2d ed., Church Educational System manual (Salt Lake City: The Church of Jesus Christ of Latter-day Saints, 2000), 616–17.

24. Nduka B. Ojaide, in John L. Hart, "Nations Will 'Never Be Same' after Lengthy Africa Trip, *Church News,* 28 February 1998, 4 (see also 3–6, 8–9).

NOTES TO CHAPTER 21—THE CHURCH IN THE MIDDLE EAST

1. See David B. Galbraith, D. Kelly Ogden, and Andrew C. Skinner, *Jerusalem: The Eternal City* (Salt Lake City: Deseret Book, 1996), 332.
2. Orson Hyde, as quoted in Joseph Smith, *History of The Church of Jesus Christ of Latter-day Saints*, 7 vols., 2d ed. rev., ed. B. H. Roberts (Salt Lake City: The Church of Jesus Christ of Latter-day Saints, 1932–51), 4:375–76. Hereafter cited as *HC*.
3. See ibid., 4:113.
4. Galbraith, Ogden, and Skinner, *Jerusalem,* 336.
5. Orson Hyde, in Smith, *HC,* 4:455.
6. Ibid., 4:456–57.
7. George A. Smith, as quoted in Galbraith, Ogden, and Skinner, *Jerusalem,* 342.
8. Jacob Spori, *The Turkish Mission 1884–1900,* 6 September 1887, available at the Historical Department, The Church of Jesus Christ of Latter-day Saints, Salt Lake City, Utah. Hereafter cited as LDS Church Archives.
9. In ibid.
10. See Rao H. Lindsay, "A History of the Missionary Activities of The Church of Jesus Christ of Latter-day Saints in the Near East, 1884–1929" (master's thesis, Brigham Young University, 1958), 22–23.
11. "The Gospel in Armenia," *Relief Society Magazine* 8 (June 1921): 367.
12. Lindsay, "Missionary Activities of The Church of Jesus Christ of Latter-day Saints in the Near East," 72.
13. In ibid., 76–78.
14. See Hugh J. Cannon, "Around-the-World Travels of David O. McKay and Hugh J. Cannon," 199, in LDS Church Archives.
15. In *Cherished Experiences from the Writings of President David O. McKay,* comp. Clare Middlemiss (Salt Lake City: Deseret Book, 1955), 80; see also Cannon, "Travels," 202–03.
16. Cannon, "Travels," 199.
17. David O. McKay, in *Cherished Experiences,* comp. Middlemiss, 82–83.
18. See Palestine-Syrian Mission Annual Reports, 1934, 400, in LDS Church Archives.
19. See ibid., 1938, 516.
20. See ibid., 1951, 319.
21. Galbraith, Ogden, and Skinner, *Jerusalem,* 452.
22. See ibid., 453.
23. See Galbraith, Ogden, and Skinner, *Jerusalem,* 454–467.
24. Howard W. Hunter, *The Teachings of Howard W. Hunter,* ed. Clyde J. Williams (Salt Lake City: Deseret Book, 1997), 100.
25. James A. Toronto, "Middle East," in Arnold K. Garr, Donald Q. Cannon, and Richard O. Cowan, eds., *Encyclopedia of Latter-day Saint History* (Salt Lake City: Deseret Book, 2000), 749. Hereafter cited as *Encyclopedia of LDS History.*
26. Ibid., 749.
27. James A. Toronto, "Jordan," in *Encyclopedia of LDS History,* 584–85.
28. Parviz Morewedge, as quoted in Kathryn Baer, "BYU Translates, Publishes Islamic Text," *Church News,* 14 February 1998, 6; see also *Church News,* 3 April 1999, 6.

NOTES TO CHAPTER 22—THE CHURCH IN NORTH AMERICA

1. See S. George Ellsworth, "A History of Mormon Missions in the United States and Canada, 1830–1860" (Ph.D. diss., University of California, 1951); Lamar C. Berrett, "History of the Southern States Mission 1831–1861" (master's thesis, Brigham Young University, 1960).
2. Leonard J. Arrington, "Colonizing the Great Basin, *Ensign,* February 1980, 18.
3. Ibid., 19.
4. In Arthur M. Richardson, *The Life and Ministry of John Morgan* (n.p.: Nicholas G. Morgan Sr., 1965), 231.
5. Andrew Jenson, *Encyclopedic History of The Church of Jesus Christ of Latter-day Saints* (Salt Lake City: Deseret News Publishing Co., 1941), 821.
6. George Albert Smith, "How My Life Was Preserved," in *A Story to Tell,* comp. General Board of the Primary Association and Deseret Sunday School Union Board (Salt Lake City: Deseret Book, 1959), 156.
7. In Richardson, *The Life and Ministry of John Morgan,* 356.
8. Ibid., 357.
9. See Richard O. Cowan and William E. Homer, *California Saints: A 150-Year Legacy in the Golden State* (Provo: Brigham Young University Religious Studies Center, 1996), chapter 11.
10. Heber J. Grant, in Cowan and Homer, *California Saints,* 265–66.
11. Joseph Smith, *Teachings of the Prophet Joseph Smith,* sel. Joseph Fielding Smith (Salt Lake City: Deseret Book, 1976), 363.
12. See Jenson, *Encyclopedic History,* 396; see also James C. Vandygriff, "Kelsey Texas: The Founding and Development of a Latter-day Saint Gathering Place in Texas" (master's thesis, Brigham Young University, 1974); see also Texas Mission Annual Reports by President Charles E. Rowan, 1931, 580; 1932, 560; manuscripts available at the Historical Department, The Church of Jesus Christ of Latter-day Saints, Salt Lake City, Utah.

NOTES TO CHAPTER 23—THE CHURCH IN THE CARIBBEAN

1. Heber Meeks, *Autobiography of Heber Meeks: Second Period* (n.p., 1983), 204.
2. See ibid., 204–9.
3. See ibid., 206.
4. Glen L. Rudd, "Keeping the Gospel Simple," *Brigham Young University 1987–88 Devotional and Fireside Speeches* (Provo: Brigham Young University, 1988), 103.
5. Ibid.
6. See Glen L. Rudd, "Puerto Rico," in Arnold K. Garr, Donald Q. Cannon, and Richard O. Cowan, eds., *Encyclopedia of Latter-day Saint History* (Salt Lake City: Deseret Book, 2000), 969. Hereafter cited as *Encyclopedia of LDS History.*
7. See *Deseret News 2001–2002 Church Almanac* (Salt Lake City: Deseret News, 2000), 388.
8. See Glen L. Rudd, "Dominican Republic," in *Encyclopedia of LDS History,* 302–3.
9. *Church News,* 21 March 1981, 3.
10. In Spencer W. Kimball, "Rendering Service to Others," *Ensign,* May 1981, 45.

11. See *Church News,* 21 March 1981, 4.
12. Spencer W. Kimball, in ibid.
13. See Patrick Cannon, "Haiti," in *Encyclopedia of LDS History,* 455–56.
14. See *2001–2002 Church Almanac,* 347.
15. See David R. Crockett, "Jamaica," in *Encyclopedia of LDS History,* 566.
16. See David R. Crockett, "Virgin Islands," in *Encyclopedia of LDS History,* 1295–96.
17. See ibid.
18. In Jason Swensen, "Prophet Teaches, Motivates Caribbean Islanders," *Church News,* 24 March 2001, 6.
19. Gordon B. Hinckley, as quoted in ibid.
20. In Swensen, "Prophet Teaches," *Church News,* 24 March 2001, 6.
21. See *Church News,* 4 December 1993, 3–4.
22. In Jason Swensen, "Caribbean's First Temple Prompts Rejoicing," *Church News,* 23 September 2000, 4.
23. In ibid.

NOTES TO CHAPTER 24—ADMINISTERING THE INTERNATIONAL CHURCH

1. See Andrew Jenson, *An Encyclopedic History of the Church* (Salt Lake City: Deseret News Publishing Co., 1941), 237–38.
2. See *Church News,* 1 July 1961, 6.
3. See *Church News,* 19 June 1965, 3–5.
4. Kahlile Mehr, "Area Supervision: Administration of the Worldwide Church, 1960- 2000," in *Journal of Mormon History* 27 (Spring 2001): 193.
5. Ibid.
6. See Larry Skidmore, "Conference," in Arnold K. Garr, Donald Q. Cannon, Richard O. Cowan, eds., *The Encyclopedia of Latter-day Saint History* (Salt Lake City: Deseret Book, 2000), 236. Hereafter cited as *Encyclopedia of LDS History.*
7. Dean L. Larsen, "The Challenges of Administering a Worldwide Church," *Ensign,* July 1974, 18; see also Harold B. Lee, Conference Report, September 1967, 103–4.
8. See *Church News,* 28 December 1963, 6.
9. See *Church News,* 3 May 1975, 3, 12; 17 May 1975, 3.
10. Spencer W. Kimball, in Conference Report, October 1976, 10.
11. David O. McKay, in "Status Changed for Seventy Council," *Church News,* 17 June 1961, 3.
12. See Alan K. Parrish, "Seventy," in Daniel H. Ludlow, ed., *Encyclopedia of Mormonism,* 4 vols. (New York: Macmillan Publishing Company, 1992), 3:1300–3.
13. Spencer W. Kimball, in Conference Report, October 1976, 10.
14. See Conference Report, October 1986, 63–64.
15. See Conference Report, April 1995, 71–72.
16. Gordon B. Hinckley, in Conference Report, April 1997, 4.
17. See "News of the Church," *Ensign,* February 1977, 91.
18. See *Church News,* 1 April 1978, 4.
19. See "News of the Church," *Ensign,* February 1977, 91.

20. See Doyle L. Green, "The Church Sends Its Message to the World Through the Unified Magazine," *Improvement Era,* August 1969, 4–7.

21. Henry D. Taylor, in Conference Report, April 1967, 35–37.

22. In Jack E. Jarrard, "Unique Mission Serves World," *Church News,* 1 February 1975, 12.

23. Bernard P. Brockbank, as quoted in ibid., 3.

24. Birgitta de Linde, in "Church Family Style in Tanzanian Home," *Church News,* 22 February 1975, 6.

25. See *Church News,* 8 February 1975, 6, 13.

26. See "News of the Church," *Ensign,* January 1981, 77–78.

27. See "Diplomatic Affairs Consultant Appointed," *Church News,* 13 April 1974, 17.

28. See *Church News,* 5 January 1980, 11.

29. In LaVarr Webb, "Poland Dedicated by President Kimball," *Church News,* 17 September 1977, 4.

30. Spencer W. Kimball, as quoted in Edward L. Kimball and Andrew E. Kimball Jr., *Spencer W. Kimball* (Salt Lake City: Bookcraft, 1977), 328, 329.

31. See Paul Hyer and Jeffrey Ringer, "People's Republic of China," in *Encyclopedia of LDS History,* 201

NOTES TO THE CONCLUSION—HOW FAR HAVE WE COME?

1. Joseph Smith, *History of The Church of Jesus Christ of Latter-day Saints,* 7 vols., 2d ed. rev., ed. B. H. Roberts (Salt Lake City: The Church of Jesus Christ of Latter-day Saints, 1932–51), 4:540.

2. James R. Moss, "Patterns of International Growth" in James R. Moss, R. Lanier Britsch, James R. Christianson, and Richard O. Cowan, eds., *The International Church,* (Provo: Brigham Young University Publications, 1982), 305.

3. William Cowper, "God Moves in a Mysterious Way," *Hymns of The Church of Jesus Christ of Latter-day Saints* (Salt Lake City: The Church of Jesus Christ of Latter-day Saints, 1985), no. 285.

4. See Orson Pratt, in *Journal of Discourses,* 26 vols. (London: Latter-day Saints' Book Depot, 1854–86), 18: 63–64.

5. Moss, "Patterns of International Growth," in *The International Church,* 298.

6. Gordon B. Hinckley, in Conference Report, October 1999, 94.

INDEX

missionary work, 27; Mormon
Colonies (Mexico) visited by, 243;
responsibilities of, 482; role of, 503
Arabic, Book of Mormon translated
into, 441
Area Authorities, role of, 491–92
Area authority seventies, 492
Area conference: Hong Kong's first,
352; Taiwan's first, 355–56
Area presidencies, creation of, 289
Areas, Church: division of Church into
administrative, xvi, 484; map of,
486–87; worldwide, 488–89;
supervision of, by seventies
presidencies, 491; membership and
facilities in, chart, 521
Argentina: customs in, 259; first
missionary work in, 259–66; first
baptism in, 263; Saints experience
gift of tongues in, 263–64; early
missionary work among Germans
in, 266, 268; early membership
statistics in, chart, 267
Arias, Manuel, 278
Arizona, early Mormon colonies in,
448–49
Armenia, emigration of Saints from,
435
Armenian, Book of Mormon translated
into, 441
Armenian Mission, closure of, 434;
reopening of, 434
Armenians: early missionary work
among, 426–28; challenges of
missionaries, 427–28; Church
members offer humanitarian aid to,
431; missionary work among
American, 435
Armstrong, Richard, 153
Arrington, Leonard, on colonization by
Mormon pioneers, 448
Articles of Faith, ix
Aruba, first branch in, 478
Asay, Carlos E., as a missionary to
Middle East, 435
Ashley, Mary, 223
Asia: early missionary work in, xiii;
postwar Church growth in, xiv;
geography of, 303; religions

practiced in, 303; challenges to
Church growth in, 303–4;
Christians a minority in, 303–4;
political changes in, 304;
beginnings of Church in, 305; first
branch in, 307; LDS servicemen in,
326–27; nations of, dedicated for
preaching of gospel, 327; Gordon
B. Hinckley tours, 329; first temple
in, 334, 334–35; Joseph Fielding
Smith tours, 337; first temple in
mainland, 344; map, 366; south
and southeast, Church expansion
in, 367; south and southeast,
Church membership in, 368;
assessment of missionary work in,
390–91; Church membership and
facilities in, 391; southeast, impact
of LDS servicemen in, 510;
present-day Church influence in,
516. See also individual countries
Asioli, Roberto, conversion of, 107
Assistants to Twelve, 489–90
Asuncion Branch, as first branch in
Paraguay, 271
Atlanta Georgia Temple, 458
Aunuu, 173
Austin, Homer, 406
Australasian Mission: 165; creation of,
165; headquarters of, moved to
New Zealand, 166
Australia: early missionary work in, xiii;
highlights of early missionary work
in, 160; background of, 160–61;
establishment of Church in, 160–64;
first missionaries arrive in, 161; first
converts in, 161–62; opposition to
Church in, 161–63; first branch in,
162; emigration of Saints from,
162–63; missionaries sent home
from, 163; reasons for slow growth
of Church in, 163; temporary
decline of Church membership in,
163–64; David O. McKay's visit to,
199; effect of World War II on, 204;
wartime efforts of Church members
in, 208; first stake in, 218; faith of
Saints in, 220–21; additional
temples built in, 221–22

Colombia-Venezuela Mission, 283
Colonia Juárez Chihuahua Temple,
    296
Colonization, by Mormon pioneers,
    448. *See also* Mormon Colonies
Colorado, early Mormon colonies in,
    448–49
Colorado Mission, 454
Commandment, to do missionary
    work, x–xi
Communication, worldwide, among
    Church units, 519
Communism, 93; Church entrance
    into countries controlled by, 115;
    in Poland, 500; fall of, in U.S.S.R.
    and Eastern Europe, 509. *See also*
    Europe, Eastern; Iron Curtain;
    Russia
Condor, James Riley, martyrdom of,
    451
Condor, Martin, martyrdom of, 451
Conferences: as Church units, 485;
    general, 492–93; satellite
    transmission of, 493; area, 493;
    stake, 493
Confucianism, 303
Congo, beginnings of Church in, 414
Cooke, William, 164–65
Coombs, M. Vernon, 200; founds
    Church school in Tonga, 203
Copenhagen Denmark Temple, 97, *98*
Ćosić, Krešimir: as member
    missionary, xvi–xvii, *127,* 127–28;
    as ambassador, 128
Costa Rica: first missionaries and
    branch in, 276; first native
    missionaries from, 276
Counselors, to mission presidency, first
    use of, 206–7
Couple missionaries, 500. *See also*
    Missionaries
Courage, of early missionaries, 15–16
Court, Thomas S., 179
Cowan, Richard O., vii
Cowdery, Oliver, as second elder of
    Church, 537–38n. 4
Cowley, Matthew: as president of New
    Zealand Mission, 204; his love of
    the Maori people, *207;* plans

expansion of Maori College,
    213–14; prophesies regarding
    Church in Japan, 326; rededicates
    China for preaching of gospel, 348;
    supervises postwar missions in
    Pacific, 484
Cox, Fern, 374
Cox, John, conversion of, 97
Cox, Soren, 374
Cox, Thomas L., 167
Creation, Mosaic account of, 61
Croatia, 126–28; Church membership
    in, 128
Crosby, Caroline, 145; opens school on
    Tubuai, 146
Cuba: evaluated for possibility of
    missionary work, 470; Communist
    takeover of, 470
Cultures: Polynesian, 210–12; Pacific
    and Church, blending of, 228–29;
    acceptance of other, 505–6; relating
    gospel to other, 517
Cummings, Donald, faith of, 220–21
Cuna Indians, 278
Curaçao, first branch in, 478
Curriculum materials, Church,
    495–96; translated into Portuguese,
    xvi. *See also* Magazines, Church
Cuthbert, Derek A.: first resident
    Briton called as General Authority,
    96–97; called to First Quorum of
    Seventy, 103–4
Cuthbert, Muriel, 96
Czechoslovakia (Czech Republic),
    119–20; evacuation of missionaries
    from, 80–83; political changes in,
    115; members at baptism in, *118;*
    Communist takeover of, 119;
    official recognition of Church in,
    120; dedicated for preaching of
    gospel, 120; mission in, 120;
    Church membership in, 120; first
    meetinghouse in, 122;
    Communism in, 509
Czerwinski, Fryderyk, *121*

Damron, Joseph W., 147–49
Daniel, prophesies God's kingdom will
    roll forth, x

Pacific Islands, 140–49; as
missionary to Tahiti, 142; as
missionary to the Tuamotus, 143
Growth, Church, 507–16; prophecies
regarding, x; indicators of, xvii–xxii;
in Scandinavia, 61; in Italy, 106–7;
in Spain, 107–9; in Greece,
111–12; in Czechoslovakia,
119–20; in Hungary, 120–22; in
Australia, 162–63; in New Zealand,
169–70; in Pacific Islands, 181; in
South America, 265–66; in Latin
America, 284; in Philippines,
363–64
Guam: early missionary work in,
225–26; first meetinghouse in, 226;
dedicated for preaching of gospel,
226, 327; Church membership in,
226; included in Southern Far East
Mission, 348–49
Guatemala: first missionaries sent to,
276; first baptisms in, 276; Saints
in, *277, 283*; recognition of
Church in, 278
Guatemala City Guatemala Temple,
296
Gudmundsson, Gudmundur, 32
Guicci, Domingo, conversion of,
264–65
Guzman, Jose D., conversion of, 278

Hagoth, voyages of, 135
Hague Netherlands Temple, The, 97
Haifa, Palestine (now Israel):
"Templers" in, 424–425; early
missionary work among German
colonists in, 425–26
Haiti: first Church members in, 475;
first branch in, 475; dedicated for
preaching of gospel, 475; first
mission in, 475–76; first stake in,
476; Primary children in, *476*;
missionaries withdrawn from, 476
Hallam, Arn, 386
Halvorsen, Gail, 89–90
Hamilton New Zealand Temple, 217;
building missionaries work on, 214;
building and dedication of,

219–20; attendance at open house,
220
Hammer, Paul, 64
Hammond, Francis A., 158–59, 183
Han In Sang: translates Book of
Mormon into Korean, 340; heads
Korean translation department,
341; as first native Korean mission
president, 343; called as first
Korean General Authority, 345
Handcarts, 55–56
Hanks, J. Phillip, on importance of
Building Missionary Program,
215–16
Hanks, Knowlton F., as missionary to
Pacific Islands, 140
Hanks, Marion D., 381; assists with
Asian missions, 331; visits
Thailand, 369; assists in
humanitarian aid project, 372
Hansen, Jonetha, 73
Hanson, Peter, 30–33
Harris, Franklin S., reviews
colonization plans, 434
Haven, Jesse, prophesies regarding
Church in South Africa, 397
Hawaii: early missionary work in, xiii,
149–53; economy and geography
of, 136; milestones of early
missionary work in, 139;
establishment of Church in,
149–59; government of, 150;
dedicated for preaching of gospel,
150; first mission in, 150; first
branch in, 152; early Church
growth in, 153; learning language
of, 154; departure of missionaries
from, 156; apostate activities of
Walter Murray Gibson in, 157;
decline of Church activity in, 157;
General Authorities visit, 157–58;
new gathering place selected in,
158–59; Laie as LDS gathering
place in, 183–84; temple built in,
187–90; David O. McKay's visit to,
190–92; spiritual highlight of
David O. McKay's visit to, 191–92;
Church schools in, 202; wartime
efforts of Church members in, 208;

Jackson County, Missouri: as heart of Zion, 47; prophecies regarding, 444
Jacksonville Florida Stake, first stake in American South, 458
Jamaica: first missionaries in, 469–70; persecution of early missionaries in, 470; first branch in, 476; first convert in, 476; first mission in, 476; dedicated for preaching of gospel, 476; branch members in, 478
Japan: David O. McKay's visit to, 190; political structure in, 313; early missionary work in, 313–19; first missionaries arrive in, 314; dedicated for preaching of gospel, 314–15; opposition to Church in, 314–16; early Saints in, 315, 318; challenges of missionary work in, 315; slow growth of Church in, 316; work schedule of early missionaries in, 317; closing of early mission in, 317–19; earthquake in, 318; nationalism in, 319, 322–23; anti-U.S. sentiments in, 319, 509; milestones of postwar Church growth in, 322; Saints in prewar, 322–23; mission president visits, 323; religious restrictions in, 323–24; political changes in, 324; first mission home in, 324; first postwar missionaries enter, 325; baptism in, 325; favorable conditions for missionary work in, 325–26; first postwar convert in, 326; branches added in, 326–27; included in Northern Far East Mission, 327; native missionaries serve in, 327; rapid postwar Church growth in, 328; new branches in, 328; meetinghouses built in, 328; local leaders in, 328; building program in, 329; first temple excursion from, 330; second mission created in, 331; Spencer W. Kimball's visit to, 332; further division of missions in, 332; first stake in, 332–33; second temple built in, 335; late twentieth-century

membership in, 335; impact of LDS servicemen in, 510
Japan East Mission, creation of, 333
Japan Mission, 326, 332
Japan West Mission, creation of, 333
Japanese Americans, 320–31
Japanese Mission (in Hawaii), 320–21
Japanese-Central Pacific Mission: success of, 321; notable converts from, 321, 331
Japan-Okinawa Mission, creation of, 332
Jerusalem: rededicated for preaching of gospel, 432; opposition to Church in, 438. See also Israel; Palestine
Jerusalem, New: prophecies regarding, 444. See also Jackson County, Missouri
Jesperson, Norval, 281
Jesus Christ: second coming of, 444–45; as head of Church, 502–4
Johannesburg South Africa Temple, 413
John Benbow home, 18. See also Benbow, John
Johnson, Joseph W. B.: conversion of, 408; on revelation on priesthood, 409–10
Johnson, Kenneth, called to First Quorum of Seventy, 104
Jones, Daniel Webster: called as first missionary to Mexico, 234; early life of, 234–35; on first LDS meeting in Mexico, 238
Jones, J. Talmage, 388
Jones, Nathaniel, 310–11
Jones, Thomas S., 148
Jones, Wayne A., 386
Jordan, Church center established in, 439–40
Journal of Discourses, publication of, 68
Juárez, Benito, 237, 510
Juárez Academy, 239
Juárez Stake, first stake in Latin America, 242–43

Kailimai, David, 191
Kauai, Church schools in, 153; first meetinghouses in, 153–54

Malaysia: local missionaries serve in, 375; beginnings of Church in, 375–76; first district in, 375–76; Church officially recognized in, 375, 500

Malta, early missionary work in, 41–42

Mandeville (Jamaica) Branch, 476

Manila Philippines Stake, 361–62

Manila Philippines Temple, xv, 362

Manoa, Samuela, missionary work of, 173–74

Mantano, Gilbert, 385

Maori Agricultural College, 203; expansion of, 213–14

Maori boys, photograph of, *207*

Maori building, photograph of, *215*

Maoris: gospel introduced to, 164; widespread acceptance of gospel by, 166–73, 227; first convert among, 167; reasons for acceptance of gospel by, 170–72; culture and beliefs of, 171–72, 192–93; missionaries' acceptance of culture of, 172; use gift of tongues during meeting, 193–94; Church schools for, 203; prophecy regarding, 546n. 3

Maps: British Isles, 2; Western Europe, 28, 92; Mormon emigration routes, 44; Eastern Europe, 114; Pacific Islands, 138; South America, 254; Central America, 273; Mexico, 273; Asia, 366; Africa, 394; Middle East, 419; Areas of the Church, 464–65; North America, 466–67; Caribbean, 466–67; United States of America, 486–87

Mapusaga, Samoa, as LDS gathering place, 183, 185–86

Marcos, Ferdinand, *361*, 362

Mariana Islands, 225–26; first missionaries in, 226

Maritime Provinces (Canada), missionary work in, xi. *See also* Canada

Markow, Mischa, 66, *72*, 128; conversion and service of, 70–75; courage and faith of, 75

Marriage, plural, 60, 453; Australian opposition to Church due to, 161–63; leads to establishment of Mormon Colonies in Mexico, 242–43; opposition to Church in South Africa due to, 397

Marriages, temple, in eastern U.S., 461

Marsh, Thomas B.: receives promise regarding missionary work, 7; on responsibilities of Quorum of the Twelve, 503

Marshall Islands, 225–26

Martin handcart company, 55–56

Martins, Helvecio, first black General Authority, 289

Materials, Church, effects of globalization on, xxii–xxv; translation of, 495–96, 518. *See also* Magazines, Church

Maturity, as stage of Church growth, 514–15

Maui, challenges to early missionary work in, 152–53

Maui: success of early missionary work in, 150–53; Church schools in, 153; first meetinghouses in, 153–54; early LDS chapel in, *158*. *See also* Hawaii

Mauss, Vinal G., 326–27

Maxwell, Neal A.: on challenges of growing Church, xxiii; visits Mongolia, 358; organizes first stake in Thailand, 372; organizes first stake in Singapore, 375

Maycock, Philip, 429

Maypan (Jamaica) Branch, *478*

McCombs family, 477

McConkie, Bruce R., *376;* on future of Church in Chile, 285–86; on dedication of Indonesia for preaching of gospel, 377

McCune, George W., 459

McCune, Matthew, 310; conversion of, 307

McDonnel, William, 167–69

McKay, David O., *195;* background of, 93; worldwide tour of, 431; inspired to find missionary, 431–33; on function of First Council of Seventy, 490

Samoa, 174; evacuated from Pacific, 204–5; Christian, in Asia, 303, 347–48; challenges of early, in India, 307–8; six-lesson teaching plan adopted by, in Japan, 328; sent to Mongolia, 357; Christian, in Thailand, 368
Missionary: inspiration received by, 13, 425–26; prayer of, answered, 23; child healed by, 34–35; death of, in Turkey, 427–28. *See also* Missionaries; Missionary work
Missionary work: Saints commanded to do, x–xi; first international, xi; member, xvi–xviii; Joseph Smith receives inspiration regarding, 4–5, 7; spiritual promptings in, 13; success of early, 13–14; without "purse or scrip," 17; inspiration in, 23, 70–71, 141, 151, 280–81, 507; effect of World War I on, 77–78; overcoming obstacles to, 115; challenges in, 278; government laws restricting, 384; language barriers as challenges to, 504–5

North America:

beginnings of, in Mexico, xiii–xiv; in North America, 46–47; early, in Mexico, 237

Central America, South America, and the Caribbean:

beginnings of, in South America, xiii; in Latin America, 297–98

Europe and Africa:

in Great Britain, success of, xi–xii; in Scandinavia, xii; beginnings of, in Europe, xiii; by Krešimir Ćosić, xvi–xvii, 127–28; in England, prophecy regarding, 3–4; opposition to, in England, 22, 25; success of, in British Mission, 26–27; opposition to, in Scandinavia, 33; in Germany, 62–63; in Holland, 63–64; in Finland, 65; European, aided by publications, 66; in Hungary,

70–75; in Eastern Europe, 70–75; early, in Yugoslavia, 127–28

The Middle East, Asia, and the Pacific:

in Pacific, xii; beginnings of, in Hawaii, xiii; early, in Pacific Islands, 137; early, in Hawaii and French Polynesia, 139; in Tubuai, 140–42; reasons for challenges of, in Japan, 315–16; language challenges of, in Korea, 338; challenges of, in Hong Kong, 354
Missions: international, as indicators of growth, xx–xxi; European, chart, 132–34; counselors called to assist presidents in, 206–7; in Pacific Islands, chart, 230; in Latin America, chart, 300–301; in Asia, 391; in Africa, 417; in Middle East, 442; in Caribbean, chart, 481; supervision of, 483–85; division of, 483–84; U.S., chart, 486; worldwide, chart, 521
Missouri: gathering of Saints to, 47–48; expulsion of Saints from, 47–48
Mobs, missionaries threatened by, 450–53
Mol, J. J., on success of Church in Pacific Islands, 227
Molokai: Church schools in, 153; first meetinghouses in, 153–54; Joseph F. Smith's experiences in, 154–55
Mongolia, 357–58; government of, 357; missionary couples sent to, 357–58; first missionaries enter, 357–58; challenges to Church growth in, 358; legal recognition of Church in, 358; Church membership in, 358; first meetinghouse in, 358; first visit of General Authority to, 358
Monogolia Ulaanbaatar Mission, organization of, 358
Monroy, Rafael, 245–46
Monson, Frances, 103
Monson, Thomas S., *476*; dedicates Yugoslavia for preaching of gospel,

in, xiii; highlights of early missionary work in, 160; first missionaries in, 164–66; establishment of Church in, 164–73; first converts in, 165; first branches in, 166; Maori people of, 166–73; early meetinghouse in, 168; first Maori branch in, 169; rapid growth of Church in, 169–70; Maori culture in, 171–72; Western Samoa controlled by, 178–79; David O. McKay visits, 192–94, 199; Church schools in, 202; Maori Agricultural College founded in, 203; missionaries evacuated from, 204; hui tau meetings suspended during World War II in, 206; wartime efforts of Church members in, 208; Church high school in, 210; building missionaries in, 213–14; Church College of, 214; Church members in, 215; first stake in, 217; temple site selected in, 218–19; success of Church in, 227

Nhat, Dang Thong, 382

Nicaragua: early missionary work in, 278; first convert in, 278; missionaries withdrawn from, 299–300

Nigeria: first missionaries in, 405–6; rapid growth of Church in, 405–8; unofficial groups wait for baptism in, 406; official recognition of Church in, 410; spiritual experience in, 411; couple missionaries sent to, 411–13; legal record of Church in, 412; first stake in, 414; announcement of first temple in, 416

Nisei, definition of, 325

Noall, Matthew, 183

North America: missionary work and gathering within, 46–47; first temple outside, 188; first stake outside, 216–17; Church in, 393; Church milestones in, 443–44; missionaries from, 444; Church history in, 445; expansion of

missionary work in, 453–56; approaches goal of having all areas within stake boundaries, 459; strengthened by LDS influence, 459–60; map of, 466–67

Northern Far East Mission, division of, 332, 337

Northern Rhodesia (Zambia), 402

Northern States Mission, 453

Northwestern States Mission, 454

Norway, early missionaries in, xiii, 31. See also Scandinavia

Nugent, Victor, 476

Nuku'alofa Tonga Temple, 221; royal family tours, 222

O'Donnal, Carmen, 296

O'Donnal, John: as member missionary in Central America, 276; as temple president, 296

Oahu: Church schools in, 153; first meetinghouses in, 153–54; Stake, as first stake outside North America, 216–17, 319

Oakey, James H., 399

Oaks, Dallin H.: on bringing gospel to China, 360; visits Aruba Saints, 479

Ogunmokum, Adeqole, 405

Okazaki, Chieko: conversion of, 321; service of, in Relief Society general presidency, 321

Okinawa, dedicated for preaching of gospel, 327

Okkers, Alice Johanna, on receiving temple endowments, 410

Old Testament lands, 420

Olives, Mount of, construction of BYU Jerusalem Center on, 438

Operation Smile, 383

Oriental Exclusion Law, 318–19

Origin of the Species, 60–61

Orson Hyde Memorial Garden, 437

Ortega, Jose, conversion of, 277–78

Other Side of Heaven, The, 506

Pacific Islands: early Church growth restricted by travel challenges in, 135–36; beginnings of Church in,

Pratt, Rey L., as Mexico mission president, 243, 248; death of, 250–51; visits Argentina to establish missionary work, 261

Prayer, answer to, 7, 23

Presiding Bishopric, supervises translation of Church materials, 494

Preston, England: early missionary work in, xi; branch in, 10; temple in, 97

Priesthood: revelation on the, xxiv–xxv, 400, 406, 408–9, 470, 473; Fijians authorized to hold, 223; Melchizedek, 298–99; emphasis on, in Japan, 328; emphasis on, in Korea, 343

Proclamation to the People of the Coasts and Islands of the Pacific, A, 161

Prophecy: Church globalization a fulfillment of, ix–x; Old Testament, regarding worldwide growth of Church, x; regarding Eastern Europe, 115; fulfillment of, 132; regarding Church in Japan, 326; fulfillment of, in Korea, 344

Public Affairs Department, 463

Publications, Church, 23, 38, 66, 161; reduction in volume of, 518. *See also* Magazines, Church

Puerto Plata Branch, President Kimball's kindness to members of, 474–75

Puerto Rico: first missionaries in, 471; first branch and district in, 471, 473; early Church members in, 471–72; first visit of Church president to, 473–74

"Purse or scrip," early missionary work without, 17

Quiche, unwritten language, 278

Quorum of the Seventy, organization of, 482

Quorum of the Twelve: organization of, 482; assistants to, 489–90

Railroads, immigrant travel by, 58

Rappleye family, 473

Records: Church, 204; mission, during World War II, 207

Regional Representatives, 488; release of, 491

Regions, as Church administrative units, 488

Religion, freedom of, 511–12; in Japan, 324

Resources, natural, in Pacific Islands, 136

Restoration, the, 520

Revelation: on priesthood, xxiv–xxv, 400, 406, 408–9, 470, 473; regarding missionary work of the Twelve, 15; impact of, on missionary work, 509–10

Reynolds, George, on apathy of British Saints, 60

Rhee Ho Nam, 342; called as first stake president in Korea, 343

Rhodakanaty, Plotino, 240–41

Rhodesia (Zimbabwe): beginnings of Church in, 401–2; first convert in, 402; Northern (Zambia), 402. *See also* Zimbabwe

Rich, Charles C., colonizes California, 448

Richards, Franklin D., 63; Brigham Young's advice to, regarding immigrants, 54–55; supervises publication of Pearl of Great Price, 67; presides over British Mission, 483

Richards, Jennetta, conversion and courtship of, 11–12

Richards, Joseph, 307–8, 310

Richards, Willard, 10–11; as missionary to England, 5–6; courtship of, 11–12; serves in British Mission presidency, 14; ordained an Apostle, 21

Richey, Benjamin, first to share gospel in India, 306–7

Ricks College (BYU–Idaho), founding of, 37

Ringger, Hans Benjamin: called to First Quorum of Seventy, 104; works toward Church recognition in Czechoslovakia, 120; visits Polish

Sino-Japanese War, 347
Skousen, Samuel J., 270–71
Slover, Robert H., 337–38, 340–41; as
   temple president, 345
Slover, Rosemarie, 345
Smith, Alma L., travels to Hawaii to
   resolve problems, 157–58
Smith, Cecil B., 223
Smith, E. Wesley, 189; travels with
   David O. McKay, 191
Smith, George A.: as missionary to
   England, 21, 23–25; rededicates
   Palestine for preaching of gospel,
   423
Smith, George Albert: reunifies
   Mexican Saints, 252–53; on
   experiencing danger as missionary,
   451–52
Smith, Jenny, 180
Smith, Joseph F., 189; visits Europe,
   69–70; as missionary to Sandwich
   Islands, 154; on learning Hawaiian,
   154; travels to Hawaii to resolve
   problems, 157–58; selects
   Hawaiian gathering place, 158–59;
   instructs missionaries to teach
   Maori people, 167; announces
   Hawaiian temple, 182; chooses site
   for Hawaii Temple, 187;
Smith, Joseph Fielding: helps evacuate
   European missionaries, 81–83;
   prophesies safe evacuation of
   missionaries, 82–83; helps prepare
   materials for Swiss Temple, 96;
   dedicates Guam for preaching of
   gospel, 226; dedicates Asian nations
   for preaching of gospel, 327; tours
   Asia, 327, 337; dedicates Korea for
   preaching of gospel, 337–38; visits
   Hong Kong, 348; dedicates
   Philippines for preaching of gospel,
   360
Smith, Joseph: prophesies regarding
   Church growth, ix; receives
   inspiration regarding missionary
   work, 4–5, 7; on significance of evil
   spirits, 9; on inspiration given to
   missionary, 13; calls Apostles home
   from British Mission, 26; on

purposes of gathering, 43–46; sends
   missionaries to Pacific Islands, 137;
   prophesies concerning Lamanites,
   234; martyrdom of, 447; on stakes
   of Zion, 456–57; on worldwide
   expansion of Church, 502; as first
   elder of Church, 537–38n. 4
Smith, Willard L., as first mission
   president in Tonga, 179–80
Smith, William, prophesies regarding
   missionary work in England, 3–4
Smoot, Reed, on selection of site for
   Hawaii Temple, 187–88
Šnederfler, Jiři, works toward Church
   recognition in Czechoslovakia, 120
Snow, Erastus, as missionary to
   Denmark, 30–33
Snow, Lorenzo: steel engraving, 30;
   dedicates Italy for preaching of
   gospel, 34; as missionary to Italy,
   34–36; dedicates Switzerland for
   preaching of gospel, 36; as
   missionary to Switzerland, 36–37;
   travels to Hawaii to resolve
   problems, 157–58; sends
   missionary to India, 307;
   announces mission in Japan, 313
Snyder, John, 10
Snyder, John, as missionary to
   England, 5–6
Society Islands, early missionary work
   in, 142
South Africa: arrival of first
   missionaries in, 396; history of,
   396; diversity of people in, 396;
   beginnings of Church in, 396–98;
   dedicated for preaching of gospel,
   397; persecution of early
   missionaries in, 397; first branch
   in, 397; first baptism in, 397;
   emigration from, 398; missionaries
   leave, 398; mission reopens in,
   398–99; growth of Church in, 399;
   opposition to Church in, 399;
   government changes in, 399–400;
   first meetinghouse in, 400;
   challenges to missionary work in,
   400; Church growth in, 402;
   rededicated for preaching of gospel,